The
SURVIVAL KIT
for the
Elementary
School
Principal

ABBY BARRY BERGMAN   **JUDY POWERS**   **MICHAEL L. PULLEN**

The SURVIVAL KIT for the Elementary School Principal

CORWIN
A SAGE Company

For information:

Corwin
A SAGE Company
2455 Teller Road
Thousand Oaks, California 91320
(800) 233-9936
Fax: (800) 417-2466
www.corwin.com

SAGE Ltd.
1 Oliver's Yard
55 City Road
London EC1Y 1SP
United Kingdom

SAGE India Pvt. Ltd.
B 1/I 1 Mohan Cooperative Industrial Area
Mathura Road, New Delhi 110 044
India

SAGE Asia-Pacific Pte. Ltd.
33 Pekin Street #02-01
Far East Square
Singapore 048763

Printed in the United States of America

Library of Congress Cataloging-in-Publication Data

Bergman, Abby Barry.
The survival kit for the elementary school principal/Abby Barry Bergman, Judy Powers, Michael L. Pullen.
   p. cm.
Includes bibliographical references and index.
ISBN 978-1-4129-7277-2 (paper)
   1. Elementary school principals—United States—Handbooks, manuals, etc. 2. Education, Elementary—United States—Administration—Handbooks, manuals, etc. I. Powers, Judy.
II. Pullen, Michael L. III. Title.

LB2831.92.B47 2010
372.12'012—dc22   2009038068

This book is printed on acid-free paper.

10 11 12 13 14 10 9 8 7 6 5 4 3 2 1

Acquisitions Editor:	Arnis Burvikovs
Associate Editor:	Desirée A. Bartlett
Production Editor:	Jane Haenel
Copy Editor:	Nancy Conger
Typesetter:	C&M Digitals (P) Ltd.
Proofreader:	Cheryl Rivard
Indexer:	Molly Hall
Cover and Graphic Designer:	Michael Dubowe

Contents

All forms, letters, and checklists included in *The Survival Kit for the Elementary School Principal* can be found at corwin.com/elementary survivalkit.

About This Resource

The principal is at the center of action within the elementary school. She or he is the person that parents, staff members, and students turn to when they have a concern, an issue, or even a good bit of news that they wish to share. The principal sets the tone for the entire school community, and the degree to which she or he is organized for peak performance can affect the daily and long-term operation of the school.

School leaders learn by experience, and this can be a long process taking many years. Beginning and experienced principals often comment that the administrative training programs in which they were involved did not prepare them for the day-to-day, "nitty-gritty" challenges that they face in schools. *The Survival Kit for the Elementary School Principal* is designed for the busy practitioner. It is a virtual library of essential information, forms, letters, charts, and checklists that can be readily used in any elementary school. Full of pragmatic advice gleaned after many years of successful experience in the position, this book can be invaluable to principals. Very often, principals do not have the time to "reinvent the wheel" and write letters, memos, or draft procedures when they have already been done successfully by others. This book contains many sample letters, easy-to-adapt procedures, and forms that will be relevant to any elementary school situation. It can save countless hours of time and energy!

How does the principal set and implement goals for the school? How can the school community be organized to participate in shared decision-making and site-based management? What are the most effective practices for ensuring student discipline? How can effective teacher observations and evaluations be conducted so that they will result in professional growth and development? These questions and many more are answered in the book. All of the recommended practices are tried and true; they have been culled from years of experience and have emanated from discussions with countless principals in a variety of settings—urban, suburban, and rural. The suggestions are suitable for schools large and small, regardless of the way they are organized.

The Survival Kit for the Elementary School Principal does not promote a specific instructional or administrative philosophy, so it will be applicable to a wide range of situations. It is intended to be helpful rather than prescriptive.

This book is designed for principals and assistant principals as they seek to implement quality programs in elementary schools. It covers all important aspects of the principalship and the elementary school program. It will allow for more effective and efficient planning, communication, and administration of the school and the instructional program. It can be thought of as a desktop reference for practitioners.

There are over 90,000 elementary schools in the United States. The vast majority of schools have a principal, and in some of the larger buildings there are one or more assistant principals. This book might also be used as a textbook, or an adjunct resource, for college courses in educational administration. Aspiring principals may also find this an invaluable resource as they consider this exciting new career and prepare for interviews.

HOW TO USE THIS RESOURCE

The Survival Kit for the Elementary School Principal is arranged topically, by areas that all principals face within a school year. Exactly how each person uses this portfolio will depend upon the intention and needs of the reader. Some may want to read the book cover to cover, others will go first to the chapters that are of immediate importance in their own schools, while still others will glean the table of contents for a very specific item for which they need assistance. In any case, it should be kept close at hand for ready reference and assistance. There is no specific sequence of organization for the book. Each chapter represents an important area of school administration that all principals will encounter.

All of the forms in the portfolio can easily be reproduced or adapted for use in any elementary school. Permission is granted by the publisher to reproduce or alter these forms, letters, and checklists for local needs. *The Survival Kit for the Elementary School Principal* was designed for flexible, broad use; each reader will find a way to make it most meaningful and helpful.

All of the forms, letters, and checklists included in this book can be found online in both pdf format and in an editable form at corwin.com/elementarysurvivalkit. The editable version allows you to simply open the appropriate file, launch it with your own word processor, and place your own name or school name in the letter or form, thus saving valuable time in reproducing any of the resource materials. You can customize the letters, reformat the text to add your own special information, and print the letters on your school stationery. In this way, this book truly is a portfolio of letters, forms, and other resources.

SPECIAL NOTE

Throughout this resource, school and principal names are occasionally used to create a sense of realism for some of the forms and letters included. Although some of the names are generic enough to be the names of real people or schools, there is no intention to refer to any specific individual or school. The names are purely fictitious and any resemblance to an actual school or principal is purely coincidental.

Abby Barry Bergman

Acknowledgments

The preparation of any meaningful book in education is never a solitary enterprise. Over the years, we have benefited from the ideas and encouragement of friends and associates. We have learned from the hundreds of professionals with whom we have worked—sharing joys and triumphs, frustrations and roadblocks. We have learned how be principals from those individuals with whom we have worked shoulder to shoulder each day. Our gratitude and esteem go out to the staff of the schools in which we have practiced. Our administrative colleagues and trustees of the boards of education with which we have worked have always been supportive, helpful, and have led the path for successful leadership.

We thank Arnis Burvikovs, senior editor at Corwin, for his vision and encouragement. We also express sincere appreciation to associate editor Desirée Bartlett for her ongoing patience, wise judgment, and friendly, reasoned advice; to our production editor Jane Haenel for leading us through the production process; and to Nancy Conger, who provided crisp, sensitive, and artful copyediting.

We each owe debts of gratitude to our families, our spouses, and our children, who have continually been a source of support and encouragement. They were always there, ready to listen to an idea, offer a bit of advice, and most importantly, to understand the need to juggle the responsibilities of being school professionals, spouses, parents, and authors of this book—by no means an easy act!

Abby Barry Bergman
Judy Powers
Michael L. Pullen

SPECIAL ACKNOWLEDGMENT
FROM THE FIRST EDITION

No advice can be more valuable than that offered by other administrative colleagues. Most notably, I thank my good friend and fellow principal, Ella Reiss Urdang. She provided invaluable feedback in the preparation of this volume. She read the draft of each and every chapter and suggested substantive revisions, always with her inimitable style and sense of humor, which helped me to see more clearly the direction in which I was headed. The other principals with whom I work, William S. Greene and Patrick M. Westcott, offered suggestions and advice that have been of considerable help. I was privileged to work with an esteemed group of educators at the Ralph S. Maugham School in Tenafly, New Jersey—a finer staff no principal could hope to work with.

Abby Barry Bergman

PUBLISHER'S ACKNOWLEDGMENTS

Corwin gratefully acknowledges the contributions of the following individuals:

Jill Gildea, Superintendent
Harrison School District
Wonder Lake, IL

Roseanne Lopez, Performance Pay Coordinator
Amphitheater Public Schools
Tucson, AZ

Neil MacNeill, Principal
Ellenbrook Primary School
Ellenbrook, Western Australia

Jacie Maslyk, Principal
Crafton Elementary School
Pittsburgh, PA

Pamela B. Maxwell, Principal
E. E. Oliver Elementary School
Fairview, AB, Canada

Ruthann Ryan, Principal
Algonquin Lakes Elementary School
Algonquin, IL

About the Authors

Abby Barry Bergman has been involved in the field of education for over 40 years, in both private and public educational settings. Initially a kindergarten teacher, he has taught at the university level and has filled a variety of positions in school administration. Since 2002, he has served as the Regional Science Coordinator for Putnam/Northern Westchester BOCES, a service organization for a consortium of school districts in New York State. Previously, he was principal of the Ralph S. Maugham School in Tenafly, New Jersey, for over 20 years—an elementary school in a nationally reputed "lighthouse" school district.

Having received his bachelor of arts degree from Hunter College of the City University of New York, he went on to engage in graduate study, earning the master of arts, master of education, and doctor of education degrees from Teachers College, Columbia University. In 1996, Dr. Bergman received the Administrative Excellence Award presented by the Bergen County Administrators Association.

Dr. Bergman has also served as an independent consultant in educational product development and evaluation. He has authored books in the field of science education and written several professional articles, pamphlets, and curriculum guides. He authored *Learning Center Activities for the Full-Day Kindergarten* and coauthored *The Complete School-Age Child Care Resource Kit*, both published by The Center for Applied Research in Education. He resides with his wife in New York.

Having earned degrees at both Barnard College and Teachers College, Columbia University, **Judy Powers** began her career teaching at the elementary level for 10 years. As both a teacher and a policy board chair of a New York State Teacher Center, Judy conducted professional development courses in the areas of mathematics and classroom management. During her 16 years as an elementary school principal, Judy continued to conduct district- and building-based training and led schools based on a continuous improvement model. While a teacher, principal, and interim assistant superintendent, Judy consistently worked to build strong connections between school and community stakeholders. She led several regional workshops on teacher evaluation, supervision, and staff development. Judy now is a consultant to educational organizations. She has coordinated a mentorship program and now coordinates regional professional development, oversees curriculum development, coaches elementary administrators, and conducts staff development in the areas of leadership and curriculum development in both public and private schools.

 **Michael L. Pullen** currently works as an elementary school principal in upstate New York—a capacity he has served in for the past six years. Prior to becoming an elementary principal, his teaching career saw him work in urban, suburban, and rural districts in upstate New York. As a principal, Michael has led several district curriculum initiatives and had made regional presentations about science curriculum development. Under his leadership, his buildings have been recognized by the state education department as either high-performing or gap-closing schools four times.

Michael received his B.A. from St. John Fisher College, his M.S. from Nazareth College, and his Certificate of Advanced Study (CAS) from the State University of New York at Oswego. He and his wife currently reside outside of Rochester.

1

Your Role As Principal

"All Things to All People" or "Principle-Centered Leadership"[1]

Ask any elementary school principal to describe her role, and that principal is likely to respond that it depends on what's needed at the moment. Within any given period, a principal might be an instructional leader, a gatherer of supplies, a nurse, an arbitrator, a disciplinarian, the chairperson of an important school district committee, or a message taker. The school leader's role is so diverse that a single description cannot fully capture the nature of the position. The term *principal* in a school context is derived from the notion of a "principal teacher." Most principals would cherish this function, but the role is much more complex and all-encompassing.

THE NATURE OF THE PRINCIPALSHIP

The principal is the focal person in a school—the person who must be aware of the water leak in the library, the child who is struggling with math concepts, the teacher who is preoccupied because her son is at home ill without good supervision, the youngster whose parents are in the midst of a bitter divorce, and the first grader who just "discovered" how to read and is now reading everything in sight. School leaders are faced with everyone's problems, but they also have the joy of working with lively, interested students and adults, witnessing the exhilaration of learning, and helping people identify and solve problems.

Note: All forms, letters, and checklists included in this chapter can be found at corwin.com/elementary survivalkit.

As principals, we often find ourselves in a "squeeze play" between parents, teachers, and students. We would like to think that we all have the children's best interests at heart, but there are times when the needs and wants of these constituencies do not mesh. For instance, a parent might demand (preferably ask) that a teacher make certain accommodations for her son's learning style. The parent feels that the teacher should record her son's homework in his assignment pad as the youngster often forgets to do it himself. The teacher may not see the situation in the same light as the parent, might feel pressured by the demand, and wonder how such accommodations can be made when working with a group of 25 other students. She may insist that the child learn to assume this responsibility for himself. Without a meeting of minds, this clash of positions will more than likely wind up in the principal's office. Wanting to do the right thing, the principal must negotiate a path for a solution—understanding the nature of the child's learning style and problem (if there is one), the level of flexibility and skill of the teacher, and the parent's perspective. Such situations call forth the best elements of tact, diplomacy, instructional leadership, and problem-solving skills. Often, the actual solution is not as important as how the principal can help others to see opposing points of view and find the ground for compromise. (By the way, a simple solution in the above case might be for the teacher to remind the boy to record his assignments and then have him show his pad to her at dismissal time.)

DEFINE YOUR OWN BELIEF SYSTEM

It is often difficult for principals to find their grounding in the complex demands that they face day in and day out. Many principals want to please everyone. After all, the role is often perceived as being "all things to all people." This does not always work, though, and trying to please everyone can bring principals into direct conflict with competing views and demands. What is the best approach to take? Which underlying assumptions should guide decision-making? How do opposing views become reconciled? School leaders must find their own footing and apply their best instincts and skills to each situation. It helps, though, to define a basic belief system with which to judge all decisions. This set of guiding principles will not be the same for all, but the exercise of defining them for yourself is worthwhile. What do *you* think are the most important functions within a school? Many principals declare that it is best to always judge situations by applying the rule, "Is it best for children?" There may, of course, be varying views of what indeed *is* best for children. It is often best to define a belief system involving all stakeholders in a school (see Chapter 3), but for our purposes here, you might begin by asking yourself the following questions:

- What are the most important functions of the school?
- What are the best practices and attitudes evident at school that promote these functions?
- What evidence do I have that these functions are being fulfilled?
- What do I do that enhances or impedes the realization of these functions?

Reflecting upon these questions can help to clarify a few guidelines for decision-making.

Clearly, different principals in different schools will find unique answers to these questions, but the exercise itself is instructive. A simple belief system we have developed for our own use is as follows:

- All children can learn and benefit from an active, engaging, quality learning environment.
- Do what is best for all students, that is, for the *community* of learners.
- Promote the best practices that are consistent with sound research.
- Support the close ties that we value between home and school.

Some may argue with that belief system; clearly, it won't work for all in all schools. It can be argued, for example, that our emphasis on the community of learners might serve to diminish the needs of an individual. Usually, however, if an action is good for the group, eventually that decision will be good for the individual. Let's see how these key principles could have been applied to the situation discussed above. The school leader might have understood and shared the parent's concern that her son was not recording his homework assignments. The school leader might also have understood the teacher's point of view that it would take too much time away from the group if she were to record his assignments each day. By suggesting that the teacher provide a reminder for the child to enter his homework and then check it at the end of the day, the needs of the group were protected and the importance of honoring the parent's concerns also fostered the preservation of close ties between home and school.

Keeping your own set of priorities in the forefront of decision-making helps to build consistency and reliability. People like to know that a school leader's behavior is somewhat predictable. Acting from your own belief system can also give you the peace of mind of knowing that you are treating issues fairly and objectively. Holding to your beliefs does not mean that you are inflexible; rather, it implies that you have a yardstick against which to measure actions and decisions.

SYSTEMS THINKING, THE LEARNING ORGANIZATION, AND STRATEGIC PLANNING

Progress, planning, and problem solving in any organization can be viewed through the systems thinking approach. Best articulated by Peter Senge in his landmark work, *The Fifth Discipline*,[2] systems thinking implies that the component parts of any organization can best be interpreted in the context of their relationships with one another and how they affect the total picture. In systems thinking, the approach focuses on how the various components (lets say parents, students, central-office administrators, teachers, teacher organizations, the board of education, state education officials, and so on) are linked, interconnected, and affect one another. A decision that seemingly involves only one constituency may, when put into place, have effects that reverberate through the entire system. For example, a neophyte principal decided to change the lunch schedule thinking that adding an extra lunch shift would reduce crowding in the lunchroom and also reduce the density of children on the school grounds during lunchtime recess. It made good sense. She had no idea that a unilateral decision of this nature would have caused such a stir! Everyone was upset—teachers, lunch aides, parents, and students. After weeks of consultation and the inclusion of all parties, a far more effective pattern of lunch scheduling emerged. It was a tough lesson, but an important one. Clearly, this principal was not applying the principles of systems thinking. School leaders may think that they are taking systems thinking into account instinctively, but a deliberate sense of awareness of how the system operates can aid in the planning and response process.

In schools, systems thinking is often used and promoted through a "learning organization." A learning organization is a group of individuals who seek to continually enhance their capacities to envision and create the results that they want. Structures are put into place in which the members of groups see divergent points of view, are committed to shared goals, and feel free to suggest a wide variety of ideas and approaches to achieve the stated mission. Membership in a learning organization often includes representatives from several positions that may contribute divergent, yet helpful, points of view. They learn to solve problems together. Their involvement fulfills a sense of personal meaning and commitment.

One of the important tools often used in systems thinking and by the learning organization is strategic planning. Simply put, this approach identifies where the organization wants to be at some point in the future and how it is going to get there. Strategic planning determines the mission, philosophy, and goals of the organization and the design and roles of how to achieve these essential guiding principles. The plan sets performance goals, specifies objectives, defines roles, and allocates resources to achieve the plan, and then sets guidelines for how you will know when you have gotten to where you wanted to be.

The mission, philosophy, and goals of an organization become a decision screen through which a principal and stakeholders can decide whether a program or strategy is congruent with the shared views of the school community. It is easy to see how systems thinking, learning organizations, and strategic thinking can all apply to a school as an organization. These applications are further discussed in the next two chapters.

INSTRUCTIONAL LEADERSHIP

Most school leaders would say that, first and foremost, their role is to be the instructional leader of the school. This means that we stay focused on what is being learned. Countless distractions may keep us from this primary task, but the goal is to maintain instructional focus. This is always a challenge in the midst of the unique demands of our positions, yet there are several deliberate actions that we can take to provide instructional leadership.

Work With Staff to Develop Curriculum

School leaders invoke committees to study or reassess existing aspects of the curriculum. There will always be volunteer teachers to serve on such committees, and some staff members may be willing to assume leadership of the effort. (Whether or not parents are included in such a committee is a matter of the tradition within the school or district.) Studying curriculum is a healthy activity in any school. Even if the staff and the community seem to be reasonably well satisfied with a curriculum, periodic examination of content, practices, and materials will engender interesting discussions, new insights, and a genuine sharing of ideas.

Define, clearly and from the outset, the goals of the curriculum study group. (Figure 1.1 is a sample of a flyer asking for volunteers to work on a curriculum committee.) Are you looking to conduct a brief examination of the curriculum? Is the expectation to conduct an intense review, including a survey of staff, students, and parents? Is there a need to simply update the curriculum, or is a complete overhaul in order? Do you need to consider a new approach or set of materials? The principal does not necessarily have to be involved in every aspect of curriculum work, but leadership is provided by orchestrating and defining

Figure 1.1 Sample Flyer Seeking Volunteers for a Curriculum Committee

WE'RE LOOKING FOR A FEW GOOD VOLUNTEERS!

Elementary school science is the curriculum area next up for review within our school district. In September, we will enter Phase I of our three-year Curriculum Renewal Cycle. In Phase I review, our goals will be

- to read current literature about science content and practices;
- to study the best practices currently employed in the field;
- to examine our current curriculum by comparing it with national and state standards for science education, assessing teacher and parent opinions about our current science program, and studying the results of student achievement in the area of science;
- to confer with colleagues in surrounding communities to gain information about their science programs;
- to meet with publishers' representatives to see what new materials are available; and
- to make recommendations for Phase II (Pilot Projects) for the following school year.

The Science Curriculum Study Group will meet once every month throughout the next school year. It would be best if we had one teacher representative from each of our grade levels and two parents on our committee. If you would like to suggest specific parents, please indicate their names on the slip below and I will contact them.

If you would be willing to serve as a volunteer for our Study Group, please return the slip below to my office May 31.

____, Principal

Chair of the Science Curriculum Study Group

____

☐ I would be willing to serve on the Science Curriculum Study Group next year.

☐ I would also like to suggest the following parent(s) be asked to participate:

___________________________________   ___________________________________

Name: _____________________________   School: _____________________________

the work of the committee. Providing motivation and inspiration are other aspects of the principal's role. The results of any curriculum study should be reported to staff, school district administrators, and the community.

Provide Resources for Curriculum Development and Implementation

One of the most important resources a school leader can provide for curriculum development is time. Teachers will ask when in the day they will be able to do this important work. If funds are available, hiring substitutes to cover teachers is a popular alternative. In many school districts, teachers are required to remain after school on certain days for meetings and professional work. Curriculum work could be accomplished at this time. Another possibility is to cover the items required at faculty meetings by memo, e-mail, and response forms, and save faculty meeting time for curriculum development.

As committees look at curriculum and practices, new materials and information about approaches must be provided. School leaders call publisher representatives to acquire sample copies of books or kits for examination. They secure relevant articles and distribute them to the study group. Instructional leaders also bring new approaches and practices or state requirements to the committee's attention.

Supervise the Implementation of Curriculum

Through formal and informal observations, the principal should check on the implementation of curriculum. If a new program is adopted, you can ask to witness a lesson in which the new practice or material is incorporated. Feedback to teachers is essential. When observing the implementation of new programs, though, it should be remembered that teachers are taking somewhat of a risk.

Just how much latitude teachers have in how they deal with the stated curriculum is a matter that is decided within each school district. If you need to know that an adopted curriculum is being covered, then classroom observations are a sound way to supervise curriculum implementation. Chapter 4 is devoted to the process of supervision and evaluation.

Assess the Impact of the Curriculum

As the instructional leader, you have the responsibility to assess how well a curriculum or particular practice is being accomplished. Assessment devices are generally embedded in lessons or units of study. Also, there is usually some form of summative evaluation that can inform teachers and administrators about how well the objectives of the program are being achieved. Along with teachers, principals discuss what standards are appropriate for class attainment and how to interpret an individual youngster's achievement.

The success of any curriculum is judged on the basis of achievement on a wide variety of measures. Performance assessment and portfolios of student work should be incorporated into the view of a curriculum's impact. Samplings of teacher satisfaction, ease of implementation, quality of materials, and parental reactions can also provide valuable information about the effectiveness of a curriculum. All of this translates into important commitments for school leaders; however, the time and involvement devoted to the process of curriculum development and supervision is essential for instructional leadership.

THE IMPORTANCE OF DIPLOMACY

The principal must be a diplomat. As we negotiate the minefields often set before us, we may not always have a choice of *what* to say, but we do have a choice about *how* to say it. There are many occasions when we must convey information to parents that they might not be happy to hear, but if we demonstrate sincerity and a genuine concern for the dignity and integrity of the person to whom we are speaking, the most difficult messages can be delivered. When talking about their children's learning or social difficulties, parents may feel that they are in some way responsible for the problem. In such discussions, we should be ready to say what the school personnel will do to help the child who may be struggling.

Parents or teachers who meet with the principal may be angry about one thing or another. How we handle this anger can affect the outcome. Sometimes, people just want to ensure that their views are heard. You can acknowledge that you have understood a sentiment or viewpoint by restating it or paraphrasing it in the conversation. Understanding someone's position does not necessarily mean that you agree with it, but it's a way to promote open communication. With such an approach, parents or teachers will more than likely leave your office feeling that they have been heard, even if they did not leave with the outcome they may have originally wanted.

Any school system has its own set of politics. Educators often bemoan the fact that the educational process can become politicized, but this is a fact of life. School board members often run for office endorsing a specific ideology or approach. They may want to "bring back memorizing math facts" or are in support of some favored innovation. Principals cannot avoid being brought into the fray, but tact and diplomacy are needed in these situations. Again, it is wise to acknowledge that you understand the point of view. Clarification of your own position, while respecting the reality that people of goodwill may disagree, will help to ease the way through such situations.

In all dealings with the various constituencies you face, and especially when confronted with problems, try to achieve a "win-win" solution. This requires artful negotiation, a respect for divergent opinions, and a true desire to find a compromise that embraces each party's core beliefs. Such a compromise is not easy to accomplish, but with a will to solve problems and the desire to be viewed as someone who can be flexible and truly listens, even the greatest of challenges is not insurmountable.

THE NEED FOR POSITIVE COMMUNITY RELATIONS

The principal is a leader who fulfills many community functions. In many respects, the principal represents the school and the school district. This role comes with important responsibilities. Education and the schools that provide it are increasingly under public scrutiny and attack. This is a fact of life that we must face. We all hear parent and community member memories of a more orderly, well-disciplined society in which everyone learned to read, write, and compute with great ease and simplicity. (We're not certain that such a world ever existed, but times have become more complex.) The cost of education has also been a matter of heated public debate. Increasingly, there is a cry for accountability and a summary of the results of educational initiatives and practices. Citizens expect proof that their tax dollars are working for them in their schools. All this means that the principal must be aware of the need to promote and explain what schools do and to foster positive community relations. There are several deliberate actions that we can take to accomplish this.

Promote Your School

When talking about the school, it is important to be positive and upbeat. Convey all the good things that are happening and the opportunities that exist for children. Use every opportunity you can to talk about the school, a particular program, and what you believe in. Invite parents and other community members to the school for special days to witness firsthand the activities that occur. Open school days, in which visitors can sit in on classes, are particularly effective. Special programs, such as grandparent days, writing celebrations, assemblies, field days, and class plays, provide ideal ways to involve the community in school events.

You should ask to be put on the agenda as a "guest speaker" at PTA meetings. This is a good chance to explain the school's programs and gain support for new initiatives. Send out flyers publicizing the event and always leave time for a question-and-answer period. The members of the PTA will provide a captive audience and can serve as a sounding board to gain a sense of community perceptions.

Newsletters are essential communication tools. Use them to promote the school and explain its programs. If the PTA produces a monthly newsletter, make sure that a principal's column is a regular feature. If the school office produces a newsletter, focus on educational practices and items of interest to the entire parent body. Student writing samples, classroom news, special events, and community happenings all deserve ample coverage. It is often useful to have a friend, spouse, or neighbor read your column and offer feedback to make sure that the terms used will be understood by those who do not live and breathe school concerns.

Bring Your Community Together

Schools can be the center of community life. Few towns and neighborhoods have the close-knit associations these days that they had in the past. Some people prefer anonymity; others miss the sense of community they enjoyed in earlier times. There is much that we as principals can do to bring people together and develop a sense of community. School fairs, picnics, and other special events unite parents and their neighbors. The school can be the glue that holds everyone together. Of course, such events will attract the parents of schoolchildren, but there is no reason why other citizens—not necessarily associated with the school—should not be included. Flyers announcing these events can be posted in nearby stores, supermarkets, and libraries. When neighbors come together, they are likely to associate, share common interests, and appreciate the uniqueness of their community.

In many neighborhoods, schools are used for a wide variety of community functions; after-school programs, recreation programs, Girl Scouts and Boy Scouts, and adult education classes may all be held in school buildings. Just how you relate to these various groups is also important. Although each school district will have its own policies on this matter, in most communities, school buildings are viewed as public resources, to be used for a wide variety of functions. School leaders are expected to cooperate with outside agencies or community programs in making the school available. School leaders who feel that they have no role in this area are likely to be tried in the court of public opinion.

View Parents as Partners

Principals and schools benefit when parents are viewed as partners. It is important to build enduring alliances so that parents and school personnel work together to promote school goals and programs. PTAs often provide funding for school equipment and initiatives. Parents expect, and are entitled to, reports or demonstrations of how their fundraising efforts have benefited the children. For example, when parents in one of our schools purchased GPS (Global Positioning System) devices for student activities, we took part of a PTA meeting one night to show how the children were using this new technology.

Parent education is also necessary if we hope that parents will understand and support school programs. This is particularly true in the case of pilot programs or new initiatives. It is always best if the individuals closest to the new program provide the demonstration.

Teachers are generally happy to attend such meetings, share their views about a new program, and explain how it is affecting the children. Such practices go a long way toward building credibility and support. Figure 1.2 is a sample of such a program announcement.

| **Figure 1.2** | Sample Flyer Announcing Information Meeting About New Instructional Program |

LEARN MORE ABOUT OUR NEW SCIENCE PROGRAM

As a part of our regular PTA meeting on November 17 our principal and members of our school faculty will make a presentation on our new science program.
    Some of the issues that will be addressed include the following:

- How is our new science program different from the program used in the past?
- What is "inquiry learning" anyway?
- What can you expect to see at home as a result of our new science program?
- How can parents support children as they explore science?
- How are current issues in science and technology incorporated into the program?
- How will student learning in science be assessed?

A question-and-answer period will follow the presentation.

Where: School Library

When: Tuesday, November 17, at 7:30 PM

    Refreshments will be available following the meeting, courtesy of your PTA.

Organizing seminars or discussion groups on topics of interest to parents can also promote positive parent relations and involvement. An approach that can be most helpful is to develop (along with your parent leaders) a survey of topics that parents would be interested in learning more about. Issues such as child development, discipline practices, homework expectations, sibling rivalry, and drug resistance skills are generally of interest to parents. It is not hard to find individuals who are willing to lead a discussion on these topics. School personnel, community leaders, and local professionals can all be approached to conduct such meetings. Programs of this nature go a long way toward building good relations and promoting the school as a center of community life.

Work Actively With Families

All school leaders realize the importance of being available to families. Demonstrating an interest in the lives of children and their families can make the difference between a principal who is perceived as being distant and aloof with one who is viewed as warm, accessible, and compassionate. School leaders who show a genuine interest in the lives of children are appreciated within their school communities. Some children simply want to share that an aunt is having a birthday, or to discuss their anxieties about the arrival of a new brother or sister. We know that in many ways there are no limits to the role of the principal. We are often called upon to be an advisor to youngsters and their parents. When families are troubled, it is important to exercise good listening skills to get to the heart of a problem. But it is also necessary to know our limits. We cannot provide family therapy, but we can maintain a list of local agencies that will provide assistance and support to families in crisis. Figure 1.3 is a sample letter to families in which an assistance program for students is offered.

Figure 1.3   Sample Letter to Parents About Pupil Assistance Committee

November 23, _________

Dear Parents,
    At our school, we have a standing Pupil Assistance Committee, or PAC. This committee is a school-based problem-solving team designed to assist teachers in developing intervention strategies that help students who are for any reason experiencing difficulty at school. The PAC serves as a vehicle to develop instructional goals, accommodation plans, and assessment plans through collaborative discussion and planning.

WHAT CAN THE PUPIL ASSISTANCE COMMITTEE DO TO HELP?

- Offer structured support and assistance to teachers, students, and parents.
- Plan a program of assistance to meet individual student needs.
- Foster positive communication between the student's parents and the school.
- Assist teachers in developing alternative strategies to promote student competence in basic skills and socioemotional areas.
- Provide a means for teachers to share and increase their skills and knowledge.
- Track the student's response to intervention in terms of targeting assessment techniques.

The core committee is composed of the principal or her designee, a member of our child study team, the school nurse, the speech/language teacher, a guidance counselor, and support-services staff. In addition, the teacher of the child for whom we are seeking assistance is always a part of the group.
    If you would like additional information about our Pupil Assistance Committee, or if you would like to schedule a meeting to discuss concerns you may have about your child, please contact your child's teacher or me.

Sincerely,

Principal

Most school systems require that principals participate in the development of a crisis response plan—a systematic procedure for dealing with family or community tragedies. Typically, a crisis response plan will spell out those individuals (usually the principal, teachers, a counselor, a school nurse, parents, police officials, and sometimes religious leaders) who will be called in case of an emergency. Such events might include the death of a student, staff member, or parent, or a natural disaster like a severe storm or earthquake that leaves families disrupted. Assembling the group is one matter, but predetermining the ways in which the group will respond is not only at the center of the plan, it is the most important aspect. Who will notify the parent body? Who will deal with the media? Which community representatives will be called upon to help? How will a communications center be established? Where will the children be evacuated in the event of an emergency during the school day, such as a furnace explosion or fire? These are just a few of the items that need to be addressed in a crisis response plan. Often, principals conduct simulated or "mock" crises to gain practice in walking through the steps of the plan. The plan should be well publicized, and the community will undoubtedly appreciate the initiative the principal has shown in developing this level of preparedness in the event of a crisis or community emergency. (More about crisis response planning appears in Chapter 16.)

Get Out Into the Community

Another part of community relations is the alliances created outside of the school building. Many school leaders are members of local service organizations like Rotary, Kiwanis, or Lions Club. Speaking at meetings, or simply mingling with local business and professional people, can do much to promote goodwill for the school in the community.

It is also helpful to establish relationships with local businesses and institutions in the school vicinity. Through such links, principals are often able to garner services or equipment for their schools. Even if nothing material is gained from such associations, local proprietors are often willing to come to school to speak with children about their business or craft, to read to youngsters, or to become involved in other ways.

Ties with senior citizen groups can be mutually beneficial for the students and the seniors. Children can perform at senior centers and, if possible, the seniors can visit the school. Many school leaders have spearheaded "grandparent" programs by matching seniors with students at the school. The youngsters can host a breakfast or lunch and interview the seniors about their occupations, life experiences, or memories of the area. Students can also visit and develop interchanges with residents in local nursing homes—a positive intergenerational experience.

There are countless ways in which you can reach out into the community, invite involvement, and establish positive public relations for the school. It would be a mistake to underestimate the importance and the benefits that can be derived from fostering good community relations. This is key to the role of the elementary school principal.

LEARN FROM EXPERIENCE

As in all life processes and positions, experience is a great teacher. As we wend our way through the obstacles and opportunities that are inherent in the principalship, we must be alert to the signals that inform our practice. Many school leaders have learned the hard way that introducing a new program, curriculum innovation, or new school procedure without involving (or at least listening to) those individuals who will have to live with the decision can lead to resistance, blocking, and even deliberate undermining of the effort. For example, a neophyte principal reasonably concluded that having a Halloween Parade during the school day simply took too much time away from the instructional program—a whole day was essentially wasted. A few teachers had put this idea into his head, and it seemed like the right thing to do. He announced that this year there would be no parade. He had no way of gauging the uproar in the community. Aside from the parents, the students, and other school personnel, neighborhood residents with no official ties to the school always came out to view the students marching around the school grounds. This principal learned, rather quickly, that such decisions, despite their apparent justifications, may indeed fly in the face of long-held traditions and backfire. Of course, all of us will make mistakes, but the benefit of making mistakes is to learn from them.

EFFECTIVE TIME MANAGEMENT PRACTICES

How do active, involved school leaders juggle all the simultaneous demands and priorities that are a part of the position and still keep their heads above water? Time management is key. Each one of us must find the system that works best for her to keep all the balls in the air and not let them fall. A few tips and techniques can help to organize and apportion time within the day.

Get to know the "ebb and flow" of the day. It is a good idea to record your activity in 10- or 15-minute blocks each day for a few days, and then analyze your patterns of interaction. A few predictable time slots may emerge, including

- returning telephone calls;
- meeting with the school secretary and/or office staff;
- working on correspondence;
- doing walk-throughs of the building;
- attending to building and site needs;
- completing teacher observations;
- working on special projects or reports;
- supervising the lunchroom; and
- attending meetings within and outside of the school.

Some school leaders decide upon a specific time of day to meet with their secretaries. For example, once all of the children have settled into their classrooms, you might sit down with the school secretary and go over correspondence, outline jobs for the day, and review schedules and the week's activities. Secretaries generally appreciate having time devoted to outlining priorities and regular meetings to review the stream of tasks that need to be accomplished. Finding a specific time of day to return telephone calls has also helped some principals to develop a sense of order to the day. If possible, being available to chat with teachers at the end of the school day can be very rewarding. Again, this creates a predictable time within the workday. Teachers learn that you are available and appreciate the opportunity to discuss concerns, triumphs, or frustrations. While we all know that school days are highly unpredictable, the extent to which we can build in a level of routine will help to organize our time.

Maintaining a calendar is another important dimension of time management. Record appointments the moment they are made. (Many principals like to maintain their calendar electronically or in pencil since so many meetings and commitments are often changed.) It has worked well for some principals to keep their calendars on their desk and allow the secretary to record any appointments that she makes. Appointments can also be posted electronically in e-mail programs. As an additional reminder, whenever an appointment is recorded, it is also noted in an office log—a notebook in which you and your secretary can record important notations for one another.

The office log is an extremely useful tool. In it you can record times of telephone calls, internal messages, the names of parents who come in to sign their children out, important incidents, and other items that require attention. Make sure that you check it frequently, as it serves as a running log of important events and reminders in the school day and can be referred to as needed. It is a comprehensive account of all office activities. Figure 1.4 is a sample page from an office log.

Another important time management device is the "to do" list. Sometimes, this is incorporated into the calendar alongside times for appointments or in an electronic

Figure 1.4   Sample Page From an Office Log

Monday, December 7, ——

8:05 Mrs. Jacobs called. She will not be able to make the 10:30 A.M. appointment she had with you today. She will call to reschedule.

Please call Jill Adler, 552-1306. She wants to sign up as a substitute and would like to come in for an interview (She sounds nice!)

8:15 Frank Somers called. Please call him back.

8:20 Mrs. Foley came in with a check for tomorrow's assembly. I put it in the safe. The performers will be here at 1:30 AM.

8:45 Dr. Perotta's secretary called. Your meeting with him and the Business Manager has been scheduled for Thursday at 9:30 A.M. (I marked it in your calendar.)

9:05 Mrs. Talbert called to say that Keisha (4-K) will be out all week. She has chicken pox. I have alerted the nurse.

9:10 Emma Jones - Re: Feb. 8th performance of the Middle School Band. She will need 26 music stands and 48 chairs and an extension cord.

9:35 Please call Ellen Duffy,   352-0131.

9:40 Mrs. Forman called. She's very upset about something that happened between James and Ryan Hogos on the bus yesterday. (I tried to calm her down!) Please call her after 1:00 P.M. at 362-6441.

10:05 The "Computer Doctor" arrived. I sent him to the library to check the hard drive that is broken.

10:30 Dr. Biondi called. The Chapter I visiting team will be here next Tuesday, Dec. 15th around 10:00 A.M. (I marked your calendar.)

Please see me about next Wednesday's workshop. There's a problem!

calendar. This list guides the work of the day, and the tasks included can be given time allocations. When you leave the office, take your "to do" list along with you. As you walk through the school, invariably you will come upon things that will need to be remembered. Simply add them to your growing list. The kinds of items in the list might include a need to prepare a work order, a phone call to make, something that must be ordered, and so on. If we don't mark down reminders as we think of them, a busy school leader can often forget them.

At the end of the day, it is beneficial to review the day. Which tasks were accomplished? Which tasks need to be recorded on tomorrow's to-do list? Take a moment to reflect upon the day, preview the next day's calendar, and reprioritize the to-do list. Prioritization is an important activity, and there is no one formula for all school leaders. Some school leaders like to begin the day by accomplishing a few relatively simple tasks to gain momentum and obtain a sense that they already have something under their belts; other school leaders like to forge ahead into the most time-consuming and complex task first and work intensely and uninterruptedly for a while. Each of us must consider various approaches but also know our own work style and personality and make appropriate changes and adjustments to task commitment. Sometimes, it is really useful to force yourself to attempt a new way of doing things, trying out a new working pace or prioritization. This may require moving away from your comfort zone, but the results may be surprising.

MAINTAIN PERSPECTIVE

Maintaining perspective and a sense of humor are essential to success as an elementary school principal. It is easy to become lost in the problems that we all face. Some are truly important; others are really trivial. If we choose to focus on the obstacles (and we encounter many within the course of a day), we are likely to get bogged down and not see the true joys of working with children. We cannot always solve every problem, but if we tell ourselves that we are only human and continue to work to the best of our capacities, there is much pleasure and fulfillment in the sense of accomplishment that accompanies a day in the life of a principal.

When encountering a funny incident with children, teachers, or parents, nearly every principal has at one time or another said that they are going to record it in the book he's going to write when he retires. Cherish these moments and incidents. They are truly special and they bring joy to our work. As you review your work at the end of each day, think of one positive achievement or triumph and one thing from which to learn. Our jobs are indeed difficult to define, but if we continually ask ourselves if we are trying to be "all things to all people" or if we are leading by keeping a few basic principles in mind, we will probably all sleep better at night.

NOTES

1. The phrase "principle-centered leadership" is attributed to author Stephen R. Covey. This concept is best articulated in his book, *Principle-Centered Leadership* (New York: Summit Books, 1991).

2. Systems thinking is often associated with the work of Peter Senge, *The Fifth Discipline: The Art and Practice of the Learning Organization* (New York: Doubleday, 1990).

2

How to Plan for the School Year

Setting Goals and Maintaining Focus

The success of most outstanding schools derives from the desire of the staff to continually improve its own performance and provide meaningful opportunities for students. Goals help to provide a focus for school improvement and the refinement of programs and practices. Members of an effective organization continually examine their own craft and seek ways to enhance performance. One important way to ensure this is through setting and implementing school goals.

THE CONTEXT FOR SCHOOL GOALS

School goals are part of a larger strategic plan. Setting school goals usually follows a definition of the beliefs, vision, and mission for the school. A vision is often thought of as an image of the future you seek to create. A mission is a statement of what the school does to advance the vision. In creating a vision, those who craft it draw on shared beliefs about the environment and the organization. A school leadership team (see Chapter 3) is an ideal body to create a statement of beliefs, because its members usually have broad representation from the school community. A *belief statement* is a philosophical summary of the key values that members of the school community hold dear. In a way, it is a statement of how the school defines itself. The process for developing a statement of beliefs and a vision or mission is somewhat similar. Divide the members of the team developing the statements into three or four groups with mixed constituents in

---

Note: All forms, letters, and checklists included in this chapter can be found at corwin.com/elementary survivalkit.

each group. That is, each group should contain a parent, a teacher, perhaps a secretary, school aide, or custodian.

1. Provide each group with chart paper and a distinct marker color.

2. Have each group brainstorm some of the essential elements or key terms that they feel should be a part of the belief statement or mission.

3. After each group has had enough time to record its thoughts, ask the groups to rotate, read one another's charts, and add comments or questions (with their own marker color) to some of the statements made by the other group.

4. After each group has had time to consider the work of all the others, form new groups to consolidate and refine the statements.

5. As a whole, consider the charts produced and seek the commonalities that will make for a unified document that embraces all of the ideas.

This may seem like a simple task, but it is not. Skilled negotiation, compromise, and goodwill must prevail to perform this task successfully. Often, groups grapple with the idea that some ideas or statements seem "bigger" or more far-reaching than others. Some members of the group may be more adept at refining these statements than others. Rely on the strengths in the group to help develop documents with which everyone feels comfortable. Sometimes, meeting to review subsequent drafts will help to bring a new perspective.

A sample of school vision and mission statements appears below. A school philosophy appears in Figure 2.1.

◖◔ VISION AND MISSION STATEMENTS ◕◗

Our **Vision** for our school is to provide a supportive, nurturing environment in which all students flourish, attain academic excellence, and enhance their self-worth.

The **Mission** of our school community is to help each child identify and cultivate his or her greatest potentials and to provide a curriculum that will foster the skills, knowledge, and attitudes necessary to live a successful, healthy, fulfilling, and informed life.

Figure 2.1 School-Community Philosophy

SCHOOL-COMMUNITY PHILOSOPHY

1. We strive to provide a nurturing environment in which all children can flourish and grow and enhance their self-worth.

   - We care about and accept responsibility for all of the children within our school family.
   - We strive to meet the individual needs of all of our children.
   - We believe in our ability to create programs and secure the resources required to meet our needs.
   - We believe in our ability to solve problems.
   - We respect one another and believe in setting and modeling appropriate behavioral standards for all students.

---

2. We strive for academic excellence in a stimulating school environment.

- We try to instill in all children a love for learning.
- We value problem-solving skills and critical-thinking skills.
- We value creative expression in all of the arts.
- We believe instruction should be relevant to children's lives.
- We value bright, attractive, inviting, and stimulating classrooms.
- We continually examine our curriculum and instructional practices to ensure educational growth and the best possible program for children.

3. We value close ties among children, staff, parents, and the community.

- We value frequent contact between parents and staff to ensure a connection with all aspects of school life.
- We value the mutual sense of appreciation within the school community.
- We work together and plan whole-school experiences as well as activities across grade levels.
- We strive for mutual understanding and respect between the school and the community.

**WE ALL SHARE A SENSE OF PRIDE IN BEING ASSOCIATED
WITH OUR SCHOOL FAMILY!**

It is natural that once a statement of beliefs, a vision, and a mission is created, the goal-setting process will be the next step.

THE POWER OF GOALS

One of the many advantages of setting and maintaining goals is that the process has the potential to bring the staff together. Goals can rally people who exhibit divergent styles and approaches around common purposes. In explaining the importance of developing goals, a wise superintendent used to invoke the old adage, "Your reach should exceed your grasp, or what's a heaven for." The clear implication of this quotation is that goals can help us to reach, stretch, grow, and achieve an ambitious vision.

School goals take many forms. They can define a specific academic target such as improving test scores in a particular area, or developing alternative assessments such as performance tasks or portfolios. Goals can also address a community need such as increasing parent participation in school functions. Goals can also be aimed at improving a certain aspect of school life such as homework practices—both in terms of student completion of homework as well as enhanced teacher communication about homework expectations. Some goals can be directed toward the improvement of an instructional practice like the refinement of cooperative learning approaches.

GOALS SHOULD MAKE A DIFFERENCE

One of the challenges in setting goals is to strike a balance between making them manageable and, at the same time, making them important. Administrators are sometimes tempted to set goals that are trivial—that they know are easy to accomplish, or are simply an acknowledgment of something that is already part of normal school routine. Goals, though, should make a difference; they ought to have the potential for significant school improvement.

Goals that have the greatest promise of bringing about significant results usually cannot be achieved within a single school year. Therefore, many schools set multiyear goals. Each year can build upon the accomplishments of the prior year, or a goal may require several distinct steps to full implementation. For example, if the use of performance-based assessment is a goal, then the staff would probably need to spend a year learning about the approach—reading, attending conferences, and having deliberate conversations. A second year might involve the staff in studying exemplars, designing and implementing performance assessments, and gathering information about use of the practice. Finally, in a third year, the staff might assess how the new approach has impacted student learning and school culture.

SETTING GOALS: BROAD-BASED INVOLVEMENT

Some districts or states require that schools set improvement goals as a part of a monitoring or self-assessment process. Whether required or not, establishing goals is a most worthwhile activity in any school. Not only do goals have the potential to bring improved opportunities to students, they can also help staff members unite on common purposes and directions. Broad-based involvement can yield meaningful, important goals. Diverse viewpoints often result in unique outlooks and perspectives. When several constituents have been involved in setting school goals, they are more likely to "buy into them" and support them. A fairly straightforward sequence for setting goals is outlined below:

1. Form a committee or other group to work on establishing school goals. It is important to involve as many stakeholders as possible—teachers, parents, support personnel, and, naturally, the principal.

2. Review district goals with the committee and consider how school goals address them.

3. Review the needs of the students. Sometimes, a needs-assessment survey precedes the goal-setting process. In other instances, a prescribed state benchmark, such as pupil achievement in a testing program, may dictate that a specific target be set for pupil performance. Baseline data from formal and informal assessment instruments can provide the foundations for creating data-driven goals. What do we want to have happen? What do we need to get there? How will we know that we have arrived? These are all questions that need to be answered to create data-driven goals. (See Chapter 7 for more information.)

4. Once needs and data patterns have been identified, brainstorm broad initiatives that might be undertaken to address those needs. List all of the ideas and do not reject any reasonable thoughts at this point. Sometimes, the needs identified will lead directly to an effort that needs to occur.

5. Discuss each of the ideas put forth. Consider feasibility, resources required, and whether or not the idea would address the identified needs.

6. Select a few broad goals that align with previously established district goals for further discussion and development.

7. Have each member of the committee think about ways that the potential goals might be achieved. What are some specific activities that would support fulfillment of the goals? What resources would be needed? How will we know that we have achieved our goals?

8. Adjourn the meeting.

9. Meet a second time to refine the development and definition of the goals. Sometimes, after a period of time has passed, new insights will be forthcoming and ideas that may have seemed feasible at one time no longer seem appropriate after a period of reflection.

THE ELEMENTS OF WELL-DESIGNED SCHOOL GOALS: SMART GOALS

School goals should begin with a general goal statement. This is a summary of the major intent or purpose of the goal. The need for a connection to district goals should be explained.

A process for the development of goals that is used in many schools is the design of "SMART Goals." SMART is an acronym that usually stands for: Specific, Measurable, Attainable, Relevant, Time-Based. (Different groups use variations of these terms.) Generally, the terms can be described as follows:

Specific

- Is the goal well defined?
- Is the goal clear to anyone who has basic knowledge of the goal?

Measurable

- Can the goal can be measured and by what means?
- What evidence will indicate achievement of the goal?

Attainable

- Is the goal realistic in terms of its reach and time frame?
- Does the goal represent a true stretch in achievement?

Relevant

- Does the goal address the need(s) identified?
- Will it "make a difference"?

Time-Based

- Does the goal have a clear time frame including a target date?
- Are the assessment devices available prior to the target date?

The specific activities required to achieve the goal statement should be identified. Following that, identify the resources required, staff involved, timeline, and means of assessing achievement.

Sample School Goal Statements

School goals should be relevant and related to individual school needs; however, listed below are a few sample goal statements. Data-driven goals might include the following:

- Provide a new science program and instructional strategies that will result in 95% of fourth-grade students attaining a score of 3 or better on the spring state science assessment.

- By June 15, the number of K–5 students will improve their reading comprehension skills 5% in each grade level as measured by the District Reading Assessment.
- By the end of the school year, 90% of fourth-grade students would have prepared a "proficient" persuasive essay about an environmental issue as measured by a teacher-prepared rubric.
- Develop new strategies and review activities so that, by June 15, 90% of all third-grade students will achieve or surpass the minimum level of proficiency on the state mathematics test.

The following examples of more general goals are not necessarily data-driven, but can have elements of measurement that will allow for determination of success:

- Develop ways to incorporate technology into all subject areas.
- Find ways for all teachers to collaborate in the development of integrated instructional units based upon a central theme.
- Improve the level of communication with parents and students about homework expectations.
- Increase awareness within the entire school community and coordinate resources to help children exhibit more inclusive behaviors.
- Study and design alternative assessment techniques for student growth in reading, writing, mathematics, and science.
- Study alternative school scheduling patterns with the intent of providing longer blocks of uninterrupted classroom instructional time and reducing student "pullouts."

A sample of a school goal-planning form appears in Figure 2.2.

Figure 2.2   Goal-Planning Form

_______________________________________ School

GOAL-PLANNING FORM

Activity	Resources	Staff	Timeline	Assessment/Outcomes

KEEP THE BALL IN THE AIR

Once school goals are established, a challenge is to maintain focus on the goals throughout the school year. It is easy for staff members to become bogged down in the routines and problems of daily teaching, and goals that may have seemed important when they were first developed no longer have the same sense of urgency. Here is where the principal must "keep the ball in the air." You can use a variety of techniques to maintain focus and attention to school goals, such as the following:

- Organizing staff in-service programs to address the goals
- Conducting faculty meetings that are concerned with progress toward the goal or that deal with key learnings about the goal
- Having committee members provide brief updates about the accomplishment of specific goal-related activities
- Helping teachers identify how they might support the goal as they develop their own individual professional improvement plans
- Issuing memos and reminders for key dates and deadlines for activity accomplishment reports or assessments
- Talking about progress with staff members during informal conversations

Some principals actually tape the goals to the top of their desks. In this way, they are always within their view. Each day, they glance at activities, timelines, and assessments as a way of keeping the goals in mind.

It is often helpful to inform parents about school goals and initiatives at PTA meetings and other community forums. A letter to parents outlining school goals is also a good communications device. A sample of such a letter appears in Figure 2.3.

Figure 2.3   Letter to Parents Outlining School Goals

OFFICE OF THE PRINCIPAL

______________________ (date)

Dear Parents,

   It was wonderful to see so many of you at Back-to-School Night. There will be many more opportunities throughout the year to participate in such school events.

   Each year, our staff, in collaboration with the School Leadership Team, sets goals for the school. We consider these "challenge goals"—new directions for us to stretch and to grow. In a sense, it's our way to make an already very good school even better! We have outlined three major goals for the current school year:

- **The Assessment of Integrated Learning.** All youngsters will participate in learning experiences that tie together activities from a variety of disciplines around a central theme. In some of these units, children will see how music, art, literature, movement, math, and technology can all contribute to enhancing meaning, making their studies "come alive." Teachers will be designing assessments in which youngsters will ***demonstrate*** what they know and are able to do.

(Continued)

Figure 2.3   (Continued)

- **Improved Science Performance Test Results.** Our classroom teachers are focusing on improving science performance results. They have devised performance assessments set up at stations for the students to accomplish at the end of each science unit. This will give them practice with the format of station assessment that is a part of our fourth-grade state science test. As an added benefit, teachers are finding that the students truly enjoy these experiences.
- **Internet Site Selection.** All students use the Internet at school to support research, conduct simulations, and communicate with others. Some Internet sites are appropriate and relevant to specific units of study. Teacher collaborative groups will identify safe, relevant, and stimulating Internet sites to enhance and support student learning.

Should you have any questions or suggestions regarding our implementation of these school goals, please do not hesitate to contact me.

Sincerely,

Principal

REPORTING ON GOAL FULFILLMENT

Interim reports can be generated to convey progress toward the achievement of school goals. Such reports can take several forms. A sample of an informal letter to parents reporting progress on school goals is shown in Figure 2.4.

Figure 2.4   Letter to Parents Reporting Progress on School Goals

OFFICE OF THE PRINCIPAL

______________________ (date)

Dear Families,
    Happy New Year! I hope that the year ahead is filled with peace, good health, and personal fulfillment. I would like to take this opportunity to provide a brief update on our school goals for the current academic year.

Homework Study

As you may recall, we conducted surveys of parents, teachers, and students last spring concerning the issue of homework. Basically, our goal was to improve the level of communication with parents and students about homework expectations and also to witness an improvement in the level of quality with which homework is completed. Teachers have been taking extra steps to be more explicit about homework expectations—especially in connection with long-range projects in which parental assistance may be requested. A letter was sent to all parents in October in which general homework guidelines were outlined. It is fair to say that we hope parents will support their children's efforts in completing homework without "taking over." Later in the spring, we will be conducting surveys to assess the effectiveness of our efforts in this area.

Integrated Learning

This year, all youngsters have been involved in integrated learning units centering on the central theme of "relationships." These instructional themes usually include well-defined student activities in which several disciplines are brought together to enhance children's learning experiences. Youngsters work in reading, writing, music, art, technology, physical education, and other areas that build upon one another and encourage children to see the natural connections in all areas of study. As always, we will be assessing the impact of our instructional practices. We hope you have seen evidence of these exciting new approaches.

Sincerely,

Principal

In many school systems or states, the results of goal fulfillment must be documented. Even if this is not the case, it is good practice to produce a report on the accomplishment of goals for the staff and the school community. Sharing the results of school goals demonstrates accountability and commitment. These reports can be rather detailed, incorporating graphs, charts, and anecdotal comments—or they can be brief, executive summaries in which the major findings are analyzed and discussed. In any case, the goals statements should be summarized, a review of the goal activities offered, and the results reported along with a discussion of their impact or implications. The format of this report will depend upon the importance of the goals, local reporting requirements, and the degree to which the school community has been involved. A sample of a brief goal-fulfillment report is shown in Figure 2.5.

Figure 2.5 Report on Goal Fulfillment

SCHOOL GOAL NO. 2 (COLLABORATION/ASSESSMENT)

June _______

Goal Statement

For all teachers to collaborate on the development of integrated instructional units based upon a central theme, to identify student outcomes, and to assess student learning through a variety of performance-based techniques.

Summary of Goal Activities

A central theme, "Relationships," was selected by the staff at the end of the ______–______ school year.

Four planning/study groups were formed to develop integrated instructional units based upon the central theme. The following study groups were formed:

- First and Second Grades: "Steps to Friendship"
- Kindergarten and Fifth Grades: "Partners and Relationships"

(Continued)

Figure 2.5   (Continued)

- Third Grades: "Studies of States, Geography, Biographies, and 'Tall Tales'"
- Fourth Grades: "Immigration and the Relationships of Newcomers With Existing Residents"

Classroom and special teachers met to develop the thematic units. Each study group identified the following elements for each of the units planned:

- The expected learning and performance outcomes
- The generalizations and essential questions for the theme
- The disciplines that lend themselves to meaningful integration in the theme
- The kinds of performance/products that will be used to assess the outcomes
- The rubrics or other means to assess the quality of student performance or product

The staff worked with a consultant for one day to provide on-site advice and guidance for the development of assessment techniques.

A variety of performance assessments were developed to evaluate student achievement of the stated outcomes.

Unit planning charts were developed and posted in the staff lounge so that teachers could see each other's efforts and share ideas, activities, and resources with one another.

Teachers conferred and considered how the results of the implementation of the integrated units (and their assessment) informed instructional practices.

A compendium of the results of the performance assessments was compiled and shared.

Analysis of the Results

A great deal of honest and intense collaboration was evidenced in the planning and implementation of the integrated units. Teachers made the time to meet with one another. Teachers of various grade levels planned jointly and special-subject teachers were involved.

The planning process was most effective. Teachers submitted comprehensive unit outlines and defined all of the above-stated elements. Considerable evidence of student involvement was noticed. New and novel learning experiences were afforded to the students. In particular, the units that involved more than one grade level were particularly meaningful. For example, fifth graders observed and studied the ways in which kindergartners play and learn and then drew conclusions. They also considered some developmental differences between how the younger children learn and how they learn.

Teachers became quite analytical of their own practices. In reports submitted that summarized the implementation of the units, the educators reflected upon the assessments used and described how the information obtained might change or alter future approaches.

Implications of the Results

New and unique learning opportunities were planned and implemented with all youngsters. Teachers who might not have worked collaboratively in the past were intensely involved in planning and implementing thematic units. There was anecdotal evidence that these individuals saw the benefits of collaborative relationships and the richness of ideas that can emanate from this work. Classroom teachers realized new strengths—both within themselves and within special-subject teachers—and capitalized upon them.

The units were most stimulating. Teachers designed authentic performance assessments to evaluate the attainment of the anticipated outcomes. The teachers learned how to craft good assessments—learning from experience and analyzing results. Our consultant, ___________________________, met with all teachers at the school on January 23. She worked with each planning group on refining the assessment activities. An increased level of teacher reflection and collaboration was evidenced.

Teachers' analysis of instruction intensified as they indicated how this involvement informed their own practices. They produced novel and engaging assessments and reflected upon which assessments were effective and which were not. Educators found evidence of learning in ways that might not have been previously recognized. They became more explicit in their ability to identify tangible outcomes of learning.

New intensity of collaboration was witnessed among teachers and between teachers and students. An impressive and well-documented compendium of teacher reports was assembled and distributed so that teachers could witness the results of each other's work. The outcomes of the units were shared with the shared decision-making team.

School goals help to bring staff members—and perhaps other members of the school community—together for common purposes. Goals are aimed at student achievement and school improvement and provide a focus for staff involvement and initiative. All organizations benefit from self-examination and the identification of areas for growth and development. The benefits of setting and implementing school goals go far beyond the goals themselves. They announce to the community that in your school, you seek ways to examine programs and practices and continually improve operations. This, in itself, is a purposeful and powerful statement.

3

Shared Decision-Making

The Key to a More Effective School

As a school leader, you are called upon to make countless decisions each day. Some can be dealt with by relying on your instincts. Which substitute will you assign to which classroom? How will you deal with a disruptive student, an irate parent, or a school bus that is late? All are on-the-spot decisions that experienced principals make in the course of a day without consultation. In other matters that principals face—important matters, such as new directions for the school, staff development initiatives, or restructuring—would benefit from broad-based, participatory decision-making. Collaboration in the formation of school policies, priorities, and resource allocation not only enhances the outcomes, it also promotes leadership within the staff and community, and can result in increased levels of commitment to the school and its programs.

WHAT IS MEANT BY SHARED DECISION-MAKING?

Shared decision-making, one of the major educational reform items of the 1990s, is a structure in which all the major stakeholders in an organization work together to define goals, formulate policy, and implement programs to enhance operational effectiveness. Essentially, this means that those individuals who will be charged with carrying out a decision or implementing a program will be involved in making the decision or designing the policy. Shared decision-making is an attempt to place the responsibility and accountability closest to the level where the decisions will be implemented. There are

Note: All forms, letters, and checklists included in this chapter can be found at corwin.com/elementary survivalkit.

many degrees of shared decision-making ranging from an informal advisory group for a principal all the way to a strong, empowered school leadership council in which the principal is but a single member with a single voice. Several terms are often used interchangeably in describing shared decision-making, but each of them has important distinctions. Some of these terms include

- principal's advisory committee,
- school advisory council,
- administrative decentralization,
- participatory management,
- school improvement committee,
- school-based management,
- site-based management,
- school-based leadership council, and
- school-based decision-making.

Each of these terms has a different implication and refers to a distinct form of shared decision-making. The *school advisory council* or *principal's advisory committee* are the terms that suggest the least degree of external empowerment. Principals may select a committee of teachers and/or parents (at their own pleasure) and bring issues to the group for which the opinions or reactions of others are desired. In this form of shared decision-making, the principal may solicit input regarding alternative approaches to a problem or situation, but since the group is advisory in nature, its decisions are not at all binding. In *administrative decentralization*, important decisions are made at the school site, rather than at a district office, but the principal can decide upon how much authority is shared and to what extent members of the larger school community are involved in making decisions and setting policies.

Participatory management suggests that individuals aside from the principal are involved in decision-making at the school. This may be restricted to assistant principals, team leaders, grade-level leaders or advisors, or a broader segment of the school community. It just means that others participate in formulating and carrying out programs, policies, and procedures.

A *school improvement committee* is a specific form of shared decision-making in which a group of staff or community members sets specific goals for school improvement and also specifies means of accomplishing tasks associated with the goals. State education departments sometimes mandate school improvement committees, particularly when student performance falls to substandard levels. The group may have a narrow scope or it may be somewhat broad in its influence, depending upon how the committee is constituted and designed.

Perhaps the most common terms that are used to signify shared decision-making are *school-based decision-making*, *site-based management*, *school-based management*, or *school-based leadership councils*. These phrases refer to a process in which the school becomes the primary unit of decision-making. Decision-making in this context usually involves staff members, parents, and often community members who are not necessarily affiliated with the school. These decision-making bodies are often associated with school reform—the removal of bureaucratic obstacles to bring new opportunities to students—that is based upon the collective inquiries and recommendations of the members of a school's shared leadership group or other leadership forum. This form of shared decision-making is the basis for the assumptions and premises in this chapter.

Shared decision-making was not invented by anyone. It has developed as a response to a traditional model of top-down, authoritarian school control. The delegation of power, decision-making, and responsibility to the local school unit has the potential for divergent and creative responses to school operations and problems.

WHAT ARE THE BENEFITS OF SHARED DECISION-MAKING?

Any attempt to broaden the base of decision-making in a school is likely to result in greater commitment on the part of others in the implementation of those decisions. When staff and community members feel influential, their creative potential is released. The collaborative nature of school-based management has the added benefit of reducing faculty isolation—a problem that plagues professionals in many school systems. It has been found that when people work together, they are less likely to press for special interests or idiosyncratic approaches, since their involvement in shared decision-making helps them to see the "larger picture."

Shared decision-making sends a signal to staff and community members that their opinions and expertise are valued. Improvement in faculty morale is a frequent outcome. Collaborative decision-making can also match resources and programs to locally developed instructional goals. Leadership among staff and community members is likely to emerge and be nurtured through such a process.

The nature of collaboration, although not without its problems, often results in increased communication. People involved with the school—often with a variety of points of view—bring their perspectives to the table and everyone involved can benefit from the broadened outlook. With the necessary professional development required to operate as an effective school advisory or governing body, school improvement will be at the forefront of the agenda. Shared decision-making is a forum in which all segments of the school community can "buy into" the school program and feel that they have had an important role in crafting it.

In addition to the very real benefits outlined above, some states and school districts *mandate* the creation of shared decision-making groups in schools. These same groups are so helpful in school improvement efforts and collaborative involvement that they may also be used for a variety of other functions: Title I committees, grant development groups, or mandate compliance groups. A shared decision-making group (or a subcommittee from such a group) can provide the forum for these mandated discussions to occur.

WHAT DO EFFECTIVE SCHOOL LEADERSHIP GROUPS DO?

Shared decision-making emerges when there is broad support for this form of school leadership. The principal who feels coerced into forming a group will not really support its operation and may in fact undermine its success. It is wise to visit schools that have had positive experiences with shared decision-making structures, interview participants, and ask about the benefits as seen from the point of view of each of the constituents.

In general, effective school leadership groups will be committed to enhancing student performance, improving school climate, fostering professionalism, increasing broad participation, and endeavoring to reach more effective, long-lasting decisions for the school.

The specific areas in which such groups become involved are variable. It depends on the school district and the views of the principal and the members of the team. Some of the kinds of activities that are appropriate for school leadership groups to deal with include

- school safety concerns,
- improvement of student performance,
- homework policies,
- staff development initiatives,
- cultural arts opportunities,
- school climate,
- school scheduling,
- discipline,
- the needs and maintenance of the physical plant and school grounds,
- enrichment opportunities for students,
- parent involvement,
- budgeting, and
- staffing.

Not every school can deal with all of these issues each year, and this is simply a list of the possibilities that can be a part of the team's agenda. Some of the more complex (and "touchy") issues, such as staffing, budgeting, and instructional practice, may not be appropriate until the group has "gotten its feet wet" and matured. As effective teams evolve, the members feel more confident to tackle some of the more "thorny" and controversial issues and often "morph" into school learning communities.

In this section, you'll find a few specific activities and skills that are important for the group members to consider as they launch into shared decision-making and site-based management.

Communicate, Consult, and Collaborate

Whatever happens in a meeting, it is important to communicate with various constituents to check the perceptions that may have emerged at the meeting. One pattern of communication that has proven quite useful is for each member of the group to agree to consult with 7 or 10 colleagues to test ideas and gain input. In one successful team, primary-grade teachers met with other primary teachers, special-subject teachers "touched base" with other special teachers, and other teachers defined a group of parents with whom they would confer. Each person within the team selected an "outside-of-the-team" school constituent group to gain feedback on ideas and the work of the leadership team: One parent chose to work with members of the Asian parent community, and the principal opted to contact members of the school's Hispanic community. In this way, when important issues were discussed, the team members obtained a broad cross section of the feelings and opinions of others in the school community. Through such interchanges, the team members benefited from the ideas of others, refined their perceptions, became attentive to a variety of audiences, and raised collective consciousness. The graphic in Figure 3.1 depicts such patterns of communication.

Figure 3.1   Patterns of Communication

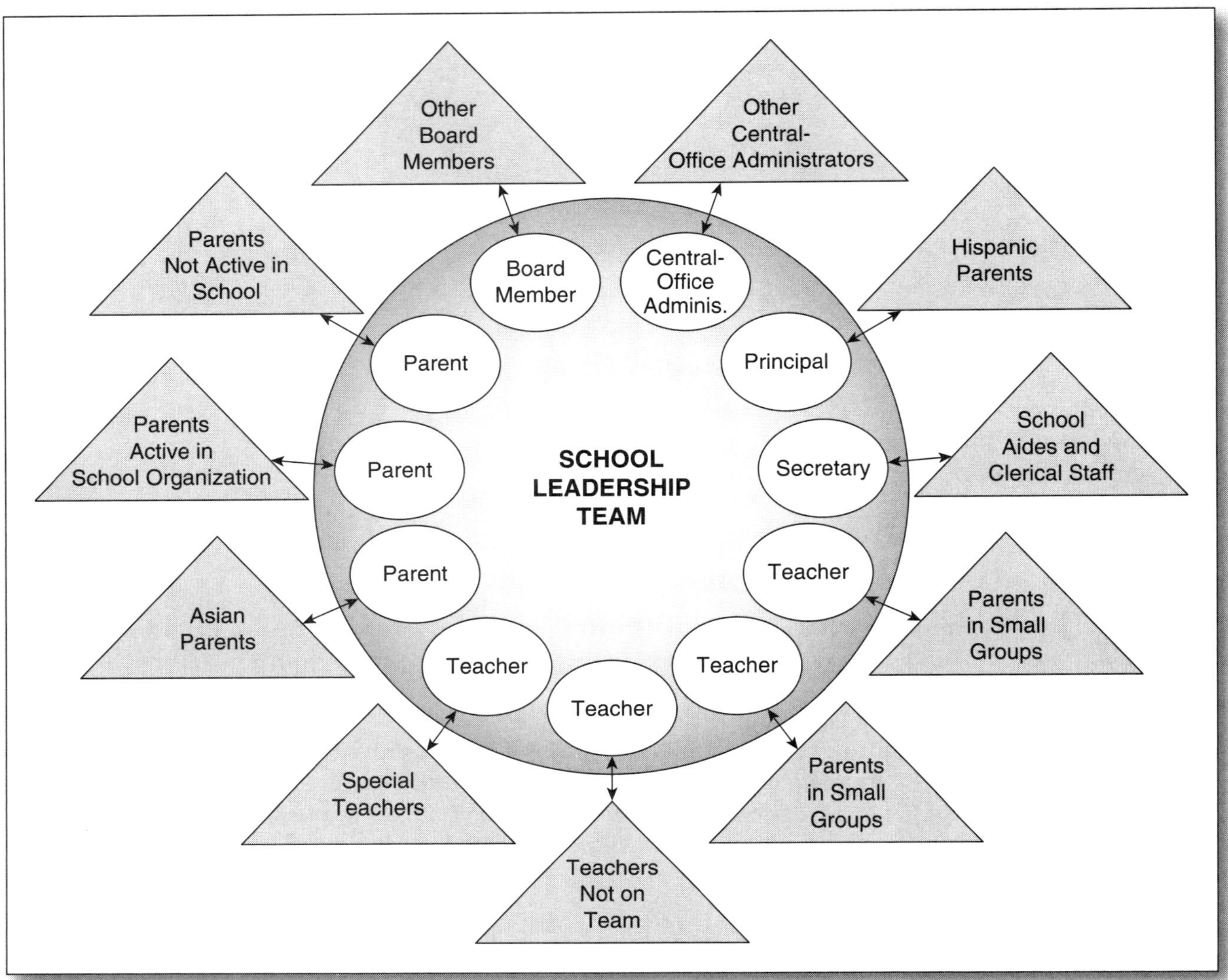

Define a School Statement
of Beliefs, Vision, Mission, and Goals

A good, productive activity for a leadership team to begin with is to define a school philosophy or statement of beliefs and vision and mission statements. There are some distinctions among these terms. A school *philosophy* is basically a statement of the guiding principles that drive decision-making and action at the school. A *mission* is an organization's "reason for being." It is a concise view of what a school, institution, or corporation strives for. It should be specific and focused and give a clear sense of direction. The mission statement should clearly be action oriented. *Goals* constitute the operational plan for achieving the vision and mission, consistent with the school beliefs. (See Chapter 2 for a more thorough discussion of preparing school belief and mission statements and goals.)

Conduct Needs Assessments

Members of school leadership groups can conduct needs assessments to begin to consider issues of common interest. A needs assessment can be a fairly simple instrument—just a questionnaire that taps what individuals feel are the greatest needs for the school from their point of view. Fairly complex and scientific needs-assessment instruments are available, but a very straightforward one appears in Figure 3.2. Once the members of the group have filled out their needs assessments, the sheets can be shared, discussed, and prioritized. When needs have been identified and the members of the group feel that they are legitimate and important, plans can be made to investigate these needs further and to draft action plans to meet them.

Figure 3.2 Needs-Assessment Form

NEEDS-ASSESSMENT IDENTIFICATION FORM

1. What do you think are the greatest needs facing our school in the following areas?

   Curriculum and Instruction: ____

   ____

   ____

   Community Relations: ____

   ____

   ____

   School Climate: ____

   ____

   ____

   The Physical School Plant and Grounds: _______________________________

   ____

   ____

2. Why do you feel that the items identified above are significant needs?

Name: ____

Consider School Climate Issues

School climate is an important matter for such groups to consider. School spirit, parental involvement, openness, student discipline, and staff facilities are all aspects that affect school climate. Do parents feel welcome? Do children feel valued? Do staff members feel appreciated? All of these items are appropriate topics and issues for school leadership teams to address.

Discuss Matters of Interest to the School Community

Sometimes, matters important to the parent community are not apparent to staff members. In some schools, parents' perception of preferential treatment in class placements, homework expectations, and staff availability for parent conferences are items that may be of interest to the parents. Certainly, all members of the school community have a stake in the school's physical facilities, and this is a topic of great interest and appropriateness for school leadership groups.

Act as a School Learning Community

In education, new instructional programs and techniques constantly emerge. Sometimes, staff members jump right on the bandwagon only to find that the trend has passed. Teachers often say that they see trends come and go with new approaches quickly falling out of favor; "they have seen it all!" Such a cynical view, though, can never really result in educational improvement and development. Therefore, a very legitimate activity for school leadership groups to engage in is to study new programs and instructional methodologies, read literature, conduct action research, and decide in an informed manner as a school learning community about which new programs to pilot or which ones need further clarification or development.

Distribute Resources

All schools have resources that are available. Such items might include computers and other technological devices, furniture, building spaces, and the like. Aside from these physical items, there are of course financial resources. There are times when school principals would appreciate group input and problem solving regarding how best to distribute such resources. If such decisions are made by the principal alone, staff members might cry "favoritism." However, when such allocations are determined (or recommended) by a leadership group with broad representation, the decisions are more likely to be accepted without resentment.

Establish Budget Goals and Priorities

All members of the school community have a vested interest in the school budget. Some leadership teams are not ready for this responsibility, but it is an important one. School budgets are often political matters. If the principal can demonstrate that a budget request was developed with broad-based input, including the advice of community members, the process will be viewed as more democratic, collegial, and representative. All voices will be heard in the process—from the practitioner in the classroom to the taxpayer who may not have any children in school.

Intense interest in the needs of the school building and capital projects also exists in school communities—whether it be considering if replacement windows are more important than improving the school fields, or resurfacing a gymnasium floor, or replacing hallway lighting. The leadership team is an ideal body to discuss and prioritize such needs. Again, the broad-based input from all school stakeholders will undoubtedly result in greater support for school budgets, capital programs, or even bond issues.

Provide Input Into Personnel Decisions

Whether or not a school leadership team will have input into personnel decisions is usually a matter determined by the district office or the board of education. In some cases, a school team, or a subcommittee of the team, will conduct paper screening or interview candidates for positions in the school. In other cases, this function is a centralized one. The exact role that a school team will have in personnel decisions should be determined at the time the group is organized so as to avoid any misunderstandings. Members of any interview committee must be trained to learn about legal matters related to hiring and personnel practices.

Assess the Effectiveness of School Programs

School programs and practices benefit from fair and honest assessment. Sometimes, the effects of programs are measured by standardized tests; in other cases, portfolios and other forms of authentic assessment are more appropriate. Many times, an integral part of assessing school programs is an open discussion of the impressions of those who deliver and receive such instruction. School leadership teams can have important conversations about school practices, and such dialogue will yield important insights and information.

Through shared decision-making, school leadership groups can support or make recommendations for school organization, class-size ranges, and the incorporation of new initiatives, among other things.

Engage in Positive Public Relations

One of the functions of a school leadership team is to promote the school. Positive public relations are an essential activity. Newsletters of team initiatives; a simple brochure explaining the group, its functions, and membership; and reports to the wider school community are all effective means of promoting good public relations. A school leadership group can assign a member as a public relations liaison who can issue press releases and coordinate efforts to inform others about team activities. Two samples are included. The first is a letter from a principal announcing the formation of a school leadership team (Figure 3.3), and the other is a letter that provides a report on the recent accomplishments of such a group (Figure 3.4).

Figure 3.3 Letter Announcing the Formation of a School Leadership Team

_______________________________ (date)

Dear Members of the School Community,

Greetings! At our school, we believe that the people responsible for implementing school decisions should be a part of the process of arriving at those decisions. That's one reason why so many schools across the nation have begun to change their decision-making process by moving to a system of school-based management.

Several states have mandated school-based management, and a number of schools have now instituted shared decision-making as a part of their routine operation. We are fortunate that our staff is committed to implementing this promising practice as well.

(Continued)

Figure 3.3   (Continued)

School-based management has a number of advantages for teachers, for parents, for non-parent taxpayers, and—most importantly—for our students. For parents, there is mounting evidence that parent participation in education is a critical component for student success in school. Research clearly shows that school programs designed with strong parental involvement result in improved student performance. Also, with the dramatic increase of working parents, there are fewer parents available during the day for traditional parent volunteer activities. Schools need to accommodate the needs of working parents if they want to build relationships that can lead to increased communication. Finally, school-based management raises parent and community enthusiasm and is a positive force in gaining support for school budgets.

Our school's Leadership Team will be representative of all constituencies of our school community when making decisions. It will be comprised of four of our teachers, three parents, the school secretary, our assistant superintendent for instruction, and myself. Our team has begun to develop a school philosophy statement. Through "focus meetings" (dates and times to be announced), we will be able to share our vision with our community at large. Our ultimate philosophy statement will enable the council to shape decisions within our school and help the school community become more aware of its resources and needs.

I am most enthusiastic about this wonderful opportunity for shared decision-making. We all hold a precious stake in the education of our youngsters. As stakeholders, our school-community partnership will surely be strengthened and more enduring.

Sincerely,

Principal

Figure 3.4   Letter About School Leadership Team Accomplishments

__________________________ (date)

**HOW HAS THE SCHOOL LEADERSHIP
TEAM AFFECTED YOUR CHILD?**

The school's Leadership Team is our shared decision-making group. Composed of parents, teachers, the principal, the school secretary, and a member of the Board of Education, the team meets once each month to consider issues of importance to teachers, parents, and the community at large. All meeting dates are listed in our school newsletter, and interested parties are always welcome to sit in on meetings and witness our deliberations.

You might be wondering how the actions of the Leadership Team have influenced programs and practices and affected your own child at our school. Highlighted below are just a few of the many initiatives undertaken by the team.

- **A New Way of Scheduling.** In response to teacher and parent concerns about a highly fragmented school day for students, a subgroup of the Leadership Team conducted a two-year school scheduling study. As a result of an increase in the number of "pullout" programs, e.g., Speech/Language, Instrumental Music, Remedial Reading and Math, and E.S.L., we found that some classroom teachers have their whole class with them for less than 50% of the school day. The team's findings and recommendations led to an improved school schedule that has allowed teachers to have their entire class together for longer blocks of time. Teacher planning time was also rearranged so that teachers at the same grade level can plan together to allow for increased curriculum coordination. Parents, teachers, and students have all attested to the positive effects of our practices in school scheduling.

- **Homework Practices.** A yearlong study of homework practices led to a clearer understanding of the purposes of homework, improved teacher communication about homework expectations, and a greater degree of independence for homework completion on the part of most of our students.
- **Reconfigured Support Services Program.** The Leadership Team was instrumental in the development of a plan to restructure the ways in which we provide academic assistance to youngsters. The redesign of our program and staffing patterns resulted in a greater level of service to students at times during the school day that were more convenient for both teachers and students. We made the "program fit the child," rather than the "child fit the program."

This year, our meetings have focused on a consideration of alternative means of assessing student progress in a variety of areas. We are also exploring ways to help students become more sensitive to the feelings of one another and are considering a peer mediation program. We are also planning a series of school spirit get-togethers in which we will be able to chat more informally with all members of the school community about school projects and initiatives.

Principal

WHAT STEPS ARE REQUIRED TO ESTABLISH A SCHOOL LEADERSHIP TEAM?

Starting a school leadership team requires advance planning. Where does the initiative come from? The principal? The central office? Interested staff members? Parents? Whatever the source of initial interest, the principal must take a key role in getting the ball rolling. One of the first things is to call a meeting of concerned parties to define some of the purposes and possible configurations of a school leadership team. (Sometimes, you will be responding to a state or district mandate to form such a group.) Once there is sufficient interest and support for the development of a school shared decision-making body, some of the more concrete activities can take place.

Decide Upon Team Composition

One of the important decisions that will have to be addressed by an emerging shared decision-making body is the composition of the group. How many members will the group have? What constituencies of the school community will be represented? How long are the terms of membership? School leadership teams might include representatives from the following groups:

- Teachers
- Parents

- Nonteaching staff members: a secretary, custodian, school aide, crossing guard
- Nonparent member of the community
- A district office representative
- A member of the board of education
- Principal

The matter of parent membership was a somewhat controversial issue in the early days of school leadership teams. More recently, however, parents are considered essential participants. Indeed, in some schools it is sometimes an issue whether teachers or parents will represent a majority of the group membership. Some schools make a point of seeking a nontenured teacher for the group so as to provide a different perspective than the one provided by more "seasoned" faculty members. The matter of whether or not to include students on a school leadership team is another matter that should be considered. Most leadership teams in elementary schools do not include students as regular members but may find, from time to time, that it would be beneficial to invite student representatives to a meeting to join in the discussion of particular issues. Some states dictate the composition of school leadership teams.

The size of a school leadership team is another matter that must be considered. Generally, a group of 10 to 15 members seems to be most common. More than 20 members can result in an unwieldy group, yet fewer than 8 may be too few members to be truly representative. Three sample configurations for a school leadership team are listed below:

1 Principal	1 Principal	1 Principal
3 Teachers	4 Teachers	4 Teachers
		1 from K–2
		1 from 3–5
		1 Special
		1 Nontenured
3 Parents	3 Parents	4 Parents
1 Support Staff	1 Secretary	1 Noncertified Staff
1 District Office	1 District Office	1 Teaching Assistant
	1 Community Member	1 District Office
		1 Board of Ed Member
		1 Nonparent Community
		1 Student __________
__________	__________	
9 Members	**11 Members**	**15 Members**

Just how each of these members is selected is another matter that must be considered. The principal may appoint teachers and parents. In some cases, a teacher association official appoints teachers, though their peers may also elect them. A selection committee of the school PTA might secure parent representatives and a similar selection committee of the school faculty might secure teacher representatives.

The length of terms of team members is another factor that must be decided. In most cases, team members serve for one, two, or three years. It makes good sense to establish a term of more than one year so as to provide continuity. Some teams build in a "staggered term" procedure. For example, when the group is first formed, half of the members will join for three years and the other half will join for two years. In this way, the entire team will not all change at once, and at least half of the members will overlap in order to provide continuity.

Define Which Decisions the Leadership Team Will Make

Based upon the degree of latitude allowed by the school district, the interests of the team members, and the needs of the school, a list of the kinds of decisions that are appropriate or desirable for the team to make should be prepared.

Fledgling groups may not have the experience or training to make some kinds of decisions, for example: personnel recommendations, staff assignments, budget priorities, and other such matters. However, as the group matures, these kinds of decisions can be considered.

Create a Constitution for the School Leadership Team

A wise consultant to a school leadership group once recommended that its members not be in too much of a hurry to encode its operating procedures. Instead, she suggested that the group "live for a year" without too many restrictions so that the members themselves might determine the best ways to operate, tailored to their own situation. What kinds of decisions have been made? How have these decisions been arrived at? What have been the various roles within the school leadership team? What are the communication patterns? What are some of the obstacles? These questions and others should be considered before actually writing a constitution.

A sample constitution from an elementary school leadership team appears in Figure 3.5.

Figure 3.5　Sample School Leadership Group Constitution

**SAMPLE CONSTITUTION FOR
AN ELEMENTARY SCHOOL LEADERSHIP TEAM**

The school's Leadership Team was initiated in the spring of _______ to provide a structure for shared decision-making within the school community. This document was designed to create a structure and operational plan for the Leadership Team.

  I. Official Name

    The official name of the site-based decision-making group at (name of school) Elementary shall be the "(name of school) School Leadership Team."

 II. Operating Guidelines

    A. The school Leadership Team's constitution is developed by the team members and is subject to annual approval by its membership.

    B. Copies of the Leadership Team's constitution shall be distributed to members of the team and a copy shall be kept in the school office and the district office for review by the staff and the public.

    C. It is understood and expected that members of the team will act as communication liaisons to their constituent groups.

(Continued)

Figure 3.5 (Continued)

III. Membership and Election Procedures

A. The Team will be composed of the following eleven (11) individuals from the school community:

- The School Principal;
- Four (4) teachers to be elected by their peers. Two teachers will be elected each year for two-year terms. If possible, included among the four shall be one teacher from the primary grades, one from the intermediate grades, one special-subject teacher, and one nontenured teacher.
- Three (3) parent members should include a current PTA president, an active member of the PTA, and a third member not necessarily affiliated with the PTA. Parents will be selected by the PTA to serve for a term of two years.
- One (1) support staff person (e.g., secretary, custodian, lunchroom aide, teacher aide, clerical aide, library aide) to be elected by his/her peers for a two-year term at a meeting chaired by the current support staff team member.
- One (1) central-office administrator to be selected by the superintendent for a two-year term.
- One (1) Board of Education member to be selected by the board president for a two-year term.

B. Members may serve for no more than two consecutive terms.

C. A staggering process of team membership will begin during the _____–_____ school year in order to ensure continuity.

D. In the event of a resignation, a new member will be selected according to the above procedure.

IV. Selection and Responsibilities of the Leadership Team's Chair

A. The chairperson of the Leadership Team shall be elected for a one-year term by the team from among its members. To promote a greater sense of shared decision-making, it is agreed that the principal shall not serve as chair.

B. The chairperson will work with the facilitator to set the agenda for each meeting using input from the members of the team and the school community.

C. A facilitator, a recorder, and a timer will be selected for each meeting.

V. Meetings

A. Meetings will be held on a regular basis, at different times of the day, in order to accommodate the schedules of as many members of the team as possible.

B. Schedules of meetings shall be listed in the school's monthly newsletter.

C. The agendas shall be posted in a conspicuous place in the school one week before the meeting. Items may be added at the discretion of the chairperson.

D. All meetings shall take place in the school, unless otherwise noted.

E. It is recommended that each team member encourage visitors to attend meetings. Visitors may speak to agenda items but shall have no vote.

F. If special circumstances prevent attendance, members will notify the chairperson.

VI. Committees

    A. To broaden involvement among staff and parents, standing committees may be established by the Leadership Team to provide recommendations and information to the team as needed.

    B. *Ad hoc* committees shall be established by the team as needed and will serve until their tasks are completed. These may be buildingwide, grade-level, or subject-specific committees.

    C. The leader of each of these committees shall communicate about their activities and progress to the Leadership Team and chairperson on a regular basis.

VII. Voting

    A. A quorum is defined as 7 (including the principal) of the 11 team members and is required for any decision necessitating a vote.

    B. Each member of the team shall have one vote on any issue. Voting is by voice or show of hands, unless otherwise agreed upon.

    C. Decisions shall be made by consensus whenever possible unless any member present requests a formal vote. When a vote is taken, a majority of the entire team (6 of the 11 members) must approve.

    D. The principal may exercise the right to call for a reconsideration of a team vote within a reasonable time period (one to two weeks). Whenever the principal exercises this right, a meeting of the team will be convened as soon as possible. At that meeting, the reconsidered vote must receive a 75% majority (8 of the 11 members) in order to pass.

VIII. Minutes

    A. Minutes shall be recorded and distributed to team members, to the superintendent of schools, and to the president of the teachers association. Minutes shall be made available to members of the Board of Education and the school community. Individual copies may be requested of the school secretary.

    B. Minutes shall be kept on file in the school office for a period of five years.

IX. Changes and Amendments

Changes or suspensions in provisions of this document adopted by the Leadership Team would require approval by at least 75% of the team.

Constitution adopted: March 6, _________   LAST AMENDED 1/21/____

Set Specific Goals for the Leadership Team

In addition to operational procedures, the members of a school leadership team should consider its purpose or goals. These will vary from school to school, and from district to district. The purpose will depend upon the degree of authority that the group has—whether it is a true decision-making body or simply an advisory group. In some cases, the goals of the team can be incorporated into the constitution. A sample of the goals set for a school leadership team is shown in Figure 3.6.

Figure 3.6   Sample Statement of Goals for a School Leadership Team

STATEMENT OF GOALS FOR A SCHOOL LEADERSHIP TEAM

The school's Leadership Team was established to broaden participation and decision-making within the school community. The specific goals of the Leadership Team include the following:

Chart a Vision for the School

The Leadership Team will define the guiding principles for the future of the school. This will support and enhance our school philosophy and be developed with broad input from the entire school community.

Address Concerns of the School Staff and Parent Community

The Leadership Team will solicit agenda items from the staff and the parent community, and consider these issues and make recommendations based upon discussion and deliberation.

Serve in an Advisory Capacity to the Principal

The Leadership Team will provide the principal with input concerning specific decisions related to budget and staffing and other issues for which the principal seeks advice.

Function as a School Learning Community

The Leadership Team will help research, plan, and support instructional practices and programs. The team will serve as a "sounding board" in the assessment of such programs and practices. The team will also help to develop staff development plans to ensure that instructional programs are carefully implemented.

Be Involved in Meeting State Requirements as They Arise

Since the State Education Department requires that school-community committees be established to review school goals and annual plans, the Leadership Team will be the group that fulfills this function.

Interface With the School District Quality Council

The Leadership Team will provide regular and ongoing communication with the District Quality Council through its elected representative. The Leadership Team will support and reinforce district goals and priorities.

Promote Positive Public Relations for the School

The Leadership Team will actively promote positive public relations for the school by effectively communicating the accomplishments of the school and the team.

WHAT IS THE RELATIONSHIP OF THE LEADERSHIP TEAM TO THE LARGER SCHOOL COMMUNITY?

It is only natural for a school leadership team's authority to be questioned in the larger school community. Should this group make decisions for the staff and announce them as done deals? Should this group make decisions that will have an effect on the parent community and then announce it as a *fait accompli*? Such matters have caused lots of problems for school leadership groups and may undermine their effectiveness or even spell their demise. There are times when the members of a team feel frustrated about going back and forth to their constituencies to test ideas and gain feedback on decisions. Admittedly, this does slow down the proceedings; however, without such communication, decisions will more than likely be resented, and some members of the school staff and parent community may work to sabotage the group's efforts. Members of school leadership teams are well advised to do a lot of conferring and gathering of input before arriving at important decisions that will affect the lives of others. This is not to say that teams cannot make significant determinations, but effective communication and a sense of responsibility to the larger school community are likely to result in decisions that are met with greater acceptance and appreciation.

WHAT ARE THE SKILLS REQUIRED FOR EFFECTIVE TEAM MEETINGS?

The conduct of meetings sets an important tone for the overall operation and effectiveness of a school leadership team. Meetings should always follow an agenda with a time allocation for each item, along with a clear sense of individual roles and responsibilities. Members should be respectful of diverse points of view and learn to listen to what others have to say. Good meetings don't just happen; specific skills are necessary for effective, cooperative, and productive team meetings.

What Are the Characteristics of Successful Meetings?

The following is a list of the characteristics of successful meetings:

- Agendas are distributed prior to the meeting with a time allocation for each item.
- All group members focus on agenda topics during the meeting.
- All members have equal access to relevant information.
- Various viewpoints are respected.
- Someone serves as facilitator, process observer, recorder, and timekeeper.
- A recorder takes minutes of the meeting.
- The effectiveness of the meeting is assessed.
- The minutes are disseminated after the meeting so as to form a collective memory.

Define Clear Roles and Responsibilities

Specific roles for team members will help to move meetings along in a productive fashion. These roles should be rotated among the group members so that all participants have experience performing each of the functions. Some of the roles cannot be learned at a single meeting, so many teams rotate the roles every three months. Following is a list of the more important roles and responsibilities for team meetings:

Facilitator

- Remains neutral during the meeting; does not take sides on issues
- Moves the meeting along according to the agenda

- Focuses the group on the topics at hand and discourages extraneous discussion
- Encourages participation by all members; deliberately elicits opinions from those reluctant to speak
- Protects individuals from criticism or personal attack
- Suggests strategies and methods to resolve complex issues
- Summarizes what others have said and reviews decisions

Recorder

- Takes minutes of what takes place at the meeting
- Checks for accuracy, occasionally asking the group if what is being recorded clearly matches the collective memory of what has happened
- Organizes ideas, decisions, and accomplishments
- Copies important material that may have been recorded on charts
- Prepares or submits minutes in a timely manner

Timekeeper

- Keeps track of timelines allowed for each agenda item
- Provides reminders to the group when time allotment is about to expire
- Seeks approval from the group to extend beyond the allowed time limit for a specific item
- Assesses how well the group has kept to time limits

Group Member

- Contributes to group discussion
- Maintains focus on agenda items
- Helps facilitator remain neutral during discussions
- Encourages all members to participate
- Actively listens to what others are saying
- Works to achieve consensus
- Maintains a positive and productive attitude

Aspects of Active Listening

During team meetings, each member should listen to what others are saying—really listen. Active listening is a skill that should be discussed and practiced by all team members. Some of the essential aspects of active listening include the following factors:

- *Maintain eye contact.* Look at the speaker. Your body language says a lot about how intently you are listening. Leaning in toward the speaker also demonstrates that you are focusing on what is being said.
- *Seek clarification.* If you do not fully understand the content and intent of what someone else is saying, ask for clarification. When individuals are asked to clarify what they are saying, their ideas are likely to become more precise and accurate.
- *Paraphrase.* Restating what someone has said is another means of seeking clarification. If you paraphrase a group member's statement or point of view, it is a good check to see if you really understood what the other person was saying. Some phrases that you might use to paraphrase include: *Are you saying that . . . ? Do I*

understand correctly that . . . ? Do you mean that . . . ? Essentially, what you are saying is . . . ? If your restatement was inaccurate, the person has an opportunity to clarify what was said and you can check again.

- *Define areas of agreement and difference.* When there are differences among group members about issues or ideas, it is helpful to define the areas where various members agree or differ. Determining where people stand can help the group reach a resolution or compromise.

Active listening doesn't just happen. It is an important skill that must be learned and practiced.

How to Achieve Consensus

Consensus decision-making is not an easy process, but it can be very powerful and advantageous for effective team meetings. Consensus means a general agreement. It is a decision in which key points of view have been integrated. All members of the group feel that their ideas have been incorporated into the consensus decision. Consensus decision-making may take more time than decisions based upon polls or votes, but the outcome is more likely to be better supported. All members must contribute to the formation of a consensus. Differences are clarified and viewed as helpful to the process. Consensus does not require unanimity, but it is a carefully crafted amalgam of all ideas pertinent to an issue. Consensus decision-making requires open and honest communication, a high level of trust, and a belief that issues can be resolved by including a wide variety of opinions.

In working toward consensus, all members of the group have an obligation to explain and clarify their perceptions, convey their feelings, listen carefully to others, maintain flexibility, and be willing to negotiate. Achieving consensus does not mean that a vote has been unanimous, but it is a decision that everyone in the group can live with and support. Once a consensus is reached, all members agree to take responsibility for implementing the final decision.

How to Overcome Obstacles and Conflicts

There are inherent obstacles in any shared decision-making process. Awareness of these obstacles and acting to overcome them can help to move the work of the team along. One of the most common obstacles is lack of agreement. This is why it is important, early on, to define just what the team will and will not do.

Another obstacle to effective team progress is *unrealistic* expectations. Some members expect that all of the major problems facing the school and community will be solved in short order by the school leadership team. The team is not a panacea. It *can* increase the level of participation in decision-making, but clearly it will not be able to make all decisions that need to be made in a school. The members of school leadership teams should be realistic and practical about the impact that they can have.

Some teams take on too much too soon and then may feel thwarted in their efforts. Sound advice given to beginning groups is to start small but deal with issues that are important. Try not to take on too many issues too quickly.

Respect for collective bargaining agreements must be maintained if leadership teams are to be effective. All members of the group should be given copies of the various contracts that guide the responsibilities of all staff members. A conflict is likely to emerge if a team takes an action or makes a decision that is in clear violation of an existing collective bargaining agreement. This should be understood at the outset. Another option is for you to have that information on hand for the group.

Time, or the lack of it, is an obstacle faced by many school teams. How much can realistically be done when a team meets once or twice a month? Important decisions take time, especially if a variety of viewpoints are incorporated into those decisions. Some observers of school leadership teams believe that it takes three to five years for them to fully take hold and have a significant impact upon the school and its operations. Be patient and allow sufficient time for deliberations, decisions, and the process.

Blocking or skepticism is another obstacle that many leadership groups face. If the members notice that one member is blocking the work of the team or being unduly negative or stubbornly resistant, the group should first consider whether or not the individual may feel threatened by the group. Working effectively as a team is a responsibility shared by all of the members. Negativity should be discussed openly with the goal of uncovering some of the sources of frustration experienced by individual members. The person who blocks or sabotages the work of the team should be confronted with skill and sensitivity, being careful not to demean the individual, but always keeping the success of the group in the forefront of the discussion. Occasionally, school leadership groups need to identify resource persons who may provide mediation or conflict resolution for the group.

How to Set the Agenda for the Team Meeting

One of the most effective ways to set the agenda for a team meeting is to agree on the items to be discussed at the end of the previous meeting. Some items are standard ones and will probably be on the agenda for every meeting. If the members of the group agree to the major portion of the agenda while they are still together, unusual issues will not come as a surprise. A sample agenda worksheet appears in Figure 3.7. A form like this can be completed at the end of each meeting and will form the basis for the next meeting's agenda.

Figure 3.7   Agenda Worksheet for Team Meeting

LEADERSHIP TEAM MEETING AGENDA WORKSHEET

1. Welcome

2. Approval of Last Meeting's Minutes

3. Review of Meeting Agenda and Roles

4. Report From the District Leadership Council

5. Reports From Faculty and PTA Representatives

6. New Agenda Items:

    a. ____

    b. ____

    c. ____

    d. ____

    e. ____

7. Review of Action and Decisions

8. Assessment of Meeting

9. Agenda Setting for Next Meeting

10. Adjournment

Notes or information to be included with the next agenda:

Whoever prepares the agenda should check it for accuracy against the minutes of the prior meeting and with the facilitator of the meeting to make sure that they are accurate. Try not to overcrowd agendas. Allow sufficient time to allow for full discussion of the items. It is also advisable to assign time allocations to each of the items to ensure that you will be able to get through the agenda within the allotted time for the meeting.

The agenda should be distributed to all group members at least one week before the meeting. If background material is required for meaningful discussions about a particular topic, relevant information or documents should be attached to the agenda so that all members will have a chance to review them before the meeting. In some groups, the agenda is also printed on a large chart so that it can be referred to throughout the meeting. If it is asked that a new item be added to the agenda—one that was not anticipated at the previous meeting—the team chairperson (or whoever sets the agenda) should discuss the need for and advisability of including the item with a few key group members.

THE ROLE OF THE PRINCIPAL IN SHARED DECISION-MAKING

Principals who have helped usher their schools into shared decision-making do not usually feel that they have lost power or authority. On the contrary, they often feel that a greater appreciation for the complexity and difficulty of their roles emerges from the process. In site-based management, the principal is seen as a facilitator of consensus. However, the principal must be genuine about the intentions of shared decision-making. If you go into the process with a half-hearted attitude or feel that a new structure for decision-making will only be more work, this feeling will quickly be perceived by others. Principals most often find that they will be responsible for all of the usual tasks associated with their jobs. As a result of shared decision-making, though, principals find new roles. They must become resource providers, information gatherers, and encouragers. When groups make decisions, the level of commitment to those decisions is greater than if an edict came from the principal and all are expected to comply. Most principals have found that when members of the school community are involved in setting programs, standards, and evaluative structures, they all assume greater responsibility for ensuring success. In many ways, this makes the job of principal easier.

When a school leadership team is first organized, be clear about the kinds of decisions you want to retain for yourself. The selection of staff and teacher assignments are often options that principals wish to keep. As long as you are clear about the prerogatives you want to retain, this will be respected, and will help to outline for the team the decisions with which it will be involved. As the group matures, the principal may wish to share more decision-making and extend its sphere of influence.

School leaders make hundreds of decisions each day. It is not always easy for them to trust others to make the decisions that come so naturally. Clearly, decisions made by a leadership team will not be as quick or timely as those made by a principal alone, and many experienced principals may feel that projects conducted by members of a team will not be executed as well. It is important not to take over once you give a group responsibility for the completion of a project. This will not help to engender trust and confidence or leadership. With training and experience, the decisions made by groups can be highly effective because they encompass a broad cross section of viewpoints and perspectives and represent broad-based commitment.

In some leadership team constitutions, principals maintain the right to veto a decision. This is understandable, since principals are the ones who are often responsible for implementing decisions and policies. Along with the accountability of the principal should come some discretion about what will work best for the entire school community. The overuse of a veto, though, can undermine the confidence of the group. Experience in shared decision-making and learning from mistakes and triumphs can help to ease the way for those principals who may have been initially reluctant or skeptical.

HOW TO ASSESS THE EFFECTIVENESS OF A SCHOOL LEADERSHIP TEAM

At the end of each team meeting, it is a good idea to assess its effectiveness, and there are a variety of ways to do this. A simple yet fruitful technique is to go around the table and have each member make a brief statement assessing the meeting. What went right? What could be done differently? What was a high point and a low point of the meeting? What was interesting? How well did we accomplish our agenda? These are all questions that can be answered as you go around the table to get a quick sense of everyone's impressions of the meeting. If someone records the remarks, they can be reviewed at a later time and compared to other meeting assessments to consider the group's progress.

If time permits, there are a variety of evaluation forms, questionnaires, or checklists that can be completed to assess the effectiveness of a meeting. Filling out these forms does take some time, but it also helps to focus group members on the factors that are important for effective meetings. A sample of a leadership team meeting assessment form appears in Figure 3.8.

Figure 3.8 School Leadership Team Meeting Assessment Form

SCHOOL LEADERSHIP TEAM MEETING ASSESSMENT FORM

	Yes	No	Not Sure
1. An agenda was distributed prior to the meeting.			
2. Members arrived and meeting started on time.			
3. There were ways to make sure that items important to me were included on the agenda.			
4. We reviewed the agenda at the beginning of the meeting.			
5. Participants assumed the roles of facilitator, recorder, and timekeeper.			
6. All members of the group actively participated in the meeting.			
7. We developed alternative approaches and solutions.			
8. Group members felt free to express divergent views.			
9. Participants practiced the principles of active listening.			
10. An issue was clearly understood and clarified before action was taken.			
11. Participants had an opportunity to consider more than one solution to a problem or issue.			
12. When assignments were accepted, it was clear who will do what.			
13. We summarized what was accomplished at the meeting.			
14. We planned the agenda for the next meeting.			
15. We assessed the effectiveness of the meeting.			

What were the major accomplishments at this meeting?

How might we improve our meetings?

There are other means of assessing the performance of a school leadership team. Some are relatively easy to accomplish: a quick and easy one is to simply list the accomplishments of the group or the issues with which it has dealt. The members of the team can review this inventory and have conversations about how the deliberations and decisions have made a difference for students and teachers. These accomplishments can be "published" in a school newsletter or an open letter from the leadership team to the school community (see Figure 3.4).

Another means of assessing the work and progress of a school leadership team is to review meeting agendas and make a list of "content" and "processes." The content is a catalog of the issues or topics that the group has dealt with. The processes are the techniques, skills, and methods that were employed at the meetings. Such a list might include such things as active listening, agenda setting, meeting assessment, strategic planning, achieving consensus, brainstorming, active participation, and goal setting.

Reports from the school leadership team to the district office or to the school community are also a form of assessment. Perhaps a school superintendent or a community person can interview team members to gain insights into their perceptions of the effectiveness of the leadership group.

Shared decision-making and site-based management have shown that they are structures that can help people rethink the ways that schools operate. These approaches help to build commitment and accountability within a school. The mistake that many principals make is to expect too much too soon. Effective group decision-making takes time, experience, a high level of trust, and the ability to learn from mistakes. Once you have seen the many benefits of site-based management, you will reap the rewards and advantages that come with a community of stakeholders that is committed to school improvement, better opportunities for students, and increased levels of support for the school.

4

Improving Teacher Observation and Evaluation

One of your most important roles as principal is the observation and evaluation of staff members. A well-thought-out supervisory process can enhance the skills of all personnel and help individual teachers engage in a continuous cycle of self-improvement. Guiding the growth of teachers is much more than occasional formal observations and the preparation of an annual evaluation report; it is a systematic approach for helping them to refine their instructional practices and to define areas for professional development.

Teacher evaluation is sometimes perceived as an onerous process—something to go through or endure. However, if the process is approached from the standpoint that the great majority of teachers are competent and interested in learning new techniques and strategies, as well as charting areas for continued development, then the observation and evaluation cycle can be met with enthusiasm and cooperation.

THE PURPOSES OF SUPERVISION AND EVALUATION

The development and implementation of a supervisory model should focus on the teaching-learning process. The goal of such a program is to attain high-quality instruction. If a supervisory process is to be effective, its purposes and principles must be clearly understood by all involved. Basic to any evaluation structure is a shared understanding of what constitutes good teaching. Teaching is a complex enterprise that requires continual reflection, analysis, and decision-making. These functions are best performed in a collaborative atmosphere where ideas and insights are shared and

---

Note: All forms, letters, and checklists included in this chapter can be found at corwin.com/elementary survivalkit.

directions for continuous improvement are discussed. The basic goals of any program of supervision and evaluation include the following:

Improving Instructional Performance

Improving the quality of instruction is the key element in any supervisory process. As curriculum is developed and refined, teachers need new tools, strategies, and skills to implement the instructional program. As teachers gain a deeper understanding of the process of teaching and learning, they are in a better position to assess their own techniques and methodologies. "Another pair of eyes" in the classroom can help teachers focus and reflect on their own instructional performance and judge in an objective way what has worked for them and what has not. As teachers and supervisors discuss goals and strategies, refinement of practice is the general goal. Research about effective techniques can be shared, as well as what seems to work best for a particular group of youngsters.

Promoting Professional Development and Growth

One of the important purposes of supervision and evaluation is to promote professional development and growth. Reflections upon teacher observations and conversations about perceived strengths and needs lead to the identification of areas for continued improvement—new skills to learn, new approaches to employ, new content to be mastered. Engaging staff in open and honest dialogue about areas for improvement can lead to the identification of resources and an action plan for individual development. Such resources might include attending conferences and seminars, reading journals, visiting other teachers, joining a faculty study group, or creating a professional learning community. One of the outcomes of staff evaluations should be the formulation of an individual professional growth plan for the following school year.

Providing a System for Bringing Assistance to Teachers

The process of supervision and evaluation can lead to the identification of teacher and program needs. Some teachers may benefit from additional assistance in the use of technology or the use of cooperative learning strategies. Such needs can easily be an outcome of the observation process and professional discussions. Resources can be provided from staff within or outside the school system. The important thing is to identify the needs and then discuss ways to bring about desired changes or growth.

Reinforcing Effective Instructional Practices

As you conduct teacher observations and evaluations, you have the opportunity to reinforce those practices that are valued in your school or school district. Identifying and labeling teacher actions and approaches are essential aspects of the observation process. If teachers demonstrate effective classroom management techniques, take note of what they do that is successful. If the classroom atmosphere is positive, state the evidence. If the teacher promotes active participation on the part of the students, specify those actions to support your observation. Teachers need to know that you notice what they do to foster student progress. Sometimes, teachers do things as a matter of good instinct, but they are unaware of these effective practices. Take note and label them in the observation report. Praising and labeling effective practices in specific terms builds a common vocabulary for teachers to use in professional conversations that will encourage them to reflect on and refine specific techniques and approaches.

Pointing the Way Toward Professional Goals

An essential aspect of the process of teacher evaluation is the establishment of a professional improvement plan. The main features of this plan may be an outgrowth of multiple observations and discussions. An open, frank assessment of teacher needs and areas for desired growth can lead the way to such a plan. The formulation of professional growth plans will be discussed later in the chapter, but goal setting is an important element of the observation and evaluation cycle.

Suggesting Areas for Organizational Goals and General Staff Development Needs

A series of observations of many teachers can help to identify areas for organizational improvement. Do teachers need more information and development in a particular instructional approach or curriculum area? How strong is the school's science program as evidenced from classroom observations? How well have state and national standards been incorporated into classroom practice? Are teachers differentiating instruction to meet the diverse needs of their students? Generalizing and reflecting upon your observations can help reveal patterns of organizational need and staff development directions.

Providing a Basis for Personnel Decisions

One of the most difficult decisions that we face as principals is whether or not to reemploy teachers. A well-thought-out and clear evaluation process can form the basis for rational personnel decisions. Nobody likes surprises, and principals can get themselves into serious trouble if they make important personnel decisions without having followed an appropriate process, and without proper documentation. Although shedding light on personnel decisions is not the chief purpose of teacher supervision and evaluation, the gathering of information and evidence for this important function cannot be overemphasized.

Building a Professional Community Built on Reflection and Inquiry

Reflection and inquiry can be generated via unannounced classroom walk-throughs, which are brief, two- to three-minute visits to classrooms. As the instructional leader in your school, you should place these on your calendar so they don't get lost due to other managerial duties. The purpose of a walk-through is to gain information about all aspects of the classroom setting—climate, instructional strategies, curriculum, student behavior and attitudes, and student engagement, to name a few. This type of visit does not represent an opportunity to evaluate a teacher, but rather to give you a picture of what is going on in your school. Teachers should be trained to know the purpose of walk-throughs and how reflective thinking improves practice. Feedback is given to teachers only after several walk-throughs have taken place and can be in the form of a question that will stimulate a teacher's reflection about classroom practice, which will, in turn, promote a professional dialogue between you and your teachers. The number of visits to classrooms allows you to be a visible instructional leader in your school. Think about the opportunity to visit ten classrooms in thirty minutes! Longer informal visits to classrooms can be reserved for new teachers and teachers who are marginally competent.[1]

HOW TO ESTABLISH A POSITIVE CLIMATE FOR TEACHER SUPERVISION

Teachers may be nervous or uncomfortable about the supervisory process. For this reason, it is important to set a comfortable tone for the conduct of observation and evaluation conferences. This requires sensitivity and human relations skills. Teachers must be assured that the purpose of supervision is to help them to become more effective teachers and not to "catch them" or to focus on perceived deficiencies.

The first step in building trust in the supervisory process is to make teachers aware of the purposes of evaluation. Emphasize that it is a collaborative, constructive enterprise. A review of the process, the forms used, and the expectations of the supervisory cycle should be provided to teachers in writing, reviewed at staff meetings, and also reiterated in individual conferences. A sample letter to staff, to be distributed early in the school year, outlining the purposes and process of staff supervision appears in Figure 4.1. The process described in Figure 4.1 should clearly reflect the district's established process, which is often negotiated and outlined in the teacher contract. Many districts have a different evaluation process for probationary teachers than for tenured teachers, and it is important for personnel serving as mentors to new teachers to be very familiar with the supervision and evaluation process.

Figure 4.1   Letter to Teachers Outlining Supervision Process

Name of School and District

Dear Staff,

Welcome to a new school new year! One of the important areas to clarify at the beginning of each school year is our process for teacher supervision and evaluation. We believe that effective teacher evaluation is essential to the achievement of the educational goals of our school district. We also encourage teachers to assume greater leadership and be self-reflective about their own professional growth through collaboration and the formulation of a professional improvement plan. With these ends in mind, the purposes of our supervisory program are as follows:

- Improve instructional performance
- Promote professional development and growth for the district
- Reinforce effective instructional practices
- Point the way toward areas for individual professional goals

The supervisory process follows a specific sequence in which all teachers will be involved:

Early Fall	Goal Review Conference: Each teacher will meet with the principal to review the Professional Improvement Plan outlined in the prior year's Summary Evaluation Conference. New teachers will develop the plan at this time.
Fall/Winter	Informal and Formal Observations: Informal observations will be conducted to gather information about classroom climate and curriculum implementation. Informal feedback will be provided after each observation. Formal Observation(s): Each teacher will be asked to schedule one or more formal observations. These will last for one class period or a minimum of 30 minutes. Each observation will be preceded by a Pre-Observation Conference at which goals, instructional strategies, and assessment techniques will be discussed. The observation will be recorded on the standard Teacher Observation Form. A Post-Observation Conference will also be conducted.
February	Mid-Year Review With Superintendent: Each supervisor will have a conference with the superintendent to review the observations of teachers.
May/June	Summary Evaluation Conference: At this conference, the observations made during the course of the year will be discussed as well as general performance indicators and the accomplishment of the professional improvement plan. A plan for the next school year is established as a part of the conference.

The specific evaluation forms to be used have been previously distributed.

All meetings between teacher and supervisor should take place in a comfortable location, be devoid of interruptions, and occur in an atmosphere that fosters mutual respect. Assure the teacher that your goal is to be helpful, to engage in a conversation that will lead to professional growth, and to capitalize on noted strengths.

The term *clinical supervision* describes the process followed in many school districts. This process involves the following elements: (1) a pre-observation conference between supervisor and teacher concerning elements of the lesson to be observed; (2) classroom observation; (3) a supervisor's analysis of notes from the observation, and planning for the post-observation conference; (4) a post-observation conference between supervisor and teacher; and (5) a supervisor's analysis of the post-observation conference. For many practitioners, these stages were reduced to three: the pre-observation conference, the observation, and the post-observation conference. A diagram depicting a common model for supervision and evaluation appears in Figure 4.2. It is important to be aware of the local state and/or contractual requirements for formal and informal observations.

Figure 4.2 A Model for Supervision and Evaluation

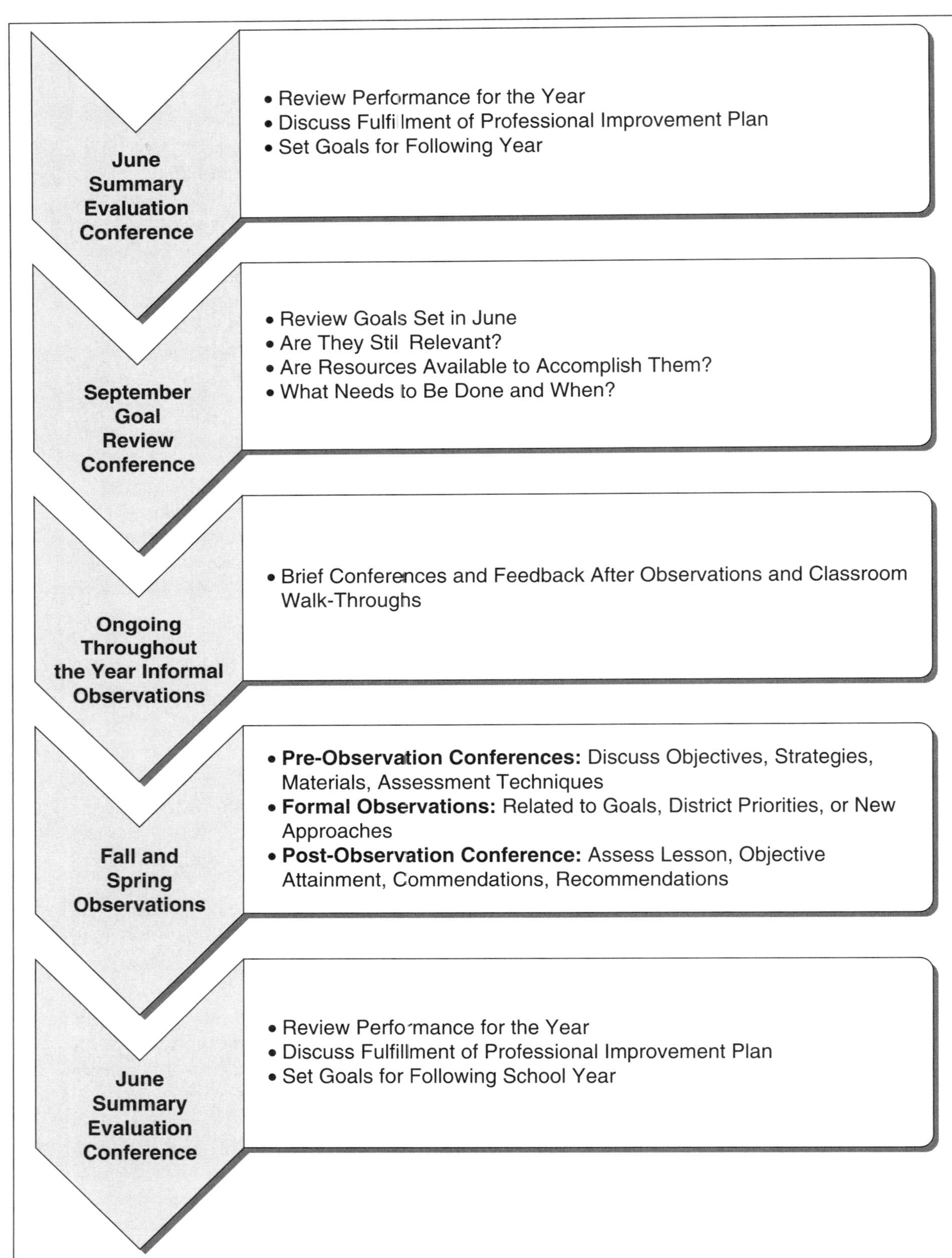

HOW TO CLARIFY THE CRITERIA
FOR SUPERVISION AND EVALUATION

It is necessary to let teachers know the criteria that will be used in the process of supervision and evaluation. These criteria may vary from district to district, but there are undoubtedly some common features that underlie any supervisory process. Criteria for evaluation should evolve from the instructional priorities and program objectives of the school system as well as individual teacher professional development goals. Standards for teacher performance should include, but should not be limited to, instructional skills, knowledge of content, classroom management skills, human relations skills, professional responsibilities, and knowledge of child development. What supervisors look for in teacher observations and evaluations should be closely linked to the teacher job description (see Chapter 19).

Flexibility must also be a part of the system. Clearly, no single model is appropriate for all teachers in all situations. Supervisors should identify a variety of teaching strategies designed to meet the needs of a particular groups of students. Teachers should be helped to apply the most effective general principles and instructional techniques, as well as those specific methods and strategies most appropriate for particular content. Some criteria cannot be seen in lessons alone but should be reflected in supervisory reports and discussions. A sample set of criteria for teacher evaluation includes the following:

Instructional Skills

- Plans effectively for lessons and activities
- Establishes and communicates the goals or expectations of the lesson to students
- Previews and reviews material as needed
- Displays clarity in presentation
- Uses techniques to stimulate students and maintain focus
- Differentiates materials, activities, resources, and assignments to meet group and individual needs
- Checks for pupil understanding of concepts
- Monitors pupil comprehension and adjusts pace accordingly
- Provides work that is relevant and at an appropriate level of difficulty for students
- Summarizes lessons

Knowledge of Content

- Demonstrates knowledge and sensitivity of subject matter
- Skillfully integrates subject matter into activities and discussions
- Is familiar with multiple resources related to subject matter
- Demonstrates the relevance of content to students' lives
- Anticipates and helps students answer their own questions
- Identifies enrichment opportunities linked to topics under study

Classroom Management Skills

- Maintains clear and appropriate standards for student behavior
- Disciplines students in a fair, objective, and constructive manner
- Uses class time efficiently
- Demonstrates consistency in treatment of students
- Provides constructive, positive feedback for actions and efforts

- Displays behavior that focuses student attention on learning
- Creates a positive, supportive atmosphere for learning
- Fosters mutual respect in the classroom
- Displays tolerance and promotes acceptance of differences

Human Relations Skills

- Communicates and interacts positively with students
- Provides for the social and emotional growth of students
- Displays sensitivity to students and listens to their concerns with care and compassion
- Works cooperatively with other staff
- Reports student progress in an effective manner
- Maintains positive relationships with parents and other members of the community
- Respects others and earns the respect of colleagues and parents

Knowledge of Child Development

- Employs developmental considerations in planning and organizing for instruction
- Displays knowledge of a broad range of age-appropriate student behaviors
- Structures experiences that are appropriate for the social development of students
- Maintains high, but realistic, expectations for students
- Recognizes students' special needs and strives to meet them

Professional Responsibilities

- Contributes to the overall goals of the school
- Self-assesses performance and willingly sets goals for professional development
- Displays a commitment to the growth of students
- Upholds rules, regulations, and professional responsibilities
- Carries out routine duties with dependability and promptness
- Assists in the selection of instructional materials
- Keeps abreast of trends and activities in curriculum areas
- Participates willingly in staff development activities
- Maintains membership in professional organizations

ACHIEVING A BALANCE BETWEEN FORMAL AND INFORMAL OBSERVATIONS

Most school districts mandate a minimum number of formal teacher observations each year. Usually there is a difference in the requirement for probationary and tenured teachers. Formal observations are important tools in the supervisory process; however, informal "drop-in" observations can yield a great deal of significant information about teaching skill and day-to-day performance. If you intend to conduct unannounced observations, make sure that teachers know that this is your policy and that lessons should continue as normal when you enter the room. It is a matter of individual choice, but it should be considered that such informal observations are not the ones to be recorded on a formal observation report. While classroom walk-throughs provide an informal way to help you gain a sense of the climate in every classroom and the rhythm and flow of the day, longer informal observations can be used for new teachers and teachers who are marginally competent.

Some principals prefer drop-in observations and classroom walk-throughs because they feel that even marginal teachers can muster up a more than adequate lesson if they have enough time to prepare for it. In all fairness, though, it makes sense for teachers to also be able to demonstrate the best that they have to offer. Teachers can be asked to "invite" the principal in to witness a lesson, activity, or event that they are particularly proud of. For example, much can be gained from observing writers' celebrations, reenactments, informal plays, student reports, and the like. In any event, whether the observation is scheduled or unannounced, teachers deserve prompt feedback. In the case of a formal observation, a written report usually summarizes the feedback. After conducting an informal observation, the feedback can be a brief note or a quick meeting in which the focus is on a specific item or technique noticed. Feedback for two- or three-minute classroom walk-throughs can be given periodically, but not necessarily after each occurrence.

REVIEWING PROFESSIONAL DEVELOPMENT PLANS

A part of the end-of-year evaluation for teachers should be the development of a professional improvement plan for the following year. This is usually based on areas of warranted growth defined in the summary evaluation or the particular professional development interests of the teacher. In any case, teachers and administrators often forget the thrust of these plans once the next school year begins. A good way to begin the cycle of supervision and evaluation is to have a conference with each staff member in which you review the professional development plans set at the end of the previous school year. A sample of one objective from such a plan appears in Figure 4.3. Depending on how ambitious an individual objective is, a teacher's professional development plan may consist of one or more goals or objectives.

Questions that may guide the goal review conference include the following:

- Is the plan developed last spring still relevant and applicable?
- Are the materials and resources available to accomplish the specifics of the plan?
- Is the plan consistent with emerging district and school priorities?
- Has anything in the teacher's assignment changed that should cause you to rethink the plan?
- What additional resources, conferences, materials, or personnel can aid in the implementation of the plan?
- What modifications are necessary to accomplish the plan?
- Are the timelines established realistic?
- What is a reasonable sequence of activities to monitor the progress of the plan?
- How will you assess progress toward the attainment of your goals?

It is important to demonstrate flexibility if there are legitimate reasons to alter or modify the plan. It also helps if you show your willingness to provide resources, coaching, or other activities that can aid the teacher in the fulfillment of the plan. It is useful to jot a note to the teacher summarizing some of the major understandings that emerged as a result of this conference.

Figure 4.3   Sample of an Individual Professional Development Objective

Name of School and District

INDIVIDUAL PROFESSIONAL DEVELOPMENT OBJECTIVE

Name: _______________________________________ **School Year:** _______________

Objective:

To learn more about the cooperative learning approach and to implement it regularly in the classroom.

Activities:

Attend a conference about the approach with another colleague.

Discuss the implications and applications of the approach with colleagues and the principal.

Read books, articles, and pamphlets about the approach.

Observe one or two teachers who are successfully using the approach.

Develop a plan for the implementation of the approach in my classroom.

Designate specific roles for youngsters in implementing the approach.

Maintain a log of the implementation of the cooperative learning approach.

Assess the implementation of the approach.

Timeline:

Gather all information and learn about the approach by November 15.

Observe other teachers by December 15.

Develop an implementation plan by January 15.

Maintain an ongoing log of the implementation of the approach.

Implement the approach between February 1 and May 1.

Assess the implementation of the approach by May 15.

Collection:

Maintain a log of learnings about the approach.

Methods:

Discuss questions about the approach with the principal and colleagues.

Provide written reflections and questions about the observation of the approach and share with the principal and colleagues.

Share the implementation plan with colleagues and the principal and make adjustments as necessary.

Develop questionnaires for students about their reactions to the approach.

Assess the student reactions.

Invite the principal and colleagues in to observe and provide feedback for the implementation of the approach.

Teacher self-assessment.

THE PRE-OBSERVATION CONFERENCE

The purpose of the pre-observation conference is to help provide focus for the lesson to be observed. In a well-thought-out pre-observation conference, the principal should do the following:

- Help teachers to clarify the purpose and goals of the lesson.
- Probe for specific observable pupil behaviors or attitudes.
- Clarify the strategies and techniques to be employed.
- Set the context for the lesson. What came before? What will follow?
- Discuss the teacher's hopes and concerns about the lesson.
- Define the role of the observer in the lesson.

One of the benefits of the pre-observation conference is that the discussion can help teachers to reflect upon what they intend to do and perhaps make some adjustments or incorporate some new ideas that may result in a more effective experience for the youngsters. Asking the teacher to help define a role for the observer can also be a tremendous aid to teachers. Sometimes, teachers may ask the observer to focus on how long they wait for pupil responses after asking a question (wait time), how they promote student participation, whether they tend to call on boys more than girls, or any other such matter that only another pair of eyes in the classroom can reasonably assess. Stress the importance of teachers informing their students in a positive way that the principal will be observing teaching and learning in their classroom. Through the classroom walk-through process and other informal observations, your presence should be a natural and expected part of the day.

The benefits of a pre-observation conference are apparent; however, if you have a large number of teachers to supervise and there is simply not enough time for this aspect of the observation cycle, you can gain insights into the teacher's purposes by asking them to complete a simple form, Pre-Observation Notes, prior to the scheduled observation. A sample of such a form appears in Figure 4.4.

Figure 4.4   Pre-Observation Notes Form

Name of School and District

PRE-OBSERVATION NOTES

Name: **Grade:**

Date of Observation:

Subject Area:

Specific Topic:

Goals for the Lesson:

Materials to Be Used:

Special Techniques to Be Used:

Assessment Techniques (How will pupil achievement be checked?):

What in particular would you like the observer to look for?

HOW TO CONDUCT EFFECTIVE TEACHER OBSERVATIONS

The classroom observation provides a unique opportunity to witness firsthand the performance of teachers, and then to engage in a professional dialogue about instruction, options, and teaching decisions. Be upbeat about the experience, but also understand that classroom observations provoke anxiety and nervousness even in some of the most seasoned professionals. Do all that you can to help teachers feel at ease about your presence in the classroom. Once a date for the observation is set, make sure to be on time. Teachers are often unsure whether to proceed with a scheduled lesson if the observer is late. This situation can increase the intensity of a teacher's natural anxiety about a classroom observation.

When you enter the classroom, greet the class and find a convenient spot to sit where you will be able to witness all of the major interactions between the teacher and students. Many principals feel free to interact with the students during the observation as long as the teacher is comfortable with this approach. In other cases, the setting is more clinical and the principal maintains the role of the quiet observer. Make sure that you remain in the classroom for the entire lesson or experience. (If your schedule is tight, it is wise to determine at the pre-observation conference the anticipated time frame for the lesson.)

During the observation, some principals maintain a running record of the dialogue between the teacher and students, recording a script of what is said. In some school systems, a checklist is provided for recording observations. Other principals try to record data in specific categories according to predetermined criteria as might be outlined in a classroom observation report form. (See Figure 4.5.) Sometimes, it is helpful to maintain notes in two columns—one for teacher actions and one for pupil actions.

The observer should have the criteria for outstanding performance clearly in mind. Following is a list of some of the items on which you may wish to focus and jot notes about:

- Did the teacher make the objectives or intent of the lesson explicit to the students?
- What did the teacher do to motivate the students or create a sense of enthusiasm?
- Was there evidence of careful planning for the lesson?
- Were the teacher's explanations clear?
- What did the teacher do to ensure maximum participation?
- Were materials used appropriately?
- Was the pacing too fast or too slow?
- How did the teacher check for pupil comprehension?
- Were questioning techniques appropriate?
- Did the teacher monitor student progress and adjust the approach as needed?
- Did a positive, enthusiastic tone pervade the classroom?
- Did the teacher demonstrate sensitivity to the students?
- Did the teacher differentiate aspects of the lesson for divergent abilities and learning styles?
- Was pupil management effective?
- Were transitions handled smoothly?
- Was the physical atmosphere of the classroom attractive and inviting?

| **Figure 4.5** | Sample Teacher Observation Report Form |

Name of District and School

CLASSROOM OBSERVATION REPORT

Name:

Position: **School:**

Lesson/Class Observed: **Specific Activity:**

Date: **Time:**

Materials: Which materials were used in the lesson?

Planning: What evidence is there of planning and preparation for the lesson?

Instructional Techniques: What evidence is there that the teacher states objectives, reviews and previews, maintains task orientation, signals transitions, emphasizes important aspects, provides clarity in presentation, checks for comprehension, utilizes materials well, maintains an attractive physical setting, and summarizes the lesson?

Student Involvement: What are students doing during the lesson?

Teacher-Pupil Relationships: How does the teacher display and foster mutual respect and enthusiasm while maintaining student discipline and responsibility?

Commendations:

Recommendations:

Evaluator's Signature: **Date:**

Conference Date:

Staff Member's Signature: **Date:**

Notes taken during a classroom observation should not be judgmental. They should simply be a record of what was observed. As you finish the observation, make sure to say something positive to the teacher about the lesson, or at the very least acknowledge the opportunity to have visited the classroom.

Later, in your office, you will have a chance to analyze the lesson according to the teacher's stated objectives, defined criteria, or instructional decisions. Techniques and approaches employed are worthy of analysis. Were the methods appropriate to the content and the group? Did the strategies seem to work well in the particular situation? As you record statements of performance in preparing the observation report, make sure to cite examples to substantiate your judgments. The observation report should summarize commendable aspects and also include recommendations for improvement for how teachers can further refine their practice. The basis for both commendations and recommendations for improvement should be reflected in the lesson description. Care should be taken to prepare these reports thoughtfully and with sensitivity and professionalism. It is unwise to skimp on the time needed to prepare accurate, well-written, and reflective observation reports. They honor the efforts of the teacher and the importance of the supervisory process. Also, remember that observation reports are often read by other district administrators, may be brought in as evidence if teachers contest formal evaluations, and may be reviewed by the Board of Education prior to granting tenure.

THE POST-OBSERVATION CONFERENCE: A TIME FOR SHARING AND LEARNING

The post-observation conference is an invaluable opportunity for engaging teachers in professional dialogue and exercising instructional leadership. These conferences should be scheduled as soon as possible after the observation. This will ensure that events, strategies employed, and the sequence of the lesson will be fresh in the minds of both the observer and the teacher. A timely post-observation conference also helps to relieve any anxiety the teacher might feel about your perception of the lesson. Teacher contracts often specify how much time may elapse between the observation and the post-observation conference.

As in all such conferences, it is important to set a positive, professional tone. Welcome the teacher into your office and make sure that she or he is comfortably seated—preferably without a physical barrier between the two of you. Try to ensure that there will be no interruptions during the conference. If you allow your secretary or other persons to interrupt you for seemingly insignificant matters during the conference, it conveys to the teacher that you do not place too much value on the process.

Begin the conference by stating the purpose of the meeting, that is, to share and review impressions of the lesson, to celebrate successes, and to plan for professional improvement. Invite the teacher to convey his or her sense of how the lesson went. What worked well? What student behaviors support the impressions? Would any changes be made now that it is over? Having a teacher self-assess and reflect upon the outcomes of a lesson is a very powerful technique for fostering professional growth. Indeed, such self-evaluation is in itself a goal of supervision.

Part of any post-observation conference should be a review of the teacher's intended goals for the lesson. Were the goals met? What did the teacher do to promote the achievement of the goals or to foster student learning? Listen to the teacher's assessment. Even if it is not consistent with your own impressions, ask what evidence the teacher has for his or her conclusions.

After listening to the teacher, you can offer your own observations and impressions. Present data to substantiate your statements and compare your own views with that of the teacher. Be honest and forthright about differences in perception if any exist. With the teacher, probe for inferences about why the stated purposes were achieved, or why they were not. After you state your own impressions, check for the teacher's understanding of what you are trying to convey. Are you making yourself clear? Paraphrase any agreements you may have about the impact of the lesson as well as any differences in perception that may have emerged from the conversation.

Usually in post-observation conferences, a summary of commendations and recommendations is made. Commendations should be sincere, not trivial, and crafted to encourage the teacher to continue to utilize those practices that you feel are most effective. Keep the recommendations focused, and do not offer so many that the teacher is not able to absorb what you are trying to convey. Specify those recommendations that are the most important and that you feel can have the most impact on the teaching/learning process. State your recommendations in nonthreatening language; use facts and observations to back up your statements. What might be done differently? What skills must be refined? When evaluating any lesson, it is essential to consider the teacher's level of expertise, years of experience, and specific staff development experiences. Although we may have absolute standards of excellence in our own minds, teacher observations should take note of growth and improvement of performance over time.

Allow the teacher to react openly to your comments and analysis. Always seek common ground. Try to elicit areas in which the teacher would like to refine techniques or practices. In some cases, it is appropriate to develop a plan for follow-up. If the teacher wishes to practice a suggested technique or strategy, a date can be set for a subsequent observation, at which time specific coaching or focused feedback is offered.

Finally, the post-observation conference itself should be assessed. Ask the teacher whether or not the conversation was useful. Solicit feedback about anything the teacher learned from the conference. The teacher's reaction to the conference, as well as his or her acceptance of suggestions offered, provides important feedback to you about your own conferencing skills and instructional leadership.

OTHER MEANS OF OBSERVATION AND EVALUATION

There are many other ways to collect information about teaching performance. Alternative data about teaching performance cannot replace the classroom observation, but taken together with it, other means can offer a comprehensive view of the results of instruction. Teachers can submit videotapes of lessons. A video recorder set up in the back of the room, or one handled by a student or technician, can record lessons and experiences that supervisors do not or cannot observe themselves. Then the teacher and principal can view the tape together and form a collaborative analysis of what they observed.

Student projects, performances, plays, writing celebrations, community service initiatives, and test performance can all be analyzed and provide much important information about teaching effectiveness. Even if you did not see the execution of certain projects, the results of those projects can reveal a great deal about what went into creating the products.

Peer observation, in which teachers sit in on one another's classes and offer constructive feedback, is becoming a more popular adjunct to the observation performed by supervisors. This system requires some training and a great deal of trust among colleagues. As principal, you can set the idea into motion, but once it has caught on and peer observations occur, they should be considered a confidential matter between teachers. Principals who interfere in this process have often found that the system can break down. Regular peer observation can be a most effective practice, but it is recommended that it be kept independent of the formal supervisory process.

Just as portfolio assessment has proven to be an effective means of evaluating student growth, it can also be used in the supervision of teaching performance. A teacher's portfolio may be considered a record of instructional accomplishments. Portfolios can include lesson plans, samples of student activities, work samples, letters from parents and students, photos of class projects, and videotapes of classroom explorations and performances. A portfolio can be most effective when teachers share its contents with the principal in a meeting. Formal teaching portfolios should be presented in an organized manner, perhaps including a table of contents or guide to what is included. As teachers guide a reviewer through their portfolios, they reflect upon their practices and can be encouraged to make their own judgments about instructional performance and professional needs and priorities. Developing a portfolio can be part of a probationary teacher's requirement to demonstrate growth through reflective practice. New teachers who are required to create a portfolio should have a clear outline of what is expected and a wide variety of samples to view.

Another means of promoting teacher evaluation is the self-assessment. A sample self-assessment form appears in Figure 4.6. This is something that a teacher can do in the privacy of the classroom or home. The results need not be reported to anyone. The purpose of the self-assessment is for the teacher to reflect on important aspects of teaching, learning, and professionalism. The questions themselves guide the individual to think about their own performance and perhaps set personal goals for improvement.

Figure 4.6   Teacher Self-Assessment Form

Name of School and District

TEACHER SELF-ASSESSMENT

Consider the questions below and reflect upon your performance in each area.

Planning and Preparation

- Do I prepare for lessons adequately and assemble all materials prior to instruction?
- Are goals, objectives, and outcomes clear in my own mind?
- Do I anticipate questions from students or problems with the lesson?
- Are key questions specified?
- Am I clear about the instructional strategies I intend to employ in lessons?
- Do I specify assessment techniques?

Instructional Skills

- What do I do to motivate students for learning?
- Do I communicate objectives to students at the beginning of lessons?
- Are instructional materials varied and intrinsically interesting?
- Do I ask questions to probe student understanding of the learning?
- Do I adjust lessons as necessary depending on student comprehension?
- Have I anticipated and made adjustments for individual learning styles?
- What do I do to make lessons relevant to children's lives?
- Do I provide opportunities for students to share and collaborate?
- Are students actively involved throughout my lessons?
- Do I invite students to share and elaborate upon their ideas?

- What do I do to foster higher levels of thinking?
- Do I maintain accurate records of student growth and progress?
- Do I encourage students to assume responsibility for their own learning?
- Do I provide opportunities for students to reflect upon their own learning?
- Do I ask students to summarize what they think they have learned at the end of lessons?

Learning Atmosphere

- Is my classroom attractive, inviting, and cheerful? Is student work displayed?
- Am I respectful of all students regardless of their ability or background?
- Do I take steps to ensure maximum participation on the part of all students?
- Do I maintain clear and appropriate standards for student behavior?
- What do I do to promote student self-discipline and responsibility?
- What do I do to promote a positive, enthusiastic attitude?
- Are students in my class excited and enthusiastic about learning?
- What do I do to create an atmosphere in which students feel free to take risks?

Human Relations

- Am I sensitive to the needs of students? Do I treat all students fairly and objectively?
- Do I make myself available to students who have concerns or issues that they want to discuss?
- Do I work cooperatively with other staff and the school administration?
- Do I work to promote harmony among the school staff?
- Do I communicate effectively and regularly with parents?
- Do I listen compassionately to parents' concerns?

Professionalism

- Am I personally committed to student growth and development?
- What do I do to promote and become involved in the total school program?
- Am I open to new ideas and approaches?
- Do I strive for improvement through involvement in professional development activities?
- Am I willing to serve on school and district committees?
- What do I do to keep abreast of professional literature in teaching and curriculum?

HOW TO MAKE THE MOST OF AN ANNUAL EVALUATION CONFERENCE

The annual evaluation conference is a summary, usually held near the end of the school year, at which the general performance of the teacher for the past year is discussed and assessed. In most school districts, such an evaluation is a contractual or a state education department requirement. The purposes of the annual evaluation should be clear to all parties. Generally the goals of the conference are to

- judge professional performance,
- review accomplishment of growth plans for the current year,
- define exemplary areas of commendation,
- identify areas for improvement, and
- set a professional growth plan for the next year.

If the yearlong evaluation process has been implemented well, there should be no surprises in the annual evaluation conference. Ongoing professional discussions, informal notes, and formal observations should set the stage for this meeting. As in all important contacts between principal and teacher, it is wise to set an appropriate tone for the meeting. Be friendly, helpful, professional, and review the purposes of the conference. Reinforce that the goal is professional improvement, and the participants should consider themselves colleagues who operate within a constructive framework. New teachers should know well in advance if they are being rehired.

Some principals have completed the summary evaluation form prior to the conference and simply present it to the teacher for signature. In current practice, however, it is more common to review the performance indicators on the summary evaluation form and discuss both the teacher's and the supervisor's perceptions of teacher accomplishment in each of the areas. Principals often distribute an Annual Summary Sheet (Figure 4.7) so that principals can be reminded of the variety of professional activities in which teachers were involved during the year. Have teachers bring this sheet to the annual conference and then, following the conference, you can include the information as you prepare the Summary Evaluation Form. (See the Teacher Summary Evaluation Form in Figure 4.8.)

One important aspect of the summary conference is to reinforce and commend teacher practices that are clearly effective and that result in student growth and progress. Another important function is to identify areas for improvement and to chart collaboratively a plan to accomplish some goals. Some teachers are nervous, even defensive, at the summary conference, and a smooth, constructive meeting requires the exercise of good

Figure 4.7   Sample Annual Summary Sheet

Name of School and District

ANNUAL SUMMARY SHEET

Name: _______________________________   **Assignment:** _______________________

Formal university courses completed:

In-service workshops attended:

Committee assignments:

Special assignments:

Professional associations:

Extracurricular assignments:

Other (awards, published materials, research, travel):

Figure 4.8   Sample Teacher Summary Evaluation Form

Name of School and District

TEACHER SUMMARY EVALUATION

Teacher Name:	**School:**
Grade or Subject:	**School Year:**
Date of Conference:	**Years of Experience:**

Rating Key:

O (Outstanding): Performance of duties that merits special commendation.

S (Satisfactory): Performance that produces the intended or expected effect. Satisfies the district standard for professional performance.

I (Needs Improvement): Below district standards and specific improvement is needed.

I. General Performance

	Rating		
	O	**S**	**I**
Instructional Skills			
1. Sets appropriate objectives and communicates them to students.	☐	☐	☐
2. Displays clarity in presentation.	☐	☐	☐
3. Varies materials, resources, activities, and assignments.	☐	☐	☐
4. Uses probing questions to check for student understanding.	☐	☐	☐
5. Monitors pupil progress constantly and adjusts pace accordingly.	☐	☐	☐
6. Provides assignments that are relevant and developmentally appropriate.	☐	☐	☐
7. Fosters higher levels of thinking.	☐	☐	☐
8. Provides opportunities for all students to experience success.	☐	☐	☐
9. Summarizes lessons.	☐	☐	☐

(Continued)

Figure 4.8   (Continued)

	Rating		
	O	**S**	**I**
Learning Environment			
1. Maintains plans for instruction based upon district curriculum.	☐	☐	☐
2. Uses class time efficiently.	☐	☐	☐
3. Uses student ideas.	☐	☐	☐
4. Promotes maximum student participation.	☐	☐	☐
5. Displays behavior that focuses attention on learning tasks.	☐	☐	☐
6. Maintains clear and appropriate standards for student behavior.	☐	☐	☐
7. Maintains attractive instructional spaces that reflect student work.	☐	☐	☐
8. Displays a positive and enthusiastic attitude.	☐	☐	☐
Interpersonal Relations			
1. Communicates and interacts positively with students.	☐	☐	☐
2. Provides for the social and emotional growth of student.	☐	☐	☐
3. Is readily available to students.	☐	☐	☐
4. Treats students fairly and objectively.	☐	☐	☐
5. Works cooperatively with other staff.	☐	☐	☐
6. Reports student progress in an effective manner.	☐	☐	☐
7. Maintains positive relationships with parents.	☐	☐	☐
Professional Responsibilities			
1. Displays mature and reasonable judgment.	☐	☐	☐
2. Is supportive of school and district policies.	☐	☐	☐
3. Assumes additional responsibilities to contribute to the total school program.	☐	☐	☐
4. Completes routine duties with dependability and promptness.	☐	☐	☐
5. Assists in the selection of instructional materials.	☐	☐	☐
6. Strives for improvement through participation in professional growth activities.	☐	☐	☐
7. Keeps abreast of trends in curriculum and instruction.	☐	☐	☐

OVERALL EVALUATION

Commendations:

Recommendations:

II. Professional Growth Plans

Objectives for the Current School Year:	*Comments About Accomplishments:*
Objectives for the Following School Year:	*Assessment Techniques:*

III. Recommended Actions

Reemployment _______   Tenure _______   Salary Increment _______   Withhold Increment _______

Signature (Evaluator): ____   **Date:** ______________

TEACHER SUMMARY EVALUATION

IV. Teacher Response

I have received a copy of this evaluation and understand that if I do not agree with its contents, I have 10 (ten) working days in which to attach a reply. The original reply should be submitted to the evaluator and a copy sent to the superintendent along with the signed summary evaluation form.

Signature (Teacher): ____   **Date:** ______________

Reply (If additional space is required, attach copy):

V. Superintendent's Approval

Signature (Superintendent): ____   **Date:** ______________

human relations skills, a high level of trust, and the firm belief that all professionals seek ways to grow and refine their practice.

Ask the teachers to come to the conference prepared to discuss their own impressions of their performance for the school year and to provide evidence of the accomplishment of their professional growth plans.

Begin the conference by inviting the teacher to self-assess strengths and areas for growth. Confirm areas of agreement and talk frankly about those attributes in which your own judgment does not match that of the teacher. The summary conference should be an honest appraisal of perceptions. The areas covered can be listed directly from the summary evaluation form. Ideally, this form is closely linked to the teacher's job description (see Chapter 19). The conference should be a professional growth experience bringing to bear your best leadership skills. One of the goals of the meeting should be to help the teacher find ways to collaborate with other staff members and the school administration. During the conference, it is important to substantiate claims and judgments with data collected throughout the year. When applicable, refer to formal and informal observations. Try to avoid subjective impressions. Although the life of a principal is busy, you may find time to drop brief notes into a file with a brief phrase to remind you of conversations or interactions you've had during the school year. This will make the summary conference come alive with anecdotes and examples.

An essential aspect of the summary conference is a review of the teacher's professional growth plan. Consider each goal separately and ask the teacher to demonstrate the extent to which the goal was achieved. Remember that all goals, especially complex and ambitious ones, may not be completed in a single year. If this becomes an unyielding expectation, teachers will only want to set simplistic, clearly achievable goals, and risk taking may be compromised. In most summary evaluation reports, principals make comments about the achievement of each of the goals. The report should be an accurate representation of the conversation held at the annual review conference. Make certain that the report contains no surprises that were not discussed at the conference. Often, if the evaluation report coincides with the end of a probationary period, the report contains a section in which the principal must check a box or make a formal recommendation for rehiring or granting tenure.

The cycle begins again by setting new goals for the next school year. Sometimes, the new goals will be continuations or extensions of goals in progress. Ask teachers how you can be of assistance in working toward the goals. In most school districts, teachers have an opportunity to append a statement to the summary evaluation report, especially if they do not agree with some of the appraisals and statements made within it.

The summary evaluation conference can be a most rewarding, enriching, and growth-producing experience. If this is to happen, the experience must be serious, professionally conducted, and based upon mutual trust. Open, honest appraisals and careful definition of challenges can help to set the tone for ongoing instructional improvement and personal renewal.

HOW TO MAKE EFFECTIVE DECISIONS ABOUT REHIRING TEACHERS

One of the least pleasant aspects of the evaluation process is making decisions about whether to retain a teacher's services for another school year. Not rehiring a teacher is never an easy matter. Beginning teachers who are sincere and personable probably will have made some ties among staff, parents, and students in the school. As the school leader, however, you have the obligation to secure the best possible teachers for your school. Principals often struggle with this decision, especially if they are not certain that perceived areas of need are a matter of inexperience or if the individual will just never be a wonderful teacher. The best way to wrestle with this dilemma is to reflect on the individual's track record of growth during your period of supervision. Has she or he been open to suggestions? Has he or she understood and incorporated suggestions that have been made? Do you see the potential for an outstanding professional even if the individual still has a great deal to learn about the process of teaching and learning?

Some people feel that great teachers are naturals—they have all that it takes for excellent performance. Certainly, many aspects of good teaching are a matter of a positive, enthusiastic attitude, and a sincere fondness for children, but even the best-intentioned teachers need to develop effective instructional skills, and this process takes time and effective coaching. Sometimes, the decision of whether to rehire a probationary teacher is a matter of instinct, but in all cases, it should be considered most seriously. A wise superintendent once observed that deciding to award tenure to a teacher (in states where tenure is indeed granted) is a "million-dollar decision." She was referring to the salary that may be paid to a mediocre teacher during a professional career, or the expenses that can be incurred in attempting to remove a tenured teacher. If you have any doubts about a teacher's desire and ability to grow and to sustain a long and fulfilling career in education, it is best to err on the side of caution. Depending upon the pool of qualified teachers available in the marketplace, it just might be best to endure the discomfort of not rehiring a probationary teacher and seeking the best possible replacement you can find. Usually, districts have teacher contracts that include dates by which a teacher must be told if he or she is being rehired. It is of utmost importance that you be aware of and adhere to these procedures.

HOW TO DEAL EFFECTIVELY WITH THE MARGINAL TEACHER

Not all teachers in a school are enthusiastic, cheerful, creative, knowledgeable about the curriculum, and well organized for instruction. When several of these important attributes are lacking, you may be facing a teacher whose lack of teaching competence is truly harmful to children. This is not only difficult to tolerate in your desire to maintain a positive school climate, but beyond this, it is not giving your local residents their fair share for their tax dollars.

It is sad to see a previously well-respected professional lose teaching effectiveness. Sometimes, this can occur as a result of personal and family difficulties or the "sameness" and routine that often accompany many years of teaching. Burnout is by no means a natural or normal outcome for all long-term teachers, but it does happen for some. There are teachers who simply "run out of steam" and become unwilling to examine new approaches. Some teachers bring a negative outlook to their work; others are downright mean to children or are incompetent. As the principal, you have to exercise the responsibility to deal with teacher incompetence.

First, you must distinguish between someone who can benefit from intensive and sincere effort to improve and someone who refuses to recognize problems that they are having and is completely resistant to any kind of constructive feedback and assistance provided. An ineffective teacher may well be a decent human being who is simply not cut out for teaching. In confronting such teachers, it is important to maintain the individual's dignity. Other staff members will be watching on the sidelines, and there could well be ripple effects of a clearly adversarial relationship.

Do not hesitate to let marginal teachers know about your concerns. Act on what you notice right away; don't let bad habits continue because you do not feel comfortable confronting the teacher with frank observations. Go through the normal process of supervision. Even informal observations should be followed up with a conference and a memo summarizing the outcomes of your discussion and the suggestions made.

When you are certain that you want to go ahead and try to remove a teacher, be prepared for a complex, time-consuming, and exhausting process. In some school systems, terminating a teacher can take two or more years. You must be clear in your resolve and make a commitment to the dismissal process. Although this is a very important topic, a comprehensive treatment of this matter is well beyond the scope of this book, but a few suggestions are offered here on how to work with marginal and incompetent teachers.

The first thing you should decide to do is to provide help to the marginal teacher. Develop an assistance plan. Call in others, provide resources, and be very clear about your expectations for improvement. State directly and with concrete examples what is unacceptable about the current performance and what the desired improvements are. Define effective practices and how they can be incorporated into the teacher's instructional repertoire. Suggest specific activities—classrooms to visit, seminars or workshops to attend, articles to read. Always be professional in your demeanor and avoid an air of contentiousness.

Sometimes, a transfer to a new school or grade, if not punitively suggested, can help bring about a change in a teacher's performance. Consider this alternative, but continue to be specific about expectations for good teaching. Nothing can destroy a relationship among a principal's colleagues more than being less than honest about the purpose and promise of such a transfer.

While working with the marginal teacher, collect samples of student assignments, parent complaints, and notes to and from the teacher. The rule of thumb here is "document, document, document." Meet frequently with the teacher and write summaries of these meetings with a list of the understandings or plans developed. Be mindful of timelines that must be followed for obtaining signatures of observation reports and other written notifications.

It is also important to make sure that you are following an established process in your attempt to remove a teacher. Contact the head of your district's personnel office and attorney to make sure that your procedures and actions will not jeopardize your case if it is contested at a later date in court. This is a critical time to be a close partner with district administrators who will be playing a central role in the process.

The whole matter of working with and planning for the termination of incompetent teachers is neither easy nor pleasant. However, most principals would agree that to witness and tolerate the negative effects on children of an ineffective teacher is more uncomfortable for any school leader who is a proud professional.

EVALUATING THE SUPERVISORY PROCESS

No matter how many forms and procedures are put into place, the entire system of evaluation and supervision is sometimes viewed as subjective. You can gain important insights if you ask teachers at the end of the conference to assess the evaluation process. What were the benefits? Did the process help them to reflect upon their performance and chart areas for growth? Was it anxiety provoking? The answers to these questions can give you information about your own conferencing skills. Of course, you might expect more negative responses from those teachers who may have been disappointed with the outcome of the conference, but fair and honest professionals, regardless of some of the recommendations made, will more than likely give an open, truthful assessment of their impressions of the process.

Teacher supervision and evaluation is a relatively complex activity for the principal. The whole process must be well thought out and conducted with sensitivity. Few activities, however, are more important. A well-designed system of observation and evaluation can make the difference between a staff that just continues to conduct "business as usual" and one that is engaged in a continuous cycle of learning, professional development, and self-actualization. In the end, the ultimate beneficiaries of this essential aspect of the principal's role are the children.

NOTE

1. The how-to's of a specific approach to classroom walk-throughs has been described in a book authored by Carolyn Downey, Betty Steffy, Fenwick English, Larry Frase, and William Poston, Jr., *The Three-Minute Classroom Walk-Through: Changing School Supervisory Practice One Teacher at a Time* (Thousand Oaks, CA: Corwin, 2004).

5

The Principal's Role in Curriculum Development and Renewal

As instructional leader of the school, the principal assumes a key role in the process of curriculum development and renewal. You don't have to write the curriculum yourself, but you have important responsibilities for setting a process into motion that will ensure a well-thought-out, up-to-date, research-based instructional program that meets the needs of all students. The exact role of the principal will depend upon the size of your school or school district. In small districts with a few elementary schools, principals are significant players in the curriculum development process; in larger school districts, principals may sit on curriculum committees and be responsible for monitoring the instructional program and making sure that the stated curriculum is what is being taught. In any case, the principal must be visibly and actively involved.

An essential function of any instructional leader is to keep the discussion of curriculum and instruction in the forefront of professional conversations. Engage your staff in considering alternatives, discussing current research, and talking about approaches that have proven successful as well as those that have not. This leads to reading, discussing curriculum, and researching education theory becoming part of the culture of the school. Show that it is also important to gain the perspective of parents.

WHAT *IS* THE CURRICULUM?

Finding an inclusive answer to this question is not as simple as it may seem. Educators have different views of what constitutes the curriculum. For some, it is the content or "course of study" in which teachers engage children; for others, the curriculum is a more comprehensive term encompassing the entire fabric of the educational experience, including basic assumptions about the nature of learning, social interactions, the instructional environment, and ways of knowing—all in addition to the mere content to be learned. However, most educators would agree that a curriculum is a written plan for what students should know and be able to do. This would include all aspects of cognitive, affective, and psychomotor learning, as well as the skills and attitudes that we would hope children develop as a natural outcome of their involvement with the curriculum. The curriculum also deals with the methods of delivery (instructional strategies), assessment strategies, and instructional options that are available.

At the heart of the curriculum are four important questions that any group studying or developing curriculum must answer:

- What is worth knowing?
- What is best practice?
- What evidence will educators accept that students have learned the content?
- What constitutes excellent performance?

As simple as these questions might seem, providing comprehensive answers can require considerable effort and study on the part of teachers, administrators, and curriculum personnel.

The Framework of Assumptions

Usually, a written curriculum begins with a framework of assumptions about the learner and the social milieu of the school. It encompasses research about teaching and learning. Some possible assumptions might include ideas such as:

- All children can learn.
- Through differentiated instruction, all students will have equal access to programs and experiences regardless of gender, race, ethnicity, or disabling condition.
- The curriculum prepares students for responsible citizenship in a rapidly changing society.
- The curriculum is relevant and related to real events in the students' lives.
- The curriculum helps each child to achieve his or her greatest potentials.

In some situations, a philosophy statement about the curriculum and the learner precedes or takes the place of the delineation of a framework of assumptions.

THE CONTENT OR "COURSE OF STUDY"

The written curriculum includes the content and concepts that students will encounter. Selection of what children should learn is always the challenge. In the past few decades, we have witnessed an explosion of knowledge. What do we want our students to know and be able to do? State departments of education have identified both content and performance standards that specify what students should know and be able to do, and the development of curriculum should refer to those standards. Sometimes, the question is not what to include, but rather what to exclude from the curriculum.

In modern practice, curriculum designers are not starting with specific content topics of study; rather, they are defining the outcomes, lasting understanding, thinking skills, and habits of mind that students are expected to acquire. Some of these larger, overarching expectations of the curriculum are as follows:

- Students will become independent, self-reliant learners.
- Students will exhibit intellectual curiosity and a desire to learn more about the world around them.
- Students will understand high levels of quality and be able judge their own work against this standard.
- Students will work in a collaborative fashion, valuing and building upon each other's ideas.
- Students will exhibit perseverance in their work and studies.
- Students will make meaningful contributions to the community at large.
- Students will be able to identify and solve problems.

So, what do we really want our students to know and understand? One model of curriculum development known as backward design is described by Grant Wiggins and Jay McTighe.[1] They ask curriculum designers to formulate enduring understandings and essential questions for courses of study and translate them into learning opportunities (lessons) that lead to the understandings and answer the essential questions. An example of an enduring understanding is that within our ecosystem, living organisms are interdependent. Once enduring understandings are defined, then, and only then, does the hard task of selecting the content, concepts, experiences, and methods of delivery become the next important step. Whatever is chosen for inclusion in the curriculum, the pieces should fit together; there ought to be a logical coherence and sequence to the topics to be studied. Youngsters need to build on prior skills and knowledge to form a logical sum of experience. As teachers and principals work to define a curriculum at the elementary school level, it is important to map out the entire sequence. For example, if each grade is left to establish its own curriculum, students might be engaged in learning about electricity in three of the grades, but never study the basics of energy. An understanding of electricity is tied to an appreciation of various forms of energy. Mapping out the whole curriculum (see below), over the period of the child's elementary school experience, helps them see the logical connections, overlaps, and gaps.

THE METHODS OR TECHNIQUES TO BE USED

How the curriculum is to be delivered, or how students will be involved in the learning, is another essential aspect of a written curriculum. Teachers use a wide variety of techniques to engage children in their schoolwork. In devising instructional techniques, curriculum planners should be informed by research in the fields of child development, brain research, and multiple intelligences. Just as there is variety in human abilities and talents, there is no one way of learning. For this reason, it is important to build a variety of techniques and practices into the curriculum so that all learners will be engaged. Some students work best alone; others thrive in group situations; some work best with their hands; others learn by absorbing visual material. In planning learning experiences, teachers match techniques and instructional methods to the topic at hand, the group of learners, and the learning context. Cooperative learning, direct instruction, reading in the content area, interviews, community work, research projects, reports, and other such activities should all be incorporated at one time or another to balance the methods of delivering the curriculum. Research-based strategies that translate theory into practice should be implemented in the instruction of all students regardless of ability. When reviewing the literature, there are well-documented state-of-the-art techniques for instruction that cite the source of the research. One example of this is the Response to Intervention approach, which integrates assessment, curriculum-based interventions, and systems of prevention to maximize student achievement and to improve behavior problems. Schools monitor student progress, provide appropriate interventions, and adjust them depending on the student's response. It is designed to provide early, effective support to students who are having difficulty learning and to identify students with learning disabilities.

The Role of Inquiry and Integrated Learning

In any curriculum, students should have opportunities to conduct meaningful inquiry. Active involvement with the curriculum helps students to assume responsibility for their own learning and to develop a process for learning in general. In inquiry learning, children are prompted to ask questions about a particular topic or area of study and plan how they will find answers to those questions. They use a variety of materials, technological tools, and resources. The teacher guides children in their investigations and asks questions to prompt further inquiry. Student inquiries can be individual, group oriented, or a combination of the two. An important aspect of any inquiry is to present or report the results obtained. By following a sequence for inquiry, students learn how to conduct further and future studies. They become authorities on their own knowledge and develop the skills to assess, act upon, and communicate knowledge for a variety of purposes and in a variety of settings. In this sense, inquiry learning promotes learning-to-learn skills and may form the basis for lifelong interests.

Curriculum integration involves developing the natural relationships of content and process into meaningful problems and issues across several curriculum areas. Planning for curriculum integration accomplishes many educational purposes. An integrated curriculum

- mirrors the real world,
- has the power to motivate students,
- can help address the problem of the overcrowded curriculum,
- helps students make sense of their world, and
- fosters collaboration among students and teachers.

In planning integrated learning experiences, teachers must emphasize the natural connections among subject areas and be careful not to trivialize these connections. Designing integrated units takes time. Teachers need to work collaboratively and cooperatively. Special-subject teachers and teachers of students with special needs should be provided the opportunity to plan along with classroom teachers. If time for planning is an issue, such work can take place during faculty meetings, through electronic forums, or on days a district has dedicated to staff development and collaboration.

To the degree that we can integrate the curriculum, students will gain a deeper understanding of concepts and phenomena because their knowledge will be connected in ways that are meaningful to them. We are living in an information age where knowledge is literally exploding every year. As issues and concepts become more complex, student understanding is enhanced when information from several disciplines is related in ways that mirror the skills and habits of mind they will need to solve problems. Most problems are not situated in a single discipline with narrow solutions, but rather require the integration of skills and knowledge from several disciplines.

The Role of Differentiated Instruction

It has become a best practice to differentiate instruction to address the diverse needs of students found in every classroom. Differentiating instruction refers to designing lessons that address varied learning styles, interest, and readiness. When differentiating, it is important to ensure that all students achieve the same enduring understandings, concepts, knowledge, and skills. A teacher can address the varied learning needs of her students by creating tiered lessons that address the same key ideas and skills, but at different levels of complexity. For example, in a second-grade classroom where students are learning the skill of sequencing, one group of students may sequence a story using sentence strips prepared by the teacher, while another group orders the sentences by placing a number beside a sentence that indicates the order of events in a story. Simultaneously, the more advanced learner might create a written piece using signal words such as "first," "next," "then," and "finally." Learning opportunities and assessments may be differentiated for students without compromising designated understandings, concepts, knowledge, and skills.

The Assessments to Be Employed

How will you know what the students have achieved? How is excellent performance judged? These and other questions form the basis for considering the assessments to be a part of any curriculum. Ideally, assessment is an ongoing part of instruction. Standards of excellence can be used so that students know how they will be assessed and what constitutes outstanding performance. Evaluative measures are built into all instructional episodes, so that teachers—and students—know if they're on course. Teachers can continue the planned curriculum with relevant information to adjust the content and methods, based upon an ongoing judgment of student understanding and application. These assessments inform both teachers and students. If rubrics are used to evaluate student performance, they should be shared with students as they get nearer to excellent performance.

Assessments must be designed so that students can demonstrate evidence that they have learned the content, acquired the skills, and have developed the habits of mind identified during the curriculum review process. It is important for teachers to design assessments that reflect the desired content and skills. Both formative and summative assessments must be selected in developing any curriculum. A combination of short formative assessments, authentic assessments, performance tasks, and more traditional forms of evaluation should be included. In designing the curriculum, assessment techniques are matched to the learning. For example, if students are learning about circuits, then a performance task might be to provide batteries, bulbs, and wires, and ask the children to demonstrate a complete circuit. Curriculum developers must have at their disposal a broad knowledge of a wide variety of assessment tools and devices. In this way, a comprehensive evaluation of student learning can be planned and implemented, and mid-course corrections can be made by both teachers and students.

ESTABLISHING A TIMELINE FOR EXAMINING THE CURRICULUM

All areas of the curriculum cannot be examined at the same time. Basic outcomes for students in an elementary school can be defined, but redesigning the total curriculum is a huge undertaking. Administrators must establish curriculum priorities. Which areas are most in need of review? Which areas are witnessing the most development in the field? For example, when whole language was making its way into the language-arts curriculum in the late 1980s and early 1990s, schools began to examine their practices in this area. Likewise, when the National Council of Teachers of Mathematics published its standards for mathematics education, educators in schools all over the country began to asses their own mathematics programs and compare them to the new practices being advocated.

Principals and teachers must talk about areas of need in the curriculum, discuss trends and developments in the field, and then establish a plan for the review of each major curriculum area. These reviews should be spaced out over time in order to preserve the energy and human resources needed to study current programs. Curriculum review also requires financial resources. Teachers must meet, examine materials, and study current and proposed practices. This requires many meetings and time to conduct surveys, read current literature, and attend conferences or institutes. Such work has financial implications for teacher release time, materials, and other expenses. A five-year plan for curriculum review and renewal makes a great deal of sense. A sample plan for a K–5 curriculum renewal cycle appears in Figure 5.1.

Figure 5.1 Timetable for K–5 Curriculum Renewal

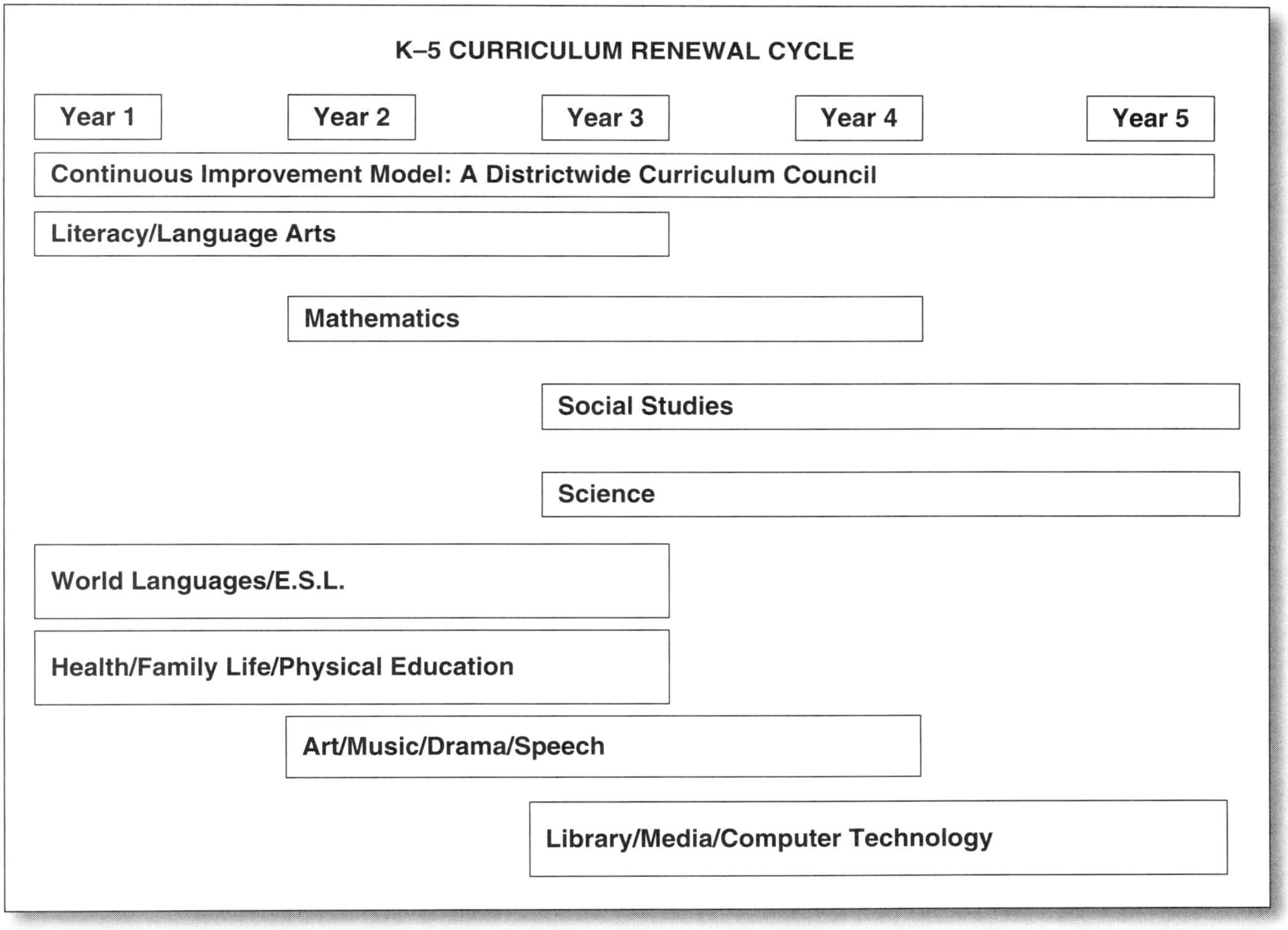

K–5 CURRICULUM RENEWAL CYCLE

| Year 1 | Year 2 | Year 3 | Year 4 | Year 5 |

Continuous Improvement Model: A Districtwide Curriculum Council

Literacy/Language Arts

Mathematics

Social Studies

Science

World Languages/E.S.L.

Health/Family Life/Physical Education

Art/Music/Drama/Speech

Library/Media/Computer Technology

A new principal may discover a window of opportunity, a curriculum area that the staff is interested in reviewing. These windows of opportunity are openings for change—places for a new principal to begin the curriculum renewal process and become a curriculum leader in the school.

A PROCESS FOR CURRICULUM RENEWAL

Before offering a process, it is important to say that all elementary school principals would be wise to work hand in hand with their central-office administrators before undertaking a process for major curriculum renewal. Any renewal will impact other schools, as well as the community.

First, a committee or study group should be formed. The membership of this group is important. Teachers will be the primary members, but administrators, curriculum specialists, and parent representation should also be considered. In some schools, staff members may be resistant to parents being a part of the committee, but as principal, you can help teachers understand the important role that parents can play. Just as a curriculum will be delivered with greater commitment when teachers are involved in developing it, so, too, the school and what is taught will be better supported by parents who have had an opportunity to voice their hopes and dreams for what their children will learn. (See Chapter 1, Figure 1.1, for a sample letter soliciting volunteers for a curriculum renewal committee.) It is essential that each member of the group be responsible for making regular progress reports to their constituent groups. This makes the process transparent and inclusive of the entire school community.

There are distinct phases of curriculum renewal, and the process should not be rushed or hurried. The plan proposed here consists of three major parts or phases: research and development, pilot studies, and implementation. Each of these parts usually takes a full school year to complete—sometimes more. Depending upon the results of the first phase, pilot projects may not be needed, but this determination cannot be made until a comprehensive examination of the existing curriculum has been completed.

Phase One: Research and Development

In the first year of the study, the members of the curriculum committee examine current practices, review current literature, establish a philosophy and general goals for the curriculum, survey programs in comparable districts, and examine and compare products in the marketplace. The committee chair should gather relevant literature for the members to review and discuss. Classical statements in the curriculum area as well as current research and organization position papers should be read. Once this process is well under way, the members of the group should define their own philosophy and general goals for the curriculum.

Current practices can be surveyed by use of a questionnaire. A sample curriculum assessment questionnaire appears in Figure 5.2. We are in the age of technology, when a questionnaire such as the one in Figure 5.2 can be created using software that collects and analyzes data. Once results have been compiled, the implications should be discussed. A wide range of comparable school districts can be contacted through the use

Figure 5.2   Sample Curriculum Assessment Questionnaire

SCIENCE CURRICULUM STUDY QUESTIONNAIRE

Name: ________________________ **Grade:** ________ **School:** ________________________

(Use additional pages if necessary)

1. What are your major goals for your science program at your grade level?

2. What are the major topics you plan to cover this year in your science program (please be specific, e.g., air and atmosphere, circuits, habitats, ecosystems, etc.)?

3. What materials do you employ for science instruction (please specify science kits used, textbooks, teacher-made materials, literature, etc.)?

4. What methods do you employ in your science instructional program (e.g., inquiry, lecture/demonstration, laboratory work, cooperative investigations, field trips, reading in the content area, nature-center work, etc.)?

5. Are you satisfied with the methods and materials you are using? Why or why not?

6. What changes (or directions) would you like to see considered in our examination of our science program? Please note any units, materials, or series you would like us to consider.

7. How many minutes do you devote to science instruction each week? Check one:

   ☐ Less than 30 minutes   ☐ 30–60 minutes   ☐ 60–90 minutes   ☐ More than 90 minutes

8. Additional comments:

---

of an electronic survey tool as well. The questions in Figure 5.3 can be used to create an electronic survey for educational leaders of comparable districts to complete.

With this information, the group should begin to think about next steps. What is the general level of satisfaction with the current program? Is it considered effective? What measures of student achievement are available? What changes, if any, are in order? These are all important questions, which the members of the group will have to answer. If it is decided that a new program is warranted, then the group must consider whether the new curriculum will be locally developed or if a commercial program will be purchased. In any case, the program and practices considered should be consistent with the

Figure 5.3   Science Curriculum Telephone Interview or Electronic Survey Form

SCIENCE CURRICULUM TELEPHONE INTERVIEW/ELECTRONIC SURVEY FORM

Name of School District: _______________________________ **Date:** ____________

Person Interviewed: ________________ **Position:** __________ **Phone No.:** __________

1. What science program is currently used in your elementary grades?

    Name of program: ____

    Publisher: ______________________________ Grade(s) using: ________________

2. If a text is used, what provisions are made for "hands-on" laboratory work?

3. What is your general assessment of the effectiveness of the program(s)?

4. What is the general level of teacher and parent satisfaction with the program(s)?

5. By what means do you assess the effectiveness of your science program?

6. Who handles the ordering of science materials and supplies in your school district?

7. What opportunities for differentiation does the program offer?

Name of Interviewer: ____

philosophy and goals outlined by the group. If a search is conducted for a commercial program, a systematic way of evaluating materials examined must be established. (See Figure 5.4 for a sample of a program evaluation form.)

The final aspect of Phase One of curriculum renewal is the identification of pilot studies for the next year. This may be a comparison of distinct programs and practices in different schools or grades, or the use of a single new program judged against existing practices. In any case, the committee must decide how the pilot programs will be assessed. Will pilot teachers be surveyed? How will student achievement be measured? How will you decide which of the various pilot programs will be adopted for future implementation?

Figure 5.4   Commercial Program Evaluation Form

COMMERCIAL PROGRAM EVALUATION FORM

(Complete this form after reviewing any commercial program considered)

Program or Series Title: ____

Publisher: ____

Edition or Level Reviewed: ____

1. Does this program seem to be consistent with and supportive of our philosophy and goals for science instruction in our schools?

2. Do the topics and related concepts seem age/grade appropriate?

3. Are there provisions for "hands-on" exploration of concepts and phenomena?

4. Are the investigations easy to set up? Are materials readily available?

5. What possibilities for integration of the curriculum and inquiry are evident?

6. Are there provisions for teachers to differentiate the curriculum for students who need a challenge and those who need additional help?

Name of Reviewer: ______________________________________   **Date:** ____________

Phase Two: Pilot Studies

Once pilot studies have been determined, the committee must continue to monitor progress. If a new curriculum is to be locally developed, when will this be done and who will create it? If a commercial program is used, problems with vendors and materials should be discussed and solved. Feedback should be gathered during the pilot study year.

A multifaceted assessment of the pilot programs should be implemented. Teacher questionnaires, parent surveys, and student achievement measures should all be designed. (A sample parent questionnaire appears in Figure 5.5.) In this way, different programs and practices can be compared and conclusions drawn about the relative effectiveness of the various programs. At the end of the pilot study year, recommendations for future action should be made. Implementing new content and practice can have its challenges, so teachers need to be clear about where to give ongoing feedback and to whom they can pose questions. Student work collected during the pilot program must be studied and

Figure 5.5 Sample Parent Questionnaire About Science Pilot Programs

_______________________ (date)

Dear Parents,

   As you may be aware, we have embarked upon a major effort to renew and revitalize our science instructional programs in our elementary schools this year. As we assess our pilot projects, we are interested in the extent to which students' involvement in science at school has been reflected at home. Kindly take the time to answer the questions below and return this form to your child's school office within one week. This information will assist us in the evaluation of our new science programs.

Sincerely,

THE SCIENCE CURRICULUM STUDY GROUP

	YES	NO
1. Were you aware that your child was involved in a new or revised science program this year?	☐	☐
2. Has your child related any of the specific science experiences he or she has had in school this year?	☐	☐
3. Have you noticed an increase in your child's interest in science?	☐	☐
4. Do you feel that science has received greater emphasis in our schools this year than in the past?	☐	☐
5. Has your child conducted any science experiments at home?	☐	☐

Any additional comments or remarks would be appreciated.

If you have any special talents, interests, or abilities in science that might enhance our science programs, please note this.

Name: _______________________________ **Grade Level of Child(ren):** _______________

compared to the criteria formulated in the curriculum renewal process. Once recommendations have been developed and forwarded to the superintendent, the members of the committee may be called upon to make a presentation to the board of education. This is particularly necessary if the implementation of a new program has major budgetary implications.

Phase Three: Implementation

Once pilot programs have been assessed, plans for full-scale implementation must be made. An important aspect of any implementation effort will be designing a staff development program that will help teachers become familiar with the new program and recommended practices and teaching strategies.

Once the adopted program is in place, the usable life of the curriculum may be considered five years. Although the formal curriculum renewal cycle may seem complete, efforts must be made to sustain, maintain, and improve the existing programs. Annual budget allocations for replenishing materials, kits, and other supplies are a continual requirement. The professional support program must also be kept alive to help teachers incorporate new ideas and approaches into their instructional practices.

PREPARING A CURRICULUM DOCUMENT

Before attempting to prepare a curriculum document, several questions should be considered. These questions may lead to further study that must be accomplished before actually sitting down to write the new curriculum.

1. What changes in the existing curriculum are being recommended? What is the educational rationale for these changes? Will the scope and sequence be changed? Will new topics be introduced? Will new methods or techniques be employed? Will topics be omitted from the existing curriculum?

2. Have recommendations from national curriculum studies been incorporated into the curriculum? What research and professional literature was reviewed and how are the findings reflected in the proposed curriculum?

3. What state content and performance standards are met by this curriculum?

4. What impact will the new curriculum have on other subject areas or grade levels?

5. How has articulation with other levels of the school district (elementary, middle, high school) been addressed?

6. How will critical-thinking skills and habits of mind be addressed in the new curriculum?

7. What technology will be incorporated into the curriculum?

8. Is any special equipment or materials required for adoption of the curriculum?

9. Has the curriculum been reviewed for bias and equity issues?

10. Does the curriculum allow teachers to differentiate the activities and assessments for students of varied abilities?

Once these questions have been considered, the study group can begin to prepare the actual curriculum document.

Statement of Philosophy

Most often, a curriculum guide begins with a statement of philosophy. This should express the views of the curriculum developers and also incorporate current research findings and best practices in the field. A statement of philosophy should be brief and stated in language that will be understood easily by all constituencies. A sample philosophy statement for an elementary school science curriculum follows:

> Experiences in science are essential for the intellectual development of children. In science, children have an opportunity to handle, manipulate, and otherwise experiment with the materials of the physical and natural world. Children are exposed to the experiences that form the foundations of logical thought. It is becoming increasingly evident that these kinds of experiences early in life are critical for optimum intellectual development.
>
> Children have a natural curiosity about the world in which they live. Children learn as a result of this natural curiosity. As they poke, prod, and explore, they will develop answers to some of their questions. The science curriculum supports children in their quest to know. Science is one way that we seek to interpret the world in which we live, but it is also a way in which each individual investigates and interprets. Beyond this, science is also humanity's quest to know. Scientists have studied the rocks at our feet and the stars above our heads. They have probed the atom and peered into the living cell. To a large extent, they are asking the same kinds of questions as the curious child.
>
> No child needs to or can duplicate the work of thousands of scientists. The children can make use of what has already been learned. Certainly, one of the purposes of science learning is to tap the knowledge that has been accumulated and distilled over the ages. An important dimension of every child's science education is the opportunity to relate his or her developing view of the world with that which has been developed in the past. The role of the teacher in science is to support children's natural curiosity, to foster the process of inquiry, and to lead them to find the answers to their own questions and those of others.

Define Outcomes

What do you want students to know and be able to do after being involved in the curriculum? What are the broad outcomes? An outcome is a broad statement of expectations for learners. An outcome might be for students to use multiple resources in researching their questions. Another might be for students to make contributions to the community at large and to assess the impact of those contributions. For each outcome, observable behaviors that indicate student accomplishment should be defined. These become attributes of student assessments.

State Goals

Goals may be thought of as targets for student learning. A goal might be for students to evaluate online services as they gather information for the completion of a report. Another goal might be for students to formulate hypotheses about the needs of plants after observing their growth in a terrarium. Goals should encompass specific issues, concepts, and questions that students will explore. Several goals should be defined for each of the major outcomes within a curriculum.

List Concepts and Objectives to Be Promoted

The concepts that students will be exposed to or expected to understand are listed next. Concepts are broad generalizations or "big ideas." For example, a life cycle is a concept that can be applied to several animal and plant species studied. Diversity of life forms in nature is another broad concept. For students to gain conceptual knowledge, specific objectives will need to be outlined.

Specify Techniques or Strategies to Be Employed

In any curriculum, a wide variety of approaches and instructional strategies will be utilized. Teachers must use practices that have been shown to be effective so that all students have an opportunity to learn under the best of circumstances. Some way of assessing the students' familiarity and current level of knowledge should be assessed. This can help teachers choose the entry point for students and highlight misconceptions that need to be corrected.

Instructional techniques should also be specified. Instructional techniques should be research based, and not just chosen from current fads. If cooperative learning is to be used, for which activities and investigations is this approach best suited? When are teacher demonstrations or simulations most appropriate? At what point and for what purposes should students create individual or group reports? What means of technology must be incorporated into the study and what specific skills need to be learned? How will the student acquire these skills?

It is important for a principal to create a culture where both new and tried-and-true instructional strategies are shared, and where differentiated instruction is an expectation. Whether it is communicated in the weekly staff news, discussed at faculty meetings, or shared by distributing the abstract of a current article to staff, the culture of using best practices can and must be created by the principal. Teachers' use of best practice in the classroom is as important as doctors' use of best practice in the field of medicine.

Major Activities and Assignments

In any curriculum, a set of activities and major assignments will be created that will allow students to accomplish the outcomes and goals. These learning opportunities need to be specified so that they can be replicated and modified as needed. The degree of specificity needed to outline the activities depends upon local needs and the complexity of the activities. Is a great deal of background information needed prior to involvement in an activity? What resources and materials are required? What techniques are to be employed?

How Will the Learning Be Assessed?

How will we know that students have accomplished the goals and outcomes of the curriculum? A variety of assessment techniques need to be incorporated. Some will be embedded in each activity or assignment; these may include observational checklists, skills lists, photographic records, or student journal entries, just to name a few. More formal, summative assessments must also be planned. These can be paper-and-pencil tests, performance tasks that require students to apply new learning to real-life situations, portfolios, projects, research reports, or other forms of presentation. Teachers implementing any curriculum must create common tests for students designed to assess the expected outcomes. An analysis of student work will establish levels of proficiency.

Staff Development Implications

In planning any curriculum, staff development implications need to be considered. What skills, background knowledge, or abilities will teachers need in order to implement the curriculum? Are specific attitudes or habits of mind required in order to lead children successfully through the course of study? What in-service offerings are required in order to support teacher efforts? What opportunities are provided for teachers to share their joys, frustrations, and reflections about implementing the curriculum? In this day and age, if time to meet is at a premium, school wikis (Web sites created for a specific topic or project) and blogs can allow teachers to communicate in another venue.

Just as we expect teachers to differentiate instruction for students, staff development should be differentiated for teachers who are at varied career points. For there to be equity in the curriculum, it is critical that there are structures in place for all teachers— both new and experienced—to learn how to implement the curriculum in ways that are consistent with expectations.

Finally, any curriculum is considered a "living document." A course of study that is set in stone is not likely to be strictly followed. Teachers should have opportunities to keep notes, make adjustments, and otherwise adapt the written curriculum to individual situations and the needs and interests of a particular group.

A Continuous Improvement Model

In the spirit of continuous improvement, and to ensure that the curriculum is, in fact, a "living document," a district can create a structure in which staff is always studying research in every discipline. Within this structure, a "curriculum council" can discuss, review, and suggest ideas about curriculum, and new content and state-of-the-art instructional strategies can be infused into existing curriculum on an ongoing basis. The ongoing improvement structure was shown at the top of Figure 5.1. A checklist designating the critical attributes of a coherent curriculum design, instruction, and assessment can be provided to teachers as they design lessons and assessments.

CURRICULUM ARTICULATION

Curriculum articulation may be thought of as the degree to which student learnings are consistent and flow naturally from one year to the next, and from one level of the school system to the next. If teachers at each grade level are left to design their own curriculums, they may not know what was covered the year before or what is planned for the next year. Web-based curriculum maps, described below, allow teachers to keep track of the curriculum at their own grade level and also compare their grade-level curriculum to the curriculum at other grade levels. The development of any curriculum or course of study must be informed by the experiences that students have already had and what the long-term plans are for their general education in the future. Figure 5.6 is an example of how a curriculum can be mapped to ensure articulation across the school system.

Figure 5.6 Curriculum-Mapping Grid by Grade Level

CURRICULUM MAP FOR SCIENCE INSTRUCTION

Elementary School

Grade	Outcomes	Goals	Objectives	Assignments	Assessments
Kindergarten					
Grade One					
Grade Two					
Grade Three					
Grade Four					
Grade Five					

Middle School

Grade	Outcomes	Goals	Objectives	Assignments	Assessments
Grade Six					
Grade Seven					
Grade Eight					

High School

Grade	Outcomes	Goals	Objectives	Assignments	Assessments
Grade Nine					
Grade Ten					
Grade Eleven					
Grade Twelve					

In many school systems, curriculum articulation committees are set up for the purpose of studying the coherence of the curriculum across the school system. Usually staffed by one representative from each division of the school system, the members of an articulation committee can see the "big picture" by defining the learner outcomes for the students at the exit grade of each level of the school system. Some of the purposes of such a committee might include

- studying gaps and overlaps within each curriculum area and between and among the various divisions of the school system,
- recommending adjustments to the curriculum so that it will be better articulated,
- recommending areas needing further study and development within the curriculum,
- recommending time and resource priorities within the curriculum,
- exploring opportunities for curriculum integration, and
- serving as a forum for problem solving, resource acquisition, and debate.

Curriculum Mapping

Mapping the curriculum provides a technique for all teachers to examine what is taught, how instruction occurs, when instruction is delivered, and what assessments are used. Figure 5.6 shows how a district map can ensure alignment across grade levels. There are several Web-based tools on the market designed so that school systems can map a curriculum, facilitate communication among teachers, and update it on an ongoing basis— essential facets of the curriculum renewal process. The curriculum map will change over time as teachers implement any curriculum, new or existing. Writing publicly when a topic is taught is a commitment to teaching it.[2] After articulation across the levels of a school system is ensured, teachers on each grade level can create their own curriculum maps that indicate when during the school year concepts and skills are taught, and when assessments are administered. Figure 5.7 shows examples of curriculum maps that indicate what month a topic will be taught. Maps ensure that all teachers, experienced and new, know what to teach and when to teach it, thereby ensuring that students are equitably equipped with knowledge and skills as they enter new grades and levels of the school system.

Figure 5.7   Curriculum-Mapping Grids

ELEMENTARY CURRICULUM MAP FOR SCIENCE INSTRUCTION

Grade Level

Month	Outcomes	Goals	Objectives	Assignments	Assessments
September					
October					
November					
December					
January					
February					
March					
April					
May					
June					

CURRICULUM SUPERVISION AND ACCOMMODATING TEACHER CHOICE AND FLEXIBILITY

Principals know that teachers need some degree of autonomy in personalizing or customizing a curriculum to the group with which they are working. How much choice and flexibility teachers ought to have versus the need to cover the stated curriculum is never an easy matter. Very often, the implementation of a curriculum will depend upon the makeup of a particular group of students and their interests, talents, and abilities. However, it would be expected that teachers address all students' needs through a variety of assignments, projects, and assessments that are differentiated. This is in connection to the view that a curriculum is intended for *all* students regardless of individual aptitude, interest, or background. In trying to find the middle ground, principals must analyze each classroom separately. There are situations in which some teachers are legitimately and sensitively adapting the curriculum to group needs and managing to deal with the major concepts in a sincere fashion. They match strategies to the group based upon a careful assessment of needs. On the other hand, there may be some teachers who resist any curriculum mandates—teachers who figure that when they close the classroom door, they can teach what they like and how they like without regard to district priorities. That is tougher for principals to deal with. These teachers—however talented they may be—must be confronted and asked, specifically, how they have provided an education for their youngsters that is equitable to that being provided to other students at the same grade level. When students exit our schools, we must ensure that each of their toolboxes is equally equipped with knowledge, skills, and habits of mind that allow them to become lifelong learners. Teachers must teach the core content, outcomes, and skills included in any curriculum to all students while employing the best instructional strategies.

As instructional leader of the school, you are indeed responsible for curriculum supervision—ensuring that the stated curriculum is taught so that all students, regardless of gender, race, socioeconomic status, or special needs, are provided with opportunities to learn and succeed as a result of the district's plan. At the same time, responsive principals create an environment that encourages teachers to exercise flexibility and to take risks to do what is best for students. As in many such matters, you must rely upon your best instincts and professional knowledge to judge whether teachers are abusing the freedom and flexibility to which they are entitled, and not providing the best possible education for students consistent with district standards.

What we engage children in and *how* we engage them are fundamental considerations in planning for school experiences. Developing a curriculum is a complex process that encompasses many considerations and a contemporary understanding of what is important for students to know and be able to do, and how best to convey the skills, knowledge, and attitudes for them to become effective citizens. This task can seem awesome—and indeed it is—but nothing can be more important in education than making these critical decisions.

NOTES

1. Backward design is well articulated in the work of Grant Wiggins and Jay McTighe, *Understanding by Design*, 2nd ed. (Alexandria, VA: Association for Supervision and Curriculum Development, 2005).

2. Curriculum mapping and curriculum integration have been described with many examples in the work of Heidi Hayes Jacobs, *Mapping the Big Picture* (Alexandria, VA: Association for Supervision and Curriculum Development, 1997).

Assessment in the Elementary School

Purposes and Practices

Reform in the way we view assessment in the elementary school carries significant implications for instruction in general. The No Child Left Behind (NCLB) Act of 2001 made assessment the cornerstone of education reform as we know it. Whether termed "authentic" assessment, "alternative" assessment, or "performance" assessment, one principle prevails: We must examine children's growth within the context of *what they can do, how much they can do, and how well they can do* it. NCLB has caused schools to restructure methods of instruction and how we measure student achievement; it has also demanded high-quality assessments that are aligned with state standards. Any consideration of changing the practices of assessment should begin with an examination of the purposes of assessment.

THE PURPOSES OF ASSESSMENT

Assessment is a primary means of determining whether stated goals and intentions are being met. In order to judge whether goals are realized, standards for achievement must first be set—then student performance can be compared to those standards or benchmarks. A broad variety of assessments must be brought to bear in order to provide useful information about the success of school programs, but the first step in designing and using assessments is to think through the purposes of those assessments. Some of these include

- providing an understanding of children's conceptual background, prior experiences, and attitudes (preassessment);

Note: All forms, letters, and checklists included in this chapter can be found at corwin.com/elementary survivalkit.

- diagnosing students' strengths and weaknesses;
- providing information for individual program planning;
- measuring student growth in concept and process attainment and the development of new attitudes;
- providing feedback to school personnel about the effectiveness of school programs and instructional strategies;
- providing opportunities for students to reflect upon their own learning and growth;
- providing input for a continuous cycle of programmatic examination, development, improvement, and change; and
- gaining information about student accomplishments for purposes of reporting to parents, administrators, and other interested groups.

Assessment is an ongoing process; it is not something that happens only at the end of an instructional unit. Progress is monitored on a continual basis so that instruction may be modified or adjusted appropriately. It is folly for teachers to continue with a plan regardless of the students' ability to deal with the material. When assessment is a natural part of instruction, teachers receive continual information and feedback, which helps them to adjust what they are doing. Assessments increase our understanding of the children in our classrooms and how they learn. They help us make informed decisions about planning opportunities, approaches, and materials. Assessment may be viewed as a cycle for ongoing refinement of instruction. (See Figure 6.1.)

Figure 6.1 Feedback Model for Planning, Instruction, and Assessment

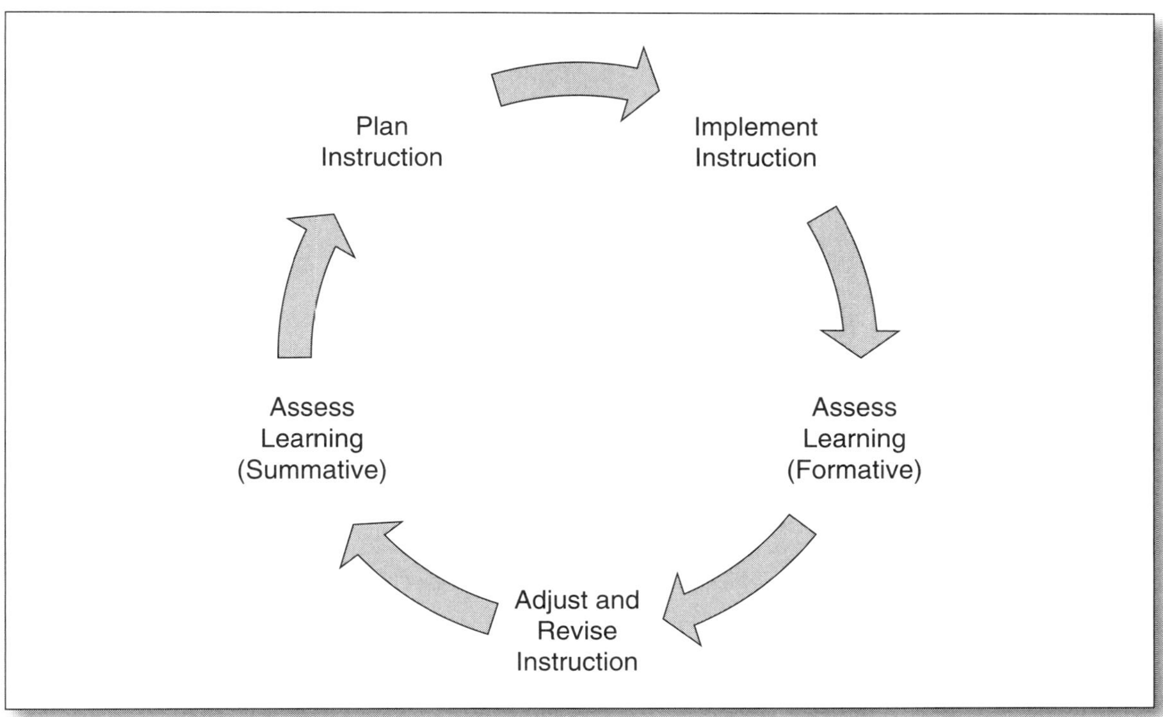

A FEW USEFUL DEFINITIONS

The current emphasis on assessment in educational practice has resulted in a host of terms that are used frequently in educational circles, but some of the distinctions are not well understood. Sometimes, these expressions are used interchangeably, and there is a natural overlap among some terms. A few helpful definitions are listed below:

Alternative Assessments represent tasks given to students in which they must demonstrate a skill or knowledge in a form other than on paper-and-pencil, standardized, or norm-referenced tests. Example: Students make up a travel brochure that invites visitors to the state they have been studying.

Authentic Assessments are activities students are asked to complete that are relevant in the world outside of school. The assessment is meaningful to students because it naturally extends the classroom learning to its broader application in the "real world" and often integrates skills from many disciplines. Example: Fourth graders who study immigration prepare an orientation booklet for newcomers to their school that reflects their learnings about the needs and wants of immigrants and U.S. customs and practices.

Benchmarks are defined levels of performance that students are expected to demonstrate within and across grade levels. Benchmarks are often stated for fourth, eighth, and eleventh graders. Example: Fourth graders use a variety of resources, including print, electronic media, and audio-visual components, to prepare a presentation about one of the states in their region.

Curriculum-Based Measures (CBMs) is an approach or assessment system for monitoring student progress, on an ongoing basis, within the context of the curriculum. At the elementary level, CBMs are brief, focused tests of basic skill development, usually in the areas of reading, writing, and math. Example: In reading, for instance, the student may be asked to read aloud for one minute. The teacher might record the number of words read correctly. These assessments tend to be administered as "quick probes" taking approximately two to four minutes to administer.

Formative Assessments are used to measure students' knowledge and understanding of a particular topic, to monitor and adjust future instruction, and to account for gaps or deficits in order to improve achievement. These tend to be nongraded assessments that inform teachers as to how to guide their instruction. Example: Students will fill out a concept map to show their understanding of checks and balances after a lesson on the three branches of government.

Instructional Outcomes are broad statements that describe what students should know and be able to do at the completion of a unit of study, course, or sequence of instruction. Outcomes are also sometimes referred to as "exit behaviors." Example: At the end of the fifth grade, students will demonstrate that they can collect, graphically organize, and interpret data.

Performance Assessments are tests that require students to demonstrate, in a natural, active, context, what they have learned and can do. Performance assessments evolve naturally from a student's involvement in an instructional activity. Example: To demonstrate their classification skills, kindergartners are asked to sort shapes into distinct categories, based upon a single attribute—shape, color, thickness, or size.

Portfolio Assessment is a collection of student work samples gathered over a period of time and used to demonstrate growth or accomplishment. Students develop guidelines for what to include in their portfolios, as well as what about their learning is evident in the work sample. Periodic examination of student portfolios to note growth and progress is an important aspect of student assessment. Example: Students keep successive drafts of a written report in a portfolio. At each stage of development, they examine their work, self-assess, and set goals for the next phase of their report and, along with a peer or the teacher, assess their progress.

Product Assessment is another way that students demonstrate what they have learned. By producing a specific product, students incorporate the concepts and skills that they have assimilated. Products reveal a great deal about student learning and thinking. Usually, teachers develop a rating scale, or a rubric, for assessing the product. Examples: Artwork, dioramas, an article of clothing, a scale model, a brochure or poster, a patchwork quilt, and so on.

Scoring Rubrics are statements or guidelines used to characterize different levels of performance. Literally, a rubric is a heading or rule. To assess a student project or paper, a scoring rubric may be developed that defines the criteria used to rate or judge a sample of student work. Rubrics may be designed according to a point scale, that is, 1 to 5, with the criteria for each number defined. They may also use word categories, for example, "novice," "practitioner," and "expert." These descriptors are then referenced to the overall quality of the product or, preferably, to its discrete elements.

Self-Assessment is an important component of evaluation; given a set of criteria, students can examine their own work or products and rate how well they did. An added benefit of self-assessment is that students can set goals for continued improvement. Self-assessment also promotes meta-cognition—the ability of students to become aware of their own thought processes and learning strategies.

Standards are statements of content learning or performance. Content standards specify what students should know in a particular area. They may be considered curriculum outlines or frameworks. Performance standards specify what students must do in order to exhibit mastery in an area of learning. Some educators consider a standard a measure of exemplary performance that serves as an ultimate benchmark. For example, the musicianship of Pablo Cassals is a standard of performance to which all cellists might aspire. Realistically, though, standards must be adapted for a population of students.

Summative Assessments measure students' achievement at the end of a unit of study or learning activity to assign a grade. Final exams, oral competencies, performance assessments, portfolios, and end-of-the-year evaluations are examples of summative assessments.

ASSESSMENT VERSUS TESTING

Assessment of student work and instructional outcomes provides different information than do the results of traditional testing. Authentic assessment helps us to evaluate the outcomes of learning, look at the evidence of student achievement, and measure student growth against preestablished criteria. Assessment is not testing, although testing can be a part of it. Assessment allows us to learn about the value and impact of what we do in classrooms. Testing, on the other hand, provides information about a "slice in time"; it does not tap the whole picture or help us gain insights into the approaches of the learner. Assessments should focus on improved learning. They should help your staff to be better educators and provide quality feedback to students. Standard paper-and-pencil tests often measure unrelated fragments of information, but they do not tell us what students can do with that information. Can they apply it? Can they use it in new contexts and situations? Multiple means of assessment, including performance measures, can better provide the answers to these kinds of questions, and the answers will be more comprehensive.

Modern means of assessment are more active than traditional measures. Most standardized tests, state-mandated tests, and norm- and criterion-referenced tests consist of brief tasks, "snippets" that demonstrate a narrow range of performance. More authentic assessments involve students in meaningful, relevant tasks that have some application to students' daily lives. They require students to apply skills and to integrate their knowledge from several areas and subjects. Authentic assessments usually provide students with information that helps them evaluate their own learning and set goals for continued growth.

In performance assessments, students usually come to realize that there is no single way to solve problems; there are multiple approaches. Teachers gain important information by noting and analyzing how students solve problems. Often, this provides as much useful information as whether or not the student arrives at the "right answer." Teacher observations, notes, and judgments are essential aspects of the assessment process. When teachers review and reflect upon their jottings, they gain important insights about how children learn and can then act upon the information that they have gained. Authentic assessment tasks are almost indistinguishable from the learning—the evaluative devices often being embedded within the learning activities themselves.

By studying children's problem-solving strategies, we gain essential glimpses into their thinking and how they are processing the information they have acquired. In this way, assessment is intricately linked to learning. In using performance assessments, teachers help students to understand the criteria that define the desired outcomes. Models of successful strategies and examples of excellent performance are shared, studied, and understood by the students before any assessments occur. Authentic assessments often tap higher-level thinking skills and can demand complex tasks and the integration of diverse learnings.

Some general characteristics of authentic learning and assessment include the following:

- Students are encouraged to discuss their emerging ideas and impressions as they learn.
- Children are asked to recall personal experience that is relevant to the new teachings.
- Youngsters apply new knowledge to new and unique situations.
- Activities are planned that place a premium on problem solving.
- Activities are planned that call for the use of higher-order thinking skills—analysis, synthesis, and evaluation.
- Choice and alternatives in approaches or solutions are provided.
- Children share impressions of, and reflect upon, new experiences.
- Students reflect upon their learning and then set goals for continued growth and progress.

- Students give input into the establishment of evaluation standards.
- Students are informed of the criteria upon which their work will be judged.
- Real-life applications and experiences are used to reflect and demonstrate learning.
- The connections among the various things that children are studying are made explicit.
- Students are provided with opportunities to work collaboratively.

Once the members of the staff have a sense of what authentic assessment is, it is time to devote attention to defining the important learning outcomes.

GAINING CONSENSUS ON LEARNING OUTCOMES

In any educational community, it is advisable to achieve consensus among the members about general learning outcomes. Among the endless possibilities within the instructional program, it is essential to determine which skills, attitudes, and knowledge are the most important for students to acquire. Such a discussion is the first step in defining instructional outcomes. As in any such important conversation, it is wise to gain the perspective of various stakeholders in the school district—teachers, administrators, staff development personnel, curriculum specialists, parents, and even members of the business community. It is indeed a challenge to achieve consensus on setting instructional priorities, but the results of such collaboration will be well worth the effort. Many principals have had to defend curriculum choices and instructional programs only because broad consultation did not take place at the beginning stages of curriculum and assessment design.

You may wonder about the best forum for obtaining community input. A wide variety of choices is available. Parent representation on curriculum committees is the most likely choice, but there are other avenues. Questionnaires, focus groups, and PTA meetings with a single curriculum agenda are all ways to secure community input about instructional priorities.

To define the most important aspects of instruction and assessment, there are key questions that must be addressed:

- What skills and attitudes are essential for successful contribution to society?
- What are the big ideas and concepts that students should develop?
- What information-finding and research skills are essential for students to develop?
- What kinds of problems do we want students to be able to solve?
- What important issues do we want our students to consider?
- What evidence will we accept that students have attained the goals we have set?

Once some answers to these questions are formulated, you can begin to define the specific outcomes for the instructional program. It is important to state the outcomes in language that is observable and measurable. The projects, performances, or products that students must present should be outlined next. For example: Students will collect, organize, and chart data after studying electricity use among the families in the community and will make recommendations for reduced usage based upon their findings. The sequence of defining outcomes, planning instructional activities, and developing criteria to assess student performance can be charted for each major outcome. A sample outcome-development worksheet appears in Figure 6.2.

Figure 6.2   Outcome-Development Worksheet

OUTCOME-DEVELOPMENT WORKSHEET

1. State the outcome:

2. What activities and projects are planned to help students achieve the outcome?

3. What, specifically, must students do to demonstrate that they have acquired the knowledge, skills, and attitudes required by the tasks?

4. What are the criteria for performance used to assess learning outcomes?

   Excellent Performance:

   Admirable Performance:

   Acceptable Performance:

   Poor Performance:

In defining learner outcomes, be careful to be specific about what teacher input and student activities will be required to promote achievement of the expectation. What will achievement of the outcome look like? How will you know that the students have accomplished what you planned? What evidence will convince you that they can demonstrate their learning? The best way to answer these essential questions is to be clear about the criteria that will be used to assess student work. For example, if one of the outcomes is for students to use multiple resources in researching a topic, the specific resources to be used should be stated—that is, books, interview data, online research, DVDs, pamphlets, exhibits, and the like. How will you expect the students to document and prove their use of multiple resources? Such definition of how you will know that students have accomplished the outcomes is an essential part of the assessment planning process.

ALIGNING ASSESSMENT TO INSTRUCTION

Authentic assessments look a lot like the instruction they are intended to measure. The two are inextricably linked. In designing assessments of instructional outcomes, educators must think about the entire learning process. How will students be engaged? How is their work relevant to their everyday lives? How will their work help them to construct new knowledge and understand new relationships? How will their involvement cut across several disciplines and help them to integrate learnings from a variety of areas? Thinking through answers to these questions can help to link assessment and instruction so that the assessments themselves will be instructive and will demonstrate to the students what they have learned and accomplished.

Consider an activity in which young children sort a collection of objects based upon a specific criterion such as color, size, or shape. To assess whether or not a youngster internalized the process of sorting, you could ask her to sort a new set of materials and describe the rule used for sorting. At once, you observe whether or not the child can perform the task. What could be a simpler or more valid assessment? Some assessment programs might ask children to choose the one object pictured among an array of others that does not belong to the group. Although there may be some relationship between selecting a picture of an object that does not belong in a given group and the operation of sorting, why stray so far from the original activity to assess the learning? Performance assessment evolves naturally from activity-oriented instruction.

Some general strategies for linking instruction and assessment include the following:

- Analyze the instruction and determine what students should know and be able to do.
- Think about real-life applications of the learning.
- Imagine situations in which the new learning can be applied to situations that affect the students.
- Plan ways to embed the assessments into the instruction.
- Plan on both short-term and long-term assessments.
- Short-term assessments should occur each time youngsters are involved in the learning.
- Culminating experiences should be designed to incorporate the learnings, skills, and attitudes that emerged and evolved over the course of the study or project.

These general suggestions should be considered when planning for instruction and assessment. To the extent that it is practical, involve students in designing assessments and setting standards for performance. For example, when developing rubrics to rate a project, ask them what they think constitutes outstanding or just barely acceptable performance. Such reflection will help students to understand that quality work requires attention to the fundamental goals of the project.

DIFFERENT ASSESSMENTS FOR DIFFERENT NEEDS

Fortunately, educators have at their disposal a wide variety of assessment strategies that can be used to provide information about student learning. The first step in selecting the right instrument or practice is to determine the purpose of the assessment. How will you use the results? What do you hope to learn about student performance? For example, if you want to find out how well students have learned some of the basic principles of electrical circuits, then you would design a performance assessment in which students are given wire, batteries, and bulbs and ask them to use the materials to build and demonstrate the operation of closed and open circuits. If, on the other hand, you want to know how well students can decode unfamiliar words, you might present them with a new book, listen to them read, and take notes on the kinds of errors and self-corrections that they make. If you want to assess a student's comprehension, you might take advantage of a Curriculum-Based Measure (CBM) and administer a Maze probe (a quick standardized measure requiring the silent reading of graded passages) to collect some baseline data and select an appropriate target. This is a simple, short, and efficient type of assessment that can help teachers plan better instruction in the area of comprehension. When the results are charted and monitored over time, a determination can be made about a youngster's progress. Both assessments provide diagnostic insights into what strategies and experiences students will need in order to become more effective readers.

In the section that follows, we will discuss different assessment techniques and the purposes that they can serve.

Observation of Students

Direct observation of students is a primary and powerful method of gathering information about their functioning and performance. When observing students, you take notice of what they do and how they do it. The teacher who is a careful "kid watcher" will quickly notice differences in children's learning styles. Some youngsters need to manipulate objects or use their hands to understand new concepts; others are active listeners and can grasp what teachers are saying and readily follow a train of thought; still others need visual cues and diagrams to help them deal with new material. One child may need a list of step-by-step procedures in order to perform a specific operation; another child pays no attention to instructions and dives right in, learning by trial and error. Teachers can uncover these individual differences through systematic observation.

Teachers need to be somewhat "scientific" in their methods of observation. They should be objective and dispassionate and be aware of the time and context of their observations. What happened before? What is happening next (snack, recess, a visit to the media center) that the child might be anticipating?

Some of the aspects on which teachers may focus during observations include

- children's behavior during basic school routines,
- children's use of materials,
- children's relationships with other students,
- children's ability to solve problems,
- children's ability to function well in a group situation,
- children's sense of independence in completing assigned tasks, and
- children's relationships to other adults.

As teachers become more skillful at making observations, they need to structure the notes that they take and how they record the information obtained from the observations. Anecdotal records are perhaps the most common form of keeping track of observations. How specific the records are, and what aspects of the child they focus on, again brings us back to the purpose. Anecdotal records should always be dated so that they may be reviewed and interpreted. If appropriate, the setting should also be noted.

Making effective observations is an acquired skill. It takes practice and consultation. One way that you can help the effort is to take notes along with the teacher and then compare the observations and inferences. Both you and the teacher can improve observational skills by such sharing and reflection.

Checklists

When you want to focus on specific behaviors, skills, or abilities, it is best to record observations on a checklist. After the activities or skills are defined, you simply have to check off whether or not the behavior has been observed. It is often helpful to date when you notice the skill so that you can track an individual's progress and growth. Checklists can serve a wide variety of purposes. Cooperative behavior can be charted by defining the characteristics you are looking for and then listing the children in the group or class. Checklists are particularly handy if you have set up learning or activity centers. By marking whether or not certain tasks are completed, you can note at a glance who has and who has not had a chance to work at the particular station or center. A simple checklist in which a teacher noted a kindergartner's accomplishment of specified tasks appears in Figure 6.3.

Figure 6.3 Performance Checklist for Kindergarten Skills

	performs yes-no sorting	sorts into more than 2 categories using a rule	creates a serial order	separates objects using a magnet	states weather looking out of window	can name six body parts	counts objects to 20	balances an object > 20 pennies
Bryan	✓ 10/1	✓ 10/14	✓ 11/1	✓ 12/4	✓ 1/6	✓ 10/24	✓ 10/1	✓ 1/8
Willie	✓ 10/4	✓ 10/15	✓ 11/8	✓ 12/3	✓ 1/8		✓ 10/3	✓ 1/9
Monica	✓ 10/2	✓ 12/17	✓ 11/1		✓ 12/18	✓ 10/30	✓ 11/18	✓ 1/13
Thomas			✓ 12/3		✓ 12/2	✓ 10/15		✓ 1/30
Julie	✓ 10/30		✓ 12/3		✓ 12/11	✓ 11/18	✓ 10/17	
Phyllis	✓ 10/3	✓ 11/1	✓ 11/18	✓ 12/4	✓ 12/5	✓ 11/1	✓ 11/18	✓ 1/27
Sebastian	✓ 11/16	✓ 12/4	✓ 12/9	✓ 12/14		✓ 12/19	✓ 1/6	✓ 1/6
Jack			✓ 12/6	✓ 12/13	✓ 1/8	✓ 12/3	✓ 12/19	✓ 1/15
Ken	✓ 10/15	✓ 11/18	✓ 11/18			✓ 12/3	✓ 12/13	✓ 1/17
Chris	✓ 11/18	✓ 12/3		✓ 12/19	✓ 1/9	✓ 12/9		✓ 1/17
Jennifer	✓ 11/20	✓ 12/5	✓ 12/18	✓ 12/19		✓ 11/11	✓ 12/11	✓ 1/21
Charlie	✓ 10/3		✓ 12/11	✓ 12/18	✓ 11/19		✓ 12/13	✓ 1/30
Shelly			✓ 12/19		✓ 12/2	✓ 12/3		✓ 1/9
Adam	✓ 10/10	✓ 11/12	✓ 12/3	✓ 12/13	✓ 12/11	✓ 11/12	✓ 12/10	✓ 1/22
Herman	✓ 10/2	✓ 11/12	✓ 12/19	✓ 12/13	✓ 12/5	✓ 12/9	✓ 11/30	✓ 1/27
Olivia	✓ 10/29	✓ 10/15		✓ 12/3	✓ 1/22			✓ 1/30

✓ = witnessed in context

Structured Interviews

The use of structured interviews helps teachers gain invaluable insights about individual youngsters. There are many different kinds of interviews, each with its own distinct purpose. You can find out much about a child in general—her likes and dislikes; learning style; homework habits; comprehension of a book studied; attitudes about self, family, and school; understanding of science and social studies concepts; and so on. Whatever the purpose of the interview, you have to prepare a set of questions that you might want to find out about a student—his likes, dislikes, what he does in his spare time, TV shows enjoyed, family information, books read, and so on.

If the purpose of the interview is general, that is, to get to know more about a youngster, you might ask any of the following questions:

- Tell me about yourself.
- How do you like to learn?
- How, where, and when do you do your homework?
- What kinds of books do you like best?
- What do you do in your spare time?

Conducting an interview about a book studied can help teachers gain insights into the child's understanding of plot, setting, and character. Clearly, this will also yield important information about a youngster's level of comprehension.

Asking children about phenomena in their everyday lives will provide insights into their comprehension of scientific concepts. One favorite question is to ask young children where water comes from. Don't be surprised if many children say that it comes out of the wall—a reasonable assumption for a five-year-old!

In general, children love to be interviewed. It makes them feel important and also demonstrates in a very concrete way that the teacher cares about them as individuals. It does require time, though, to design the interview questions, conduct the interviews, and then study the results. Most teachers who have used interviews feel that it is well worth the effort.

Performance Assessments

Performance assessments are particularly appropriate if you want to see whether or not students can perform a specific operation or activity or demonstrate a learned skill. Writing a persuasive letter might be an example of performance assessment if it follows instructions on how to construct such a letter. A performance assessment in science might be to have students determine the mass of an object using a balance. The assumption, of course, is that this skill has been taught, and the assessment is a check to see whether or not the student has mastered the skill.

Having youngsters read aloud is also a form of performance assessment. Teachers can use specific strategies to help them interpret student reading patterns and skills. Miscue analysis is one of these strategies. To conduct a miscue analysis, teachers typically prepare a transcript of a reading passage in double-spaced type. Then, as the child reads the passage, the teacher places a check over each word the youngster reads correctly on the transcript. Errors, substitutions, and omissions are recorded as well as student success at self-correction. Analysis of the records helps teachers to determine an appropriate level of student reading ability. More importantly, however, studying the kinds of errors that students make provides important insights into reading skill and development and can also point the way toward strategies to bolster progress.

One of the added benefits of constructing performance assessments is the thoughtful reflection that teachers must go through in designing the tasks. This process helps them to think through their expectations and how they might alter their instructional techniques to align them with assessment expectations. In this way, designing performance assessments has great potential for enhanced professional development.

Product Assessment

Student products and projects can provide comprehensive demonstrations of skills and knowledge covering a broad range of competencies. As a culmination of their involvement in a unit or thematic study, students often produce something, give a demonstration, or make a presentation. The possibilities are endless. A list of possible student projects and products appears in Figure 6.4.

Figure 6.4 Examples of Products and Projects That Can Be Used for Assessment of Learning

POSSIBLE PRODUCTS AND PROJECTS THAT CAN BE USED FOR ASSESSMENT OF STUDENT LEARNING

Oral	Visual	Written
☐ audiotape	☐ art show	☐ advertisement
☐ debate	☐ cartoon	☐ biography
☐ discussion	☐ chart	☐ book report
☐ dramatization	☐ collage	☐ brochure
☐ explanation	☐ collection	☐ captions
☐ improvisation	☐ design	☐ crossword puzzle
☐ interview	☐ diagram	☐ editorial
☐ narration	☐ diorama	☐ essay
☐ newscast	☐ display	☐ investigation report
☐ oral report	☐ drawing	☐ journal
☐ play	☐ explanation	☐ lab notebook
☐ poem	☐ film/filmstrip	☐ letter
☐ puppet show	☐ game board	☐ log
☐ rap	☐ graph	☐ magazine
☐ role play	☐ hypercard stack	☐ newspaper

(Continued)

Figure 6.4 (Continued)

☐ skit	☐ map	☐ notebook
☐ song	☐ model	☐ poem
☐ teach a lesson	☐ multimedia presentation	☐ proposal
	☐ overhead projection	☐ questionnaire
	☐ painting	☐ research report
	☐ pantomime	☐ script
	☐ photographic display	☐ test for others
	☐ poster	☐ word search
	☐ scrapbook	
	☐ sculpture	
	☐ storyboard	
	☐ videotape	

For example, young children might study a particular tree throughout the seasons. As a part of this activity, they visit the tree each month and draw what they notice about the tree after each observation. Examining the children's drawings will provide insights into their learning. Did the child capture the overall shape of the tree? Did she include leaves or buds? Did he place the tree within an environment? Was there an attempt to reproduce any of the actual colors? Children's drawings can reflect their observational skills and growing knowledge. Of course, at times, children illustrate those characteristics that they find easy to draw rather than all of those that they observed. As student drawings are evaluated, it is important to ask them questions. The accuracy of assessment increases when more than one approach is applied.

When students make a presentation or report, it is important that teachers have clear criteria in mind as they evaluate the product. For example, when assessing a math project, teachers may judge each of the following criteria:

- Clear statement of purpose
- Accuracy of figures used
- Validity of content of project
- Neatness
- Effectiveness of visuals
- Soundness of conclusions
- Timeliness of project completion

As another example, teachers should develop rubrics to assess student performance, products, or presentations. A rubric used to assess an oral report would assess aspects considered important in delivering such a report. Figure 6.5 is a sample of rubric used to assess an oral report.

Figure 6.5 Sample Rubric to Assess Oral Presentation

ORAL PRESENTATION SCORING RUBRIC

Criteria	Rating		
	Outstanding	*Satisfactory*	*Could Be Better*
Eye Contact	Eye contact is sustained throughout presentation.	Eye contact is seldom maintained with audience.	No eye contact is made.
Rapport With Audience	Quickly and effectively establishes rapport.	Some attempt to establish rapport.	No attempt to establish rapport.
Speaking Voice	Speaks in a clear and strong voice and at a reasonable pace.	Difficult to hear speaker at times. Pace is either too slow or too fast.	Speaker cannot be heard. Pace interferes with understanding of topic.
Content	Content is appropriate to and meets needs of assignment.	Content is evident, but sometimes is off-topic.	Content does not address assigned topic.
Sequence	Presentation is sequential and logical.	Parts of presentation are out of sequence.	No clear sequence is evident.
Key Questions	All key questions are answered thoroughly (what, when, where, why).	Some key questions were answered thoroughly.	Key questions not answered.
Audience Questions	Questions from audience are answered with specific and appropriate information.	Speaker had difficulty answering questions using specific and appropriate information.	Speaker is unable to answer audience questions.
Delivery	Presentation is delivered with genuine and lively enthusiasm.	Presentation shows some enthusiasm.	Presentation shows no enthusiasm.
Use of Visuals	Visuals are related to the topic. Visuals reflect great effort. They are neat and legible.	Visual is not entirely related to the topic. Some effort is evident.	Visual not related to topic. Visuals show minimal effort.

Portfolio Assessment

The process of portfolio assessment is the subject of entire books, so a comprehensive treatment of the subject in this subsection of a chapter is unrealistic. In its simplest sense, a portfolio is a container to store samples of student work—drafts of writing pieces, reports, projects, drawings, checklists, forms, tests, and others. The use of portfolios, though, goes far beyond the concept of a container; it is a form of assessing student work and promoting student and teacher reflection on learning. Students should be involved in deciding on what goes into their portfolios, and each item placed into them should have a purpose. Teachers have devised useful forms for students to attach to pieces that they place in their portfolios. (See Figure 6.6.)

Figure 6.6 Sample Forms to Attach to Items Selected for Portfolios

PORTFOLIO ENTRY FORM

Name: ____ **Date:** ________________

What is attached:

I chose this piece for my portfolio because it shows:

PORTFOLIO INCLUSION FORM

Name: ____ **Date:** ________________

Type of sample:

My purpose in writing in this piece was:

I achieved this purpose because:

This piece shows that I have improved in the following area(s):

The benefit of portfolio assessment comes from periodically reviewing its contents and discussing the growth (or lack thereof) that is evident. The entire process of carefully examining work and looking for improvement is extremely valuable. Growth in expression, technique, detail, and use of vocabulary are just a few of the areas that can be considered when looking at work samples over time. After reflection on the contents of the portfolio, students can set goals for improvement. This is a very powerful and important part of portfolio assessment, because it promotes student involvement in planning and assessing their own schoolwork. It helps students take responsibility for their own learning. Portfolios also help teachers demonstrate to parents their child's growth over time. (A sample of a goal-setting form appears in Figure 6.7.) Eventually, as teachers gain more experience in using portfolios, they will develop criteria for judging or rating the work.

Figure 6.7 Sample Goal-Setting Form Based Upon Examination of Writing Portfolio

WRITING GOALS BASED ON EXAMINATION OF PORTFOLIO

Name: ______________________________ **Date:** ________________

I examined my writing portfolio today and studied the following pieces:

Sample Examined	Date of Sample

Based on this examination, I have set the following goals to improve my writing:

My goal is to . . .	So I need to . . .

Teacher's Remarks:

Portfolios can also be passed on from one grade to another. For this reason, many teachers have found it useful to provide separate folders for the collection at each grade level. At the front of each of these folders, a table of contents can be developed that lists the kinds of samples, work, and projects that are included.

Before using portfolios for assessment, principals and teachers should consider the following questions:

- What is the purpose of the portfolio?
- What materials will be included in the portfolio?
- Who will make the decision about what goes into the portfolio?
- What kinds of containers (envelopes, boxes, bins, expansion folders, binders) will be used?
- How will the contents of the portfolio be organized?
- Who will examine the portfolio?
- How often will examination of the portfolio's contents be conducted?

Self-Assessment

Involving students in assessing their own growth and progress is a very powerful process. It promotes students' reflection on their own learning and accomplishments and points the way for ongoing improvement. Children cannot gain such insights unless they are invited to examine their own learning. They also know quickly whether the teacher is engaging them in self-assessment as a superficial exercise or out of a sincere desire to have students become truly involved in their own learning. Rubrics are particularly helpful to students as they self-assess their work. The goal is for students to internalize the criteria for high-quality work.

When children read and write, they make corrections to fit their own understanding of words based upon context, prior knowledge, and their skill level in reading and writing. Their corrections are a means of self-assessment in that they realize that a word they are reading or an idea they are writing about does not make sense. Observing and analyzing such corrections can help teachers guide children to understand their own patterns of learning.

Students can be invited to assess any aspect of their learning. The process is fostered when it is structured for them. Teachers can make up any number of forms that prompt children to assess their own work. Figure 6.8 is a sample of a reading self-assessment form. Once they are comfortable doing this, they can be engaged in discussions of their progress and what they need to do to go further and take the next steps in their learning.

Paper-and-Pencil Tests

Traditional paper-and-pencil tests do have their place in the elementary school. These kinds of assessments, in which students select the correct answer from a range of choices—multiple choice, true-false items, and standardized tests—can all yield important, objective information. Paper-and-pencil tests should be designed to cause students to make comparisons, to evaluate events, and to interpret data and will promote higher-order thinking skills. Well-designed tests are easy to score, efficient, and provide reliable information about student achievement in certain areas.

Figure 6.8 Sample Reading Self-Assessment Form

READING SELF-ASSESSMENT FORM

Name: ____ **Date:** _______________________

This is a list of the books I read at the beginning of the year:

Right now I am reading:

Comparing what I read at the beginning of the year and what I am reading now, I notice that:

When I think about myself as a reader, I am proudest about:

This is what I plan to do next to improve my reading interests and skills:

Common Assessments

Teachers design and administer assessments that are given to all students in a grade level. These assessments can help to ensure that an equitable curriculum is being delivered to all students.

STEPS TO FOLLOW IN DESIGNING ASSESSMENTS

As principal, you should guide the staff through some of these questions that must be considered before you design and use assessments:

- What do you want to know?
- What are the purposes of the assessment?

- Who is the consumer of the results of the assessment?
- What needs to be assessed?
- How will you use the results?

As you begin to devise assessments, the first thing you need to do is to define the learner outcomes that are to be assessed. This is often referred to as "backward design" or "backward planning." (These terms are used commonly among educators but are usually attributed to the work of Grant Wiggins and Jay McTighe.[1]) This approach begins with the end in mind. What enduring understandings do we want our students to develop? How will they demonstrate their understanding when the learning episode or unit is completed? It is important to consider the ways that you can observe an outcome in action, in a natural context. What projects, products, or performances will provide evidence of student accomplishment? Plan for ways in which students can apply what they have learned. Think of tasks that have more than one approach or one correct answer. Finally, before actually writing the tasks or project guidelines, it is important to identify the criteria that will constitute different levels of performance—excellent, satisfactory, or poor.

In designing tasks for performance assessment, you may also want to consider giving students some latitude in choosing among a variety of assessments. Make sure that the students have the resources required to perform the assessment and that the time frame provided is reasonable. Determine who will be involved in evaluating the product or performance. Will it be the classroom teacher? A panel of teachers and administrators? The student's peers? Self-evaluation? Finally, consider how the results of the assessment will be reported back to the student. A checklist for designing performance assessments appears in Figure 6.9.

Figure 6.9   A Checklist for Designing Performance Assessments

PERFORMANCE ASSESSMENT DESIGN CHECKLIST

- ☐ Have the learner outcomes been specified?
- ☐ Have observable and measurable indicators of performance been specified?
- ☐ What tasks, products, or performance will be used to assess achievement?
- ☐ Have rubrics or performance standards been specified?
- ☐ Have the performance standards been made explicit to the students?
- ☐ Will students have a choice among products or performance tasks?
- ☐ Are adequate resources and time available for students to complete the performance tasks?
- ☐ Will students work on the task alone, in pairs, or in a group?
- ☐ Who will be the audience for the presentation or product?
- ☐ Who will judge the student performance: teacher, other staff, a panel of judges, peers, self-assessment?
- ☐ How have the individuals involved in judging the work been determined?
- ☐ How will the results be reported to the student?
- ☐ How will the results be reported to parents or on official progress reports?

Standards and Rubrics

Rubrics are criteria used to judge student work. They are standards against which a sample of student work or performance can be measured. When rubrics are made explicit to students, they can also be used to guide student work—serving as benchmarks or targets. Rubrics make the entire process of evaluation more effective, public, and meaningful. They can also lead to more efficient use of teacher time because once established, rubrics make judging or scoring student work more consistent and efficient. The use of rubrics reduces subjectivity and confusion in the rating of student work. Once rubrics are designed, they can be used over and over again, though they must be specific to the type of project they assess.

Before teachers design rubrics, they should first look at models of student work—not only the excellent examples, but also work that seems to be average performance for the class. List the criteria for the performance and then return to the original models and compare the criteria with the work samples. Discuss the rubrics with the students and brainstorm examples of each of the criteria specified. In designing rubrics, it is important to avoid ambiguities and vagueness; be as specific as possible. For example, rather than stating, "the presentation was well organized," you might specify, "the presentation had a beginning, middle, and end that addressed all essential components."

Some teachers assign a point scale to the rubric, 1 or 0 to 5. Other teachers use descriptive terms to head each of the performance categories. Some examples include:

- Poor, Inadequate, Fair, Good, Outstanding
- Novice, Practitioner, Expert
- Beginner, Intermediate, Advanced
- Lacking, Proficient, Distinguished
- Minimal, Limited, Fair, Adequate, Commendable, Exemplary

Validity and Reliability

Validity and reliability are important considerations in designing assessments. Validity deals with whether an assessment actually relates to the learning or task we hope to measure. The fundamental question is: How closely does the assessment match the learning? For example, if we want to measure how well students can locate cities on a map or globe, then the assessment ought to ask them to do just that. Does the test match the "real world" application of the skill to be measured? It is because of their validity that performance assessments are considered preferable to traditional, paper-and-pencil tests. On most multiple-choice tests, the validity comes from the fact that the question matches the content to be assessed, but is the context a natural one? Does answering a test question correctly really predict that a student will be able to use the skill in the real world?

Valid assessments are also aligned with the methods of teaching that were used; if students were working on how to make accurate temperature measurements during the learning activities, then the assessment ought to check whether they can actually conduct accurate measurements.

Reliability, on the other hand, is the extent to which the assessment will yield the same results from rater to rater and over time. How accurately does the assessment measure the learning? Are the performance standards sufficiently clear so that two judges would assign the same rating? For example, if a project is to be rated on a four-point scale, an assessment design that is reliable would probably result in two (or more) raters giving the project the same rating. One way to build reliability into assessments is to have several people design them together and agree on the rating of "anchor" or benchmark performances.

Another aspect of reliability is whether the assessment will yield the same results regardless of when the learning is sampled. For example, if the assessment is for a student to write a persuasive letter, then we would expect the performance to be essentially the same whether the letter is written first thing in the morning, right after lunch, or at the end of the school day.

When designing performance measures, all assessments should be checked for both validity and reliability. If these important features are not considered or are not evident in the assessment, then its value is greatly diminished.

A BALANCED APPROACH TO ASSESSMENT

If changes in the way we view assessment are really to result in educational reform, then we must broaden the ways that we measure and evaluate student learning. A variety of strategies exist that allow us to tailor assessments to a wide array of instructional objectives. Teachers must explore and sample the many possibilities of alternative assessments and purposefully select the ones that best serve local needs. Sometimes, the purpose of assessment is diagnosis; to do this, teachers may want to survey what students already know about a particular topic. At other times, teachers want to know how students are solving problems. How do they handle new information? Assessments in which students must collect and organize data and draw realistic conclusions may be best warranted in this case. If teachers want to evaluate whether students have assimilated specific knowledge and skills, assessments can be designed to check how well the children can apply what they have learned.

Of course, there are the times when, according to state or district mandates, global assessments of achievement are called for. Sometimes, such evaluation programs are performance based, but more often they are composed of paper-and-pencil tests. Teachers should not necessarily resist these mandates, but rather see them within the context for which they are intended. It is difficult to make state and national comparisons based upon independently administered performance tasks. More formal tests are equally fair (or unfair) to all of the students who take them, and unless some rather radical changes occur within the field of education, these kinds of assessments will more than likely remain with us. Chapter 7 deals with the principal's role in more formalized testing programs.

Balance in all things can be an asset, and since educators have such a wide variety of assessment tools at their disposal, it is best that we be careful about how we choose the techniques to measure student performance in all areas. Only then can we match content, skill, and context and work toward the provision of a responsible, meaningful, and relevant assessment program that takes into consideration our purposes, goals, and needs to communicate about student progress.

NOTE

1. The process of "backwards design" is best articulated by Grant Wiggins and Jay McTighe in several books, among them, *Understanding by Design,* 2nd ed. (Alexandria, VA: Association for Supervision and Curriculum Development, 2005).

7

Using the School Testing Program to Good Advantage

Ask school leaders how they feel about the standardized testing program and you are likely to be answered with a sigh or groan. Few meet this aspect of school life with great enthusiasm. Standardized tests can strike fear in the hearts of teachers, students, and parents. Much as we might want to, none of us can afford to dismiss mandated testing programs, and, like it or not, scores are often reported in local newspapers, and the public and sometimes board of education members make judgments about school effectiveness based upon those test results. This area of school life is rarely dealt with in administrative training courses; yet, as principals, we have a responsibility to be knowledgeable about the purposes, uses, benefits, and limitations of standardized testing. Rather than complain and bemoan this reality, we can use the results of the energy devoted to this time-consuming activity to our advantage. Wise use of and interpretation of testing programs can help better meet the needs of students and lead to improvements in learning.

THE PURPOSES OF STANDARDIZED TESTING

Standardized tests are usually developed by test specialists with the purpose of assessing student achievement in specific curriculum areas. Analysis of test results can help in evaluating school practices and programs, if the material and objectives dealt with in the classrooms are aligned with the content of the tests. Test developers claim that they make extensive reviews of textbooks and state and local curriculums to ensure that their tests measure what is generally being taught in our schools. A summary of some of the major purposes of standardized tests in the elementary school follows.

Note: All forms, letters, and checklists included in this chapter can be found at corwin.com/elementary survivalkit.

113

To Assess General School Effectiveness

General performance of the student population can provide insights into how well the school as a whole is doing on these large measures of achievement or aptitude. It may be somewhat dangerous to compare the results of several schools within a school district or a city since people often latch onto differences in performance that are not statistically significant. (This issue will be elaborated on further later in this chapter.) However, if the student population in one school is essentially similar to that in another, and one school does significantly better than another, there may be some reason to examine instructional materials, content, instructional strategies, and school culture to see whether approaches to teaching may account for true differences in student performance.

Principals also like to look at how the students in their school, on average, perform when compared to national and state norms. Most standardized testing programs provide national norms that allow such comparisons.

To Provide Insights Into Curriculum Content

If bright, able students do not perform well on standardized tests, this may be a result of the alignment (or lack of it) between the curriculum to which the students are exposed and the objectives that the test is designed to measure. Few would suggest that a school revamp its curriculum solely to have it match better what the test is designed to measure, but sometimes, it may be instructive to look at the test's purported objectives and consider whether they are legitimate for your local needs. If they are not, and there is a strong philosophical commitment to the school's curriculum, then this reason can be used to explain poor or mediocre performance. If, on the other hand, the test objectives seem to be in line with what you expect your own students to know, then you may need to take a careful look at your own programs and practices. It could be that the techniques being employed in your school are not suited to what you hope to accomplish.

To Determine Areas of Strength and Need in the Instructional Program

Assuming that there is good alignment between your school's curriculum and the objectives that the tests are supposed to measure, you can assess general strengths and weaknesses in the instructional program based upon the outcomes of the standardized testing program. You may value having your students know how to deal with fractions and apply them to word problems, but an analysis of the test results reveals that this is an area in which your students did not do as well as they did in other areas of mathematics. This might cause you to examine how you involve your students in exploring fractions and how they are asked to apply their knowledge. Most tests provide a chart of instructional objectives and key them to specific test items. You should also look at those test items that were problematic for your students. Are they included in your instructional program? If not, should they be? Are the items valid and reasonable? Was the context of the question reasonable? These are all questions that you should ask to help you determine whether there are indeed some inherent weaknesses in your instructional program or whether the test items are just not appropriate for your own situation. Involving teachers in such analysis can prompt them to reflect upon their own instructional practices, consider alternatives, and modify and adjust to meet students' needs.

Data-driven goals can be set to devote resources, define curriculum initiatives, and target instructional techniques to bolster identified areas of need. In other words, data can be used to support instructional decisions.

To Measure Individual Student Achievement

Parents often attach a great deal of weight to a child's performance on one year's test results. After all, in their minds, these scores may provide an assessment of their child's learning for an entire year. Most educators realize, however, that test results are most meaningful when looked at longitudinally. How does the child's performance compare to last year's? With two years ago? *Significant differences* and trends over time can reveal something about students. Perhaps the youngster did quite well when the expectations were concrete and straightforward. In the upper grades, as the questions tend to tap more abstract concepts and interpretations, some students' scores may begin to decline. This observation may be worthy of discussion with teachers and parents. On the other hand, perhaps as a third grader, a youngster was tested while his parents were in the midst of a bitter divorce. The upset might well affect the child's performance. As a fifth grader, though, this same child may be more stable, and his performance might show improvement. Because of the need to take a long-term view of student achievement, though, it is important to impress upon parents the importance of not making quick judgments based upon one year's test results.

If your standardized program consists of both aptitude and achievement tests, then it is theoretically possible to compare children's achievement (performance on test areas) to their innate aptitude or ability. (Different types of standardized tests are considered in the next section.) If significant differences are found in a child's aptitude and achievement, it is important to discuss reasons for under- or overachievement, since, all things being equal, aptitude and achievement scores should be similar.

To Make Multiyear Comparisons of Student Achievement Within a School

Most principals track their school's performance on standardized tests from year to year. (If principals do not do this themselves, it is probable that someone at the district office is maintaining these data.) Again, in terms of large-scale trends, it is interesting to note whether the general student population (or even a grade level) has improved or declined in performance from one year to the next. You can take the median percentiles or stanines from, say, third grade and see how these same students did as fourth graders. (Stanine is a way to scale assessments to come up with an idea of normal distribution over nine intervals from lowest to highest.) Only significant differences should be considered, but some trends may be revealed. If a group of students declined significantly, is the curriculum alignment to the test very different in third grade from what it is in fourth? Are the instructional materials and teaching techniques markedly different? (When discussing longitudinal scores, it must be clear whether you are following the same group of students or comparing a grade level from year to year that is composed of a different cohort of students.) It is easy to understand why teachers might become defensive and angry at such comparisons: They may feel that test scores are influenced by so many factors beyond their control that the professional discussion might well be sabotaged. We should measure our steps as we confront or discuss this kind of data with teachers. (There are times, however, when marginal teachers might benefit from seeing the results of their children's performance compared to prior or subsequent years—provided they are open, reflective individuals.)

THE KINDS OF STANDARDIZED TESTS OFTEN GIVEN IN ELEMENTARY SCHOOLS

There is no lack of different types of standardized tests used in elementary schools. Only special personnel such as psychologists, guidance counselors, reading teachers, speech-language pathologists, or learning-disabilities consultants can administer some of these tests. Classroom teachers can administer others, especially as a part of an annual assessment program. Discussion of the tests given by specialists is beyond the scope of this book, so consideration is given here only to those tests most often administered by classroom teachers to groups of children. Keep in mind that testing has its advantages, but there needs to be a purpose behind the testing you are going to do. Two simple questions should provide you with enough direction to see if testing is warranted: What are you looking to gain as a result of the testing outcomes, and how will you use this information to shape future instruction as a result of the data received?

State-Mandated Tests

In response to the No Child Left Behind (NCLB) Act of 2001, most states have instituted standardized testing programs. NCLB requires states to develop assessments in basic skills in order to receive federal monies. As a result, annual testing in the areas of reading and math for Grades 3 through 8, and at least once in high school, has become commonplace. These tests usually measure student achievement in basic skill areas and can be used for comparisons between schools, between similar schools, and for the state as a whole. The state sets new goals each year so that schools will improve curriculum as well as set strategies to achieve the goals. Some states are now incorporating performance tests, portfolios, and speaking assessments. In many cases, teachers are sent for special training to administer and score state tests. Usually, student results are released to the press, and the performances of local districts are compared. Schools that do not meet adequate yearly progress indicators are required to develop improvement plans.

Achievement Tests

Perhaps the most common standardized test used in elementary schools, achievement tests are designed to measure the skills and knowledge that students have acquired in particular areas such as reading, math, problem solving, study skills, science, and social studies. Most of the tests are timed and are usually arranged in a multiple-choice format. Many teachers claim that they could predict the general level of achievement of their students as well as the tests do, but the tests yield specific scores. Most standardized achievement tests are norm-referenced, that is, individual performance is compared to that which was achieved by the large group of students in the original sample.

Sophisticated techniques are used to choose these norming samples, and they do represent a broad array of students from public, private, and parochial schools in urban, suburban, and rural settings.

The data derived from achievement tests allow teachers, administrators, and parents to compare student performance with the "average" student in the norming population. Scores are generally reported as standard scores, percentiles, stanines, and grade equivalents. Each of these scores is related to the normal, bell-shaped curve, with most of the children in the center of the distribution and fewer way above or below the midpoint.

Aptitude Tests

These tests are designed to measure a student's capacity for learning. In a sense, they examine what a child *could* learn given ideal circumstances. Aptitude tests are distinguished from achievement tests in that achievement tests are designed to measure what students *have* learned. Aptitude tests are thought to provide an indication of a student's learning potential. Test publishers report that aptitude tests are good predictors of academic success, and most aptitude batteries are composed of verbal and quantitative subtests.

Criterion-Referenced Tests

Criterion-referenced tests are so called because standards (criteria) are set up in advance to measure performance, and the items in the test are linked to specified learning objectives. Construction of these tests begins with a determination of what students *should* know or be able to do. Questions are then written to assess these objectives. In contrast to norm-referenced tests, criterion-referenced tests do not tell us how students do in comparison to their peers. On the other hand, criterion-referenced tests tell us how well students have mastered specific objectives. A simple example of a criterion test would be a 20-question spelling test in which anyone with 15 or more correct answers passes the test.

Diagnostic Tests

Diagnostic tests have a specific, relatively narrow focus on a specific skill or series of skills. Most often designed to uncover particular strengths and weaknesses in the areas of reading and math, these tests may be useful in pinpointing specific information about student mastery of discrete skills. When used as part of the Pupil Assistance Committee (PAC), the results of these tests can be used to suggest remedial actions, interventions, and techniques that support learning and skill acquisition as part of the Response to Intervention plan your building has in place.

Intelligence Tests

These tests are not used as widely today as they have been in the past. The most common notion of what intelligence tests do is to gain an indication of a child's innate ability. These tests tap a child's performance in solving problems using ideas and symbols and yield a score called an intelligence quotient, or IQ. The usual uses for intelligence tests include making adaptations for individual students based upon their specific strengths and weaknesses, determining eligibility for special programs such as opportunities for the gifted and talented, and assisting guidance personnel to plan for the most effective ways to match resources to individual needs. Group-administered intelligence tests are not considered to be as reliable as those given by a psychologist or psychometrician on an individual basis.

EFFECTIVE WAYS TO APPROACH THE TESTING SITUATION

Pretending that tests are unimportant and do not matter can be tempting for school leaders. There is something about the nature of a formal testing program that goes against the grain, yet we cannot allow our own ambivalence to be detrimental to teachers and students.

It is important to talk with teachers about the testing situation. Explain that the use of data derived from tests can point the way toward improved curriculum choices and instructional strategies. Frank discussions about the realistic and political importance of tests should occur. Explain to teachers the weight that others place upon tests and the ways in which these annual rituals can yield important benefits to them. Help them to plan for the event and to be prepared for the testing situation. It is your role to familiarize teachers with the tests and test procedures. No one wants to lose points for tests that are not correctly administered. Schedule a meeting to go over the examiner's manual with teachers and go through the procedure step by step. Make sure that any questions are answered and that any problems with prior administrations of the tests are explored. Pair new teachers with experienced teachers so that the inexperienced faculty members will have someone to go to at any time during the testing process.

Review the strategies that help children become good test takers. Some teachers may resist preparing children for the tests, but lead them to realize that this is a basic responsibility. They are not "teaching to the test" but rather giving their students every fair advantage to do well.

In small elementary schools, the principal will assume all of the duties of testing coordinator. This involves many responsibilities. In larger schools, there may be a teacher, guidance counselor, or remedial specialist who can be asked or assigned to the task of school testing coordinator. If such an arrangement is possible or permissible, be sure that the person appointed pays close attention to details and has shown in the past that she or he is organized and can assume such an important task.

ADMINISTRATIVE RESPONSIBILITIES IN THE SCHOOL TESTING PROGRAM

Effectively organizing and overseeing a school testing program requires careful attention to a variety of details. Testing is a formal matter and not an area that allows much room for individual interpretation or latitude. Read the administrator's manual closely and carefully for your specific role and have a clear understanding of what is expected of you. Different states and school districts have specific regulations with which administrators must become familiar.

Following is a list of basic administrative responsibilities that should ensure that your first experience with the school's testing program is a smooth one:

- Maintain an inventory of testing materials.
- Report missing components.
- Maintain security of tests.
- Prepare a testing schedule. (A sample testing schedule appears in Figure 7.1.)

Figure 7.1 Standardized Testing Schedule

STANDARDIZED TESTING SCHEDULE: GRADES 3, 4, 5

All times specified are "working times." Additional time will be needed for distribution and collection of test materials and instructions.

Monday	Tuesday	Wednesday	Thursday	Friday
				May 6
				PRACTICE TESTS All Grades: 30 Minutes
May 9	**May 10**	**May 11**	**May 12**	**May 13**
VOCABULARY Level 13: 30 min. Levels 14/15: 20 min.	READING COMPREHENSION Level 13: 40 min. Levels 14/15: 50 min.	MATH CONCEPTS Level 13: 38 min. Levels 14/15: 45 min.	MECHANICS OF WRITING Level 13: 25 min. Levels 14/15: 30 min.	BEGIN MAKEUPS
MATH COMPUTATION All Levels: 40 min.			ENGLISH EXPRESSION All Levels: 45 min.	

- Prepare testing instructions for teachers. (A sample of such a memo appears in Figure 7.2.)
- Distribute tests to teachers.
- Arrange for makeup tests.
- Count and check test documents after the testing program.
- Handle and record test results when they arrive.
- Prepare the order for next year's testing materials.

Figure 7.2   Instructions to Teachers for Standardized Testing Program

Date:

To: Teachers of Grades 3, 4, and 5

From: _________________________________, Principal

RE: STANDARDIZED TESTING

As you know, we will be administering the Balanced Test of Basic Skills (BTBS) to all third, fourth, and fifth graders this spring. Tests are to be administered during the week of May 9, according to the attached schedule. (Practice tests should be given on May 6.) Please note that specific times for administration are not given, but the days on which the various subtests should occur and the time allocations required are outlined. It is best if the tests are conducted in the mornings, with breaks provided in between parts of a test. The levels of the test are as follows:

Level 13: Grade 3

Level 14: Grade 4

Level 15: Grade 5

The following materials are attached to this cover memo:

1. The testing schedule

2. The appropriate Examiner's Manual with all instructions for testing

3. Test booklets

4. Answer sheets

5. Practice tests

6. A group information sheet (header). Instructions for completing this form are on the back.

7. Instructions for assembling your answer sheets at the end of the testing period

Children respond best to a testing situation where they are calm and relaxed. It is advisable, though, that the importance of this test be emphasized. Children should take it seriously, focus, try their best, and go over their answers if time permits.

Special-education and ESL students must attempt to take the test, but their answer sheets are to be separated from the others and submitted separately.

Before beginning tests, have the pupils fill out the Student Data Grids on the face of their answer sheets as specified on pages 8–9 of the Examiner's Manual. Please check to ensure that the grids are properly completed. Use May 9 as the test date. Please make sure that student numbers entered on the grid match those on your attendance roster. THIS IS IMPORTANT!

The specific instructions for administering practice and regular tests are outlined in your Examiner's Manual.

At the completion of testing, please check the answer sheets for clean erasures and stray marks.

Makeup tests are scheduled for May 13, 16, 17, and 18. I must have all tests in my office by 3:00 PM on the 18th. Thank you for your cooperation in this somewhat exacting, yet necessary, aspect of school life.

Attachments

HELPING CHILDREN PERFORM THEIR BEST ON STANDARDIZED TESTS

You will always have some teachers who feel that they should not "waste their time" preparing children for standardized tests; they feel the children should "take the test cold." In essence, this is not fair to the children. Teachers have an obligation to do what they can to give children every advantage to do their best on standardized tests.

The use of practice tests is an important aspect of the testing program. Usually provided by the test publishers or state assessment offices themselves, these sample items familiarize the students with the format of the test and the way that some questions will be worded.

There are some specific suggestions that teachers can offer to students that will prove valuable to them for taking standardized tests. This is something that ideally teachers would know to do, but often a principal finds that they are reviewing test-taking strategies or tips for the successful administration of tests with teachers as a means of combating test anxiety with children.

Familiarize Students With the Test Format

Teachers should review the format and the kinds of questions that appear on standardized tests. Children can well understand that reading a passage and answering specific questions is not the same kind of reading they often do in their classrooms. They should have some practice with determining the main idea of a passage. It is sometimes interesting to give children a passage to read and have them make up their own "standardized-type" questions. In this way, the students will understand the "thinking" of test designers.

Teachers can analyze standardized tests given in the past and help children understand some of the kinds of questions that might appear. Analogies can be practiced. Some questions ask children to choose the word within a series of words that does not belong with the others. These types of problems should not be completely unfamiliar to students when they take a test.

Teachers Can Provide Instruction in Specific Test-Taking Strategies

Just as a soccer coach would not send players into a game without first making sure that they understand the strategies of the game, so, too, teachers should not give children a standardized test booklet without letting them know how to approach the testing situation. The first thing teachers can help students do is to analyze the questions. What are they being asked to do? A phrase that is helpful is, "A, Q, A," or "Answer the Question Asked." Sometimes, children select a reasonable answer that does not address the specific question. The demands of the task must be studied and analyzed. Children should be taught how to narrow down their answers to the two or three choices that seem most plausible and then take their best guess.

Help students to understand that some test items are intended to be too difficult for most of the children. Youngsters should not feel that they should know all of the answers. This attitude can be discouraging and can undermine performance.

Also, talk to children about pacing. Suggest that they first tackle the questions that they are reasonably sure of and don't spend too much time on questions that they are completely unsure about. In approaching reading passages, many experts suggest that the children read the questions first, to give them a clue of what they should be alert for in the passage. It is important to be clear about how much time is allowed for a particular subtest.

If students are using separate answer sheets (as opposed to machine-scorable booklets), they should be reminded to make sure that the number of the question they are answering matches the number on the answer sheet. Nothing is more discouraging in a standardized testing situation than a severely depressed score because a student lost his place and was marking answers that didn't correspond with questions.

Students should be prompted to listen carefully to the instructions for each section of the test. Sometimes, misunderstanding the directions can result in poor test performance.

Give Children "Standardized Test–Type" Questions Throughout the Year

Children will have an advantage if they have been exposed to "standardized-type" tests throughout the school year. Teachers should be cautioned not to go "overboard" with this approach, but certainly an occasional social studies or science quiz in multiple-choice format can help children get used to this type of test. Spelling tests in which children have to find the one word among a group of four that is misspelled can also mimic a standardized test format.

Study What Children Do When They Take Tests

It is often helpful to study what children do when they take tests. During a test, the teacher can go around the room with a notebook and record what children actually do. How do they approach questions? What strategies do they use? How do they pace themselves? How do they attack a reading passage? Discussing the answers to these questions with the children will help them to be more conscious of their own test-taking behaviors and can lead to more deliberate ways of improving test performance.

Helping Children to Be Relaxed in the Testing Situation

It is not easy to find the delicate balance between helping children be relaxed while still ensuring that they will take the test seriously. Children can be motivated; help them to realize that a test is in many ways a puzzle—a challenge that can be fun. Talk openly with the children about their anxieties and always encourage them to do their best. During the test, teachers should also make sure that they are attentive to the physical environment. Rooms should be well ventilated and not too hot or too cold.

In many communities, parents like to be informed about when their children will be taking tests. Parents can help provide conditions that can lead to good test-taking performance. A sample letter to parents that may be distributed just prior to a standardized testing period appears in Figure 7.3.

Figure 7.3 Sample Letter to Parents About Testing Program

OFFICE OF THE PRINCIPAL

May 2, _________

Dear Parents of Third, Fourth, and Fifth Graders,

Each year, school systems all over the country administer standardized tests to assess pupil performance and to identify areas of strength and need in instructional programs. At our school, we use the Balanced Test of Basic Skills (BTBS), published by Sentinel Publications. The achievement subtests that will be administered to our children include the following:

Vocabulary	Reading Comprehension
Word Analysis	Math Computation
Math Applications	Mechanics of Writing
English Expression	Study Skills

Practice tests will be administered on Friday, May 5. The formal testing will occur during the week of May 8.

Children respond best to a testing situation when they are calm, relaxed, and well rested. For this reason, we ask you to ensure that children go to sleep at a reasonable hour. Also, while makeup tests can be administered, we ask that you cooperate with us to assure *maximum pupil attendance* during the testing period. Test results will be available to you later in the spring.

Sincerely,

Principal

EFFECTIVE ANALYSIS AND USE OF TEST RESULTS

Once the test data arrive at school, the true opportunity to use them to good avail begins. Depending on your school district, different kinds of score reports and item analyses will be provided. Most often, student and group scores are reported in terms of normative data.

The kinds of scores generally reported for standardized tests are listed in the following sections.

Performance Levels

Most state testing reports provide achievement scores for individual students, but for purposes of simplicity and data management, scores are usually clustered into proficiency bands, often on a four-point scale, with levels three and four being considered proficient. There are several variations on this theme, but the definition of these clusters is usually outlined in score reports.

Percentile Ranks

Percentiles are the most common type of score reported in commercial standardized tests. A percentile is a part of a scale ranging from 1 to 99. The specific percentile rank denotes the percentage of other students in the sample who obtained lower scores. For example, a percentile rank of 45 means that 45% of the comparison group was below this score, while 55% scored above it. When talking about percentiles, it is important to be clear about the comparison group. Is it a national sample, a suburban sample, or a private-school sample?

Stanines

Stanines are scores based on a scale of nine equal units that range from a low of one to a high of nine. The term is derived from a combination of words: standard of nine. The use of stanines allows for a quick interpretation and analysis of scores. Generally, stanines one, two, and three are considered low performance; stanines four, five, and six are generally considered average performance; stanines seven, eight, and nine are considered high performance. Stanines are useful when discussing scores with parents since the intervals are broad enough to make meaningful comparisons. Sometimes when using percentiles, individuals who do not understand how normative data are actually derived will make assumptions that a percentile difference of four or five points is significant, when in most instances, it is not.

Normal Curve Equivalents (NCEs)

Normal Curve Equivalents (or NCEs) are another norm that range from 1 to 99. They are similar to percentiles but have the advantage of being related to an equal interval scale. This means that the difference between any two numbers on the scale is equal throughout the distribution. This allows you to make comparisons of student scores on one type of test and any other test that uses NCEs. The scale is always the same. In computing gain scores, NCEs are most useful. For example, if a student attained an NCE of 38 in one year on a pretest and an NCE of 52 the following year, you can say that there was a gain of 14 NCE points. Such comparisons are not usually appropriate using percentile points.

Grade Equivalents

Unlike percentiles, stanines, and NCEs, grade-equivalent scores extend across several grade levels usually ranging from K.0 (kindergarten + 0 months) to 12+ (twelfth grade plus). The decimal point after the first number represents a tenth of a ten-month school year. October is usually designated as the first month, so a score of 2.1 would correspond to October of Grade 2. Likewise, an achievement of 4.5 means that the student scored at the fifth month (February) of the fourth-grade level on the particular test or subtest. Caution should be used in interpreting grade-equivalent scores. For example, a student who scores 5.2 in reading means that this student reads as well as the "typical" student in October of fifth grade; it does not mean that the student has mastered the material that is generally taught by that time in school.

Scale Scores

A scale score is a basic score used to derive other important indicators of test performance. Scale scores achieved by a student on one subtest of a battery cannot be compared with those from another subtest. For example, a scale score of 550 on a reading test will not be equivalent to a 550 in mathematics. You can, however, compare average scale scores for a group with those of an individual.

Understanding Significant Differences

When analyzing and interpreting test scores, administrators and parents sometimes fall into the trap of attributing true differences in performance to variations that are not significant. Every test has a degree of error associated with it. The standard error of measurement is a range of scores within which there is the likelihood that a student's score actually falls. Rather than putting too much emphasis on a single number for a student's score, the performance is more likely to fall within this given range. Test-score reports, or at least administrative reports, often provide the standard error of measurement for a given subtest. This number means that a child's obtained score would fall within this range 68% of the time (one standard deviation) if the child took the test over again. Often called a confidence interval, it is important to take the standard error of measurement into account when interpreting student scores. Instead of relating a single number as a result of student performance, it is best to put the student's score within the range delineated by the standard error of measurement. This represents the range within which you can have reasonable confidence that the student's performance actually resides. Understanding the standard error of measurement is important in counseling parents and teachers who may be apt to draw conclusions on gains or drops of performance from year to year that are not truly significant.

Charting School Performance

One way that administrators can compare school performance is to make a chart of median subtest scores from year to year. This can help you to compare, at a glance, how individual grades have performed from year to year. (A sample of such a comparison chart appears in Figure 7.4.) Again, the admonition about not drawing conclusions about significant differences is important. In order to compare the performance of one group of youngsters from one year to the next, you must look at the third-grade Vocabulary score for "our school" in the year 2007 with that obtained by the fourth grade in 2008. In this case, the group gained six percentile points (93rd for the fourth graders in 2008, as compared with 87th for third graders in 2007). Except for pupils who entered or left the grade, these pupils represent the same group. By converting the percentiles, though, to NCEs or to scale scores, and then comparing the difference with the standard error of measurement as stated in the test administrator's or technical manual, you would find that this is not a significant difference, and therefore, one cannot say that a true improvement in performance occurred. In fact, almost all of the differences in this chart, including the comparison of "our school" performance to the school district medians, do not represent significant differences.

Figure 7.4 Sample Comparison of National Median Percentiles for Standardized Test Performance

SAMPLE COMPARISON OF NATIONAL MEDIAN PERCENTILES FOR STANDARDIZED TEST PERFORMANCE

	Our School 2007	Our School 2008	Our School 2009	Our School 2010	District 2010	Difference From District	Our School 2011	District 2011	Difference From District
GRADE 3									
READING									
Vocabulary	70	78	87	89	87	+2	77	79	−2
Comprehension	79	70	79	73	78	−5	78	79	−1
LANGUAGE									
Mechanics	72	76	76	77	80	−3	59	78	−19
Expression	83	75	80	72	80	−8	69	72	−3
MATH									
Computation	74	82	84	90	85	+5	74	79	−5
Concepts	89	82	90	90	88	+2	83	86	−3
TOTAL BATTERY	**83**	**75**	**89**	**89**	**88**	**+1**	**76**	**82**	**−6**
GRADE 4									
READING									
Vocabulary	91	91	89	93	80	+13	89	81	+8
Comprehension	79	80	84	78	76	+2	75	78	−3
LANGUAGE									
Mechanics	94	93	92	91	85	+6	91	88	+3
Expression	84	81	86	83	77	+6	82	81	+1
MATH									
Computation	94	93	92	90	83	+7	94	85	+9
Concepts	95	95	94	95	90	+5	96	92	+4
TOTAL BATTERY	**94**	**92**	**94**	**93**	**88**	**+5**	**93**	**89**	**+4**
GRADE 5									
READING									
Vocabulary	79	79	77	71	74	−3	81	74	+7
Comprehension	73	84	81	76	83	−7	80	78	+2
LANGUAGE									
Mechanics	88	86	87	93	89	+4	85	84	+1
Expression	83	83	79	87	83	+4	84	79	+5

	Our School 2007	Our School 2008	Our School 2009	Our School 2010	District 2010	Difference From District	Our School 2011	District 2011	Difference From District
MATH									
Computation	89	93	92	91	88	+3	90	86	+4
Concepts	94	95	95	96	94	+2	93	92	+1
TOTAL BATTERY	**89**	**92**	**91**	**91**	**90**	**+1**	**91**	**88**	**+3**

Such charts allow comparison of the group performance of each grade to the performance of the school district as a whole and, depending upon how the chart is constructed, school-to-school differences. Care must be exercised in comparing one class to another. For example, if one fifth-grade class achieved a median percentile rank of 87 for reading comprehension, and another fifth-grade class achieved a median score of 54, it is important to know whether the ability levels of the children in the two groups were even at the start. This is why it is so important to be cautious about making statements about relative group performance.

Be aware also of the limitations of standardized tests and do not use them to make evaluations of teacher performance. Remember that in most cases, teachers work with a group of children for only one year. To evaluate a teacher based upon one year's achievement on a standardized test is to ignore the learning that took place in prior years.

Using Data to Check Curriculum Alignment, Make Adjustments, Set Goals

One of the important uses of standardized testing results is to check for the relative strengths and gaps in the school curriculum. Most test publishers provide a bank of objectives that correspond to test items. For state testing programs, test items are usually keyed to state standards or progress indicators. As you analyze how well your students achieved the various objectives, you might find, for example, that children did not do well on calculations involving time with hours and minutes. As you examine your math curriculum, it is possible that these kinds of problems are not covered. Then you have to make an important decision: just because such calculations are a part of the test, do you really feel that it is worth modifying your own curriculum to include practice with such problems? This is a judgment call that each school leader and staff will have to make. No one wants to change a well-thought-out curriculum just because it does not address a single question that is a part of a test. On the other hand, if an item analysis of the test revealed that something that you deem essential is indeed missing from your curriculum, then you have the opportunity to insert some new material by creating a new curriculum module or set of lessons.

Sometimes, a "look back" of two or three years may be required to check whether the local curriculum is simply not aligned to the test specifications. In any event, test data can be used to good advantage to examine instructional priorities and approaches and to set goals to improve performance. (See Chapter 2 for a more comprehensive discussion of setting goals.)

Occasionally, school leaders find that when they implement a new curriculum, there may be a dip or a rise in the attainment of certain objectives measured by the test. Again, this can be valuable information, but whether or not to modify your program is an individual school decision.

It may be useful for principals to summarize the item analysis and prepare a report to teachers indicating the areas in which students did particularly well and those areas in which they did not do as well. A sample of such a report appears in Figure 7.5. In

Figure 7.5   Sample Memo to Staff Summarizing Test Results

Date:

To: Third-, Fourth-, and Fifth-Grade Teachers

From: ____, Principal

RE: BTBS TESTING PROGRAM RESULTS

In connection with the results of the spring _________ administration of the BTBS, an item analysis included on the school administrator's report reveals the following areas of relative strength and weakness by grade level. This information may be of some value to you. Please discuss any insights or impressions you might have, based upon this data.

	Areas of Notable Strength	*Areas of Relative Weakness*
Grade 3	*Reading Comprehension* • Literal comprehension • Identifying facts • Recognizing cause and effect *Language Expression* • Verb problems *Math Computation* • Measures	*Reading Comprehension* • Interpretive comprehension • Drawing conclusions *Language Mechanics* • Punctuation *Math Computation* • Common fractions and decimals
Grade 4	*Vocabulary* • Synonyms in context • Word relationships *Language Expression* • Modification and other usage problems • Verb problems *Math Concepts* • Geometry and measurement	*Reading Comprehension* • Critical comprehension *Language Mechanics* • Punctuation *Math Computation* • Time, money, and weight
Grade 5	*Vocabulary* • Synonyms in context • Word relationships *Math Concepts* • Geometry and measurement	*Language Mechanics* • Punctuation

It is always a challenge to make a meaningful interpretation of test results. Clearly, standardized tests have limitations. On the other hand, they do reveal information, particularly in terms of major trends or shifts in performance that may be useful for us to consider carefully.

examining this report, you and your teachers may note the apparent strength in the school's instructional program in vocabulary at the fourth- and fifth-grade levels, and also the relative weakness in student mastery of punctuation, at least as measured by this test.

In terms of using test data to examine, align, and modify an existing curriculum, a model can be used to guide this process. A graphic that depicts this process appears in Figure 7.6. This procedure calls for analyzing test results and identifying areas of need, checking curriculum alignment, making modifications or adjustments to the curriculum, setting goals for implementation of the changes, and assessing the results.

Figure 7.6 A Model for Using Data-Driven Results to Examine Curriculum

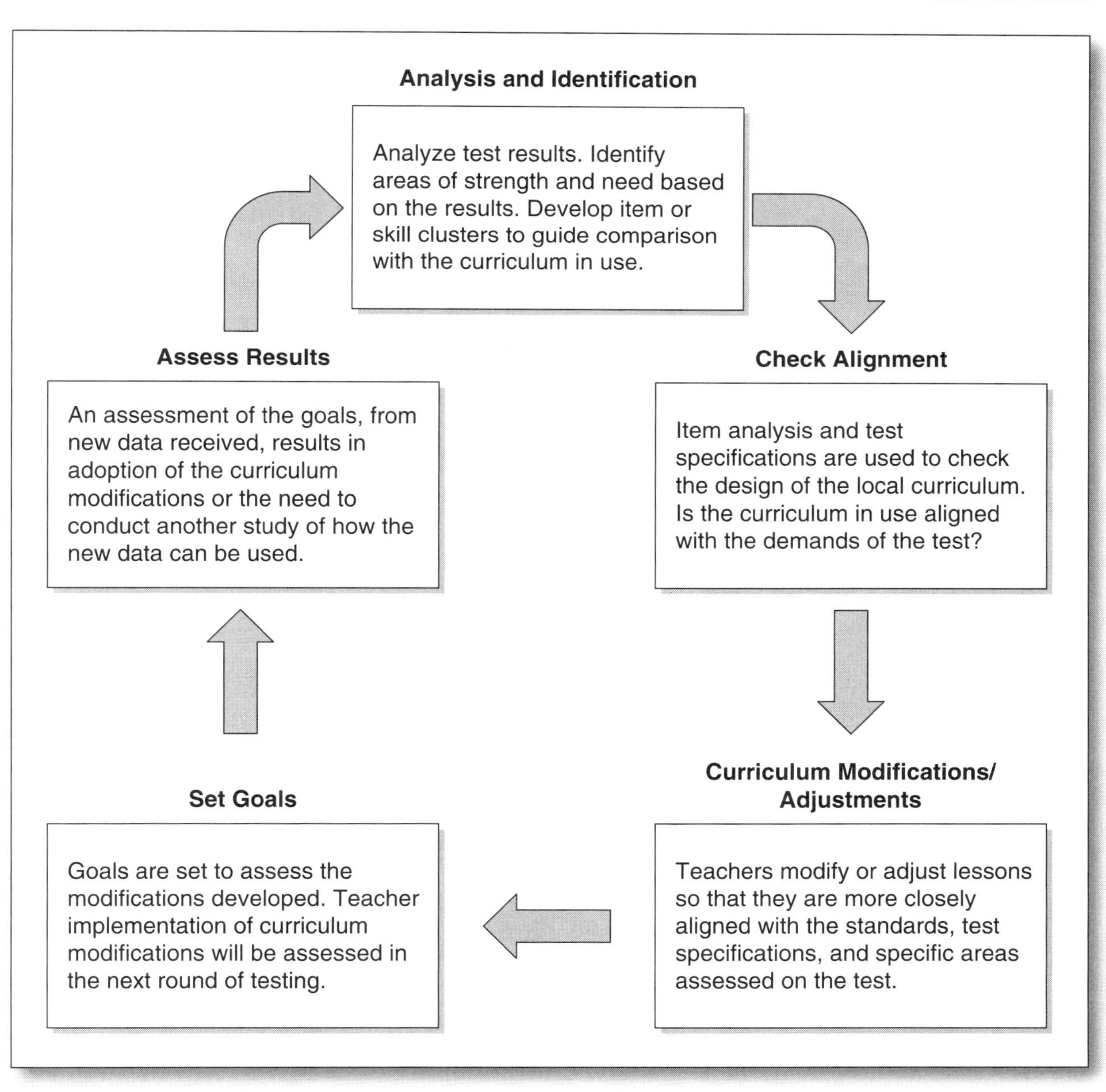

UNDERSTANDING THE LIMITATIONS OF STANDARDIZED TESTS

Despite their popularity in the American educational scene, standardized tests have some very real limitations that need to be recognized and understood. Some standardized tests do not do a good job at what they claim they do. Most good teachers could give a very accurate assessment of student achievement without the use of a test. Standardized testing has become a way of life in schools, however, and one of the reasons for this lies in the area of politics. Claims and counterclaims are made about educational systems, and the public has come to rely on "numbers," which sometimes give an air of sophisticated measurement that they do not really possess. Unfortunately, we have seen some meritorious educational programs abandoned simply because they did not "test out."

Another issue is whether standardized tests actually measure those aspects of school life that parents and teachers consider most important. Individual subtests, or even entire test batteries, never tell the whole story about student achievement. Some youngsters do "freeze up" on tests or are simply poor test takers. Tests are given throughout the year, and when the weather changes, so do the testing conditions. Any change in room temperature can make some children uncomfortable. Depression or anxiety in a student, for whatever reason, can also inhibit optimal performance. Remember that a test is simply a "slice in time" of a particular set of skills and may not accurately measure overall student achievement as exhibited throughout the year.

Some claim that tests are culturally biased. The pictures, words, and concepts may be those that are most familiar to youngsters from a rather homogeneous background. Although most test publishers do claim that their tests are free of such biases, this is still a matter that administrators, teachers, and parents are concerned about.

The multiple-choice format of most tests is another issue that educators debate. We do not often apply our knowledge in this narrow kind of way. The testing context is not a real situation in which students are able to more generally demonstrate what they know. Also, we all know that children exhibit many kinds of intelligence that standardized tests are not designed to measure. The skills of an artistically or dramatically talented youngster or those of the child who is gifted in her ability to disassemble and build models and machines are not likely to be assessed by standardized tests. If the performance of such children on these kinds of tests is not what their teachers and parents would hope, should they be made to feel that they have failed in some way? Perhaps the purposes and design of standardized tests have failed these youngsters.

"VALUE-ADDED" ASSESSMENT

Student achievement tests indicate where students are at a given point in time. However, individual student progress over a given time period is essential to monitor, especially in schools where students arrive at the school door without prior school experience, not speaking English, or without educational experiences that would place the student at an achievement level equivalent to other students in that grade. There is a trend toward examining this individual student progress, and it is called "value-added." When using a value-added model, you look at the increase over a previous score or performance and determine if the increase is more than what was expected. Subsequently, educators seek to determine the conditions that can be attributed to increases or decreases in performance change. The conditions can be a program, curriculum, teaching practice (e.g., differentiated instruction), or interventions that were implemented.

REPORTING THE RESULTS OF TESTS TO PARENTS AND STUDENTS

Different schools and school districts have different policies about how to share standardized test results with parents. In the past, some principals simply announced that the test results had been received and then invited parents to make an appointment with the teacher, principal, or guidance counselor to review the scores. In most schools, a report of the results designed for parents is mailed home.

Regardless of how your school disseminates information, it is important to be careful and clear in how you communicate the results. Help parents see the testing situation as it is. Help them understand the context of testing. Parents should have a good understanding of what the test is designed to measure, what the various scores mean (percentile ranks, stanines, NCEs, and scale scores), and what constitutes a significant difference. They should keep in mind that a gain or decline in performance based upon just a few percentile points is rarely statistically significant.

The goal of sharing test results with parents should be to encourage their participation and interest in general educational issues. Information obtained through testing can help parents understand their child's relative strengths and weaknesses within the limitations of the test and the testing situation. When sharing test results with parents, be sure to read only from their own child's test report. Again, the issue of standard error of measurement and significant differences must be reinforced.

Most state and standardized testing programs provide parent reports as a part of their scoring packages. If these reports are mailed home, you may wish to attach a cover letter that tells the parents something about the test and the purposes of the testing program. (A sample of such a letter appears in Figure 7.7.)

Whether or not to discuss scores with students is an individual matter. Sometimes, children will compare their results with their friends, and not understand what the tests are designed to do. Students, teachers, and parents should be advised about some of the pitfalls of sharing results with students. On the other hand, in some situations, good test performance can be a positive reinforcement for a child. Teachers, parents, and administrators should discuss the advisability of establishing a policy for the school in this area, understanding that some parents will take individual action according to their own values.

Figure 7.7 Sample Letter to Accompany Test-Score Reports

OFFICE OF THE PRINCIPAL

June _________________

Dear Parents,

This past spring, standardized aptitude and achievement tests were administered to all third, fourth, and fifth graders. We used the Balanced Test of Basic Skills (BTBS), published by Sentinel Publications. This testing program was selected because of its emphasis on the assessment of student thinking skills, its up-to-date norms, and its alignment with our own curriculum priorities.

Enclosed are your child's individual test results. The report is self-explanatory. It has been recommended by the School Leadership Council that parents be very careful when they share the test results with their children. Only large differences (sometimes as much as 15 percentile points) indicate a significant difference from child to child, or from one year's results to the next. Therefore, it is best to help children understand that such testing is used more as a way of assessing our own instructional practices than for individual evaluation purposes.

I am pleased to report that on the whole our youngsters did quite well. Our math scores were particularly strong, as was reading comprehension. One area that the staff and I will be looking at is the children's use of punctuation. Before we conclude that there is something lacking in our own curriculum, we need to examine the context in which these particular questions appear in the test. It may be that our children do quite well in applying proper punctuation in their everyday writing.

Test performance is only one aspect of school life. While we pay attention to these results, we also know that children possess a wide array of abilities and talents that are not readily measured by standardized tests.

Sincerely,

Principal

Current educational practice provides many ways in which teachers and administrators can assess student performance. Alternative assessments and the use of student portfolios allow us to evaluate student progress in natural, relevant settings; yet, standardized tests are still very much a reality in schools. Despite their limitations, standardized tests do have a purpose, and, used properly, they can yield important information to teachers, parents, and administrators.

8

Reporting Student Progress to Parents

Grading systems and report cards are always a matter of great debate in elementary schools. School systems go back and forth between issuing reports that include letter grades or other relative indicators of progress and the more individual or descriptive narrative reports. In any case, the basic goal of reporting to parents is to let them know how their children are doing in school. Beyond this, however, there are many other important functions that can be served in the reporting process. These include

- establishing an ongoing relationship and communication with parents,
- getting to know students better as individuals,
- having the opportunity to let parents know more about the school's programs,
- gaining support for the school, and
- helping children realize that home and school are working together.

Regardless of the system or forms you use in your school to let parents know about student performance, it should be well thought out and the goals should be clear. Oftentimes, parents are confused because schools have not clearly defined the difference between a student's progress, the process of reporting to parents, and the product or tool they use to inform others. Most commonly, these things are all lumped together as one item.

FIRST THINGS FIRST: GETTING TO KNOW STUDENTS

To set a positive climate for communicating about student progress, teachers should be encouraged to find out about their new students even before school begins. A letter sent home toward the end of the summer can accomplish several important goals. First of all, it conveys to parents that the teacher is genuinely interested in each child as an individual.

Note: All forms, letters, and checklists included in this chapter can be found at corwin.com/elementary survivalkit.

<table>
<tr><td>**Figure 8.1**</td><td>Letter Sent to Parents at the End of the Summer Inviting Information About Students</td></tr>
</table>

August 2009

Dear Parents,

I hope that you have been enjoying the summer. As I prepare for the opening of school, I want you to know how much I am looking forward to working with you and your child this year. First grade is a magical year when so much learning unfolds and children make such great strides as readers and as thinkers.

As your child's first teacher, your input, ideas, and thoughts about his or her learning will be most helpful to me as I plan for the school year. Please take the time to write me a letter about your child so that I can benefit from your thoughts and ideas. You may make your letter as open-ended as you like, but please try to address the following areas:

- What is he or she like?
- What are his or her interests or hobbies?
- What does your child most like to do?
- What activities or experiences does your child avoid?
- What strengths does your child have?
- What are your hopes for your child in the year ahead?
- Has your child mentioned any concerns about the year ahead?
- What are your child's favorite books?
- Does he or she like to write?
- Is there anything else that you feel I should know about your child?

Please send this letter to me at school as soon as possible. There are no "right answers" to these questions. Your observations of your child as a learner are the beginning of a partnership we will share throughout the year. Such positive communication can only serve in the best interests of your child. Your letters will be kept in strict confidence and will be seen only by me.

This is a great time for you to reflect on your child as a learner and to take stock of his or her unique strengths and qualities. Just before school begins, I will be sending a letter welcoming your child and outlining some first-grade routines as well as a list of needed school supplies.

I look forward to meeting all of you soon.

Sincerely,

Second, such communication provides the teacher with a richer picture of the child. Finally, this practice creates a collaborative bond between home and school in support of the learner. A sample of a letter sent to the parents of first-grade youngsters appears in Figure 8.1.

Teachers can also get to know their students better by interviewing them. Some teachers like to focus on the children's "reading lives" by asking questions about when, where, what, and how often they read. Teachers can devise any number of interview forms or questionnaires to gain more information about children's skills, strengths, interests, hopes, goals, and concerns. Such involvement and interest in the lives of their students can set the stage for close, caring relationships between teachers and children. The mere fact that the teacher wants to find out more about the children conveys to them that the teacher has faith in the partnership of learning. It makes children feel valued and important.

If student portfolios are well instituted in your school, a structured review of each child's prior year's portfolio is a very convenient and effective way of getting to know the students as learners. Even the youngest learners can tell their teachers about the contents of their portfolios. They can be prompted to reveal what each piece shows about them as learners. In examining portfolios, teachers will be able to see the children's rate of progress, the kinds of work in which the children have been involved, and particular strengths and needs.

The first few weeks of school are a critical time for getting to know students. Time spent in assessing what students already know and are able do, and how they view themselves as learners, is essential for being able make reasonable judgments of continued progress. The approaches mentioned here provide a backdrop for the meaningful assessment of student growth. Unless teachers understand where students have been and where they are coming from, they cannot realistically address the degree of progress they have made.

WHEN SHOULD STUDENT PROGRESS BE REPORTED?

Teachers report student progress to parents at various times during the school year—not just when report cards or progress reports are issued. In many cases, the very first face-to-face contact that parents and teachers may have is at Back-to-School Night. This annual event in many schools is held early in the fall and provides an opportunity for parents to meet the school staff, perhaps hear from the principal, and learn about the parent organization. Such an evening usually includes classroom visits in which teachers outline their general expectations and plans for the year. Most principals and teachers discourage individual discussions at such events, but this is an ideal time for members of the school staff to enlist parent involvement and support. Teachers set the tone for the school year, and among the many things they talk about, they should explain how parents will be informed about student progress.

Many schools have defined parent conference or report card times that coincide with marking periods. Individual parent conferences are most productive because they afford the chance for parents and teachers to have a dialogue about pupil progress. In schools where report cards are issued without individual conferences, parents should be given a chance to call the teacher to discuss questions they might have about the report issued. There is any number of variations on the report card/conference plan. Sometimes, parent conferences occur in the fall and the spring, while report cards are issued in the winter and at the end of the school year. In other situations, report cards are "delivered" at the parent conference and form the basis of the conversation. Many teachers like to report on student progress at the end of a major unit or at the culmination of a particular theme.

The purposes of the progress report should be made explicit to parents and staff. One of the thorny issues that inevitably emerges is whether or not the report is designed to assess the student's progress in relationship to his or her own abilities or whether it rates the child's progress in comparison to a predetermined standard or class average. A cover letter or some other communication should be issued that makes explicit the philosophy behind the grading or evaluative criteria used.

Parent Conferences

Parent conferences are very effective ways to report on student progress. Face-to-face interaction allows two-way communication, which can help both parties understand and explore not only how well students are doing in school, but also what might be impeding further progress, or what conditions account for good progress. Strategies and tips for conducting productive parent conferences are dealt with later in this chapter.

Parent conferences should be scheduled bearing in mind the needs and time constraints of parents and teachers. Plenty of advance notice should be provided for scheduled conference times, and teachers should be willing to accommodate parent schedules (within reasonable limits). Sending home a notice prior to the conference also provides an opportunity to solicit information and concerns before the conference. This can help teachers to better prepare for parent conferences. For a sample of such a scheduling form, see Figure 8.2.

Figure 8.2   Sample Form to Use for Scheduling Parent Conference

_______________________ (Date)

Dear Parents,

Communication between home and school is an essential ingredient for providing the proper conditions for pupil success and achievement. Discussion of a child's accomplishments and learning style supports the mutual understanding that exists between parent and teacher. In order to discuss your child's progress, I have scheduled a parent-teacher conference for:

_______________________________ (Child's Name) on _______________________ (Date) at _______________________________ (Time).

You will also receive a written copy of your child's progress report at the conference.

So that our meeting may be mutually beneficial, please fill out the form below and return it prior to the conference. Also, please confirm the date and time on the line provided below. I hope that you will make every effort to visit at the scheduled time. If, for some reason, you cannot attend the conference, please contact me so that we may schedule another meeting.

Sincerely,

____

* *

1. My child's special strengths seem to be:

2. My child's special interests (in and outside of school) are:

3. My main area of concern regarding my child's schoolwork is:

4. Other comments:

☐ I will attend the conference _______________________________ (Child's Name)

☐ I cannot attend. Please reschedule.

_______________________________________ (Conference Date and Time)

_______________________________________ (Parent Signature)

In schools that use a portfolio-assessment process, the parent conference might take the form of the child reviewing her portfolio in front of the parent and the teacher. This can be a very informative process as the parent will see concrete evidence of student achievement and accomplishment. Beyond this, there is the added benefit of gaining glimpses into the thinking behind some of the portfolio's contents and the students' assessment of their own progress. The teachers can then confirm, refute, or add relevant comments to the review. The use of portfolio assessment for purposes of reporting student progress can go a long way toward promoting student involvement and investment in their own learning. Many schools are now using electronic portfolios in which scanned samples of student work are compiled and organized according to a predetermined arrangement.

Some combination of all reporting practices is best. There should be times set aside for parent-teacher conferences. Sometimes, a written progress report or report card during the year is best. There are also times when reports specific to a project or unit will be appropriate. Ideally, reporting progress to parents will take many forms and will be ongoing throughout the school year.

CLARIFYING REPORTING PRACTICES WITH TEACHERS

School leaders have an important responsibility to help guide teachers through the process of communicating student progress. For most teachers, the cycle begins at Back-to-School Night. This is when teachers set the tone not only for the children's experiences in the year ahead but also for how student growth will be evaluated and communicated. Teachers should specify how student progress will be tracked and the kinds of instruments that are used to gain this information. The kinds of tests, performance assessments, the use of portfolios, and standardized tests should all be discussed, and the purposes served by each of these tools should be clarified.

As teachers prepare for parent conferences, principals have a key role in coaching them to conduct effective meetings. There are specific tips and techniques that principals can convey to help teachers elicit parent concerns and also communicate student progress and problems. Beginning teachers, in particular, may be reluctant to be honest with parents for fear of their reaction. In other cases, beginning teachers are *too* honest and have not had experience in how to convey concerns and issues with tact and in such a way that they will be heard by parents and not rejected outright. Conducting a professional development opportunity at a staff meeting using a think-pair-share activity between inexperienced teachers and those more senior ones who have been known to conduct tactful yet honest and productive parent conferences could produce the results you are looking for without challenging the inexperienced teacher's competence or confidence.

Although each teacher's personality and demeanor will come through in a parent-teacher conference, school leaders should try to ensure that teachers' assessments of student progress are fairly consistent within the school. We have all heard stories of one teacher being known as a tough grader and others being too lenient. Students and their parents are entitled to consistent criteria for the assessment of progress. One way to improve consistency within a school is to discuss the matter openly at a faculty meeting and also have the teachers examine and describe student work as a group.

Guidelines for Teachers

A guidebook, or at least published guidelines, should be developed for teacher completion of report cards or progress reports. Such a guide might contain the following sections:

- The philosophy and purposes of the reporting system
- The schedule for reporting to parents
- How to use the grading system (evaluation and notation keys)
- Whether or not to use +'s and –'s with letter or symbol grades
- How to ensure consistency and reliability in marking students
- Policies for retention of students in the same grade for a second year
- Procedures for special-teacher reporting practices
- Tips for conducting parent conferences

Within each school, a system will have to be established for how best to prepare progress reports, and when and where they should be distributed. In some schools, special teachers, for example, physical education, music, art, and so on, prepare a statement or two on the same page of a "special-teacher progress report." In other situations, each special teacher prepares a single page that is attached to each child's classroom report. It has become increasingly common for special teachers to prepare progress reports on a computer-based program. In any case, procedures need to be established for how special-teacher reports will be prepared and forwarded to classroom teachers for distribution to parents, either at a conference or sent home with the children. A sample memo that outlines such procedures appears in Figure 8.3.

<table><tr><td style="background-color:black;color:white">**Figure 8.3**</td><td>Sample Memo to Teacher Outlining Progress Report Procedures</td></tr></table>

MEMORANDUM

Date:

To: All Teachers

From: Principal

RE: FALL PROGRESS REPORTS

The following procedures have been established for our first marking period this year:

1. *Special-Teacher Procedures:* Special-teacher report forms will be prepared for the November and June conference periods. The folders that contain the progress report forms for each class will be kept in the staff lounge. Since parent conferences will begin on November ______, please have your reports ready before that date. When completing special-subject reports, please sign your name in the appropriate space and date your comments. Also, as you complete the reports for each class, please initial the appropriate box on the cover sheet of the folder and pass it on to the next special teacher. **Do not remove the folder from the faculty lounge!**

2. *Classroom Teacher Procedures:* The first conference day is on November _____. Have your reports ready by that date. They are to be sent home on December _____, if they have not been given to a parent in conjunction with a conference. Every effort, though, must be made to hold a conference with all parents.

3. At the conference, please review the progress report format and share work samples including items from each child's portfolio. Written comments on the report forms are helpful to emphasize areas of growth or lack thereof. Please date your comments.

4. In the upper grades, it is sometimes advisable to review the reports with the children so that they are aware of the areas in which they have performed well, as well as those areas where additional effort may be required. Students should be aware of the rating criteria and how they can work toward improving a grade.

5. Some teachers in the upper grades like to distribute blank report forms to the students for them to fill out themselves. Such self-evaluation can be a useful device for promoting student involvement in their own learning and progress.

Please review the procedures outlined in the *Handbook on Student Progress Reports*, which was distributed to you at the beginning of the school year.

HELPING PARENTS UNDERSTAND THE SCHOOL'S REPORTING SYSTEM

When designing or revising report cards, it is always important to keep the "consumer" in mind. To whom is the progress report directed? Although children can benefit from involvement in the process of assessment, progress reports are essentially for parents. The primary reason for them is to let parents know how their children are doing in school. Copies of the report are also kept in pupil files. These can be helpful in looking at patterns of progress over time, for guidance purposes, and for use when children apply to private schools or move from one community to another.

Parents should also be informed about the specific areas being evaluated in such reports. For example, in the area of reading, does the report give specific information about pupil progress in decoding, comprehension, range of reading, making reading/writing connections, classroom discussion, and so on? Parents shouldn't be surprised that report cards also address social areas such as ability to relate to other children, self-esteem, willingness to accept criticism, and self-control. New parents, in particular, should be familiarized with the categories employed in progress reports. If the report form does not contain a key or explanation of the various categories and rating codes, then a separate letter should be attached to the report form that explains the reporting philosophy, the meaning of the various grades or indications, and the subject areas evaluated.

When a new report card is developed in a school or school system, it should be accompanied by a letter explaining the process used to revise the reports and some general information about the reporting procedure. This will help to orient parents to what they can expect from the report card and what it is intended to convey. (See Figure 8.4 for a sample of such a letter.)

Figure 8.4 Sample Letter to Parents Explaining New Progress-Reporting System

OFFICE OF THE PRINCIPAL

Date: _______________________

Dear Parents,

Progress reports and conferences with teachers provide a way of informing parents, on a regular basis, about their children's growth and classroom performance. At school, we are always working to improve our reporting system. We have made several changes in our procedures this year based upon a two-year study of our existing practices. A committee, including several teacher and parent representatives, took on this monumental task. The group worked hard to survey parent opinion, examine report cards from other school districts, and consider a variety of revisions.

The reporting system that will be in effect for the current school year is summarized below:

1. Kindergarten progress reports are completed in November and again in May. The progress reports will be discussed and distributed in conjunction with a conference that will be set up by your child's classroom teacher. The progress reports focus on academic, social, and personal areas of development. Parents are welcome to request conferences with teachers at other times as needed.

2. For Grades 1 through 5, progress reports are issued in November, March, and June. Parent conferences will be held in November and March, at which time the reports will be discussed and distributed. The June progress report will be sent home on the last day of school. Again, these reports focus on major academic, social, and personal areas of development. Parents can also expect a progress report on library skills, music, art, and physical education during the first and the last reporting periods.

3. Fourth- and fifth-grade students will receive letter grades in academic areas with an additional indication of their effort as assessed by the teacher.

4. For students who participate in English-as-a-Second-Language, Resource Center, Remedial Reading and Math, Gifted/Talented, or Speech-Language classes, reports for these areas will be attached to the regular progress reports in November and June.

We believe that this new reporting system will benefit parents, teachers, and students. At the end of the year, members of the committee will meet again to evaluate the changes in structure and format and make additional recommendations as needed.

Sincerely,

Principal

IMPROVING PROGRESS REPORTS

Teachers often complain about the difficulty they experience in completing progress reports. They are time-consuming and it is often hard to find just the right way to convey information. Debates are spawned over whether to use letter grades or narrative forms.

Rare is the school staff that is totally satisfied with its reporting system. Rather than complain, though, it is far more productive to examine practices and suggest modifications and improvements.

When a group of individuals works to improve a reporting system, it should be clear about the mission of its work. Is the task to tinker with the existing system, or is the goal to accomplish a major overhaul of reporting practices? This question should be answered at the beginning of any important deliberations. Expect that any attempts to change the school's grading system will stir strong emotions. Teachers and parents tend to have definite opinions about reporting student progress. Some people prefer the apparent objectivity of letter grades; others prefer to hear more personal, albeit seemingly more subjective, descriptions of student progress.

Any group or committee that works toward the improvement of progress reports should first define the ideal attributes it would expect in a student for each area being assessed. These should be accurate and understandable descriptions of learning. They should also be reflective of current instructional practices that are assessed. If they aren't assessed, the question of whether or not they ought to be should be considered. Once that information has been clarified, a rubric can be developed that delineates different levels of performance other than the ideal. When categories and descriptors are drafted, they can be distributed to staff, parents, and administrators for feedback. Then the categories can be refined.

An example of a change in reporting progress occurred when changes in literacy instruction took place. Look at the difference between the categories in the right-hand column as opposed to those in the left-hand column:

Reading	*Literacy Development*
Vocabulary development	Demonstrates interest in books and language
Word-attack skills	Samples a variety of genres
Comprehension	Comprehends meaning using pictures and text
Oral reading	Uses appropriate reading strategies
Language Arts	Makes connections between reading and writing
Oral expressions	Generates writing ideas
Written expressions	Writes for different purposes and audiences
Grammar, mechanics, and usage	Applies standard spelling conventions
Penmanship	Attempts spelling generalizations
Listening skills	Gains and effectively uses new vocabulary
Spelling applications	Uses oral language effectively
	Listens attentively and responds to peer comments
	Shares reading and writing with others

The first thing you will notice as you examine the two lists is that the one on the left differentiates between Reading and Language Arts, while the one on the right integrates the two into the area of Literacy Development. The difference in categories also reflects a different emphasis on language development; the one on the left has a definite skills orientation, while the one on the right emphasizes language usage for distinct purposes. By the way, these two lists represent an actual revision that took place in a report card in an elementary school.

Rating scales are also important to consider when improving reporting practices. For example, look at the rating scales listed below:

Ratings	Evaluation Key	Guide
O = Outstanding	A = Almost All of the Time	A = 90–100
G = Good Progress	M = Most of the Time	B = 80–89
S = Satisfactory	S = Some of the Time	C = 70–79
I = Improvement Needed	N = Not Yet Demonstrated	D = 65–69
U = Unsatisfactory		F = Below 65

Although some might argue that these rating scales are essentially the same but use different terminology, they do convey very different presumptions about how children learn. The evaluation key in the middle column is based upon the rate of student progress, while the guide in the right-hand column refers to an absolute scale of achievement. In referring to the rating scale in the left column, it is easy to imagine that a student might have improved from unsatisfactory to satisfactory performance, demonstrating good effort and application. This youngster might receive a rating of "G" based upon his progress; his grades, however, might be in the "C" range. The scales in the left and the middle columns allow teachers to address the *rate* of progress, while the one on the right follows an absolute standard. Effective reporting practices should not note just the final results of involvement over a period of time, but also how the student got there. How did her progress change over time, and how could that progress be described? Of course, in any reporting system, space for the teacher's comments about individual growth and progress will allow this important issue to be addressed.

As you work with a group to revise reporting systems, it is best to be prepared for pitfalls. Professionals and community members will obviously have very strong opinions about rating student progress. Such procedures reflect the very fabric of the individual's view of the mission of the school and the ways to improve it. However, with an honest, open, and sincere effort, this important work can take place. It just may take longer than you think.

REPORTING PROGRESS IN SPECIAL SUBJECT AREAS

Who reports student progress in special subject areas is another matter of discussion and decision-making in examining school reporting practices. Ideally, the teacher who has contact with students in a special subject area should be the one to complete the applicable progress report. In some large schools, where an art teacher may see up to 800 students, this is not always practical. In these cases, the specialist may forward a comment or two for inclusion in the child's general progress report. In smaller schools, or where report cards are computerized, the specialist should complete the report for his or her area. (A sample form for special subjects appears in Figure 8.5.)

Figure 8.5   Special Subject Report Form

SPECIAL SUBJECTS, GRADES 1–5

STUDENT _________________ GRADE _________

SCHOOL _________________

YEAR _________________

EVALUATION KEY

S = Satisfactory
I = Improvement Noted
N = Needs Improvement

MARKING PERIODS

	1	2	COMMENTS:
LIBRARY Teacher's Name			
Understands the skills taught at grade level			
Cares for and returns materials on time			
Uses library resources independently			
Contributes during library session			
Demonstrates a positive, cooperative attitude			
PHYSICAL EDUCATION Teacher's Name			
Is developing:			
Body Awareness			
Strength			
Coordination			
Uses equipment safely			
Participates in class activities			
Is considerate of others			
Has a cooperative attitude			

(Continued)

Figure 8.5 (Continued)

	MARKING PERIODS		COMMENTS:
	1	**2**	
INSTRUMENTAL MUSIC Teacher's Name			
Is developing technical ability on instrument			
Understands basic elements of music theory			
Shows a desire to progress and works at it			
Works cooperatively in a group			
Cares for instrument			
Is prompt and consistent in lesson and rehearsal attendance			
VOCAL MUSIC Teacher's Name			
Demonstrates skills appropriate to grade level in:			
Singing			
Listening			
Rhythm			
Demonstrates an understanding of concepts			
Participates in class activities			
Has a cooperative attitude			
ART Teacher's Name			
Demonstrates an understanding of skills and concepts at grade level			
Works independently			
Uses materials and equipment with care and control			
Listens and follows directions			
Makes good use of class time			
Demonstrates a positive, cooperative attitude			

In addition to the "standard" special subject areas in which all students participate, report forms are often prepared for youngsters who are involved in individual programs such as remedial assistance, resource center (special education), English-as-a-Second Language, and gifted/talented education. (See Figures 8.6, 8.7, 8.8, and 8.9, respectively, for samples of such report forms.)

Figure 8.6 Sample Report Form for a Remedial Assistance Program

SKILLS IMPROVEMENT PROGRAM PROGRESS REPORT

Student Name: _______________________ SIP Teacher: _________________ Date: __________

Rating Key: S = Shows Steady Progress   N = Needs Additional Practice

Reading	*Mathematics*	*Writing*
☐ Decoding Strategies	☐ Computational Skills	☐ Uses Correct Sentence Structure
☐ Word Recognition/Oral Reading	☐ Problem-Solving Strategies	☐ Uses Correct Punctuation and Mechanics
☐ Reading Comprehension Skills	☐ Concepts and Applications	☐ Writes Coherent Paragraphs
☐ Displays Organizational Skills	☐ Works Independently	☐ Follows Directions
☐ Works Independently	☐ Follows Directions	☐ Understands Spelling Generalizations
☐ Follows Directions	☐ Listens Attentively	☐ Writes for Different Purposes
☐ Listens Attentively	☐ Relates Concepts to Life	☐ Relates to the Audience
Comments:	**Comments:**	**Comments:**

Parent/Guardian Comments:

Figure 8.7 Sample Resource Center Report Form

**ELEMENTARY RESOURCE CENTER
PROGRAM REPORT OF STUDENT PROGRESS**

Student: _________________________ Teacher: _________________________ Date: __________

KEY: P = Making Progress   N = Needs Continued Reinforcement

Language Arts Studies	Rating ☐	Mathematical Studies	Rating ☐	Reading Studies	Rating ☐
Comments:		Comments:		Comments:	

LEARNING AND INTERPERSONAL SKILLS:

Task Orientation	Self-Reliance	Personal Organization	Community Membership
☐ Plans approach to tasks	☐ Takes initiative	☐ Uses time productively	☐ Has a positive attitude
☐ Focuses on work	☐ Self-corrects work; is neat	☐ Takes care of materials	☐ Respects opinions of others
☐ Demonstrates persistence	☐ Works independently	☐ Keeps papers in order	☐ Exercises self-control
☐ Shows pride in work	☐ Completes homework	☐ Remembers responsibilities	☐ Follows class and school rules

Figure 8.8 Sample English-as-a-Second-Language Progress Report

ENGLISH-AS-A-SECOND-LANGUAGE PROGRESS REPORT

Student: ____

Teacher: ___________________________________ **Date:** ________________

EVALUATION KEY

G = Consistently Good

S = Satisfactory

P = Making Progress

N = Does Not Yet Demonstrate

	Marking Periods			Comments
	1	2	3	
LISTENING COMPREHENSION				
Follows directions.				
Understands basic vocabulary/expressions.				
Matches spoken words and sentences to pictures.				
Matches spoken words to written words.				
ORAL COMMUNICATION				
Uses correct word pronunciation/stress/intonation.				
Asks for/gives information/responses.				
Identifies/describes/expresses.				
Participates in conversation and free dialogue.				
Follows sequence of ideas or stories expressed.				

(Continued)

Figure 8.8 (Continued)

	Marking Periods			Comments
	1	2	3	
READING READINESS AND SKILLS				
Learns letter names and letter-sound associations.				
Identifies rhyming words.				
Participates in shared reading.				
Uses a combination of skills to decode words.				
Matches written language to pictures.				
Develops basic sight vocabulary.				
Reads language-experience stories.				
Follows and comprehends stories.				
WRITING READINESS AND SKILLS				
Writes descriptions for illustrations.				
Writes sentences/language experience stories.				
WORK AND STUDY HABITS				
Listens attentively.				
Follows directions.				
Works independently.				
Works cooperatively with others.				

Figure 8.9 Sample Report Form for Gifted/Talented Program

GIFTED/TALENTED PROGRAM STUDENT PROGRESS REPORT

Student Name: _______________________ **School:** _______________________

G/T Teacher: _______________________ **Grade:** _________ **School Year:** _________

RATING KEY

H = High Performance

A = Average Performance

N = Needs Strengthening

	Rating		Rating
ATTITUDES		**CREATIVITY**	
Respects self.		Demonstrates flexibility.	
Recognizes weaknesses.		Demonstrates fluency.	
Has self-confidence.		Is original in thinking.	
Has sense of humor.		Is elaborative in thinking.	
Accepts constructive criticism.		Makes connections between unrelated ideas.	
Respects others.		Takes risks.	
Builds on the ideas of others.		Recognizes patterns.	
Offers criticism constructively.		Is open to change.	
Accepts strengths and weaknesses in others.		Challenges assumptions.	
Becomes involved in group work.		Sees things in new ways.	
Contributes to group work.			
Accepts responsibility for own actions.			
Works diligently to achieve excellence.		**LEADERSHIP SKILLS**	
Has high standards for own work.		Is able to organize others.	
Makes important contributions to group.		Is decisive.	

(Continued)

Figure 8.9 (Continued)

	Rating		Rating
Has strong personal values.		Recognizes talents in others.	
Feels committed to group membership.		Analyzes.	
Demonstrates a "love for learning."		Synthesizes.	
Works well independently.		Evaluates using criteria.	
Asks thoughtful questions.		Is willing to delegate responsibility.	
Desires to "discover" truth.		Is cooperative.	
Solves problems on own.		Is innovative.	
Persists and perseveres.		Is open-minded.	
Demonstrates logical thinking.			
Communicates clearly.			
Acquires skills as needed.		**COMMENTS:**	
ACADEMIC SKILLS			
Acquires factual knowledge.			
Understands concepts.			
Infers from evidence.			
Displays above-average vocabulary.			
Uses research skills.			
Comprehends problems.			
Can hypothesize.			
Can construct a working plan.			

Teacher's Signature: ____ **Date:** _____________

TIPS AND TECHNIQUES FOR HOLDING EFFECTIVE PARENT CONFERENCES

Advance planning for parent conferences can help teachers to communicate important (and sometimes difficult) information about student progress and attitudes. Parents want to know that teachers know their children as people before they know them as learners. A common mistake novice teachers make is leaving out the personal side of the conference and heading right to the academic side of things. Teachers need to be gracious, tactful, and sympathetic to parents, yet realize that a conference is an important opportunity to convey essential information about school progress and to enlist parental support and cooperation.

Some guidelines for teachers for conducting successful parent conferences include the following:

- Make a list of the essential points you want to make. Too many may prove to be overwhelming.
- Have work samples, tests, rubrics, and descriptions of behavior (perhaps anecdotal records) ready at hand.
- Start with a friendly tone and thank the parent for taking the time to visit.
- Emphasize that school success is a joint enterprise between home and school.
- Sit at a conference table or a round table. Try not to use a formal barrier like a teacher desk.
- Say something nice about the student—something genuine that you appreciate about the student.
- Discuss the child's general academic performance, noting attitudes that enhance or impede progress.
- Try to have the parent respond to each point you make.
- Listen carefully to parents—not only to the content of what they say, but to the way in which it is said. Be attentive to body language, eye contact, and gestures.
- If the parent does not speak English well, arrange for a translator.
- Work toward developing practical solutions to help a situation. Offer solutions and secure the ideas and suggestions of the parents.
- Select those solutions or suggestions that show the best promise for success.
- Avoid arguments. Successful work with parents comes when parents view problems and strengths in the same light the teachers do.
- Summarize the conference and agree on how you will follow up on any plans you have made. Leave the lines of communication open for further contact either by telephone, weekly notes or reports, or additional meetings.

If the purpose of a parent conference is to chart the path for continued growth and progress, then it only makes sense to involve the students in this assessment—either prior to or during the meeting. Children learn when they reach for goals and know what they're good at and where they can improve. Bringing the child into the process can only serve to foster greater involvement in the learning process.

Effective, professionally conducted parent conferences can make teachers' lives easier. Helping teachers develop the skills for effective conferences is well worth the time and effort of school leaders. The rewards will benefit teachers and parents, and, of course, the students.

Clarifying Individual Growth and Relative Standing Within a Group

Teachers take great pains to describe and discuss individual progress, yet many parents often jump to the question, "But where does she stand in comparison to the rest of the class?" Although this is a legitimate question, teachers must be prepared for the best ways to approach this matter; it is usually a very tricky issue. Teachers should emphasize where the student started in his or her development in the class or subject and then provide concrete evidence, using work samples, to show growth. Teachers should interpret the work in relation to the expectations and intentions of the assignment. Meaning should always be attached to what students do, and this meaning should be made explicit to parents.

Some schools have developed forms that communicate effort, progress, and achievement as separate categories. For example, effort ratings indicate how much the student has applied him- or herself to the assignments and the requirements of the grade or course. Progress notes how well the child has done compared to him- or herself. Achievement ratings compare students to the class or grade-level expectations in the school. A sample of such a report form appears in Figure 8.10. Note that a separate rating is provided for each of these indicators.

Figure 8.10	Sample of a Section From a Progress Report That Rates Effort, Progress, and Achievement

STUDENT PROGRESS REPORT, GRADE 4

Student Name: ____

Midyear Reporting Form

Mathematics	*Effort*	*Progress*	*Achievement*
Understands and applies concepts.			
Displays proficiency with basic facts.			
Generates strategies for problem solving.			
Evaluates strategies for effectiveness.			
Uses mental computation and estimation.			
Applies problem-solving strategies.			
Uses calculators for appropriate computations.			
Selects appropriate operations to solve problems.			
Participates in math discussions.			

RATING KEY

Effort: EE = Exceptional Effort; **SE** = Satisfactory Effort; **ME** = Minimal Effort

Progress (student is compared to his or her own rate of growth)**: EP** = Exceptional Progress; **SE** = Satisfactory Progress; **MP** = Minimal Progress

Achievement (student is compared to class or grade-level expectations)**: EGLE** = Exceeds Grade-Level Expectations; **MGLE** = Meets Grade-Level Expectations; **BGLE** = Below Grade-Level Expectations

---

Hard as it may be to communicate relative standing in a class as opposed to a youngster's individual progress, open, frank assessments and the use of work samples as a basis for discussion will set the stage for intelligent and sensitive engagement with these kinds of evaluations of student work and progress.

Using Portfolios in Parent Conferences

Student portfolios are more than repositories of work samples. In most cases, they are designed to demonstrate student progress and be a vehicle for having children reflect on their own growth. As such, they are well suited for parent conferences and for truly looking at progress and development. Just how the portfolio is organized depends upon various factors and local initiatives, but one common element is the ability to look at student work over time and reveal trends, progress, and individual interests and talents.

In some schools, the child's portfolio is sent home prior to the parent conference. Parents can then review the portfolio with their child and respond to what they notice. Looking through a child's portfolio can also help parents frame important questions that they would like to discuss at the meeting with the teacher. A letter can be sent to parents a day or so before the portfolio is brought home, in which parents are encouraged to review its contents with their child and are given guidelines for what to observe. In some cases, the portfolio may be "electronic," and it can be transported from school to home on a flash drive or some other storage media.

STUDENT SELF-EVALUATION

Aside from the very rich opportunities for student reflection and self-assessment that accompany the use of portfolios, there are other ways to encourage children to evaluate their own learning and progress. Self-evaluation is a very powerful process because it can enable students to function independently and productively. Some teachers give the students a blank photocopy of the report form that the teacher will use to assess their progress. How to fill out the form should be modeled for the students, and then the children can complete their own report cards indicating the progress that they feel they have made in the specified areas. For smaller assignments or projects, students are often given the rubric that teachers use to assess their work. It is instructive for students to know the criteria that are being used to judge their work. Then, the students can rate their own work using the rubric provided.

In a conference with the teacher, the student's own judgments can be discussed and clarified. The teacher can explain her own assessment and compare it with the child's. Some teachers, particularly in the upper grades, like to involve their students in the parent conference. After all, the child is the one whose learning is being discussed, so why shouldn't the youngster be a part of the conversation and be able to help to set any goals that may come out of the conference?

Communication about student progress is an essential part of the total school experience. Parents want to know exactly where their students are at, in terms of their learning. Teachers want parents to know that each student's learning process is unique, therefore their individual path may look unique as well. School leaders want to know that the reporting product is meeting the needs of the aforementioned stakeholders. By reporting student progress accurately and pointing the way toward new goals and learning strategies, we can foster the continued growth and development of our children.

9

Administering Effective Programs for Students With Special Needs

Not all children are alike. No two students learn in the same way. And long gone are the days when educators teach to the proverbial "middle" of the class. Modern educational practice requires that teachers modify and adapt their instruction to meet a wide variety of needs and skill levels. Many principals remark that they spend a great deal of time helping teachers make such modifications and administering the special services in their schools.

THE ROLE OF THE PRINCIPAL IN OVERSEEING SPECIAL-EDUCATION SERVICES

Very few are the schools that have a roster composed simply of classroom teachers. The overwhelming majority of elementary schools engage a cadre of special teachers who provide additional assistance in a variety of programs to meet the individual needs of youngsters. Whether special education, remedial assistance, English-as-a-Second-Language, or the fostering of special gifts and talents fostered by unique instructional approaches, all require specially trained and skilled staff members. A school leader has an important role in overseeing and administering these programs. Basically, you must establish procedures, work to identify the needs, help to design the programs, orchestrate the services, and ensure that children are provided with the services and programs to which they are entitled.

Note: All forms, letters, and checklists included in this chapter can be found at corwin.com/elementary survivalkit.

155

There are also very specific legal requirements that principals must be aware of and implement. Ignorance of the laws that govern special education cannot be used as an excuse when appropriate services are mandated or required. There are several sections of federal law that govern school requirements and procedures. Following is a list of some of the more relevant legislation in this area:

Elementary and Secondary Education Act (ESEA)

The ESEA, Public Law 89-10, is a federal statute first enacted in 1965. It specifies funding for elementary and secondary education. The act authorized funds for instructional materials, professional development, resources to support educational programs, and parental involvement programs. Title I of ESEA distributed funding to schools based upon the percentage of students from low-income families. The ESEA has been the backbone of federal educational funding and has been reauthorized every five years. The No Child Left Behind Act of 2001 was a reauthorization of the ESEA of 1965.

Public Law 94-142

Initially enacted in 1975, Public Law 94-142, the Education for All Handicapped Children Act, requires that all children with disabilities who are found eligible for special-education services be provided with a free and appropriate education as specified in an Individualized Education Program (IEP). The IEP, which is developed when a youngster is first identified and classified, is to be reviewed annually, with reevaluations for continued eligibility for services conducted every three years. Public Law 94-142 also mandates that children with disabilities be placed in the "least-restrictive environment." This means that, whenever possible, their educational program should take place in a school as close to home as their regular public school and in the same classrooms as their nonhandicapped peers. Among other provisions, Public Law 94-142 mandates that teacher education institutions review and revise their programs to assist teachers in understanding the nature of special needs, planning for and integrating children with disabilities into their classrooms.

The Individuals with Disabilities Education Act of 1990 (IDEA)

The Individuals with Disabilities Education Act of 1990 (IDEA) is the reauthorization of Public Law 94-142, with some amendments. One of the key new provisions is the requirement to state a "transition" plan and associated services that students might require as they graduate a school or become ineligible for special-education services. The 2004 reauthorization of IDEA became effective in 2005 and requires a process similar to Response to Intervention (see discussion later in this chapter) as a prereferral model and encourages its implementation.

Federal Rehabilitation Act of 1973: Section 504

Another federal law that governs programming for students in schools is the Federal Rehabilitation Act of 1973, especially Section 504, which provides protections for all people throughout their lifetimes—not only while they are in school. Section 504 pertains to civil rights law and covers persons who have a physical or mental impairment that substantially limits one or more major life activities. Although this law has been in effect for many years, its broad application in schools is something of a recent phenomenon. There have been different interpretations (and challenges to interpretation) regarding what is an impairment that limits "one or more life functions," and this has been an area of controversy in schools.

Students who are eligible for services under Section 504 do not have to qualify for services under IDEA and may not need special-education services, instead, they may require related services or accommodations in order to benefit from the educational program. This can take many forms, from special aids for students with physical handicaps to defined modifications in the regular classroom for students who have attention deficit disorder (ADD).

Public Law 107-110: The No Child Left Behind Act of 2001

One section of a chapter cannot cover No Child Left Behind (NCLB) to it fullest extent; however, this section outlines the far-ranging implications NCLB has had in the area of special education. The basis for NCLB was rooted in the Elementary and Secondary Education Act (ESEA) of 1965. What separates NCLB from ESEA is the fact that NCLB set a standard for minimal competency for all students regardless of ability, race, socioeconomic status, and so on. NCLB's impact on special education essentially promoted a few main principles, namely, better instruction, better assessment, and more accountability. Ensuring that special-education teachers are highly qualified not only increases a youngster's chances at receiving good instruction, it is also intended to increase the collaboration between the special-education teacher and general-education teachers working to meet individual students' needs, as opposed to a special-education teacher solely modifying the workload through strategies and support. Further reauthorizations of the ESEA may specify new provisions and approaches.

State Statutes

Each state must develop its own statutes for compliance and implementation of these laws. It is the responsibility of each principal to become familiar with state statutes, regulations, and procedures.

Laws and critical timelines that govern how students are to be treated and the programs to which they are entitled change from time to time, so it is essential that you attend conferences, seminars, or other such meetings to stay abreast of the important requirements in this area.

Parental Rights and Due Process

At each step in the process of considering students for special-education services, important safeguards for parents are codified. In regard to the initial referral to the evaluation plan, the sharing of results to classification, the development of the IEP, and options for placement, all require informed consent and parental permission to proceed to the next step. You must be aware of parental rights, and you have an obligation to provide parents with copies of the local code that governs special-education procedures. A variety of forms and letters are developed to document each of these steps and individual notifications. A copy of an initial letter of notification appears in Figure 9.1. It is simply the very first step in the process of communications that is part and parcel of the special-education referral procedure.

Figure 9.1   Sample Initial Notification Letter to Parent About Referral of Child

OFFICE OF THE PRINCIPAL

Dear ____________________,

   As you are aware, your child has been experiencing some difficulty in school in the following area(s):

   The specific accommodations and adjustments that we have attempted to use in order to help ____________________ become more successful in these areas have not been as effective as we would have hoped. As a result, it is now appropriate to refer ____________________ to our Child Study Team in order to determine if further testing and assistance are warranted.

   The Child Study Team is composed of a school social worker, a school psychologist, and a learning-disabilities specialist. Our state administrative code stipulates a 15-day notification period prior to any action on the part of the Child Study Team. After approximately 15 days, the Child Study Team will need to determine if the referral is considered appropriate under their guidelines. You will receive written notification regarding the final decision of the team.

   In the meantime, should you have any questions about the reasons for the referral or the entire Child Study referral process, please do not hesitate to call me.

Sincerely,

____________________________, Principal

c: Child Study Team

Record-Keeping Requirements

There are also very specific requirements for maintaining records, not only throughout the referral and testing procedure, but also once a student is determined to be eligible for special-education services. Usually, records of referral forms and the results of any psychological and educational assessment, as well as a family social history, are treated as confidential materials and are not open for teachers to view, unless there is a specific need to do so. Parents are often worried that all of the information about their children may be "floating throughout the school." Many states require that such records be kept in a central location and in a locked cabinet.

Teachers who work with special-education youngsters must be familiar with the contents of their IEPs so that they may be aware of the specific objectives set for the youngsters and how they may address the needs identified. Special-education records should not be commingled with regular-education records—and in some districts, there can be no reference within the regular record file that a special-education file even exists. This situation must be checked with school district authorities.

Some states or school districts mandate that a special log be maintained that indicates which teachers (or other school personnel) have viewed a student's special-education file. Such a log can be placed at the very beginning of the file. A sample of a special-education record inspection sheet appears in Figure 9.2.

Figure 9.2 Sample Confidential Student Record Inspection Log

STUDENT RECORD INSPECTION LOG

Student name: ______________________________

The following persons have inspected the confidential records of the above-named student. The reason that access was granted, the date of inspection, the records studied, and the purpose for which the data will be used must be recorded.

Name:	Reason:	Date:	Records Studied:	Purpose:

Avoiding Problems in the
Referral and Classification Procedure

During every step of the referral and classification process, you must ensure that you have followed established procedures and have not violated the rights of students and parents. In many places, a district staff member is responsible for making sure that the legal rights of students and parents are protected. The following recommendations will help to make sure that correct procedures are followed and that appropriate actions are taken in the referral process:

- Document all pertinent meetings; have accurate, comprehensive records available.
- Utilize supplementary aids and services in a step-by-step, sequential manner.
- Do not predetermine or limit the number of available options.
- Utilize all services available at the local school level.
- Consider academic and nonacademic (social) factors.
- Exhaust all possibilities before suggesting a special placement.
- Utilize the expertise of resource personnel.
- Make sure that mandated timelines are adhered to.
- Make sure that required parental permission and signatures are secured at every appropriate step.

Developing a Network of Community Resources

Not every parent may choose to utilize school personnel and resources for the evaluation and treatment of learning or emotional difficulties. Sometimes, a parent will visit and ask for a referral to a private psychologist, social worker, or family therapist. It is important that principals maintain a list of community resources and private clinicians for such cases. You should always offer the school's services first, and if these are refused, private services can be recommended. It is also essential that multiple recommendations be made. Principals cannot be viewed as supporting private practitioners. Often, a list can be prepared and given to parents with a disclaimer, in which a statement is made that the list of private individuals and clinics is provided as a service to parents, but that no individual recommendations are made. The school psychologist and/or social worker should maintain an updated list of possible professionals to which families may be referred.

When such matters as child abuse, family crises, natural disasters, and other emergencies require action, you must first follow district policies. If a parental request for services or advice does not fall into one of these categories, it is appropriate for principals to tap into community services to help families. One of the benefits of experience in the principalship is that, after a long period of time, you will know from your experience with such situations which are the best individuals, services, or associations to call when assistance is needed.

Modeling an Appreciation and Respect
for Students' Abilities, Talents, and Handicaps

The principal is a role model in many aspects of behavior. You can help to build confidence in staff members by modeling, at every possible opportunity, respect for a broad variety of abilities, talents, and special needs that are exhibited among the people in the school. Staff members and parents will quickly recognize intolerance or a lack of patience for individual needs. On the other hand, the principal who respects all people and honors individual worth can help to set the tone for such tolerance throughout the school. The message conveyed is that this school is a place where we value all human beings regardless of their abilities, skills, and idiosyncrasies.

IDENTIFYING SPECIAL NEEDS OF STUDENTS

Each school district must establish criteria for the identification of students with special needs. In some cases, the classroom teacher can identify specific characteristics and determine that the student simply needs consultation with an appropriate specialist. In others, students will need direct assistance from a specialist for a period or two each day, and still others may require a program that replaces regular classroom instruction. Clear guidelines should be established for each case.

Usually, the classroom teacher is the first to sense that a child may be struggling. The great majority of teachers are quite skillful at spotting students who have problems that may need to be addressed by special services. Often, parents will alert school officials to the perceived difficulties and needs of their youngsters. Sometimes, the school nurse will sense a problem that may stem from a medical or social situation. Difficulties in getting along with other children are often overlooked in terms of an association with learning difficulties; however, the same problems that make it difficult for children to pick up the cues that make learning to read and write an easy task are often associated with difficulties in social relationships.

Some of the more subtle, not clearly academic, signs that a student is at risk for learning or emotional problems include

- excessive absences;
- excessive lateness;
- inability to maintain positive peer relationships;
- lack of productive friendships;
- inability to focus on schoolwork ("daydreaming");
- neglect of personal appearance;
- poor coordination, awkward gait;
- frequent visits to the nurse for minor complaints;
- mood swings;
- wandering in hallways or on school grounds;
- confusion, disorientation; and
- recent stress-related experience—death in family, divorce, separation, parent's loss of job.

When a child seems to be "at risk," the first thing that you should do is to collect as much data as possible. Ask the classroom teacher to take a really "good look" at the student and try to uncover any difficulties at home that may account for some of the problems observed. The teacher should begin to take anecdotal records of student behavior. You and the teacher should examine the child's school records and think about the following items:

- Has the child ever been referred for school services in the past?
- Is there any family history that seems pertinent?

- Are there any medical issues that might have a bearing on the situation?
- Have any patterns been evident in the past that might provide insights?
- Is any prior formal testing indicated in the child's records?
- What is the child's past performance in school and on tests?
- What is revealed from an examination of the child's schoolwork?
- Are the child's parents aware that school personnel are concerned?

Teachers need to be aware of a procedure that they can follow when they have serious concerns about a child and his or her learning needs or behaviors. As principals, though, we know that some teachers are more skillful than others in recognizing different learning styles and making appropriate accommodations to meet individual needs. Others may use a very limited repertoire of instructional strategies, and if children do not catch on right away, they become alarmed and call for special services. There are also those teachers who feel that they can "save any child" and will hesitate to ask for special services even when they are clearly warranted. Part of identifying and servicing special needs is knowing the teachers' own degree of flexibility and tolerance for learning differences.

In any school, teachers can benefit from a program aimed at recognizing individual learning styles and tailoring instruction so that all children can learn. Teachers need to know about visual learners, auditory learners, kinesthetic learners, and how these strengths reveal themselves in classrooms. A simple instructional strategy for all teachers is to ensure that their lessons include a variety of approaches—verbal directions, visuals, demonstrations, concrete objects, opportunity to move about the classroom, and productive student interactions.

DEVELOPING A CONTINUUM OF SERVICES FOR STUDENTS

Most schools today have a variety of services available to assist students who have special needs. General practice (and indeed the law) requires that students be served in the "least-restrictive environment." When students are referred to a child study team or a committee on special education, the team members must always consider the concept of the least-restrictive environment when deciding on placement. However, all schools should have a continuum of services that can be called into play when considering assistance for youngsters. The kinds of services, from least restrictive to more restrictive, that can be offered by a school or school district include the following:

1. *Regular Classroom Placement With Specialist Consultation.* In this situation, the child is placed in a regular classroom, but a reading teacher, learning specialist, or other professional initiates ongoing discussion and advice for the teacher about strategies to use and modifications that will best serve the youngster.

2. *Regular Classroom Placement With Collaborative Teaching or "Push-In" Assistance.* Some children require more direct support than a specialist consulting with the teacher. In such cases, a special-education teacher, learning specialist, or remedial teacher can work with the youngster in the regular classroom

setting—either individually or in a group. The specialist can work collaboratively with the regular teacher, walk about the classroom providing assistance to the youngster identified as having special needs, and help others in class who may have questions. In collaborative teaching, it is essential that the teachers plan together so that the classroom experience for the students will be integrated and seamless.

3. *Regular Classroom Placement With "Pullout" Services.* For youngsters whose needs are a bit more pronounced, or those who cannot focus well within the context of a larger class, "pullout" services may be provided. In this case, the child may leave the classroom for one or more supportive programs provided by a specialist. Such services might include extra help in reading, writing, or math, speech/language assistance, adaptive physical education, counseling, and physical or occupational therapy.

4. *Regular Classroom Placement With Resource-Center Assistance.* When youngsters are officially classified with special-education needs, they may benefit from the assistance of a special-education teacher in a resource center. The pupil-to-teacher ratio in such centers is usually small—often less than ten to one. The resource-center teacher can provide supplementary assistance with regular classroom assignments or create a "replacement program" if the regular program is considered too challenging or inappropriate for the child. In some situations, "in-class replacement" can be prescribed. In this case, the special-education teacher provides a replacement program, but it occurs within the regular classroom setting.

5. *Coteaching.* Often, a regular-education classroom teacher, a special-education teacher, and one or more instructional aides will coteach a class made up of regular-education students and students who need consistent assistance from a special-education teacher. The ratio of special-education students to regular-education students, strategies for instruction, and the relationship between the adults in the classroom have to be planned carefully. It is important that the school community is aware of the rationale for coteaching and understand how this class constellation benefits all students in the class. Effective strategies for coteaching are well documented.

6. *Self-Contained Special-Education Class.* When youngsters' needs are rather severe, they may be placed in a self-contained special-education classroom taught by a special-education teacher and perhaps instructional aides. Depending on each individual case, the child may be mainstreamed for part of the school day in certain academic subjects or special subjects such as art, music, or physical education.

7. *Out-of-District Placement—Public or Private.* For students whose needs cannot be met at the regular public school, placement may be made in a special school or class in another school district where the particular needs may better be met. These can be public or private day schools or, in truly severe cases, residential institutions.

A chart outlining this continuum of services appears in Figure 9.3.

Figure 9.3 Chart of Support Services Continuum

CHART OF SUPPORT SERVICES CONTINUUM

	Least Restrictive						*Most Restrictive*
	Regular Classroom With Specialist Consultation	*Regular Classroom With Collaborative Teaching or "Push-In" Assistance*	*Regular Classroom With "Pullout" Services*	*Regular Classroom With Resource-Center Assistance*	*Coteaching Model*	*Self-Contained Special-Education Class*	*Out-of-District Placement*
Environment	Regular classroom	Regular classroom	Support outside of classroom in special-education room or resource center	Separate resource center	Regular classroom	Self-contained special education	Out-of-district day school, private school, or institutional setting
Primary Instructor	Regular educator	Regular educator in collaboration with special educators and other teachers or aides	Regular educator with assistance from specialist	Special educator	Regular educator, special educator, one or more instructional aides	Special educator	Special educator
Curriculum	Regular curriculum	Regular curriculum with special strategies and techniques to help students	Supplementary assistance and possible adaptations	Adapted curriculum parallel to regular curriculum	Regular curriculum with special strategies and techniques for all students	Same general goals with accommodations	Special curriculum

INCLUSION AND ITS IMPLICATIONS

The term *inclusion* most often refers to addressing the needs of all students, regardless of disability, in regular classrooms. There are many interpretations and differences, however, in the way this approach is implemented in schools. Related to the concept of the least-restrictive environment, inclusion implies that almost any child can be educated in the regular-education setting, provided that the program offers the needed services and accommodations.

In many schools, students with mild to moderate learning difficulties have been successfully accommodated. In current discussion, inclusion usually refers to students with rather pervasive developmental disorders, physical handicaps, and visual or hearing impairments. In the past, these youngsters were often educated in separate schools or facilities, but parents and educators now realize that there are many benefits to providing instruction for these youngsters in their regular schools.

Administrators have an important role in helping teachers be successful in providing an inclusive educational environment. Following is a checklist of suggestions for ways you can support inclusion:

- ☐ Demonstrate, through actions and words, your own support for inclusive education.

- ☐ Secure resources and services to support classroom teachers and students.

- ☐ Welcome students with disabilities and handicaps into the school. Show that you value their presence.

- ☐ Ensure that all students can enjoy school activities and special events.

- ☐ Arrange for in-service experiences to equip teachers with skills and techniques to provide for inclusive education.

- ☐ Adapt classroom arrangements and materials to support inclusive education.

- ☐ Work with the entire parent body to support inclusive education and encourage the parents of students with disabilities to become active in the parent organization.

- ☐ Work with district administrators to ensure that the school board understands the benefit of inclusive education.

Your attitude toward inclusion is likely to influence the entire school community. Even principals who question the advisability of this approach have no choice but to welcome students with disabilities into their schools. In such cases, after a few successful experiences, they may become the most active proponents.

CREATING A PUPIL SUPPORT TEAM

In any school, there are students who have special needs that are not immediately apparent or easy to diagnose. Teachers and parents, though, may sense that something is just not quite right. Principals cannot do it all alone, and so it is helpful and wise to assemble a pupil support team that can be called together to discuss concerns about students. (Indeed, in most situations, such teams are mandated by local district or state policy.) There is any number of names for such groups. Among them are pupil assistance committee, child support group, or student resource committee, to name a few. There is an important distinction between this somewhat informal group and the more formal child study team or committee on special education. This support group should be considered an intermediary step between a teacher's recognition of a student's difficulty or problem and a formal referral for a special-education evaluation. One of the main purposes of the group is to set goals to help solve the problems identified.

For purposes of this discussion, the term *Pupil Assistance Committee,* or PAC, will be used for this group. Principals have at their disposal a number of persons whose particular skills, specialties, or points of view help to provide a multidisciplinary approach to solving problems. A possible configuration for a PAC might include

- an experienced classroom teacher;
- the principal;
- a school nurse;
- a speech/language pathologist;
- a reading or learning specialist;
- a guidance counselor, school psychologist, or school social worker; and
- an ESL teacher, if appropriate.

Depending upon your own situation, other staff members with special expertise may be available and can be included on the committee.

The ground rules for meetings should be specified in advance, and perhaps training experiences can be arranged. One approach is for the classroom teacher to be considered the "problem expert." This person requests assistance from the PAC and then provides essential backup information about the youngster. A Request for Assistance form can be developed, and once completed, this information can be distributed to all committee members prior to the scheduled meeting. (A sample Request for Assistance form appears in Figure 9.4.) Most principals find it helpful to arrange the PAC meeting at the same time each week so that it can be built into the school schedule. In this way, the special personnel can all be available at the designated time. Of course, some coverage must be arranged for the classroom teacher who will present the case. Parents are always made aware of the meeting and in some districts they are invited to attend. They are always advised of next steps arrived at by the committee.

A Problem-Solving Approach

The members of the PAC should be viewed as experts, each of whom has important insights that can help to craft a solution to the problems perceived by teachers or parents. A productive approach for problem solving may be outlined as follows:

1. *Stating the problems or concerns.* The classroom teacher, parent, or whoever has called for the PAC meeting should present the problems or concerns. Examples to substantiate the concerns may be given.

Figure 9.4 Pupil Assistance Committee Request for Assistance Form

PUPIL ASSISTANCE COMMITTEE REQUEST FOR ASSISTANCE

Student's name: ___________________________ **Grade:** _________ **School:** _____________

I. Problem Identification:

Describe what you would like the student to do that does not currently take place:

Describe what you would like the student *not to do* that is currently taking place:

II. Student's Abilities:

Strengths:

Weaknesses:

III. What Has Been Tried:

List any approaches you used to assist the student:

1.

2.

3.

List dates of any previous contacts and comments:

IV. Parental Notification of Pupil Assistance Committee Referral:

When Notified? ___________________________ By Whom? ___________________

How Notified? ___________________________ Parental Concerns: Yes or No

Signature of requesting person: ____

Job title or position: _______________________________ **Date of request:** ____________

2. *Focusing in on an identifiable problem.* When general concerns are voiced, the group may become "lost in the forest" and fail to focus in on a specific problem. The role of the facilitator is to repeat some of the concerns expressed and then ask the group members if a pattern, or more general problem, seems to emerge that can be addressed. It is important to realize that not all problems can be solved in a single meeting, and the best hope for a PAC group will be to focus on an area where there can be a reasonable expectation for assistance, intervention, or remediation.

3. *Specifying what has already been tried.* By specifying interventions that have already been attempted, the group can get some ideas as to what might work well or what can be eliminated in trying to improve the situation.

4. *Identification of the student's strengths.* A list of the student's strengths can help in the problem-solving process. This not only provides a picture of the whole child, but it is also advisable to work through students' strengths to overcome perceived weaknesses.

5. *Setting goals.* This is perhaps the most important aspect of the meeting. The group should focus on what it feels the student should be able to do that he or she is not able to do at the present time. Goals should be reasonable, realistic, and measurable. Setting goals that are too ambitious can undermine the entire process. Also, only one or two specific goals should be set. For example, a goal might be for a student to complete homework assignments on time. This is a more reasonable goal than to expect the student to focus more deliberately on schoolwork and assignments, or adhere to set behavioral expectations. The latter goal is far too global and in many instances may be doomed to failure.

6. *Brainstorming possible solutions.* Once a goal or two has been set, the group should turn its attention to thinking of possible solutions to the situation. At this point, all suggestions should be listed and accepted without comment. All members of the group should contribute to this discussion.

7. *Selecting solutions.* Each of the possible solutions should be discussed. Is the solution feasible and realistic? Are resources available to implement the solution? Does the solution build upon and take advantage of any of the student's strengths? What classroom-based interventions will be made and how will progress be monitored?

8. *Making assignments.* To implement the selected solutions, different individuals will have to assume responsibility for specific aspects of the plan. For example, perhaps a parent will be asked to take the child for an eye examination. Maybe the classroom teacher will have to initial an assignment pad before the child leaves school each day.

9. *Following up.* A date for checking on the implementation of the plan should be set. In this way, the solutions can be assessed and any further steps or actions can be specified.

It is easy to see that this approach to problem solving is applicable to many other situations in school. It is ideal for use in school leadership councils, classrooms, or parent groups.

Conducting the Pupil Assistance Committee Meeting

Each PAC should have a facilitator, and usually the principal assumes this role. It is the responsibility of the facilitator to inform all participants of the time and place of the meeting and to provide some advance information about the child who is going to be considered. Most often, the parents/guardians of the student are also informed of and invited to the meeting. (Usually two weeks' lead time is appropriate.) The Request for Assistance form completed by the person asking for the PAC meeting can be attached to the memo in which the meeting is announced.

The facilitator must keep the meeting moving and prevent it from getting bogged down in minute details. Good facilitation skills are required, as information that may be difficult for parents to hear may come out in the meeting. Each meeting should open by stating the purpose of the meeting and an introduction of the participants.

A recorder should be selected. In some situations, all of the notes (i.e., from each of the categories in the problem-solving process) are recorded on large charts, which are then taped around the meeting room. The advantage of this procedure is that everyone involved can see the notes being taken, and if any differences in interpretation arise, they may be ironed out on the spot.

The facilitator should work from a problem-solving worksheet. This will ensure that all of the essential aspects of the meeting are on the agenda. (A sample of a Problem-Solving Worksheet appears in Figure 9.5.) In meetings where the proceedings are not recorded on large chart paper, the recorder can make notes on the Problem-Solving Worksheet.

Figure 9.5 Problem-Solving Worksheet for Pupil Assistance Committee Meeting

PROBLEM-SOLVING WORKSHEET

Student name: _______________________________ **Date:** _______________

Present at meeting: ____

Problems/concerns:

Specific problem identified:

What has been tried:

Student's strengths:

Goal(s):

Possible solutions:

Solutions selected:

Assignments:

Follow-up:

The facilitator should then take the notes from the worksheet or chart and prepare a letter to the parents summarizing what occurred at the meeting. Copies of this letter may be sent to all participants. One advantage of summarizing the meeting in writing is that if the youngster does at some point in the future require a referral to a child study team, this summary will serve as a record of the prereferral interventions that were attempted.

Following Up on the Outcomes of the Meeting

As soon as a follow-up date is chosen, you should mark this on your calendar so that the meeting can be scheduled. Once again, the facilitator schedules this meeting. Sometimes, a subset of the PAC will be appropriate for the follow-up meeting.

The existence of the PAC, its purposes, membership, and the procedure for requesting a PAC meeting should be well known and publicized within the school and parent body. (See Figure 1.3.) School newsletter articles or general letters to parents and staff should be prepared so that all members of the school community know that this resource is available to them.

PREREFERRAL STRATEGIES AND RESPONSE TO INTERVENTION

Before a referral is made to a child study team or a committee on special education, principals should ensure that prereferral interventions have been attempted. This is where having a tiered approach becomes essential. Many schools have started to adopt a Response to Intervention (RTI) as their prereferral process. RTI is a framework for examining and improving instructional delivery and using data collected on an ongoing basis as the starting point for decision-making. Tier 1, instruction for all students, is research-based instruction and uses curriculum-based assessments to monitor student achievement and rate of learning. Approximately 85% of students should be successful at Tier 1 if content and skills are taught using research-based instructional strategies. This model offers you and the other members of the PAC a chance to make sound program decisions for a student based on evidence collected over a period of time while also following a very prescriptive approach to instruction. Universal screening, a brief, reliable, and valid measure, is recommended for all students so that those who are not benefiting from regular (Tier 1) universal instruction are identified. The process of formal referrals can often take weeks or months for completion. In the meantime, there are classroom-based interventions that teachers can implement to provide assistance to children. These interventions are referred to as Tier 2 targeted interventions. Unlike the discrepancy model or "wait and fail," as it has been commonly referred to, prereferral interventions may indeed be effective in solving problems that teachers encounter, thereby averting the need for a formal referral. Tier 2 interventions should address another 10% of students who experience academic difficulties. In some school systems, formal referrals cannot be made until the principal and teachers can substantiate the intermediary steps they have taken to help the child in the regular-education program. Frequent, brief progress-monitoring tools are used to assess a student's response to a given intervention. At the end of the Tier 2 intervention process, should a student need to continue to a more intensive tier of intervention (Tier 3) or to a formal referral, most of the data you have collected is so comprehensive that a teacher can implement another intervention or, perhaps, the only thing left is to formalize the child's services. Another benefit of having a tiered approach to the prereferral process is that it monitors the duration and intensity of service each student receives. A graphic that captures the essence of the tiered approach in the RTI model appears in Figure 9.6.

Pyramid of Interventions

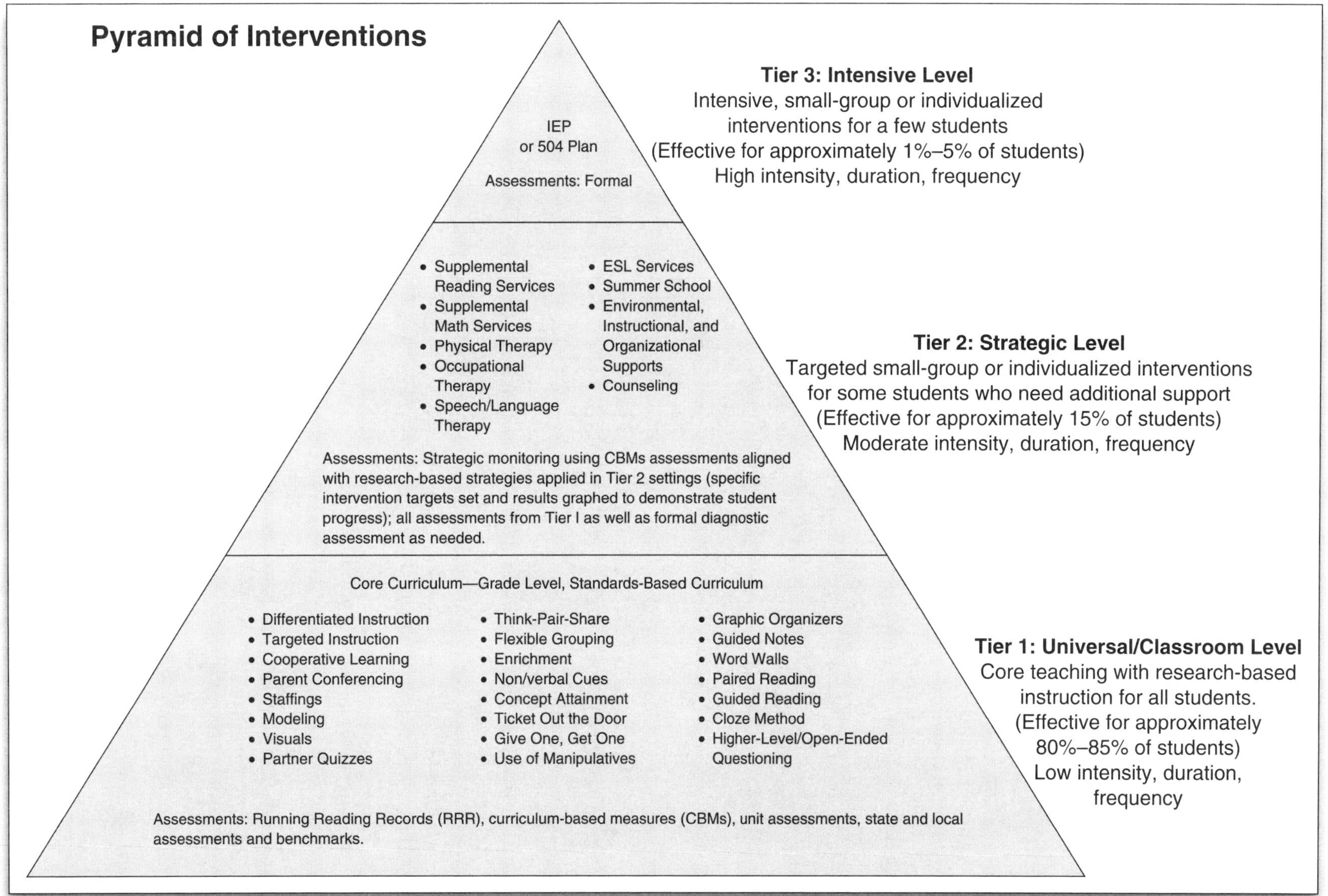

Prereferral procedures begin with data collection. Teachers should take anecdotal records on the youngster for whom they have concern. Other information that should be gathered includes a review of student records; prior test data including a school's universal screening tool, progress-monitoring tools (curriculum-based measures), standardized assessments, and state assessments; the student's basic reading and comprehension levels; the child's mathematical reasoning and calculation abilities; attendance and health records; and special teaching strategies that may have been successful or rewarding.

A PAC meeting can be fruitful in terms of suggestions, approaches, and strategies that may alleviate teacher concerns about a particular youngster. Meetings with parents may also help to better understand a child's needs and reactions. Often, setting up a communication system with parents in which regular contacts are made and student progress is monitored is all that is needed to help a youngster.

Consultation with specialists in the school and the school district may also be of assistance. Placing children in remedial classes in the regular-education program may be tried to see if the youngster responds to this kind of assistance. Speech and language assistance or guidance services may also help the youngster.

Response to Intervention is not a special-education program. It is one that involves both regular- and special-education personnel. Teachers must learn to modify their instructional strategies, implement them with fidelity, tailor them to suit individual needs, and learn how to monitor progress using brief, valid assessment tools. With some information about a child's learning style and areas of difficulty, specialists can help to develop a specific plan of assistance. Such interventions might include special (private) signals to a youngster, the use of manipulative materials, preferential seating, auditory or visual cues, or special teaming with other youngsters, among many others strategies.

PROCEDURES TO FOLLOW IN SECTION 504 REFERRALS

Section 504 of the Federal Rehabilitation Act of 1973 prohibits discrimination against qualified handicapped individuals in federally assisted programs or activities. The regulations in Section 504 cover not only students, but also adults, employees, and community members. However, it was not until the 1990s that Section 504 became broadly applied in public schools. Students who are not eligible for services under the IDEA (the Individuals with Disabilities Education Act) may indeed gain services under Section 504, since its provisions state that a person is eligible if he or she has a physical or mental impairment that substantially limits one or more major life functions. Parents and child advocates have extended these provisions to include reading as a "major life function," as well as the ability to pay attention during class. Thus, in recent years, parents have sought services and accommodations for their children who have reading disabilities or attention deficit disorder (ADD), without having to go through the special-education classification process.

You must understand the provisions of Section 504 and the rights that students may have. Any district that accepts any federal funding must comply with the provisions of Section 504. Each school district should have in place a Section 504 officer. This is the person who will receive and dispatch requests for a hearing. Usually, the request is directed to the local school, where a committee should then be established to examine the request. (Usually, a group such as the Pupil Assistance Committee described above can serve this function.) The committee should gather data, including reports from outside practitioners, and conduct its own assessment of need and eligibility. The procedural requirements under Section 504 are similar to those governed by IDEA, that is, free education, evaluation process, least-restrictive environment, due process rights, and the establishment of an assistance or accommodation plan.

Once a student is found to be "impaired" and in need of services, the 504 committee develops the accommodation plan. If a parent disagrees with the findings of the 504 committee, there should be an internal grievance process that includes appeals to the principal, superintendent, and the board of education. Ultimately, the United States Office of Civil Rights can hear complaints.

It should be noted that no federal funds are available for Section 504 accommodations and services, so some school systems will encourage parents to seek services under the IDEA (if appropriate) where some federal funding is available.

Some of the accommodations that commonly occur under Section 504 might include

- adjusting class schedules and modifying the requirements of assignments;
- supplementing verbal directions with visual instructions;
- repeating and simplifying instructions and directions;
- using tape recorders;
- implementing computer-aided instruction;
- using classroom aides;
- developing behavior modification plans;
- tailoring homework assignments;
- using the services of a sign-language interpreter and FM listening devices;
- locating special ramps, railings, and lifts for physical disabilities; and
- finding large-print materials and books-on-tape for visually impaired students.

As in all such formal procedures, meetings, accommodation plans developed, and appeal proceedings must be clearly documented in a timely fashion. As principals gain experience in dealing with Section 504 situations, they will find that they do not differ from other regular-education and special-education procedures.

REFERRAL FOR SPECIAL-EDUCATION SERVICES

Once prereferral interventions have been tried, it may be necessary to refer a youngster to a child study team or committee on special education. If there is a tiered system of interventions as shown in Figure 9.6, only 1%–5% of students should progress to this point. This process carries with it definite procedures and timelines that must be adhered to. Many school leaders have been involved in bitter challenges and court battles, only to find that they lost their cases based upon procedural or timeline errors. All principals, especially newly hired administrators, must be familiar with the district, state, and federal requirements that govern the referral and special-education placement process.

A form is usually provided to the individual who is making the referral for evaluation. This can be a classroom teacher, an ESL teacher, a school nurse, or the principal. Usually, the person who has the most direct contact with the youngster is the one who should complete the form. Parents are also able to refer their own child for evaluation.

However, once a referral is received from any source, the committee on special education, child study team, or pupil personnel services director must (within a specified amount of time, usually 15 days) determine whether or not the referral is accepted and, if so, establish an evaluation plan. At each phase of the process, parental notification and permission are required.

Most school districts can develop their own referral forms. Following is a checklist of some of the more pertinent information that should be included in a referral form:

- ☐ Name of Student
- ☐ Birth Date
- ☐ Gender
- ☐ Address
- ☐ Grade and Teacher Assignment
- ☐ Parent/Guardians' Names and Addresses
- ☐ Home and Work Phone Numbers
- ☐ Pertinent Facts About Home and Family
- ☐ Previous Schools Attended
- ☐ Physical Conditions Noted
- ☐ Medical History
- ☐ Academic Achievement
- ☐ Standardized Test Scores
- ☐ Behavioral Patterns
- ☐ Strengths
- ☐ Reason for Referral: Presenting Problems
- ☐ Prereferral Interventions
- ☐ Significant Parent Conferences: Dates and Outcomes
- ☐ Discipline Problems
- ☐ Attendance Record
- ☐ Efforts Outside of School (tutoring, counseling, etc.)
- ☐ List of Staff Members Currently Involved in Supportive Functions
- ☐ Signature of Individual Completing Referral
- ☐ Parent Notification Date

Once the referral is accepted, it is assigned to an assessment team, usually composed of individuals representing two or three disciplines, most often a psychologist, a social worker, and a learning-disabilities specialist. After the evaluation is completed, the team determines eligibility for special-education services based upon specified requirements, established categories, or classifications.

You must remain involved in the referral process from beginning to end. Apart from the importance of showing yourself to be an interested party, your leadership is essential to the integrity of the process. In most school systems, principals are the individuals who are ultimately responsible for the implementation of the Individualized Education Program (IEP) developed. This requires careful monitoring, attention to detail and requirements, and a genuine concern for students and their well-being.

DEALING WITH THE OUTCOMES OF A SPECIAL-EDUCATION EVALUATION

Once all of the reports of the examiners have been assembled, the child study team will schedule an eligibility conference to share the outcomes of the testing and determine whether or not the youngster is entitled to special-education services. These meetings are often bewildering to parents/guardians and the uninitiated, and steps should be taken to explain the process and help them feel at ease. Papers seem to be flying everywhere, signature after signature is required, and procedural requirements must be followed. Some parents have even likened the process to closing on the purchase of a home. The outcomes of this meeting, though, are essential for the education of the youngster in question. Copies of all reports should be offered to parents. It is also important to assure parents about the confidentiality of the proceedings. When faced with the opportunity to classify their youngsters for special-education services, parents are often concerned about maintaining their child's self-esteem. They legitimately require considerable reassurance that the professionals involved will do all that they can to help. It can often be pointed out to parents that without special-education services, the child might be suffering from anxiety and frustration and thus his or her self-esteem might be compromised anyway if the school were not to deal with the problem.

If the team, according to its criteria, finds that the child is indeed eligible for special-education services, an IEP and instructional plan will be developed—either at the same meeting or at a later point in time.

The IEP must contain, at a minimum, the following elements:

- An assessment of the child's current level of performance
- Certification that the child is eligible for special education according to established requirements
- Annual program goals and objectives
- Regular-program participation and modifications
- Special-education placement and justification
- A list of applicable related services
- Signatures of the child study team members
- Parent signature and statement of appeal rights
- Date for annual review

There are several placement options for special-education students. Some may be able to remain in their regular classrooms with special modifications and related services. Others will require placement in a resource center for a part of their day, and still others may need to be placed in a self-contained special-education class. There are any number of possibilities in between these options, and a program is developed to meet the needs of the student, again meeting the requirements of the least-restrictive environment.

IEPs often specify related services that are provided to assist the student, including

- individual counseling by a guidance counselor or psychologist,
- group counseling,
- speech/language therapy,
- physical or occupational therapy,
- adaptive physical education,
- note takers, and
- use of technological devices.

IEPs also include testing modifications if appropriate. These modifications might allow students to take tests without time limits, to mark their answers in test booklets instead of separate answer sheets, have small-group administration, or provisions for special lighting or special test formats such as large-print editions or increased spacing between lines and items.

Once a child is classified, an annual review meeting must occur in which the accomplishment of the goals in the IEP is assessed and new goals are set for the following year. Every three years, a classified student must be reevaluated for continued eligibility. This is called a triennial review.

You must be aware of and responsible for the maintenance of special-education records. They must be kept separately from a student's regular school files or folder and under lock and key. Access to such records is restricted, and anyone who requests the records should be entered into a pupil records log (see Figure 9.2). Regular-education files must not refer to any special-education reports or files in the school or school district. The purpose of this requirement is to ensure that the confidentiality rights of the student are protected.

School leaders often underestimate the amount of time they need to devote to parental concerns and anxieties in the special-education referral and placement process. It is often best to try to put yourself in the parent's shoes—think about your own reactions and responses to understanding your child's needs and disabilities. The process requires patience, sensitivity, and compassion.

DISCIPLINE REGULATIONS AND SPECIAL-EDUCATION STUDENTS

In federal court cases, some interpretations of IDEA have resulted in distinctions that govern the ways that principals can discipline students with disabilities. In most instances, the day-to-day decisions that principals make are certainly allowable. However, if the student's behavior is in some way related to his or her disability, you may be limited in the actions that can be taken. For example, disabled students cannot be unilaterally suspended for more than 10 days without full due process. Also, disciplinary actions may not have adverse effects on IEP goals and objectives. Recent decisions have held, however, that disabled students who have drugs or weapons in their possession may be treated in the same way as their nondisabled peers. Thankfully, drug and weapon possession rarely occurs in elementary schools.

ADMINISTERING ENGLISH-AS-A-SECOND-LANGUAGE PROGRAMS

Another area that addresses the special needs of students is the bilingual and English-as-a-Second-Language (ESL) program. Here, too, principals have important responsibilities. This area cannot be adequately covered within a small section of one chapter—indeed, entire books are devoted to administering programs for English-language learners—but there are a few suggestions that can be made. First and foremost, it is important for students who are learning English as a second language and their parents to feel like they are embraced by the school and have opportunities to participate fully in all school activities and events. Learn about the cultures of your students and some of the more relevant customs and practices. For example, in some cultures, parents may feel that they need a special invitation to participate in a school event; in other cultures, students may not look directly in the eyes of an authority figure (such as the principal) as this is considered a form of disrespect.

Bilingual and ESL programs have their own set of procedures and practices, and here, too, principals must be informed. For example, there may be a specified number of minutes that students must be involved in ESL programs for each subject each day. Class sizes may also have specific limitations. You must develop procedures for screening new students and adhering to testing cutoff scores for inclusion in or exit from programs. Beyond this, there are required reports that must be prepared each year for federal and state authorities. Regulations are very clear as to which students are or are not included in state assessments for the purpose of accountability under NCLB. It is always helpful to maintain a database of students' ethnic and language backgrounds as this information is often called for in the completion of state and federal reports.

One of the challenges that school leaders sometimes face occurs when a staff member refers an ESL student for special-education services. Does the child truly have a disability, or are the problems related to learning a new language? Often, the answer to this question is not clear-cut. Among the things that principals need to consider before referring an ESL student for a formal special-education evaluation are

- the child's level of self-esteem,
- difficulties that the child may have in developing positive social relationships,
- the use of ESL strategies in the regular classroom,
- an examination of the child's ability to complete hands-on activities,
- discussions with parents and their appraisal of the child's abilities, and
- an informal assessment of the child's abilities in his or her native language.

Prior to a referral for evaluation, it is often helpful to have a teacher who speaks the child's native language work with the child to gain an understanding of the child's competency and level of development. If possible, this step should always be considered before making a formal special-education referral.

ADMINISTERING GIFTED AND TALENTED EDUCATIONAL PROGRAMS

Just as is the case in the area of the second-language learner, one section of a chapter cannot prepare principals for administering a program for gifted and talented students. Truly gifted students are in need of special-education experiences just as much as their peers with disabilities. Often, these youngsters feel alone in their thinking and in their view of the world. They must be supported and helped to feel that they are not "oddballs," but that their views and interests are based upon unique intelligences or gifts.

There is a wide variety of interpretation as to what exactly gifted and talented education means. In some school systems, the definition is quite narrow, and programs are offered to only those students who achieve very well in academic areas, based solely upon ability testing and teacher recommendations. In other schools systems, the program for gifted and talented education is far more comprehensive and serves children who exhibit special talents in a wide variety of areas.

Programs for gifted and talented students can often become a "political football," and principals need to be aware of the pitfalls of establishing such programs. In some communities, gifted/talented programs are viewed as elitist and unnecessary. In such instances, administrators may have to educate parent groups about the unique needs of this segment of the student population. In other communities, the needs of the disabled learner and the gifted student are sometimes pitted against each other in budgetary squabbles. Here again, caution must be taken not to alienate one segment of the parent community. Like so many other areas of school administration, this is a great balancing act, but you generally cannot go wrong if you are viewed as being an advocate for the needs of *all* children.

One of the first things that principals need to do in the area of gifted and talented education is to decide upon an identification procedure. There are a variety of standardized tests that can help in the identification process, but tests alone should not be the sole criterion for identification. Other means for identifying students with special gifts and talents include

- tests of creativity,
- screening assessment measures,
- teacher checklists and recommendations,
- parent recommendations,
- anecdotal records,
- interest inventories, and
- self-nominations.

In any case, multiple criteria should be used to identify students. See Figure 9.7 for a sample of a simple teacher checklist for identifying gifted students. (It should be noted that this is *not* a standardized instrument, but rather a sampling of traits and characteristics that teachers have found in gifted and talented students.)

The next step in establishing a program for gifted students is to determine the content and context of the program. Will it be a "pullout" program? Will a specialist be required to work with the children? Can a specialist visit all of the classrooms and work with all students? Is the purpose of the program to accelerate students and simply offer them advanced courses in areas of skill or interest?

Figure 9.7 Sample Checklist for Identifying Potentially Gifted/Talented Students

CHECKLIST FOR IDENTIFICATION OF POTENTIALLY GIFTED/TALENTED STUDENTS

☐ Displays an intense curiosity about objects, concepts, and situations.

☐ Tends to view aspects of situations that other children do not.

☐ Makes abstractions and generalizations beyond his or her age level.

☐ Displays a wide variety of interests and/or hobbies.

☐ Pursues own interests in a self-directed manner.

☐ Demonstrates superior judgment in evaluating situations and events.

☐ Has an innate sense of fairness and justice.

☐ Has achieved beyond his or her peers in one or several areas of study.

☐ Demonstrates tenacity and perseverance.

☐ Is independent in work, study, and thinking.

☐ Can maintain a long attention span.

☐ Displays a questioning, inquisitive attitude.

☐ Uses a broad, appropriately applied vocabulary.

☐ Understands sophisticated nuances and interpretations of material read.

☐ Tends to learn more quickly and adeptly than his or her classmates.

☐ Displays talents in the areas of artistic, musical, or dramatic expression.

☐ Can assume and carry out learning responsibilities.

☐ Offers unusual or clever responses to ideas in classroom discussions.

☐ Can generate diverse alternatives in problem-solving situations.

☐ Can elaborate on responses and reactions with ease.

☐ Displays an intense power of concentration.

☐ Is willing to pursue matters that other children might not.

☐ Prefers to work alone and in an intense fashion.

☐ Exhibits a high energy level, especially when interested in something.

☐ Sees unique associations and relationships.

☐ Can work on many projects at one time.

☐ Can identify solutions and strategies when confronted with problem situations.

The different programs that can be offered to accommodate the needs of gifted students include the following:

- "Pullout" programs, in which identified children come together several hours each week to explore areas of interest and work on projects. Among the advantages of this kind of program is the mutual support that is engendered among the students.
- Rotating programs, in which all students can explore individual interests with the assistance of a resource teacher.
- Differentiated instruction in the regular classroom wherein teachers plan for meeting a variety of skill readiness levels, interests, and learning styles for their students. Staff development is required for teachers to develop this level of planning (such as the use of pre- and post-testing), but in this way, *all* students' needs can be met.
- An "infusion" program, in which a specialist visits all classrooms and works with the entire class while aiming to stimulate and motivate gifted learners.
- Mentorships, in which students who wish to explore particular areas of interest are paired with experts or other individuals in the community who help them in their learning journeys.
- Extracurricular clubs and classes that occur outside of the school day.
- Special groupings within the regular classroom.
- Weekend classes or special field-trip opportunities.

As you plan and develop your programs for gifted and talented students, you should form a committee of teachers, parents, and perhaps students, to assist in the effort. This group can study current literature, review successful models that exist in the area, and tailor a program to meet local needs. Just as inclusion is commonplace for disabled learners, it is becoming more and more common to equip teachers with strategies for differentiated instruction and approaches that can stimulate children at any level of achievement. In this way, the needs of gifted learners can best be met within the context of the regular classroom. Special resources, both material and human, may be required, but it can be argued that such approaches will benefit all children in the end and that students who do not possess these special gifts will flourish and find their own interests and unique abilities.

STAFF DEVELOPMENT NEEDS IN DEALING WITH UNIQUE LEARNERS

Throughout this chapter, the need to provide professional development experiences has been emphasized, as such experiences can help teachers meet the diverse needs of all students. If the school district does not offer an appropriate in-service program, you should arrange for these experiences within your own school. Partnerships can be built with local colleges to offer courses. There may also be staff in the district's child study team who can conduct workshops, seminars, and mini-courses to help teachers learn how to meet the needs of all children. Consultants can be secured to provide staff development days or faculty conferences—all designed to aid in this effort.

Many different topics or areas would be appropriate for staff development workshops or activities. These areas include

- implementing classroom-based interventions with fidelity;
- monitoring progress using brief, valid, reliable tools;
- identifying and teaching toward specific learning styles;
- using techniques for successful mainstreaming and inclusion;
- identifying specific learning difficulties;
- enhancing the self-esteem of all learners;
- implementing cooperative learning in the way it was intended to benefit all students;
- recognizing teaching/learning modalities;
- working with parents of learning-disabled children;
- using differentiated instruction;
- integrating instruction;
- teaching collaboratively;
- creating student partnerships;
- securing community resources; and
- creating successful mentorships.

You must recognize that many teachers are unprepared to deal with diverse learners. Several teachers may not have had any training in the diagnosis and teaching of students with learning difficulties. Differentiating your staff meetings based on experience is one way to model to your staff what you would expect to be happening in their classrooms. Doing so in a vertical team format will not only build capacity throughout the building, it will also put people at ease with their current level of understanding. Only through successful experiences, support, and staff development can teachers be expected to meet the array of needs and challenges they face in their classrooms each day.

ASSESSING THE EFFECTIVENESS OF PROGRAMS TO MEET SPECIAL NEEDS

As in all educational programs, practices, procedures, and offerings for children with special needs should be examined and assessed on an ongoing basis. Indeed, in most states, special-education plans require a formal three- or five-year review. This review may be external—that is, officials from the state or county may visit the school to ensure that appropriate procedures are being followed. In most cases, pupil records are inspected to ensure that files are maintained properly, principals and teachers are interviewed, and other compliance issues are examined.

Districts may also be directed to conduct self-assessments. This can be a very revealing process. Teachers, parents, and administrators are usually asked to complete questionnaires, and one individual, or a team, is charged with the responsibility to collate the responses, draw conclusions from the data collected, and make recommendations for program improvement. A sample of such a survey form appears in Figure 9.8.

Figure 9.8   Sample Student Support Services Assessment Questionnaire

STUDENT SUPPORT SERVICES ASSESSMENT QUESTIONNAIRE

The following questions are designed to promote reflection about and self-assessment of our programs and practices in meeting the individual needs of students. Please complete the questionnaire and submit it to your building principal within one week. Use the rating scale to the right of each question. Please make any comments or suggestions you might have by referencing the item number you are responding to on the back of this sheet.

Key: 5 = almost always; 4 = most of the time; 3 = sometimes; 2 = rarely; 1 = never

1. Resources and staff are available to assist in the identification of children with special needs.	5	4	3	2	1
2. Students referred to the child study team for testing are examined in a timely fashion.	5	4	3	2	1
3. A continuum of services is available to meet identified needs of students within the least-restrictive environment.	5	4	3	2	1
4. The child study team helps teachers deal effectively with students who have unique learning needs.	5	4	3	2	1
5. Students classified by the child study team are appropriately placed in supportive situations.	5	4	3	2	1
6. The Individualized Education Program (IEPs) developed by the child study team are helpful to classroom and special teachers and parents.	5	4	3	2	1
7. IEPs developed specify a full range of supplementary aids and services that would facilitate the student's learning.	5	4	3	2	1
8. Parents feel that they are a valued part of the decision-making process in developing programs for students.	5	4	3	2	1
9. The procedures for seeking assistance for children are clear.	5	4	3	2	1
10. Staff development opportunities are available to help teachers deal more effectively with students who exhibit special needs.	5	4	3	2	1

Many beginning principals, as well as their more experienced colleagues, are surprised about the amount of time and energy they must devote to administering programs that accommodate the special needs of students. This is just one of the areas that school leaders must attend to, administer, and support. With experience and practice, however, this area of school life can be one of the most rewarding and interesting aspects of the position.

10

Student Discipline

Approaches, Alternatives, and Solutions

It's 1:15 PM and you've just gone to the staff lounge after three periods of lunchroom supervision; you take your bag lunch out of the refrigerator and walk up to your office, hoping to have a few quiet moments to eat your sandwich as you read your e-mail. As you approach the office, three fourth graders are waiting to see you. They were brought to you by their classroom teacher, who heard from one of the lunch aides about a fight they had during their outdoor lunch recess period. Well, forget about your own lunch. You are now faced with a situation that requires your skill, sensitivity, and decision-making powers—on the spot. Is this a first-time incident? Are these repeat offenders? Is one of the boys a habitual bully? Is the boys' teacher one of your staff members who refuses to deal with lunchtime altercations and consistently sends children to your office without even trying to sort things out? These are all questions that will instantaneously come to your mind before you even decide how you will deal with the situation.

As long as there are schools, there will be discipline problems. The density of so many children in a relatively small place, the diverse set of personalities, and youngsters who have unhappy home lives all contribute to the inevitability of conflict. Add to the mix the fact that children have differing levels of emotional tolerance, personal idiosyncrasies, and varying stages of development; it all makes for situations that lead to discipline problems. Public surveys have indicated that one of the main concerns of parents of schoolchildren is the perceived lack of discipline in schools. However, you don't have to sit back and say that such difficulties are just a part of the nature of elementary schools. There is a great deal that principals can do to improve school climate and set into motion an effective program for ensuring positive behaviors on the part of students.

Note: All forms, letters, and checklists included in this chapter can be found at corwin.com/elementary survivalkit.

CAUSES OF DISCIPLINE PROBLEMS THAT PRINCIPALS ARE LIKELY TO ENCOUNTER

Discipline problems often occur when children are unhappy or suffer from low self-esteem. Children with behavioral difficulties frequently don't like themselves for one reason or another, and their acting out is often a reflection of emotional turmoil. Other children who cause discipline problems lack sufficient impulse control to function effectively in group situations, and this may simply be a result of developmental immaturity.

An unhappy or stressful home life can also cause students to misbehave. Changes in family structure, abuse, or turmoil can have a negative impact on the behavior of youngsters. Health or dietary problems can also contribute to difficulties in concentration, effort, and cooperation. Anger in a child, for whatever reason, is a symptom of some underlying difficulty, and the angry child is likely to have problems with personal and social relationships. Youngsters who have medical issues, such as attention deficit disorder (ADD) or attention deficit hyperactivity disorder (ADHD), may also cause difficulties for themselves or others.

Finally, at times, behavior problems can be the result of a boring, trivial instructional program or a teacher who runs a classroom that lacks any sense of structure, routine, or basic order. An environment that is not predictable can feel unsafe for children. Inconsistent expectations are confusing to children who do not know or cannot find limits or boundaries. This situation may be even more perplexing for principals than individual behavioral problems because a whole class, or a significant portion of a class, may be affected.

APPROACHES TO EFFECTIVE DISCIPLINE

The matter of effective discipline in an elementary school is not a simple issue. Many factors contribute to a happy, orderly, and stimulating environment. Children need us to be there for them, to set appropriate limits, and to be sensitive to what is going on in their personal lives. Students who lack self-discipline benefit from having structures in place that are reasonable and predictable. Routines are important for all children. They need to gain a sense of the ebb and flow of their school day. The morning meeting, jobs and responsibilities, structures for how to involve children in group investigations, and movement through the classroom and the school building all contribute to a sense of order that can do a great deal to prevent behavioral problems.

Teachers should be aware of important issues or changes in children's families; they should understand student needs—personal and social—and the students must be helped to be aware of the reasons for the teacher's expectation of cooperation and appropriate classroom behavior. There is no one way to run an effective classroom. However, with a mutual understanding between teachers and students of the structure, organization, and appropriate limits, the grounds for cooperation are established. Teachers should strive to establish positive group living skills with mutual respect and cooperation as underlying assumptions. Parents should also be made aware of classroom expectations and how their children are meeting them. Where difficulties occur, parent cooperation should be enlisted before the situation deteriorates. Sometimes, parents are simply unaware that their child is misbehaving in school.

When teachers have to talk to children or admonish them for inappropriate behavior, it is essential that they convey that it is the *behavior or actions* that they object to and not the child. Youngsters should see correction as a matter of the logical consequence of their disregard for established classroom expectations. Perhaps the most effective way to ensure a positive school climate, though, is through a deliberate program of preventive discipline.

ELEMENTS OF A PREVENTIVE DISCIPLINE PROGRAM

The old saying "an ounce of prevention is worth a pound of cure" holds quite true for a school discipline program. If a positive climate prevails and basic structures for an orderly environment are put into place, many discipline problems can be avoided. Positive reinforcement of desirable behaviors will promote these traits and attitudes. A school in which the principal and teachers are firm, but fair, and nurture mutual respect among all members of the educational community will more than likely be a school that is not unduly burdened by discipline problems.

School Structures That Promote Good Discipline

Some of the basic structures and characteristics of a school that go a long way toward promoting a positive sense of discipline are

- a visible, approachable principal;
- a sense of order in and cleanliness of physical spaces;
- collaboratively developed class rules;
- general agreement on standards for student behavior;
- respect for all individuals;
- an active, engaging instructional program;
- attractive classrooms in which student work is displayed with pride;
- a pervasive belief in good motives among all human beings;
- teachers who are willing to accept student discipline as a personal responsibility; and
- a friendly, cohesive staff.

Such a list might seem utopian, but if many of these structures are in place, the chances of discipline problems among students will be greatly reduced.

What Makes for a Positive School Climate?

Schools that are cheerful and inviting say "welcome" as soon as you walk into them. They are places where children's feelings are honored and order is apparent—definitely evident, but not obtrusive or overbearing. There is a sense that every human being is valued, and individual rights are respected. Along with these privileges comes a responsibility on the part of all members of the educational community to maintain high standards. There is a predictable rhythm and flow to the school day, and the children know what is expected of them. Routines are in place, and they are broadly understood.

Principals can do much to establish and maintain such a school climate. First and foremost, be a positive role model. Principals who demonstrate their respect for all people are likely to have this respect returned. Students know quickly when a principal genuinely cares about their well-being and is responsive to their concerns. A clear policy on student discipline is essential; the principal leads the staff in defining student expectations and implementing a plan for reinforcing those expectations. Students can and should be involved in establishing a discipline plan; if so, they are more likely to understand and follow it. Later in this chapter, sample school discipline plans are outlined.

Ascertain Potential Problems Before They Occur

One of the most important aspects of preventive discipline is to be aware of potential problems before they become true difficulties. Usually, teachers will know after two or three weeks of school which children seem to be having academic or socioemotional problems. Being alert to these signals and developing a deliberate, well-thought-out plan for individual youngsters can go a long way toward averting major discipline problems.

A good practice is to ask teachers to identify youngsters for whom they have concerns and then set up a meeting with resource personnel—a guidance counselor, school nurse, psychologist, or learning-disabilities specialist—to discuss the child

---

Figure 10.1   Memo to Teachers About Children for Whom They Have Concerns

Name of District and School
MEMORANDUM

Date: _____________________

To: All Teachers

From: _______________________________, Principal

RE: CHILDREN FOR WHOM WE HAVE CONCERNS

Now that school has been in session for a few weeks, you may have noticed some children about whom you have academic or emotional concerns. I would like to schedule a meeting, on the morning of October _____, to discuss these youngsters. The participants at the meeting will be the referring teacher, the guidance counselor, the school psychologist, the nurse, and myself. We will allot about five minutes for the discussion of each child. We cannot hope to arrive at comprehensive solutions or plans at this meeting. Its purpose is for us to determine some logical next steps.

Please list below the youngsters for whom you have concerns and a brief description of the problem you have noticed. I will schedule time for us to discuss each youngster. After I receive your responses, I will develop the specific time slots for the meeting and the schedule will be distributed to you along with information regarding the details of who will cover your class while you attend the meeting.

Please complete the form and submit it to the office by _______________. Thank you.

____

Child's name: _______________________________________

Brief description of concern:

Teacher's name ____

and what next steps might be contemplated. (See the sample memo in Figure 10.1.) Once you have collected a list of the children whom teachers have identified, schedule a "triage" meeting, in which the classroom teacher presents the concerns followed by the formulation of a brief plan of action. For this initial meeting, five or ten minutes devoted to each child can be sufficient. List the recommendations suggested for each student discussed. Some of the possible outcomes of such a meeting might include

- an individual case conference to discuss the child;
- a behavior modification plan coordinated between the psychologist and the classroom teacher;
- a meeting with the teacher, the principal, and the child's parents;
- a suggested physical examination for suspected health problems;
- individual assistance in an academic remediation program;
- counseling sessions with the guidance counselor or psychologist; and
- in extreme cases, a referral to a child study team or committee on special education for an evaluation.

Accentuate the Positive

Identifying and praising positive student behaviors is a vital aspect of any preventive discipline plan. When you notice desired behaviors, label them for the child, and offer genuine praise. It is important to be specific so that the child will know the behaviors exhibited that are so admired. For example, if you notice that a youngster held a door for another child or an adult, say, "Thank you for holding the door for Mrs. Reiss. I really like it when I see you being so considerate." When you see one child helping another, you might say, "Thanks for helping James find his coat. It's great to see kids helping each other. It's the way we want everyone to behave at our school." Educators often call this "catching kids being good."

In some schools, specific certificates, or "smile-o-grams," are filled out when any adult notices a child doing something that merits praise. This certificate can then be signed by the principal and sent home with the youngster (see Figure 10.2). Such devices may seem "corny," but school leaders know that they work. Principals also find that children know when praise is genuine and respond positively to it. Calling parents to offer compliments can also have the same effect. Such communications demonstrate that you spend time in providing praise as well as admonition.

Specific students can also be recognized for their acts of kindness or consideration by posting a brief note on a special bulletin board designed for this purpose. Praise can be offered to individuals or an entire class at school assemblies. One year, the theme for an elementary school was called CAKE, an acronym for Caring and Kindness for Everyone. Any staff member who noticed a child displaying an act of kindness would fill out a specially designed certificate in the shape of a piece of cake. Then, each week at the regular school assembly, the principal would present a "piece of cake" to the deserving youngsters. This type of public recognition announces that such behaviors are highly valued in the school. Praise must be specific and describe the behavior being honored.

Figure 10.2   Smile-O-Gram

Name of District and School

SMILE-O-GRAM

Today your child, _______________________, was awarded this Smile-O-Gram for

____.

We are all so proud!

_______________________ (Staff Member)

_______________________ (Principal)

Teach Conflict-Resolution Skills

Conflict resolution can be a component of a school's discipline plan. Teaching students to solve interpersonal problems on their own is effective and gives them lifelong skills. Conflict resolution refers to strategies that teach students to handle conflicts peacefully and cooperatively outside the typical disciplinary procedures outlined in this chapter.

Implement an Antibullying Program

Bullying is related to school discipline, and it is a widespread problem in schools. It is a problem, though, that can be solved, and the school leader is in a good position to spearhead such a program. Research from across the United States and Europe shows that when schools take specific action, bullying can be eliminated.

There are any number of commercial antibullying programs available for schools. Some work better than others, but one essential aspect is that the whole school must be behind the efforts. Effective antibullying programs involve everybody in the school community—not just the principal or a couple of concerned teachers. The administration sets a clear standard that bullying is completely unacceptable and enforces it.

When considering commercial programs, school leaders must think about which program or approaches would work best in their given school community. Even though the promoters of these programs claim to be "one size fits all," principals and others need to ascertain what will work best. Often, a school-developed program with the involvement of all stakeholders can be just as effective (or more so) than a commercial program. In any case, teachers can weave important lessons into classroom meetings, "on-the-spot" examples, and discussions to help their students understand the importance of the program and how everyone has a role in it. Children learn that by taking care of each other, speaking out against bullies, and working together, they have tremendous power.

Implement a Character-Education Program

As is the case with antibullying programs, a variety of commercial character-education programs are available. Several states provide specific curriculum guides for this area. Sometimes, character is talked about in terms of citizenship. School leaders have an essential role in encouraging the development of positive, productive citizens. Before looking into commercial programs, it is important for the members of the school community to come together to define their own set of values and expectations. Sometimes, a character education can be the core of a school discipline program, though more often it is an essential supplement to it.

Develop Expectations and Make Them Clear

If your school does not have a set of clear behavioral expectations for students, it is a good idea to organize a committee to perform this important task. Give some consideration to the membership of the committee. Certainly, teachers who are widely recognized for having established effective routines for student discipline ought to be included. You might even want to ask one such teacher to be the chair of the group. A parent or two would be good additions to the committee as well, since their perspective is so very essential in formulating behavioral expectations. Whether or not to include students in the group is a matter of individual choice. In some schools, a few students from the upper grades are asked to join the committee. In other situations, student input is elicited by classroom teachers or committee members as the deliberations occur. Figure 10.3 is a sample letter inviting individuals to join such a committee.

Once a school discipline committee is formed, meet on a regular basis. One of the first discussions should be about the development of a philosophy for student behavior. This requires considerable thought about an ideal school climate. (You'll find a sample philosophy for a school discipline plan included in Figure 10.10.)

Subsequent discussions can center on defining a set of appropriate expectations for students to ensure an orderly environment in which each child is free to learn and to develop to his or her best potential. Articles about child development should inform any decisions made by the group. Some of the questions to prompt the deliberations of the group might include the following:

- What are the characteristics of appropriate school behavior?
- What kinds of behaviors would we expect to see in an "ideal" classroom?
- Are the expectations reasonable, given the age level of the children?
- Are the expectations realistic in terms of current behavioral trends?
- How can the expectations be stated in ways that will be clear to the children?
- Do the expectations provide any alternatives for children or flexibility for a diverse student population?
- How can progress toward achieving the expectations be monitored?

Figure 10.3   Sample Invitation to Join a School Discipline Committee

Name of District and School

Date:

Dear Parents/Guardians,

Over the past few months, several parents, teachers, and students have expressed concern about student behavior. The school staff has been discussing ways to promote a more orderly school environment for all youngsters. To achieve this goal, we are forming a committee of teachers and parents to develop a school discipline plan. It is our expectation that the group will chart a set of behavioral expectations for students and then devise a plan for implementing these expectations.

Name of staff member, a second-grade teacher who has 18 years of experience at our school, has agreed to chair this important committee. We have teachers from primary and intermediate grades, special-subject teachers, and cafeteria staff. At this point, we are seeking a few parent volunteers to join our group and help us in our deliberations. Your perspective and views are essential for us to be successful in our work.

We anticipate that the group will meet twice a month, usually at 7:45 AM for about an hour. We will provide a light breakfast. If you can make this commitment and help us in our deliberations, please fill out the tear-off slip below and return it to the office by *date*. Whether you can join our group or not, we will keep you informed about the results of our work. Our joint efforts will certainly enhance our attempts to provide a sensible, appropriate structure that ensures a safe, orderly, and enriched school environment for our youngsters.

Sincerely,

Principal

____

I would like to volunteer to join the school committee that is studying student behavioral expectations.

_______________________________   _______________________________
Parent/Guardian Name   Date

Try to keep the statements simple and easily understood. Four or five statements work best—more than that can lose impact. State student expectations in positive language and avoid a lot of "we do nots" or "we will nots." Before the expectations are "published," student input should be sought. Perhaps a student council can be involved. Teachers can discuss the draft expectations with students in each classroom and return to the committee with some of the suggestions and interpretations offered by the children. Once expectations have been defined, examples of each statement should be included so that students will know the circumstances or contexts of the desired behaviors. A sample set of student expectations for elementary school pupils appears in Figure 10.4.

Figure 10.4 Student Expectations

Name of School and District

STUDENT EXPECTATIONS

1. We take responsibility for learning.

- We arrive at school on time.
- We are prepared for class.
- We demonstrate a serious and responsible attitude in daily work.
- Homework is carefully and thoughtfully completed and on time.

2. We try to settle our differences in a peaceful manner.

- We respect other people's property and personal space.
- We do not physically or verbally fight with other children.
- We do not take anything that does not belong to us.

3. We follow the directions of adults in charge, the first time they are given.

- We look at the speaker.
- We do not talk back to teachers or adults in charge, including substitutes and lunchroom supervisors.

4. We are sensitive to the needs and feelings of others.

- We use appropriate language at all times.
- We do not bully or tease other children.
- We never boo or whistle in the auditorium.
- We are willing to help each other.
- We are friendly and courteous.

5. We are expected to move safely through the school.

- We do not play around in the bathrooms or hallways.
- We do not run in the lunchroom, hallways, or up and down the stairs.

Our school is special.

Let's keep it that way!

Unveil Behavioral Expectations to the Students and the School Community

Once the set of student expectations has been developed, you have to think of how to introduce them to the students and the larger parent community. First of all, the expectations should be printed and perhaps enlarged, pasted onto poster paper, and laminated so that they can be displayed prominently in all classrooms.

The expectations should be discussed in each class by the classroom teacher. The class meeting is an ideal forum for talking about these rules. Teachers should make explicit what each of the expectations means and how they are displayed at school each day. How it is made clear will depend on the age of the students. What does this expectation look like? What does it sound like? These are ways teachers can make expectations explicit, especially for young children. Another interesting way to inform the students about the expectations is to hold an assembly program in which students from a particular grade or class volunteer to do a skit or a "role play" on what each expectation looks like in real situations. For example, two students who are just about to launch into a fight can agree to talk about their differences or seek a teacher's assistance rather than to hit, push, or shove one another. This approach helps the students to take ownership for the expectations and to see how they relate to real situations that children encounter. In some schools, small pamphlets are produced that outline the expectations and how the school discipline plan will be implemented.

Implement a School Discipline Plan

Procedures for implementing and enforcing student expectations are another important task for a school discipline committee. Some of the important issues that must be considered are: How will the expectations be monitored? What are appropriate consequences for students who do not follow the expectations? What is the role of the principal?

Teachers need to consider the important balance of rewards and consequences to help students internalize a new set of school expectations. One way to approach this is to develop a set of forms that can be used to enforce the expectations. The first is a Reminder Notice, which any adult in school may use when an infraction is witnessed. This form is then sent to the classroom teacher. (See Figure 10.5.) The next step, for

Figure 10.5   Reminder Notice

Name of School and District

REMINDER NOTICE

Date: _______________________

Dear Classroom Teacher,

   Today, I noticed _______________________ ignore the following student expectation:

____

Please issue a verbal reminder to the student.

Thank you.

____

Signature

continued difficulty in meeting expectations, would be a Warning Notice. (See Figure 10.6.) This form must be signed by the student, teacher, and parents, and indicates that a Reminder was issued and that a lunchtime or after-school detention may be scheduled. The Detention Notice indicates that a detention has indeed been scheduled. (See Figure 10.7.) To maintain records of reminders, warnings, and detentions, a Student Expectations Management Form can be developed and given to all classroom

---

Figure 10.6 Warning Notice

Name of School and District

WARNING NOTICE

Date: ___________________________

    Following student expectations has been difficult for ___________________ on at least two occasions. Continued problems in this area will result in a lunchtime or an after-school detention.

Expectation:

What I did:

What I can do to prevent this in the future:

Student Signature: ____

Teacher Signature: ____

Comments:

Parent Signature: ____

White: Teacher

Blue: Principal

Figure 10.7 Detention Notice

Name of School and District

DETENTION NOTICE

Date: _______________________________

Dear ________________________________,

   After several reminders and a written warning notice, your child, _________________, has continued to have difficulty in ____.

   As a result, we are scheduling an after-school detention for your child on Thursday, ______________________________ (date), at 3:00 PM.

   You may pick him or her up at the school office at 3:30 PM. Please know that we are always committed to working with your child to provide guidance and assistance in following established student expectations.

   Please sign the form below to indicate that you have seen this notice and discussed this matter with your child.

Sincerely,

____

I have discussed this matter with my child.

☐ My child may walk home at 3:30 PM. (School crossing guards will be on duty.)

☐ I will pick up my child at 3:30 PM.

Parent/Guardian Name	Date

teachers. (See Figure 10.8.) This will help teachers to track incidents and look for patterns with particular children. It also serves as a concrete record for discussions with parents, administrators, and guidance staff.

   Students and parents should be aware of how the plan will be implemented. A sample memo from a principal outlining the steps of the school discipline plan is reproduced in Figure 10.9. A sample letter to parents appears in Figure 10.10. It is clear that this particular system may not be appropriate for all schools, and certainly sensitive teachers will need to keep the needs of individual students in mind when issuing the various forms. Growth or progress in following student expectations should always be kept in mind. Such a system may be antithetical to the beliefs of the staff and a particular school community, but it is presented as one possible alternative for implementing a school discipline plan.

Figure 10.8 Student Expectations Management Form

STUDENT EXPECTATIONS MANAGEMENT FORM
(INSERT NAMES AND DATES)

CODE: R = REMINDER
W = WARNING
D = DETENTION

STUDENT NAME	RULE 1			RULE 2			RULE 3			RULE 4			RULE 5			RULE 6			RULE 7		
	R	W	D	R	W	D	R	W	D	R	W	D	R	W	D	R	W	D	R	W	D

Figure 10.9   Memo Outlining Implementation of School Discipline Plan

Name of School and District

MEMORANDUM

To: All Staff

From: _________________________________, Principal

RE: IMPLEMENTATION OF SCHOOL DISCIPLINE PLAN

I am grateful to all of you for your efforts in developing a school discipline plan. Listed below are the steps we will follow to implement it in our school.

1. We will have an assembly on *date and time* to unveil the plan. Specific teachers, along with their students, will talk about each of the rules in our new list of student expectations.

2. I will send a letter to all parents along with a copy of the new expectations.

3. We have agreed to use specific forms in connection with the plan:

   a. A **REMINDER NOTICE,** which any adult in school may use when an infraction is witnessed. This is sent to the classroom teacher.

   b. A **WARNING NOTICE**, to be signed by student, teacher, and parent (also filed with the principal), indicating that a reminder and a warning have been issued and that a detention may be the next step. If this form is not returned with a parent signature, the classroom teacher will call home.

   c. A **DETENTION NOTICE,** indicating the date for which a detention is scheduled. (This must also have a parent's signature.)

   d. A **STUDENT EXPECTATIONS MANAGEMENT FORM,** for use in maintaining records of when reminders, warnings, and detention notices were issued.

4. We should decide upon a period of time for which a WARNING is in effect. If we do not include a "sunset," then the likelihood that youngsters will receive detention is greatly increased. (We *do* want to recognize growth if infractions are fewer and less frequent.)

5. Along with this plan, we should continue our efforts in the areas of positive reinforcement, lessons on each of the expectations, and activities in cooperative and group living skills.

6. Situations should be referred to me after continued infractions *following* a detention. The sequence of my steps will be as follows:

   a. Talk with the child.

   b. Call the parent(s).

   c. Schedule a conference with the parent(s).

   d. Schedule a child study team meeting.

If we all use our professional judgment and maintain a clear vision of how to implement this plan, we will have an impact. Let's remember that our goal is to help children recognize and improve their behavior.

Figure 10.10 Letter to Parents Outlining School Discipline Plan

Name of School and District

Dear Parents/Guardians,

Over the past several months, a committee of teachers and parents has met to discuss student behavioral expectations at our school. Our first task was to develop a philosophy for such expectations. Our statement reads as follows:

> To foster an educational environment conducive to learning and mutual respect, clear and appropriate standards for student behavior must be established. With trust and positive support, we can work together to help students develop positive interpersonal relationships and respect for one another's right to learn in an orderly school environment. We believe that preventive discipline, through caring and instruction, positive role models, and corrective action when appropriate, will result in a cooperative educational community. It is with these beliefs that we have defined a set of behavioral expectations for our students. They are presented with love to all who are proud to be called a member of our school family.

This statement guided our development of five clear behavioral expectations for students. What emerged is the collective thinking of teachers, students, and parent representatives. Each teacher will discuss these expectations with the children so that they understand their meaning and intent. We also outlined some of the consequences that would result if youngsters ignore these expectations. These include verbal reminders, "time-out" in the classroom or at recess, a call home, after-school detention, or referral to the principal in cases of serious disruption or actions that endanger the safety of others.

We have a wonderful student body at our school, and these guidelines will not replace our continual efforts to work toward the development of conflict-resolution skills, positive values, and the enhancement of self-esteem. Our student mediator program is also helping children to solve problems they may encounter as normal conflicts arise.

Next week you will receive a copy of our new student expectations. Please take the time to review them with your child. We are confident that our efforts will result in a more pleasant school atmosphere for all youngsters.

Sincerely,

Principal

ADVICE FOR TEACHERS ABOUT CLASSROOM DISCIPLINE

In addition to general expectations for student behavior in the school, individual classroom teachers may have their own set of rules for classroom conduct. It is important that these additional (or complementary) expectations not conflict with those of the school at large. Teachers should keep classroom rules simple, easy to understand, and posted for all to see.

Some general guidelines can be provided to teachers in order for them to maintain good discipline:

- Seek opportunities to praise children who exhibit positive behaviors.
- Act from good motives, not from anger or frustration.
- Be consistent in expectations of children.
- Remember that shouting is ineffective and can give the children a sense that the teacher is not in control.
- Be sure reminders and reprimands are reasonable and commensurate with the offense.
- Do not punish an entire group for the misbehavior of one or a few.
- Do not speak negatively about a child within earshot of other children.
- Isolation from the group should be kept to a minimum.
- Avoid "power struggles" or placing children in a "win-lose" situation wherein compliance may be difficult for them in terms of their self-image and peer relationships.

Teachers can use a variety of techniques and strategies to improve discipline in their classrooms, and principals need a repertoire of strategies to give to teachers to help them in this area. The list that follows is by no means exhaustive, but it represents a few ways that other teachers have found successful.

Diagnose Classroom Climate

One way that teachers gain a better understanding of student perception of classroom climate is to conduct a simple diagnosis. This may be done through a classroom meeting in which the teacher states that the agenda will be devoted to a discussion of classroom discipline. What works well? What areas need to be improved? Do students generally respect one another? Do children feel safe and free from ridicule in the classroom? An informal survey may also be distributed to assess classroom climate (see Figure 10.11).

Figure 10.11   Classroom Climate Survey

CLASSROOM CLIMATE SURVEY

Answer each of the questions with the term that best describes how you feel.

N = Never

S = Sometimes

A = Always

1. I feel safe in my classroom.___________
2. I feel that my teacher listens to me when I have a problem. ___________
3. I feel that I am respected in this classroom. ___________
4. I feel that the kids in this class get along with each other. ___________
5. I feel that the kids in this class help each other out. ___________
6. I feel that I can be honest with my classmates. ___________
7. I trust the other kids in the class. ___________
8. I don't have to worry about "put-downs" in this class. ___________
9. I do my part to make this a pleasant classroom. ___________
10. It's "cool" to try your best in our classroom. ___________

Once the results are obtained, they should be reviewed and analyzed. As principal, you may be able to assist teachers in looking over the children's responses and developing a sense of the perceived classroom climate.

Use Active Listening

Active listening is a technique that teachers can use to gain a better understanding of how students feel about particular situations or problems. It works best with children who are verbal and are able to express their concerns. The active listener is empathetic and tries to put him- or herself in the other person's place to understand what that person is saying and feeling. In general, the teacher encourages the child to state his or her point of view. The active listener does not interrupt the child's train of thought. The child's feelings are validated and recognized whether or not the listener agrees with the sentiments expressed. The teacher shows that he or she understands what is being said by both nonverbal and verbal actions. Some of the nonverbal actions include

- leaning in to get closer to the child,
- nodding or making other gestures to show that you are really listening, and
- maintaining eye contact.

Some verbal aspects of active listening include

- clarifying what is being said by asking questions using neutral, noncondemning language;
- restating or paraphrasing what the child is saying and asking if this restatement is accurate;
- summarizing what is being said; and
- helping the child reflect on what he or she has said and helping him or her evaluate feelings.

Active listening is a first step toward understanding a child's problems or conflicts. Sometimes, just having a listener will be a tremendous source of relief to the youngster. It conveys that the teacher is willing to understand and show compassion for the child's point of view.

Be Assertive When Necessary

In certain situations, teachers must be assertive about their own rights and those of the other members of the class. A change in behavior is necessary immediately. When teachers state their expectations clearly and with great conviction, they are being assertive. They convey a very definite, uncompromising tone in their voices. Assertiveness may help when students refuse to talk about a problem or when they repeatedly infringe upon the rights of others. It is also helpful when students have refused to listen to other ways of dealing with problems. For example, if a youngster keeps sticking his leg out to trip others who pass his desk, and the behavior is persistent, then a firm, assertive demand should be given.

When delivering a message assertively, the teacher should look directly at the child and speak in a clear, firm voice. The teacher should state what the child did in very clear, unambiguous language and then state what needs to happen and why. It is best to avoid "what ifs" and simply state the expectation with such conviction that the child perceives that there is no option but to comply. Sometimes, the teacher will have to repeat the expectation more than once to ensure that it was heard and internalized.

Behavior Modification

Behavior modification stems from the belief that we can shape children's behavior based on a preestablished system of rewards and punishments. The premise is that actions can be altered because the child wants something that is valuable. That something can be praise, positive letters sent to parents, opportunities for free time, or some special privilege at school or at home. It is clear that the goal is to change the behavior that is objectionable.

The child and his or her parents should be involved in developing the plan. Usually, two or three behaviors are defined. They might be bringing homework to school, arriving in the classroom on time, or coming to school with the appropriate books and materials. Then, the student and teacher discuss a list of rewards that he or she would like to work toward. A certain point value is sometimes assigned to each positive behavior. At the end of each day, the teacher records the extent to which the child achieved the desired behavior. Whether the teacher, the principal, or the parent provides the reward can be decided upon when the system is set up. Some examples might be that if a child earns 25 points, the parent will take the child out for an ice-cream treat or the child will be the office messenger for a day. The important thing is that the rewards must be meaningful to the child; otherwise, he or she will not want to work toward them.

Behavior modification programs should be assessed regularly. Is the system working? If teacher, parent, or student forgets to keep records, or shows disinterest in the agreement, it is likely to fall apart. Behavior modification programs require commitment, vigilance, and determination.

Student Behavior Contracts

Student contracts have some similarities to behavior modification programs, but the key feature here is the development of a written agreement with the student of what behaviors are to be achieved and how they will be recognized. First, the teacher and student should be willing to work on developing a contract and then defining the specific behaviors that will be covered by it. The student must be involved in drawing up the agreement. The rules that will be followed are clarified and stated in clear, simple language. Consequences, not punishments, for not living up to the agreement are often included in the contract. A reward should be included for successful completion of the contract. A date when follow-up will occur is an important aspect of the contract. The student, teacher, and the parent sign the contract. A sample student contract appears in Figure 10.12.

The various techniques discussed in this section will not work equally well for all teachers in all situations. For example, some professionals are simply not comfortable with behavior modification approaches, and despite their general success, this approach will not work without the teacher's commitment. Each teacher, school, and principal needs to have a variety of strategies that can be used to help students exhibit responsible behaviors. There is no one best solution for all situations. What is important, though, is to keep trying to solve problems. If one approach does not work, move on to another.

Figure 10.12 Student Contract

MY STUDENT CONTRACT

I, _________________________________ (name of student), will do the following:

1. ____

2. ____

3. ____

If I do accomplish the above by _____________________ (date), then, _____________.

If I do accomplish the above by _____________________ (date), then, _____________.

Agreed to by:

Student Signature: _________________________________   **Date:** ___________

Teacher Signature: _________________________________   **Date:** ___________

Parent Signature: _________________________________   **Date:** ___________

THE PRINCIPAL'S ROLE IN THE SCHOOL DISCIPLINE PROGRAM

Some teachers wrongly assume that the principal *is* the school discipline program. The principal helps to establish discipline policies and procedures but should not be expected to handle all of the school's discipline problems. The principal should be thought of as a "last resort" after other alternatives have been exhausted. The school discipline plan should definitely include the principal—but only as part of a progressive system in which teachers work with children, contact parents, and set up individual plans, before referring students to the principal. If the office of the principal is abused, our impact is weakened. Also, the principal cannot possibly see each child who commits an infraction. Classroom teachers can refer students to a principal after a pattern is detected. Of course, severe incidents should always come to your attention. It is essential that every staff member knows and understands his or her role in the school's discipline policy and procedures.

There are times, however, when students can be referred immediately to the principal. This should be specified in the school's discipline plan or policy. For example, in some schools, theft of property, vandalism, possession of a knife, or physical fighting will result in a visit to the principal after the teacher has had a chance to sort out some of the initial details. These matters should be worked out in advance so that everyone—teachers, students, and parents—is aware of the procedures. That being said, the principal does have a distinct role in maintaining student discipline. Following are some key areas and suggestions.

Be Visible

If you are seen in the school hallways, cafeteria, and on the playground, children recognize that you are around and involved in the day-to-day life of the school. The principal "knows the rules" and can enforce them, providing praise and admonition, as incidents are noted. Principals can note classes that are traveling through the halls in an orderly fashion and provide positive reinforcement. At assembly programs, principals can announce the positive behavior of individuals or groups.

Be a Facilitator for Teachers

Principals can help teachers develop their own procedures for effective classroom discipline. You can assist in diagnosing student problems and charting strategies and plans for dealing with disruptive students. By asking appropriate, focused questions, you can lead teachers to formulate their own strategies and plans. Some important questions include the following:

- Are classroom rules specified, posted, and clear to the students?
- Are students involved in defining classroom rules and appropriate consequences?
- Are rewards and consequences reasonable and likely to result in reinforcing the desired behaviors?
- Is the classroom environment orderly and inviting?
- Is the taught curriculum engaging, relevant, and at an appropriate level for the students?
- Are classroom materials and furniture arrangement conducive to student cooperation and interaction?
- Are limits reviewed periodically?
- Is follow-through consistent and predictable?
- Is the teacher aware of and sensitive to the individual needs of the youngsters in the class?
- Is communication with parents comfortable, direct, and open?
- Is the teacher familiar with developmentally appropriate expectations for social behavior?

Another way to facilitate the development of effective teacher discipline practices is to pair inexperienced teachers with more seasoned ones who are recognized for their ability to enforce positive disciplinary procedures. A new teacher's mentor can make this an area of focus if needed. Sometimes, teachers work together in study groups to read articles, talk about effective strategies, and share experiences. As principal, you can suggest the formation of such a group and provide support in terms of resources, refreshments, and perhaps in-service credit for such pursuits.

When you notice effective techniques, parent communication devices, contracts, motivational techniques, rewards, or innovative consequences, you can publish them in faculty bulletins or newsletters. This fosters sharing and the celebration of successes among staff members.

Be a Positive Role Model

As principal, you cannot miss opportunities to be a positive role model. Praise for effective behavior and a clear sense of the school's behavioral expectations should always be forthcoming. When dealing with disruptive children, be firm, clear, and direct, but not angry. If teachers and other children witness you losing your temper, it signals that this kind of behavior is acceptable. Make it clear that you do not approve of objectionable behavior, but you accept the child as a child. When you deliver admonitions for misbehavior at lunchtime, recess, or before or after school, you should always let the classroom teacher know about what you have said and done. When all parties communicate about a student's misbehavior, children get the message that all of the adults are acting in concert and that everyone knows what is happening.

Act as a model of treating all children and adults with dignity and respect. This will be noticed, and it sends the message that this school is a place where all people are accepted and valued but still held accountable for appropriate behavior.

Secure Resources to Help Teachers

Resources are often available within a school to assist teachers in establishing a classroom discipline plan, and one of the roles you can fill is to secure these important resources. Sometimes, the resources are for a commercial program or consultants. Guidance counselors, if available, can be particularly helpful to teachers and students. Often, they know how to assist in the formulation of behavior modification plans and in the development of strategies to promote effective communication within a classroom. They may also suggest ways to maintain anecdotal records in order to help teachers recognize patterns that may predict the circumstances that trigger volatile situations or behavioral problems.

A school social worker can be of invaluable assistance in helping teachers to understand complex family structures and some of the tensions and anxieties that children from dysfunctional families may exhibit. Social workers can help teachers to become more compassionate and skillful in their interactions with families. School psychologists can also provide assistance to teachers. In some school systems, teachers must go through the office of the principal to contact such support professionals, and this is where the principal has the opportunity to be a resource provider.

School leaders and school support personnel have access to outside agencies. Some such agencies are free and provide child protective services; others charge fees but might have a sliding scale so most families can afford to take advantage of the professional help that is offered. As principal, you should maintain a file of community resources, agencies, and private practitioners that may be provided to parents who request information about such services. The school psychologist and/or social worker are good resources for this information.

Deal Directly With Students

There are, of course, times when the principal must deal directly with students who are disruptive. In larger schools, principals require teachers to fill out a referral form so that they will be knowledgeable about the offense when they meet with the student (see Figure 10.13). How often have we found ourselves asking a child why he was sent to the principal's office only to find that the youngster replies, "I don't know," or learn that his version of the offense is very different from the teacher's?

As a school leader, you should have a clearly established, predictable way of how you deal with children who are referred to you. Teachers want to know what they can expect when they send a child to see you. One system that has proven quite effective is the card

Figure 10.13	Discipline Referral Form

Name of School and District

DISCIPLINE REFERRAL FORM

Student Name: ___________________________________ Date: ______________

Teacher: ___________________________________ Grade: ______________

Nature of Incident:

Prior Actions Taken by Teacher:

Principal Action:

Parent(s) Notified: ☐ Yes   ☐ No

Parent Response:

Follow-Up:

Principal Signature: ___________________________ Date: ______________

box; a file box on your desk can have student names placed on index cards in alphabetical order. An alternative arrangement might be to keep a loose-leaf binder with a page in it for each child. A small photo of the student might be placed at the top of each page. The first time a child is referred to you, a dated notation of the circumstances is recorded on the child's card, and the youngster is asked to complete a written behavior incident report (see Figure 10.14). After the child writes the report, you discuss the infraction to make sure that the child understands what about her behavior was objectionable. The first referral is considered a "warning"; make it clear that after the second referral, the youngster's parents will be called. After a child is referred to you a third time, the parents or guardians are called to school for a conference. This system is predictable to students, and teachers appreciate knowing that the principal is using a systematic, publicly understood approach. Of course, principals have to "filter" the infractions that children are sent for. Some teachers will refer children for relatively minor infractions; others never refer children to the principal's office. There should be some discussion among the staff regarding the circumstances under which a child will be sent to the principal—for example, physical fighting, destruction of property, or the third time a particular published student expectation is ignored or disobeyed. (The three notices discussed earlier in this chapter should be helpful in the process.) You should be considered the last resort, and when you do see students, one of the main purposes should be to help students understand appropriate behavior and how they might work toward exhibiting these desirable actions.

| Figure 10.14 | Behavior Incident Report |

Name of School and District

BEHAVIOR INCIDENT REPORT

This is what I did:

This is what I could have done to avoid this:

This is what I will do in the future:

Student Signature: ____   **Date:** _________________

Deal With the Teacher Who Abuses the Office of the Principal

In practically every school, a few teachers will be too quick to refer students to the principal. They may feel that discipline problems are the domain of the principal, or they may be legitimately overwhelmed and unable to cope. It is probably not wise to refuse to see students sent by such teachers, but at the same time, for the teacher's sake (and your own), it is best to set a meeting with the teacher and help to establish ground rules for when students are to be referred to you. It is quite possible that the teacher has not thought through a classroom discipline plan and may need guidance. Organizational techniques may need to be reviewed and reinforced. Look at classroom structures. Is the classroom environment orderly? Are regular routines established? Are the students aware of behavioral expectations and the consequences for not following them? This is a fine opportunity to share strategies, consider alternatives, and tailor a plan suited to the teacher's own instructional style.

Try to convince the teacher that overreliance on referrals of students to the principal undermines his or her own ability to secure a disciplined environment. If it is perceived that an experienced teacher is simply using the principal to avoid dealing with issues that are clearly within his domain, an open, frank conversation about the situation is in order. Make it clear that the teacher is overusing the office of the principal, and that if students are referred for petty matters, you may not be in the position to support the teacher when it is essential. Another strategy is to meet with the teacher and review the reasons for each referral after it occurs. The teacher may soon come to realize that it might be best to deal with minor infractions without seeking your intervention.

THE IMPORTANCE OF PARENT COMMUNICATION

When dealing with parents of students who present discipline problems, always start with the premise that the parents are willing to help and want their children to have satisfying school experiences. Some teachers and principals feel that student behavior in school can best be dealt with in school, but the role and assistance of parents should never be underestimated. If you have concerns about a youngster's behavior, making contact with the child's parents is vital. She or he may not have been aware that the child was having difficulty with school behavior. Very often, the cooperation and communication between home and school is all that is needed to help children become more aware of expectations. If the parents are cooperative, the child realizes, at the very least, that parents and teachers are working together for her best interests. Once parents are engaged, make sure to keep them informed of trends and progress (or the lack of it) in their child's behavior. At a meeting, state explicitly when you will report on the status of the student's behavior. If it is daily, a simple device, the Daily School Progress Report, is an effective communication tool that lets a parent see, at a glance, how the child performed in school each day (see Figure 10.15). The teacher maintains

Figure 10.15 Daily School Progress Report

Name of School and District

DAILY SCHOOL PROGRESS REPORT

Date: _______________________

Student's name: _______________________________ Class: _______________________________

Rating Key: **O** = Outstanding; **S** = Satisfactory; **I** = Improvement Needed; **U** = Unsatisfactory

	RATING
Behavior	
Completion of Assignments	
Cooperation With Others	
Reports From Special Teachers:	
Physical Education	
Music	
Art	
Library	
Technology	

Teacher Comments:

Teacher Signature: _______________________________ **Date:** _____________

Parent Comments:

Parent Signature: _______________________________ **Date:** _____________

a batch of these forms and gives one to the child each day. The child presents the report to the parent after school, and the parent must sign it to indicate that it was reviewed. Opportunities for comments are provided. Parents and teachers often feel that such communications can help children understand expectations and be aware of the concerted efforts of parents and teachers. These reports may also be linked to a system of rewards and consequences.

ALTERNATIVES IN A SCHOOL DISCIPLINE PROGRAM

In addition to the measures covered so far in this chapter, you may have occasion to consider some of the following steps.

Student Mediation

Teachers and principals in schools all over the world are organizing student mediation programs. In such initiatives, older students (even fourth, fifth, and sixth graders) are trained in the techniques of conflict resolution and they offer their services to help other youngsters solve disputes and problems. Student mediators need expert training if they are to be effective. There are several organizations that can help schools initiate peer mediation programs.

There are some basic commonalities in student mediation programs. Usually, two mediators work with two disputants. Some of the steps of mediation may be summarized as follows:

Starting

1. Introduce yourselves as mediators.

2. Ask those in conflict if they would like a mediator to help them solve the problem.

3. Find a quiet spot to hold the mediation.

4. Ask for agreement on the following:
   - Agree to solve the problem
   - Agree not to put down the other person
   - Agree to let the other person finish talking

Listening

5. Ask one person to begin describing what happened.

6. Paraphrase what the first person said using active listening techniques.

7. Let the first person finish telling what happened and how he or she feels.

8. Ask the second person to describe what happened and how he or she feels.

9. Paraphrase again.

10. Ask the disputants to paraphrase each other's point of view.

Finding Solutions

11. Ask each person to state what he or she could have done differently.

12. Ask each person what he or she could do right now to make the situation better.

Choosing Solutions

13. Help both persons find a solution that neither objects to.

14. Congratulate both students on a successful mediation.

15. Fill out a Mediation Report Form.

When two students request a mediation, or a teacher or another staff member suggests that two students might benefit from a mediation, they can fill out a Mediation Request Form (see Figure 10.16). This form is then given to the faculty advisor for student mediation, who will then schedule the mediation. Once the mediation is completed, the mediators complete a Mediation Report Form (see Figure 10.17), which is then duplicated and given to each of the students in the conflict, their teachers, and the faculty advisor.

Developing a student mediation program requires some initial financial resources (basically for training) and a faculty advisor. In some schools, the faculty advisor works under the same terms and conditions (voluntary or compensated) as a student council advisor. Developing a student mediation program can indeed become one of the projects initiated by a student council.

Figure 10.16   Mediation Request Form

Name of School and District

MEDIATION REQUEST FORM

Students' names and classes:

Describe the conflict:

Please place this request form in the mailbox of the Student Mediator Faculty Advisor. A mediation will be scheduled as soon as possible.

                              Thank you.

  (Do Not Write Below This Line)

____

A mediation has been scheduled for _________________ and ___________________

Date: ___________________   **Time:** ___________________

Mediators: _______________________________ and ___________________________

Location: ____

Figure 10.17 Mediation Report Form

Name of School and District

MEDIATION REPORT FORM

Students' names:

Mediators' names:

How did you find out about the conflict?

_________________ Students _______________ Teacher _______________ Aide

_______________ Principal _____________ Yourself ____________ Referral Form

What was the conflict about?

Was the conflict resolved? ________ Yes ________ No

Resolution:

Student One agrees to:

Student Two agrees to:

Signature: ____ (Student One)

Signature: ____ (Student Two)

Mediators' Signatures: ____

Date: ________________

Time-Out

When children are excited or agitated, they may simply need some quiet time away from a frustrating situation. A time-out is an effective alternative for students who need to be removed from a large group. It should be explained to the child that this is not necessarily a punishment, but rather an opportunity to "cool down" and become ready to talk about a particular situation. Time-outs should never be unsupervised. In large schools, where guidance counselors may be employed, the counselor's office may be the best place for the child to stay. Other places for a time-out may be the nurse's office, the school's main office, and, of course, the principal's office. In some cases, the classroom itself may accommodate time-out space.

In-School Suspension

In-school suspensions are generally considered a more serious consequence than a time-out. Time-outs are often given spontaneously and for a relatively short duration. An in-school suspension, on the other hand, is usually planned in advance and is a consequence of a major infraction of school rules or student expectations. Parents should be notified in writing about in-school suspensions, and in many schools, these incidents are recorded on the child's record card or a behavioral incident chart.

During an in-school suspension, the child should be given meaningful assignments to complete. Of course, supervision must be arranged. This oversight can be similar to that provided during time-outs, but the period of supervision will naturally be longer, since the duration of an in-school suspension is usually for an entire school day.

Out-of-School Suspension

A formal suspension should be considered a last resort when all other means to help children develop better behavioral practices have failed. Each school district—and perhaps even the state—will have rules that govern how formal suspensions are to be dealt with. Most often, a suspension begins with parent notification. A meeting takes place in which the child and parent are apprised of the nature of the offense. Documentation is usually presented and notes about the patterns of the student's behaviors are reviewed. Copies of any letters previously sent to the parents are also on hand. It is a matter of the child's due process rights that he or she hears the charges leveled and is given an opportunity to respond to them. A second objective of the presuspension hearing is to work out a plan for improvement including specific behavioral details and the monitoring actions to be employed. Parent, child, teacher, and principal should work together to devise strategies aimed at behavioral improvement.

Out-of-school suspensions are often very inconvenient for parents, especially in the case of single parents or homes in which both parents work. Principals often have to weigh the benefits of suspension against the likelihood that the child may be at home— or worse yet, on the streets—unsupervised. Usually, the duration of a suspension is a day or two. Many school districts and states have a limit of five days for formal suspensions. Suspensions are sometimes helpful in getting the attention of parents or guardians in order to secure their help in student behavioral plans.

Discipline and Special-Education Students

There may be a different set of rules that apply with regard to discipline of special-education students. If a youngster's behavior is directly related to his or her disabling condition, the standard disciplinary procedure may be preempted by statements or clauses in the child's IEP (Individualized Education Program). In such situations, it is best to work collaboratively with the child's case manager to work out a discipline plan that includes appropriate expectations and consequences.

The school leader plays a key role in the development and implementation of a school discipline plan. Clearly, this does not mean that the principal is the school's sole disciplinarian. Helping teachers become effective managers of student behavior is one of the great challenges of the principalship. It can also be one of the most rewarding activities you can accomplish when you witness growth on the part of staff members, and see a true sense of community emerge from efforts to create an orderly, engaging, and stimulating educational climate in the school.

11

Improving Your School's Professional Development Program

Theongoing development and improvement of employees' professional skills is a necessary aspect of the health of any organization. In education, we tend to do less in this area than do those in American industry. In some large corporations, 10% to 20% of staff budgets are devoted to continued training and education for its employees. How many school budgets can boast even 5% of an allocation for staff development? Unfortunately, the number is few indeed—and this in a profession where our mission is so important.

In large school districts, the professional development program may be centralized, with individual schools having some say in the needs and priorities of the local staff. In other situations, the staff development program is truly up to the individual principal and faculty. In any case, the program must be carefully thought out and tailored to both individual and broader educational needs.

THE NEED FOR ONGOING PROFESSIONAL DEVELOPMENT

The continuing education of a school staff is essential to its provision of a quality instructional program. Many situations call for a staff development program designed for a specific purpose. These include the following:

Note: All forms, letters, and checklists included in this chapter can be found at corwin.com/elementary survivalkit.

- *A New Curriculum:* When a new curriculum or instructional sequence is adopted, teachers will require some familiarity and training with the new material. Sometimes, background knowledge is necessary; at other times, specific approaches and procedures must be learned.
- *Research and New Insights in Teaching and Learning:* When research points the way to new and clear directions for teaching, educators must learn more about this information and the implications for their instructional practices. For example, new discoveries in the area of brain research have pointed the way toward distinct changes in the way teachers should engage children in learning. The Web and electronic databases have made it easier to access current literature in the field of education.
- *New Methods of Instruction:* When the cooperative learning approach was first broadly recommended in classrooms, teachers needed to learn more about this method and how to apply it accurately and with careful planning in their own situations.
- *Basic Instructional Practice:* Sad as it may seem, some teachers do not enter the workforce with sufficient background in the areas of planning, classroom management, and assessment of learning. Particularly for new teachers, induction programs in which they learn some of the basics of running an effective classroom is an important part of a professional development program.
- *Advances in Technology:* Rapid changes and advances in the area of technology have also determined a specific teacher training need. Some teachers are quite adept at picking up new technologies; others need more "hand-holding" and direct assistance in order to incorporate new developments in technology into their classroom practice.

Assisting teachers in the development of individual growth plans and meeting the responsibilities of a world-class education require ongoing, carefully delivered staff development programs. Many components of a professional development program are detailed later in this chapter. Much staff development takes place on a daily basis, but in order to improve instruction, which is, after all, one of the main reasons to help teachers achieve their fullest potential, the program for professional growth must be broad and multifaceted, taking into account the needs and characteristics of the adult learner.

HOW TO BEGIN: CONDUCTING A STAFF DEVELOPMENT NEEDS ASSESSMENT

As in any major school initiative, it is important to plan carefully. One of the first steps in designing a staff development program is to determine the needs and skills of the practitioners and compare these to school and district priorities and goals. A good way to acquire this information is to conduct a needs assessment for staff development; you can gather data on the perceived needs of the staff, the skills the individuals feel they already possess, areas in which they would like to have more opportunity to grow, and any special interests or talents that individual staff members already possess and might be willing to pass along to others.

It is best to involve staff members in the design of the needs assessment and also in analyzing the data that are collected. This will help build commitment and broaden the support for the staff development program that is proposed as a result of the survey. Figure 11.1 is a sample of a diagnostic staff development questionnaire that can be used to conduct a needs assessment. The form and its contents can easily be adapted to any

Figure 11.1 Sample of a Diagnostic Staff Development Needs Assessment

STAFF DEVELOPMENT SELF-ASSESSMENT SURVEY

A committee of teachers and administrators is in the process of designing a comprehensive staff development plan for our school. As a part of this process, your input in answering the questionnaire below will help us develop a program that will best suit the needs of all staff.

	Disagree	Somewhat Disagree	Strongly Agree	Agree	Don't Know
1. Staff development activities result in changes in classroom practice for most teachers.	☐	☐	☐	☐	☐
2. Professional development is highly valued by all members of the educational community.	☐	☐	☐	☐	☐
3. Sufficient time for planning and learning exists during the school day.	☐	☐	☐	☐	☐
4. Staff development activities in our school are generally collaborative and respectful.	☐	☐	☐	☐	☐
5. The staff recognizes the need to grow professionally.	☐	☐	☐	☐	☐
6. The impact upon students of new knowledge and skills gained by staff is regularly assessed.	☐	☐	☐	☐	☐
7. Staff members regularly reflect on their own performance.	☐	☐	☐	☐	☐
8. The results of educational research are valuable for program and practice improvement.	☐	☐	☐	☐	☐

(Continued)

Figure 11.1 (Continued)

	Disagree	Somewhat Disagree	Strongly Agree	Agree	Don't Know
9. The staff works collaboratively and uses effective interpersonal skills when working together.	☐	☐	☐	☐	☐
10. Teachers' classroom management strategies increase academic learning time.	☐	☐	☐	☐	☐
11. Teachers use strategies that promote high expectations for all students.	☐	☐	☐	☐	☐
12. Student assessment focuses on what students actually know and can do in relevant contexts.	☐	☐	☐	☐	☐
13. The staff has the knowledge and skills required to facilitate the learning of special-needs students.	☐	☐	☐	☐	☐
14. The staff has the knowledge and skills required to facilitate the learning of ELL students.	☐	☐	☐	☐	☐
15. Ongoing opportunities for technology training exist for all staff.	☐	☐	☐	☐	☐

local situation. It can be used to gather information about teachers' feelings and opinions about the value of staff development in general. The more specific questionnaire that appears in Figure 11.2 can be used to determine individual needs and talents or skills. Looking at these two forms, it is clear that they are both useful in the design of a staff development program, yet they serve very distinct purposes.

Figure 11.2	Sample of a Survey to Determine Individual Staff Development Needs and Skills

STAFF DEVELOPMENT QUESTIONNAIRE

1. Considering our school goals in the areas of assessment, technological applications, and integrated learning, are there specific areas within these goals that you would like to explore this year and for which you feel you would benefit from involvement in staff development activities?

2. What kinds of activities (workshops, collaborative meetings, planning time, in-the-classroom support, formal coursework, etc.) do you feel would most benefit you in your support of the school goals?

3. Are there other areas in which you are interested, i.e., classroom management, specific projects, curriculum materials, idea exchanges, discussion groups, etc.?

4. Are there areas in which you have been working and in which you have developed proficiency to be a leader and/or resource for other teachers in the school or district?

Name: ____ **Date:** ________________

Once information from a needs assessment survey is collected, you should meet with a group of teachers to analyze the data. What are the prevailing attitudes about staff development? Do teachers seem to have faith in the benefit of professional growth activities? Do they feel that there is sufficient time and will to develop instructional skills? Do they feel that the professionals in the school work collaboratively? What are the needs and strengths of the professional staff? The answers to these questions will reveal a great deal about where to begin in designing a staff development program.

School leaders require teachers to meet the needs of their students by differentiating instruction. A needs assessment allows principals to "walk the talk" and design a differentiated staff development program so that teachers at varied stages in their careers benefit from different types of professional development. In addition, staff members require a variety of delivery methods for professional development. Some teachers are able to attend after-school offerings; others can take advantage of summer courses, while another group can attend professional development programs only within the regular school day.

STAFF DEVELOPMENT AND BEHAVIORAL CHANGE

Some of the main goals in any staff development program are to provide teachers with new skills, to change instructional behaviors, and to develop new views about the teaching-learning process. With a needs assessment completed and analyzed, it is then possible to plan a staff development program based upon local issues and requirements. In developing such plans, it is essential to keep in mind the unique characteristics of adult learners and how to effect behavioral changes.

First of all, it is important to set a context for change. All stakeholders should feel that they have a voice and can contribute true input into the planning of the program in which they will participate. It may be necessary to spend some time and energy to convince staff members of the need for change. Most people are not willing to change unless they see reasons for the change—reasons that directly affect them. How will new approaches help the professionals to meet their goals or become more effective teachers? Sometimes, it is convenient to rely on a state mandate or a newly adopted curriculum, but this attitude is usually not sufficient to bring about true behavioral change. Teachers must see how their involvement in a staff development program will help them to become more effective as evidenced by improved student results. Involving teachers in the study of important issues that face the school or school district can often help them see the need to improve skills and competencies. This is clearly the case in the area of technology. Many teachers originally resisted the trend to incorporate computers into their classrooms, but once they saw how these tools would assist their performance and in some ways ease and help organize their jobs, they became more willing to learn more about technology in general.

Programs for the adult learner have important distinctions from planning instruction for children. In devising programs to enhance the professional skills of teachers, a few factors must be considered, including the following:

- Teachers like to gain a sense of immediate application of their new learning. This is why "learn tonight, teach tomorrow" workshops tend to be so popular.
- Many teachers tend to be skeptical about university-based research. They are more responsive to classroom-based research projects in which they can see immediate results in their pupils.
- Many teachers are somewhat resistant to change. They often need to be helped to see that change is invigorating, refreshing, and nonthreatening.
- Adult learners like to think of themselves as "colearners." Rather than set up a workshop leader as "the expert," make your teachers feel that all participants are learners.
- Teachers like to see follow-through on their new learnings. The "one-shot deal" workshop has generally been considered ineffective. Ongoing support and discussion with respect to new approaches is necessary.
- New learnings are reinforced if professionals practice and share.
- Expect and deal with conflict, which is often inevitable, in the change process.
- Adult learning should be viewed as a part of a cycle of ongoing improvement and continuous professional development.

In planning staff development programs, principals should consider all ideas that are offered and realize that there are many needs that have to be addressed. Some of these include introducing and gaining background knowledge on new subject matter, improving general instructional skills, finding out about and practicing new techniques and strategies, and developing skills for collaboration.

THE PRINCIPAL'S ROLE IN DEVISING A STAFF DEVELOPMENT PROGRAM

As school leaders, we do not have to conduct the staff development program, but we do have an important role in organizing the effort. We must know what the needs are and how to secure the appropriate resources to meet those needs. The following areas are well within the principal's role to plan and implement a staff development program in an elementary school.

Organize the Effort

As instructional leaders of the school, principals have to organize the effort for beginning a staff development program. We must see beyond the mundane duties that consume the time of all of us and look toward the general health of the organization. We can get through each day by moving the paper from the "in" box to the "out" box and feel a sense of accomplishment, but unless we have the vision for the development of long-range goals and work with staff to devise a program to achieve that vision, the school will not move forward. We must involve staff in the planning and implementation of a professional development program, but we cannot conduct it ourselves; we simply (or not so simply) must lead the effort.

Survey Needs and Skills

Surveying staff needs and talents was dealt with previously in this chapter, but it is important to ensure that such a needs assessment takes place. Again, work with staff to develop the needs assessment, to analyze the results, and to plan programs and opportunities to meet the perceived needs. As a school leader, you should also encourage staff with special skills and talents to work with colleagues and share their expertise. Very often, local solutions, created by teachers working cooperatively, have great promise and power for promoting the overall growth of individuals in the entire school.

Secure Appropriate Resources

As principal, you are in a good position to know what resources are available to support staff development efforts. Educational consultants, teachers in the school district or other districts, university connections, state education department officials, and individuals from local businesses, industries, or consortiums can all be helpful with different aspects of the professional improvement program. Establishing these relationships takes time, but the results are well worth the effort. You never know where or when an excellent resource will next emerge. For example, in a school where students were studying the role of famous scientists in terms of their discoveries and historical context, a local pharmaceutical firm organized a cadre of research associates to come to the school and talk with the children about important scientific discoveries and the people behind them. Had the principal not bothered to go out into the community and work on securing diverse resources, this highly successful program might never have occurred.

Give Demonstration Lessons

When an innovation or specific technique is introduced to the staff, principals can be most helpful by demonstrating the use of the strategy or approach in the classroom. Rather than putting on a show for the teacher, though, it is best to involve the teacher in the planning of the lesson and in assessing its impact. Rolling up your sleeves and teaching in classrooms is appreciated by most teachers and demonstrates in a very concrete sense that you value and support the new practice or innovation.

Once you have demonstrated a new skill or approach, you can ask the teacher to use it on her own and then sit in on the teacher's demonstration and provide coaching and advice. When the trust level is high, teachers and administrators will both benefit from working together in this way.

Encourage Participation in Staff Development Activities

Principals have a key role in encouraging staff to participate in professional development activities. If the principal does not support the program, this attitude will be easily sensed by the staff. On the other hand, if principals attend workshops, seminars, and in-service courses along with teachers, their support is clear. Some teachers may need individual encouragement to become involved in professional development activities.

You can also support the growth effort by working with teachers to set professional improvement goals that lead to involvement in staff development opportunities. You can encourage (and sometimes assign) teachers to join curriculum committees, study groups, and teacher networks and to enroll in graduate courses that will help improve their skills and practices.

Become Involved in Professional Organizations

By joining professional organizations, you can gain a wealth of information about staff development practices and opportunities that can be brought to the school. Conferences, institutes, conventions, and regional workshops can all be used to bring new ideas to the school staff. Through membership in professional organizations, you can network with colleagues who can share triumphs, successes, and practices and programs that have promoted the improvement of staff development opportunities.

Share Professional Literature With the Staff

Through regular reading of relevant journals and professional magazines, we gain important information about trends, research, and successful practices worth replicating in our schools. Once you are aware of the needs and interests of individual staff members, a journal or copy of an article (if permitted) can be routed to those teachers who you feel would most benefit from or enjoy the article. Most teachers would be happy to know that you care enough about them and have taken the time to know about their interests to pass along articles that will foster their professional growth. There are, of course, times when a single article will be of interest and is important enough to distribute to an entire staff—especially if it deals with a major school initiative or goal. When literature is passed along to all teachers in a school, an opportunity should be provided to discuss the article and its implications for the school—perhaps at a faculty or study-group meeting. Whether you publish a weekly "staff news" electronically or on paper, an interesting, relevant research abstract can be attached. This creates a culture of learning within the school that communicates that educators are lifelong learners.

Be a Model of Lifelong Learning

As in most areas of professional behavior, the way that we act as school leaders sets the tone for the entire staff. If we show interest in school-based research and professional literature, this will send an important message about our own value system to the staff. If we discuss professional issues, we convey the fact that this is a place where the examination and improvement of instruction is a priority. Teachers must view us as intensely interested in the educative process and always willing to learn and grow in our own skills as instructional leaders. The authors have been in schools where the principal, while attending a professional development conference, has a sign on the office door saying, "Out Learning." If principals model lifelong learning, it will become an established norm in the school.

It is important to mention here that a school leader's own learning is critical and can be sustained and nourished through membership in professional organizations such as the Association for Supervision and Curriculum Development (ASCD), the National Association for Elementary School Principals (NAESP), and the National Staff Development Council (NSDC). Organizations such as these keep us well informed about what is under discussion in education at the national level.

Create Professional Learning Communities

Establishing learning as a norm within your school can foster the development of professional learning communities. The development and sustenance of these learning communities is well documented in the work of Peter Senge[1] and Richard Dufour.[2] In schools, the term *professional learning community* refers to a group of individuals working collaboratively to ensure and enhance student achievement. Both the individual members of the learning community and the group share their learning, examine data and research, and apply it to the school setting for an expressed purpose. For example, a learning community may work to infuse a school with technology. In a "learning organization," each staff member should be part of a learning community that encourages reflective practice, focuses on results, and works toward a shared vision of student success.

Effective professional development also resides in the schedule the principal creates. Scheduling common planning time for grade-level members promotes a discussion of ideas and opportunities to share successes, challenges, and best practices.

IMPLEMENTING AN EFFECTIVE
STAFF DEVELOPMENT PROGRAM

A well-planned staff development program should emanate from the active involvement of the school staff, district personnel, and perhaps outside consultants. Several elements ought to be part of the school's professional development plan, and any such effort should begin with a definition of beliefs, or the philosophy of the staff improvement program.

Defining Purpose and Intent

As in any important school initiative, it is best to begin by working together to achieve consensus about the purpose and intent of the staff development program. Is the goal to help each individual achieve his or her personal goals? Is the program focused on the achievement of district goals? Is the acquisition of specific skills the intent of the program? Such questions need to be considered and well thought out. Some schools or school districts develop a "credo" or belief statement about the professional development program. A sample of a staff development credo appears in Figure 11.3.

Figure 11.3   Sample Staff Development Credo

Name of School District

STAFF DEVELOPMENT CREDO

We believe that, as members of the *Name of District* school community, we are professionals and must continually refine our knowledge and skills to promote learning. Each staff member is a practical researcher grappling with the complex issues of teaching and learning. We need to take the time to be reflective about our work in order to make effective decisions about what to do and why.

Therefore, the *Name of District* Staff Development Model is built upon the following beliefs:

- The school district's vision, mission, and goals shape and influence professional development activities.
- All professional initiatives are marked by collegiality and collaboration.
- Educators are part of a professional community that encourages experimentation in all disciplines and provides opportunities to take risks, refine practices, implement changes, and internalize concepts.
- Educators enhance, increase, and modify their knowledge of theory and practice by actively participating in professional organizations and/or by seeking out other professional growth activities.
- Educators are active in setting goals for their own professional growth and selecting those activities best suited to achieve these goals.
- Professional growth incorporates time for learning, reflection, and sharing among colleagues.
- Professional development activities need to be assessed on an ongoing basis so that the program can be adapted to meet identified needs.
- Staff development initiatives are supported through collaborative planning, effective evaluation processes, and adequate budgetary support.

Scope of the Staff Development Program

A comprehensive staff development program fulfills many functions simultaneously. Aside from the focus on specific goals and objectives, the collaboration that accompanies professional development activities has its own set of benefits—reducing teacher isolation, promoting a genuine sharing of ideas, and small-scale classroom-based research projects. Ongoing action research—research designed to gather information and data on a small scale in one or several classrooms—emphasizes that teachers continually focus on curriculum, instruction, and student results.

One of the important aspects of a staff development program is a focus on curriculum. When a new unit, sequence, or topic is introduced, teachers need both background information and the relevant knowledge and skills required to convey the information most appropriately.

Teaching methodology is another important component of staff development. With new insights in the areas of assessment, differentiation, working with special-needs students, and the use of technology, teachers need to be brought up-to-date and be given the opportunity to gain experience in adapting and implementing with fidelity new practices in these instructional areas.

District goals, whether they are the use of technology, integrated learning, performance assessment, portfolio process, or differentiation, among others, generally require new skills for teachers. Assistance for teachers in working toward the fulfillment of district goals is another important dimension of a staff development program.

Activities designed to help professionals improve their practice can also lead to the promotion of leadership. As individual teachers become more familiar, comfortable with, and adept at implementing educational innovations, they can offer workshops, demonstration lessons, and coaching to assist the growth of colleagues. Effective leadership includes promoting teachers' expertise. Many principals first exercised leadership within their own classrooms in the areas of professional improvement. Effective principals seek teacher leaders who become important in the educational landscape because they bring expertise and credibility to the professional development of all staff members.

Individual Growth Plans

All professional educators should set goals for their own improvement. This should be built into the normal evaluation process. Procedures and forms for this process were outlined in Chapter 4, Improving Teacher Observation and Evaluation. Sometimes, larger groups of professionals wish to propose a plan for more comprehensive staff development, involving either a few individuals or the entire school. It is best to have the details of this plan specified and presented to a school leadership team or the appropriate district committee that approves such plans—especially if there are financial implications. A form that can be used to propose staff development plans appears in Figure 11.4.

Teacher Workshops

Workshops tend to be practical sessions that can be given by any person, agency, or organization. The term *workshop* implies a brief, hands-on experience that is intended to help teachers improve their instructional skills or learn some new content or teaching technique. Less formal than university courses or institutes, workshops usually give participants something that is immediately applicable to their daily work. Whether it is a way to use reflection journals, a procedure for taking running records of student reading, or how to best use a new piece of technology, workshops are oriented toward implementing a practical skill.

Figure 11.4 Sample Form for Staff Development Proposal

Name of School District

STAFF DEVELOPMENT PROPOSAL FORM

1. Please provide a brief description of the program you are proposing.

2. How does the program address school and/or district goals?

3. Who is going to participate?

4. How many students will be impacted?

5. How will participation be determined (volunteers, members of a committee or study group)?

6. When will the program take place?

7. Please itemize the costs for the program including any consultant fees, substitute time, hourly rate for participants, materials, and so on.

8. What is the plan to implement the new learnings or skills?

9. How will the effectiveness of the program be assessed?

Name: _______________________________ **School:** ____________________________ **Date:** __________

In-Service Programs

Most school districts also have a somewhat formal in-service program. Composed of individual courses, study groups, or networks, these offerings are usually supportive of district goals. In larger school systems, credit for advancement on salary guides is sometimes linked to completion of certain courses. School districts often publish a brochure that highlights the various offerings. In-service courses can also be led by local college or university staff members for local or graduate credit. In any case, the in-service program is an important component of a school district's staff development program.

Teacher Professional Days

Many school districts build teacher professional days into the annual calendar. These days can have a specific focus or a list of possibilities can be provided for the staff. Such days can have an important impact on establishing a professional, collegial tone, so the days must be carefully planned so that they will be meaningful and useful. It is wise to involve teachers in organizing the professional days so that the planning group can benefit from their ideas and gain commitment to the success of the program. A well-represented planning team also ensures that there are potential learning opportunities for every staff member and that no one is left out. Occasionally, a stimulating and important guest speaker can be brought to the school or the district.

Individual schools can plan professional days around local themes or school goals. For example, if a school goal is to improve assessment techniques, teachers can work in groups with staff developers, the principal, or a consultant in ways that will improve their skills in this area. They can design assessments or collaboratively develop rubrics for their administration, and then, at a later date, share the results. Groups can be formed on the basis of interest or need.

Most educators have found that a single-day experience is not valuable without appropriate follow-up in the classroom setting. Professionals must return to concepts discussed and assess how they have implemented them in their own classrooms. This application can test the true impact and benefit of professional days. The group of individuals who designed the professional days as well as the presenters can benefit from feedback from the participants. A sample Professional Development Activity Feedback Form appears in Figure 11.5. The information gathered from such assessments should be collated and analyzed to see how such opportunities can be improved.

Mentoring

New staff members have traditionally worked along with more experienced teachers in any number of informal relationships to help them to "learn the ropes" for surviving a first year of teaching. Recently, however, the notion of a mentoring relationship has taken on a more formal and well-thought-out structure. Some states require the appointment of a mentoring team to new teachers. Usually, this team is composed of a teacher, the principal, and perhaps a staff developer or support-services teacher.

Generally, a teacher mentor is an experienced, well-regarded teacher whose advice and counsel can help orient new staff members. Effective mentors listen carefully to the problems and concerns of the beginning teacher. They may observe (or perhaps coteach with) the new teacher and offer essential feedback designed to improve professional skills. The mentor also helps the new teacher find his or her way in the culture of the school and transmits some of the values and mores of the organization. Aware of professional development opportunities and community resources, the mentor can also point the way toward activities that are well suited to the new teacher's needs. In order to create an effective, trusting relationship, it is important that the mentor have a nonevaluative role in the professional life of the new teacher. Much information about the stages a new teacher goes through is available, along with effective interventions that can support new teachers through the stages of becoming a successful teacher. Time should be set aside for the mentor and the new teacher to meet, share, and establish plans for professional growth and development.

Figure 11.5   Sample Professional Development Activity Feedback Form

Name of School District

PROFESSIONAL DEVELOPMENT ACTIVITY FEEDBACK FORM

Staff Development Activity: ____

Date of Activity: ____

Presenter(s): ____

I. Please rate each of the following by circling a number (4 being the highest):

- Overall Rating   4   3   2   1
- Relevance to Your Professional Activities   4   3   2   1
- Content   4   3   2   1
- Presentation   4   3   2   1

Most Helpful Aspect(s):

Least Helpful Aspect(s):

II. How can you use the information, ideas, or strategies learned in your own teaching situation?

III. How do you expect to extend your learning from this activity? Please specify.

IV. Other comments or suggestions:

Thank you very much for your input!

Name (Optional): ____

Summer Workshops

Many school systems sponsor a variety or summer activities for teachers. The summer months offer a good opportunity to work in a concentrated fashion on curriculum renewal, the examination of new instructional materials, previewing technological devices, and finding ways to integrate new teaching approaches. Teachers often have a fresh outlook during the summer and can devote the time and focus required to reflect on instructional activities without diverting their energies and attention from their daily work with children.

In planning a productive summer workshop program, the needs of individuals, groups, and the district should be kept in mind. Perhaps there is a thrust in the area of science. If so, teachers could work with administrators and staff developers to learn about new programs, approaches, and techniques. If a particular group of teachers has a need to discuss and work on pupil management strategies, a summer workshop might be organized around this topic. Individual teachers might attend summer institutes at universities, consortiums, or professional associations. Opportunities for professional development during the summer or vacation months should be an integral part of a district's staff development program, and in-service credit, graduate credit, or stipends are often offered.

Working With Staff Developers

In districts fortunate enough to have full-time staff developers or teacher coaches, professionals have unparalleled opportunities to work together. Staff developers generally work on identified district and individual needs. Some have a specific focus, like technology; others are well versed in general instructional issues and can offer assistance to any teacher who is willing to work with them. Staff developers have the opportunity to follow up on the development and maintenance of new skills and practices. For example, if a group of teachers and a staff developer attend a workshop or seminar, their work together when they return to the district can be enhanced as they practice the new learning together and have conversations about its impact.

One of the great advantages of teachers working with professional coaches is the sense of collaboration that accompanies two colleagues working together. Often, staff developers will introduce themselves, explain their areas of expertise and interest, and solicit teachers to work along with them, according to a specific district model. Some of the many services that staff developers can offer include the following:

- Provide demonstration lessons.
- Assist in the use of new or complex instructional equipment.
- Help teachers to plan and craft productive learning experiences.
- Offer suggestions for classroom management.
- Model and coach teachers in the incorporation of new approaches.
- Provide resources and materials to aid instruction.
- Provide guidance and feedback as lessons are observed.
- Work with teachers to set up and carry out professional improvement plans.

Administrators in many school districts are finding that the budgetary trade-offs that may have to be made in order to secure sufficient funds to hire a staff developer are well worth the sacrifice. Such "on-the-job" training and direct assistance within the context of the regular classroom can make a significant impact on the improvement of instruction within a school.

Creating a Teacher Resource Center

A facility, or just a room, where teachers can go to examine professional journals, discuss triumphs and concerns, explore new ideas, and make classroom materials can enhance and support the professional development of all staff members. The use of such a center can expose teachers to new ideas and help them become adept at using them.

Some of the items to have on hand in a teacher resource center include

- professional journals,
- books and articles,
- curriculum guides,
- samples of commercial programs,
- brochures,
- curriculum guides from other school districts,
- tools and supplies to make instructional materials,
- computers with Internet access, and
- software to preview or practice.

A little effort to make the room inviting and comfortable will make teachers want to be there. Perhaps the PTA can be asked to purchase or seek donations of some modest furnishings—a lounge chair or two, a sofa, and work tables. The provision of coffee or after-school refreshments will also make the center more attractive to teachers. As in all dealings with a professional staff, involving them in the planning and contents of a teacher resource center will result in more willing and eager use of the area. As a school leader, you have a role in securing the resources to equip the center; you can then observe the many benefits that are derived from its existence.

Assessing Staff Development Programs

As in all major initiatives, the school's staff development program should be assessed on an ongoing basis. Is the program meeting the stated needs? Are teachers growing in their repertoire of skills and abilities? Is student achievement enhanced? Is the program flexible enough to meet the varied needs of a diverse staff? Does the program help to promote district goals and initiatives? The answers to all of these questions have important implications for the success of the staff development effort.

Teachers and administrators should work together to design the instruments and other means of assessing the effects of the program. Just as involvement in any one seminar or workshop must be followed up, so too must the larger program be measured, checked for success, and modified as needed.

THE FACULTY MEETING AS A FORUM FOR PROFESSIONAL DEVELOPMENT

Many teachers complain about faculty meetings—often for good reason. If information is shared that can readily be distributed by memo, e-mail, or a faculty bulletin, we are missing a golden opportunity to use the faculty meeting for more important purposes, such as professional development and the promotion of staff collaboration. Some principals publish a weekly bulletin of information that includes announcements, due dates, schedules, and a list of upcoming events, thus freeing the faculty meeting for more important purposes.

Following are a few tips to make faculty meetings more productive and meaningful.

Elicit Agenda Items From the Staff Prior to the Meeting

One way to do this is to have a "faculty meeting planning committee" session a few days before the meeting. A good configuration for such a group is a primary-grade teacher, an intermediate-grade teacher, a special-subject teacher, a special educator, and the principal. The group can be rotated through the faculty so that everyone has a chance to serve on the committee throughout the year. If the names of the individuals on the planning committee are published in a staff bulletin, then all teachers can give ideas to these individuals for items to be included on the faculty meeting agenda. As principal, you should be truly open to including agenda items of concern to the staff. Sometimes, an item may involve one or two individuals or an issue that is rather personal. In this case, you can suggest a different forum for dealing with the matter.

Since teachers often need a bit of refreshment at the end of the day, the teachers on the planning committee may wish to organize snacks for the meeting. This can help to set a friendly, hospitable tone.

Establish an Agenda With Timelines Devoted to Each Item

The agenda for the faculty meeting should be developed and distributed a day or two prior to the meeting. This will afford staff members time to think about some of the items, read a pertinent article attached to the agenda, or prepare materials that will be needed for the meeting. The agenda should have a time allocation for each of the items—an estimate of the amount of time needed to cover each topic. It is often difficult to stick to the agenda, especially when certain topics bring about disparate views, but the facilitator of the meeting should develop the skills to move the meeting along.

Involve Staff Members in Conducting the Meeting

Once the agenda is established, a way to promote leadership among the staff is to have the members of the planning group lead the faculty meeting. Three distinct roles can be assigned: facilitator, timekeeper, and recorder. Each of these roles requires particular skills that faculty members can practice, and faculty meetings are a natural training ground. The roles should be listed on the faculty meeting agenda. See Figure 11.6 for a sample faculty meeting agenda.

Figure 11.6 Sample Faculty Meeting Agenda

ELEMENTARY SCHOOL FACULTY MEETING AGENDA

Date

Room 214

I. OPENING (3:15–3:45): Each person will share a highlight from his/her professional life last week.

II. FACULTY DISCUSSION (3:45–4:20)

Peer pressure is a strong influence on our students. This is a normal developmental reality as children reach middle childhood. There are peer dictates regarding clothing, attitudes about learning and cooperation, and how children act toward one another.

Figure 11.6	(Continued)

Focus of discussion:

GROUP DISCUSSION A (8 minutes):

1. What are the general effects we see in this area?

2. Are there common threads we notice within the grades?

3. How is the influence of peer pressure manifested?

4. Is peer pressure necessarily negative?

SHARING (8 minutes)

GROUP DISCUSSION B (8 minutes):

1. How have we been dealing with the effects of peer pressure?

2. Can peer pressure be used to our advantage?

3. Should we try to lessen the effects of peer pressure? Can we do so?

SHARING AND SUMMARY (8 minutes)

III. PROFESSIONAL SHARING (4:20–4:30)

Name of teacher will demonstrate how she has determined which "search engines" have yielded best results for her fifth-grade study of the Civil War.

IV. ASSESSMENT OF MEETING (4:30–4:35)

FACULTY PLANNING COMMITTEE:

Facilitator: *Name of staff member*

Timekeeper: *Name of staff member*

Recorder: *Name of staff member*

Key to Staff Development Goals

The agenda and focus of the faculty meeting can be quite varied. Some topics may deal with faculty interests and concerns, others may deal with district initiatives, and still others may be keyed to general staff development goals. Sometimes, simply sharing a specific teaching technique or use of a material or resource can make for a stimulating faculty meeting. One way to promote such collaboration is to ask for teacher volunteers and then send the individuals a brief form to help them to frame their presentation. (See Figure 11.7.) Such practices tend to foster pride among the staff and a sense of collegiality. Always follow up such presentations with a personal thank-you note.

Figure 11.7 Letter to Teacher Providing Guidelines for Professional Sharing

ELEMENTARY SCHOOL, OFFICE OF THE PRINCIPAL

Dear _____________________,

Thank you for volunteering to share with faculty a project, technique, or material that you have found particularly useful in your instructional program.

You may organize your talk any way that best suits your needs, but if you would like a general guideline for the discussion, you might want to consider this suggested format:

- Was there a specific teaching/learning need that prompted you to develop the program, material, technique, or approach? If so, what was it?
- Describe what you developed and how you implemented it.
- What were the results of your use of the material, technique, approach, or program?
- Can you think of other applications for the materials or approaches?

I do appreciate your willingness to share your experiences with our colleagues. If there are any materials or equipment that you will need, please let me know.

Sincerely,

Principal

All faculty meetings ought to end with a brief assessment. This can be a brief two- or three-question form soliciting feedback on the topics covered, the value of the discussions, and how staff might want to go further in this work. Another way to assess the meeting is to go around the room and ask each staff member to say one thing about the meeting that was personally valuable and one area that might have been improved. Incorporating this feedback into future meetings will more than likely result in improved staff discussions or work sessions.

STAFF DEVELOPMENT FOR SCHOOL SERVICE PERSONNEL

It may seem from the discussion in this chapter that teachers are the only school employees who require a staff development program. This is far from the case. Secretaries, nurses, guidance counselors, psychologists, teacher aides, lunchroom personnel, custodians, substitutes, and bus drivers all can benefit from programs designed to help them improve their skills.

When technological advances first came to elementary schools, many secretaries were simply given computers without sufficient training to know how to use this tool that would ultimately enhance their work. Custodians need to know how best to organize their schedules and how to use new equipment and cleaning materials. School clerks also need to learn how to use new technologies and how to respond to children in any variety of situations. Bus drivers, too, can clearly benefit from a few sessions in which they explore the best ways to gain children's attention and to maintain order.

Many school districts provide an orientation program for substitute teachers. This helps to inform these essential personnel about the routines of working in schools, how to gain and maintain children's interest and enthusiasm, how to go about following normal school procedures, what the general instructional strategies are, and the best ways to communicate how the children fared—both to the classroom teacher and to the principal.

Working successfully in schools is a complex matter. Roles change and shift as society changes. All employees need and deserve opportunities to reflect upon their performance, to learn new ways of fulfilling their duties, and to benefit from the experience of others. Each person in an organization has a unique and important role. If we invest in helping each person see how job performance can be improved, the entire organization will flourish and grow.

NOTES

1. Peter Senge describes using professional learning communities as part of a learning organization in *The Fifth Discipline: The Art and Practice of the Learning Organization* (New York: Currency Doubleday, 1990).

2. Richard DuFour, Rebecca DuFour, Robert Eaker, and Thomas Many describe the process of implementing professional learning communities in schools in *Learning by Doing: A Handbook for Professional Learning Communities at Work* (Bloomington, IN: Solution Tree, 2006).

12

Promoting Effective Communication

Internal and External

I t's nine o'clock and a bell rings signaling the beginning of a special assembly program. The children in only half of the school's classes find their seats in the auditorium. Someone says, "Where are the third graders?" What happened? Somewhere along the line, there was a lapse in communication.

Effective communication is an essential attribute for being a successful principal. Teachers need to know what is happening in the school. This goes far beyond the awareness of scheduled events; relevant information about professional opportunities, new research about classroom practice, general items of interest, praise and admonition, and school procedures need to be communicated clearly and in a predictable fashion. Indeed, communication is a basic skill for effective school administration and management.

THE IMPORTANCE OF EFFECTIVE COMMUNICATION

You can be bright and well-intentioned, and still fall on your face without good communication skills. Although certain aspects of effective communication are related to personality, there are skills and techniques that all individuals can learn and practice that will enhance the way that they relate, interact, and communicate with others. It is often remarked that "it is not *what* is said, but *how* it is said" that allows the message to be heard.

Note: All forms, letters, and checklists included in this chapter can be found at corwin.com/elementary survivalkit.

231

How and what you communicate in many respects determines how you will be perceived by others. If we appear distant and aloof, people are apt to feel uncomfortable in our presence; if we are warm, friendly, and convey an interest in others, we are more likely to make people feel comfortable and more actively listen to what we have to say. Often, principals have to convey information that is difficult—areas of needed growth for a teacher, problems that students are experiencing, or parental attitudes that seem harmful to children. It is a challenge indeed to provide this information in a way that will permit open dialogue.

If you convey information with sincerity and sensitivity, you are better able to get their point across. Be skillful in choosing the right words that will give information, but never rob another human being of their dignity. Aside from sensitivity, timeliness of communication is another important aspect of being an effective principal. Teachers, students, and parents need information that is current and will help them to stay informed and active in the school.

You must also communicate praise for the actions of members of the school community. Such compliments, whether written or verbal, should be given for genuine purposes and be delivered with sincerity. Most people can tell when someone is being gratuitous or condescending.

Communication is clearly a "two-way street." We need to be able to sense other people's reactions, read "body language," and pick the best times to issue communications. Clearly, the degree to which a principal is an effective communicator can enhance or detract from general professional performance, success, and fulfillment.

KEEPING THE SCHOOL STAFF INFORMED

Schools, like other organizations, depend on an effective flow of information. Different communications tools—memos, e-mails, letters, oral statements, routing sheets, bulletins, and the like—are most appropriate for specific situations. Listed below are a variety of communication devices and the circumstances in which they can most effectively be used.

The Sign-In Sheet

Each morning, when staff members come into school, they can be asked to go to the school office to check their mailboxes and sign in by placing their initials next to their names on a sign-in sheet. Aside from allowing you to check whether or not a teacher has arrived at school, the sign-in sheet can be a vehicle for communication of last-minute changes in schedule, important notices, and reminders. Since the sign-in sheet contains the names of school staff members, it can also be used as a routing sheet appended to articles of interest, communications passed from employee to employee during the school day, or as a check-off sheet for collections, items due in the school office, and the like. There are countless reasons for which you will need a handy roster of staff members. Once produced, the sign-in sheet can be duplicated time and time again throughout the year. Of course, if it is saved as an electronic file, then any changes in staff or assignment can be readily made. A sample of a sign-in sheet appears in Figure 12.1.

Figure 12.1	Sample School Sign-In Sheet

ELEMENTARY SCHOOL SIGN-IN SHEET

Day: _________________   **Date:** _________________

Classroom Teachers:

Mrs. Brahms (203) _______

Mr. Bruce (212) _______

Mrs. Dannon (214) _______

Mrs. Graber (209) _______

Mrs. Hunker (109) _______

Mrs. Kang (103) _______

Mrs. McGrath (201) _______

Mrs. Philpot (113) _______

Mrs. Pinea (211) _______

Mrs. Plender (213) _______

Mrs. Simon (206) _______

Ms. Rubel (120) _______

Other Personnel:

Mrs. Bergman (Vocal Music) _______

Mrs. Chandler (Nurse) _______

Mrs. David (Classroom Aide) _______

Mrs. Day (Support Services) _______

Mrs. DeFilippo (Classroom Aide) _______

Mrs. Faster (Support Services) _______

Mrs. Fenton (ESL) _______

Mrs. Irving (Library) _______

Mrs. Jankow (Interpreter) _______

Dr. Kasten (Child Study) _______

Mr. LaRuche (PE) _______

Mrs. Limon (Inst. Music) _______

Ms. Matarri (Classroom Aide) _______

Mrs. Riesen (Counselor) _______

Mrs. Ross (Librarian) _______

Mr. Schmidt (Support Services) _______

Mrs. Sisto (Clerical Aide) _______

Mrs. Talon (Art) _______

Mrs. Winfried (Classroom Aide) _______

Mrs. Wool (Speech) _______

1. **This morning's assembly will begin at 9:30 AM instead of 10:00 AM. Please be ready when you hear the bell.**

2. **Mrs. Fenton is out today and we do not have a sub. Please do not send your students to ESL classes today.**

3. **Goal Fulfillment Forms are due in the office tomorrow!**

The Weekly Calendar

Another essential device to foster good communication is the publication of a weekly (or daily) calendar. Whether distributed in hard copy or electronically, the calendar provides a schedule of important events in the school for the week. Some of the items that can be listed in the calendar include

- names (and positions) of itinerant staff who are in the building on a particular day;
- special events such as rehearsals, assemblies, meetings;
- items due in the office on a particular day;
- special assignments such as lunch duty, bus duty, and so on;
- an item of professional interest; and
- an inspirational quotation.

If saved as a word-processed document, compiling the calendar is made much easier since many assignments, personnel in the building, and events will occur over and over again each week. A sample of a school calendar appears in Figure 12.2. The calendar can also be used as a professional development tool by reproducing an article of interest, a chart, or some other useful communication on the back side (called the "flip side" on the sample). (Some principals prepare a weekly abstract of educational research or append pertinent articles to their calendars not only to communicate current information, but also to signal that this is a staff that learns.) In some larger schools with very busy schedules, a daily calendar may need to be published.

Figure 12.2 Sample Weekly Calendar

ELEMENTARY SCHOOL CALENDAR

Week of May 17, 2009

MONDAY, 5/17		Nurse Kibel here today
		Lunch Duty: V. Cameron/C. Bergsten
		Special-Services Team (Wuhl, Rosen, Kasten) here in AM
	7:20 AM	Super Orchestra at Mulvihill School
		STORY LUNCH/Kindergarten: 11:25 AM
	8:15 AM	Child Study Meeting in Mrs. Prendergast's office
	3:15 PM	Faculty Meeting in Room 214 (agenda previously distributed)
TUESDAY, 5/18	7:30 AM	Orchestra rehearsal
		Mrs. Sienta (Clerical Aide) here AM only
		Lunch Duty: V. Cameron/L. Reilly
		ESL Checklists due in office today
	10:00 AM	Mrs. Prendergast at Principal's Meeting
		2nd Graders leave for Fairview Lake for overnight
	7:45 PM	PTA Meeting/Library

WEDNESDAY, 5/19		Nurse Kibel here today
		Joan Wuhl (Speech/Language) here all day
		Lunch Duty: V. Cameron/H. Fumiko
		STORY LUNCH/1st Grade: 12:15 PM
	8:15 AM	5th Grades visit middle school (Cafeteria)
	9:45 AM	4th Graders to Nature Center
	3:00 PM	2nd Graders return from Fairview Lake overnight
THURSDAY, 5/20	7:30 AM	Orchestra rehearsal
		Mrs. Sienta (Clerical Aide) here AM only
		Lunch Duty: J. Lehmann/L. Reilly
	10:30 AM	Mrs. Prendergast at IASA Meeting
		Jay MacDonald (Computer Technician) here AM
	1:00 PM	DARE—Ms. Rubben's 5th Grade
	2:00 PM	DARE—Mrs. Paterno's 5th Grade
FRIDAY, 5/21		Nurse Kibel here in PM
		Mary Partimer (Learning Specialist) here all day
		Lunch Duty: V. Cameron/L. Reilly
		Goal Fulfillment Reports due in office today

LOOKING AHEAD:

TUESDAY, 5/22	7:30 PM	PTA General Meeting and Spring Concert

Flip-Side Article: "Moving to Higher Levels of Thinking"

Memos

From time to time, probably more often than we would like, important information must be conveyed to the staff in the form of a memorandum. By setting up a template on your computer, these can be easily produced. In writing memos, it is wise to be concise and to the point. If you are requesting specific information or a particular response, be sure to state the deadline, and do so in boldface type. Memo writing is in some ways an art. You have to convey the essential aspects of what you want to say in an organized fashion. The use of bullets, numbered lists, and indented paragraphing will call attention to specific items. Memos can be organized to request needed information required from teachers. You can make reporting easier for teachers by embedding a form or questionnaire into the body of the memo. A sample memo calling for a report on the accomplishment of a school goal appears in Figure 12.3.

Figure 12.3   Sample Memo Form Requiring Specific Information

ELEMENTARY SCHOOL

Date: May 12, 2010

To: All Teachers

From: Principal

RE: GOAL FULFILLMENT REPORT

In order for me to compile a report on our achievement of our goal to assess integrated learning, please fill out the form below and return it to me by **May 19, 2010**. You may work on the forms in your unit planning groups, but please complete one form for each class.

1. What assessments did you design and use to measure student achievement of the goals set for your integrated unit?

2. In reviewing student performance on these assessments, please indicate what percentage of the students in your class demonstrated evidence of achieving your stated goals for each of the following indicators:

Indicator	*Percent of Students Achieving*
• extensions of knowledge	____________
• skill acquisition, growth, and application	____________
• use of multiple resources	____________
• knowledge/understanding of concepts	____________
• independence	____________
• interdependence	____________

3. Please list the forms of evidence you have to support your estimates of student achievement.

4. How did/will the results of the assessments inform your instructional practices? (Please respond on the back of this page.)

Teacher: ________________________   **Name of Unit:** ________________________

Bulletin Boards

Bulletin boards can be effective communication devices. If one is near the sign-in sheet, important items of general interest can be posted. Organize the information posted on bulletin boards. For example, staff development opportunities can appear in one section; another section can be devoted to timely messages and reminders under the heading "Important"; still another section can display district notices such as job postings, health and safety information, and required procedures. Some principals like to keep the school and district goals on the bulletin board so that they can readily be seen throughout the year.

It is important to avoid clutter on bulletin boards. Keep them neat and remove notices that are no longer timely or relevant. In some schools, a teacher or secretary may be assigned the responsibility of maintaining the office bulletin board.

Staff Bulletins

Periodic bulletins should be issued from your office to keep staff informed about upcoming events, procedures, requirements, and other school news. Staff bulletins are different from memos in that they may incorporate several unrelated items. They are different from calendars because staff bulletins offer an opportunity to expand upon a statement, a due date, or a requirement that cannot readily be explained within the body of a weekly calendar.

Staff bulletins can incorporate checklists, reminders, and items of general interest about the lives of people who work in the school. Some principals like to number staff bulletins consecutively so that they can be referred to again. Of course, staff bulletins can be distributed by e-mail as well. A sample staff bulletin, called "Keeping You Posted," appears in Figure 12.4.

Figure 12.4 Sample Staff Bulletin

ELEMENTARY SCHOOL

Date: May 5, 2009

To: All Staff

From: Principal

RE: KEEPING YOU POSTED, #14

CONGRATULATIONS RAYNEE PRADA	Our own Raynee Prada has been named as Somerville's "Teacher of the Year." Selected by a committee of teachers, parents, and administrators, this is an honor Mrs. Prada richly deserves for her unswerving dedication to her children as well as her instructional leadership.
RECYCLING SCULPTURE CONTEST	The town recycling coordinator, Mr. Vanderlind, has sent us flyers about this year's annual recycling contest. Please go over the very specific rules for the contest with your children. Any students whose sculptures are not composed of the specified materials and whose sculpture exceeds the size limitation will be disqualified.
CLEANUP OF SCHOOL GROUNDS	Our outdoor spaces could use some cleaning and sprucing up. Would any teacher be willing to organize a "cleanup patrol" during recess time? Please see me so that we may coordinate efforts.

(Continued)

Figure 12.4   (Continued)

WRITING ACROSS THE CURRICULUM	Mrs. Milanos has been asked to prepare a display of "Writing Across the Curriculum" for the new boardroom at the district administration building. Please send any student samples mounted on construction paper with the student's name, class, and school plainly printed on the front to Mrs. Milanos at Smith School by May 12. I know we would all like to have our school represented in the display.
AUDITORIUM LOBBY	Many thanks to Ann Brady and Linda McCord for decorating the auditorium lobby. Doesn't it look wonderful?
ASSESSMENT CONFERENCE	There are still four seats available for the assessment conference next Saturday. One in-service credit will be granted for participation. Please see me if interested.
PLANNING CHARTS FOR MAY	Integrated learning planning charts for the month of May are due in the office on May 7.

Letters: Formal and Informal

Letters are an essential form of communication for principals. Formal letters can summarize important conferences with teachers. When the letter includes a reprimand and may have repercussions about continued employment, copies should be sent to the superintendent and to the teacher's personnel file. Similarly, when praising a teacher for a particular accomplishment or a time when the individual went "beyond the call of duty," you should also send a copy to the superintendent and the personnel file. Such letters are much appreciated.

It is also useful to summarize conferences with parents in which information was covered that may need to be referred to again. Many principals end such letters with a statement inviting parents or guardians to call the school if they feel that parts of the letter do not accurately reflect the issues raised or the outcomes of the conference.

Informal letters, used frequently, can be a simple thank-you to a teacher or parent, a reminder, or a request for information. The tone of informal letters is lighter than formal letters, but both are useful for different circumstances and purposes.

The Staff Handbook

In every school, routines and procedures should be encoded in a staff handbook. The advantage of publishing such a handbook is that all procedures will be in one place so staff members can refer to them throughout the school year. Also, once distributed (and perhaps signed for), you can rely on the fact that a particular routine or procedure has been communicated to staff members.

Following is a list of the many sections that can be included in a staff handbook:

- Staff members, assignments, and e-mail addresses
- Special responsibilities, committee membership, special assignments

- Teachers in charge of specific areas or activities
- Faculty Meeting procedures and dates
- Attendance procedures: Pupil and staff
- Sick leave, personal leave, illness in family regulations
- Substitute-calling procedures
- School schedule: Arrival, dismissal, lunch shifts, bell schedule
- Student doors for arrival and dismissal
- Assembly procedures and seating plan
- Crisis Response Plan
- Field trips: Procedures, required forms, advance notice, bus arrangements
- Fire drills, bus drills, emergency drills, bomb threats
- Lesson plans: Regular instructional and substitute plans
- Lunch program: Lunch supervision plan, schedule, responsibilities, rainy-day plan
- Physical education procedures
- Pupil Assistance Committee procedures
- Pupil discipline plan and procedures
- Shared decision-making and school leadership team procedures
- Safety procedures: In school, outdoors

Staff handbooks should be collected at the end of each school year and updated electronically if information in particular sections have changed.

Due-Dates Calendar

A convenient device to remind teachers of upcoming events or due dates is a large calendar of the month posted in a location where most people are likely to see it. (Just above the photocopier is a good place.) A calendar with one large page for each month is a good format. You or your secretary can then write special events, due dates, and other reminders with a marker in the appropriate box. Some of the items that can be placed in the calendar include assembly times and programs; due dates for tasks like book orders, surveys, reports; marking-period dates; scheduled field trips.

OBTAIN REQUESTED INFORMATION IN AN ORGANIZED FASHION

Principals often need to secure information from teachers in order to complete state reports, district tasks, census data, and other paperwork. The principal who is effective in written communication knows how to organize the request for information in a way that streamlines the process for all parties. For example, if you need data on pupil achievement of specific goals, rather than referring to a prior memo, ask for the information in a way that is efficient and convenient for both the person who is giving the information and the person who is collecting it. (See the sample provided in Figure 12.5 in which the collection of data for specific computer skills is required.) Teachers will undoubtedly appreciate the extra attention and degree of organization exhibited to make their completion of the task simpler and less time-consuming.

Figure 12.5   Sample of a Way to Collect Required Information in an Organized Fashion

ELEMENTARY SCHOOL

Date:

To: All Staff

From: Principal

RE: REQUESTED DATA FROM THE DIRECTOR OF TECHNOLOGY

Dr. Iuzzo, our Director of Technology, has asked for each teacher to provide a report on their students' accomplishment of specific computer goals. Please fill out the information below and return the form to me within two weeks. I will collate the information for the school and forward the results to Dr. Iuzzo.

Goal	No. of Students in Class	No. of Students Who Have Accomplished Goal by May 12, _____
Student can turn computer and peripherals on and off in correct sequence.		
Student knows how to load a program.		
Student knows how to load a CD.		
Student can create a simple document using a word processor.		
Student can change font size and text appearance.		
Student can set margins and tabs in a document.		
Student can save document with a unique name.		
Student knows how to delete files.		
Student knows how to use the page setup menu.		
Student can rename a file.		
Student can create a simple spreadsheet.		
Student can create a database.		

Teacher Name: _____________________   **School:** _____________________   **Grade:** _____________

ELECTRONIC COMMUNICATION WITH THE SCHOOL COMMUNITY

We live in the age of electronic communication. It makes getting out a message to a broad audience easy and speedy. Beyond this, we are moving to more paperless forms of communication as an environmental initiative. School districts all over the country have established e-mail notification systems for emergencies, meeting information, and other timely information. Families often sign up for such notifications at the beginning of the year or during the registration process. Most school districts and individual schools maintain their own Web sites with essential information, staff rosters, program descriptions, calendars, and displays of classroom or student work. (See Chapter 13 for tips on maintaining a school Web site.)

Despite the convenience and benefits of electronic communication, we cannot always assume that every family has a computer or online services. Some families may be reluctant to divulge e-mail addresses. Because of this, there is still a need for "paper communication," and in some instances, such as essential notices that need to be signed and returned, paper communication is still necessary.

KEEPING THE PARENT BODY AND THE COMMUNITY INFORMED

Just as staff members benefit from timely and accurate communication, so, too, do the parents and the community at large. Parents like to know what is happening at school and what programs and special events their children will be involved in. Many teachers send home weekly or monthly newsletters highlighting curriculum pursuits, special programs, and class studies. These are generally appreciated, and they allow parents to connect activities at home to what is happening in their children's classroom. Similarly, as principals, we should issue monthly newsletters that convey important information about the school in general. Such newsletters can include a calendar of events, a message from the principal, staff information, health notices, PTA news, classroom news, and the like. Desktop publishing programs can readily produce attractive and professional-looking school newsletters. For a sample of a school newsletter, see Figure 12.6.

A worthwhile project to work on with parents is the development of a parent handbook. This can be an attractive booklet in which essential information about the school and its procedures is organized for ready reference throughout the school year. With the text saved in an electronic document, the contents can be modified each year to reflect current information and school routines. Items that can be a part of a parent handbook can include the following:

- Introduction from principal and representative from the parents association
- Acknowledgments
- School mission statement and philosophy
- School floor plan
- Registration procedures and requirements
- The school day: Schedule, arrival, dismissal, and lunch periods

Figure 12.6 Sample School Newsletter

PEN & PENCIL

_________ Elementary School

Vol. XXX, No. 8   **March _______**

CALENDAR

Mar. 8   Young Inventors' Meeting
7:30 PM at Middle School

Mar. 9   PARENT CONFERENCE DAY
12:45 PM DISMISSAL

Mar. 11   HSA Cultural Arts Assembly
"Oak Tree Songs" 9:00 A.M.

Mar. 15   3rd Grades to Paperbox Theater

Mar. 15   Board of Education Meeting
8:00 PM at District Office

Mar. 16   Book Fair—International Theme

Mar. 16   PTA Meeting 7:45 PM at
Library—All Parents Welcome!

Mar. 16   PARENT CONFERENCE DAY
12:45 PM DISMISSAL

Mar. 18   International Day Assembly 9:00 AM

Mar. 23   PARENT CONFERENCE DAY
12:45 PM DISMISSAL

Mar. 25   Somerville Council Meeting 3:15 PM

Mar. 29   Board of Education Meeting
8:00 PM at Central Office

Mar. 30   KINDERGARTEN REGISTRATION

Mar. 31   KINDERGARTEN REGISTRATION
1:30–3:30 SCHOOL OFFICE

THE PRINCIPAL'S PEN

Dear School Parents,

In March, a second conference will be scheduled with your child's teacher to review individual student progress. This is a wonderful opportunity to review your child's progress with his or her teacher. In order to make the conference as fruitful as possible, please begin to think about the following questions:

1. How does your child feel he or she is doing in school?

2. Are there any areas that your child finds particularly frustrating or difficult?

3. Does your child seem to understand homework assignments?

4. What growth have you noticed in your child's schoolwork since the last conference?

5. Have you reviewed your child's portfolio? What are your impressions?

6. What questions do you have for your child's teacher?

Successful parent/teacher conferences are cooperative sessions in which insights and impressions are shared and evaluations are linked to actual work samples and assessments.

As with all school practices, I am interested in your reactions to our conference procedures. Please do not hesitate to let me know your feelings.

I will be available during the conference days to speak with any parent who wishes to meet with me. Please contact Mrs. Goldstein, the school secretary, to make an appointment.

Sincerely,

Sara L. Prendergast,
Principal

KINDERGARTEN REGISTRATION

Kindergarten registration will take place at Somerville School on March 30 and 31 for children who will be five years old on or before October 1, ______.

The hours for registration are from 1:30 to 3:30 PM on each of these days. Required documents include proof of residence (original deed or dated lease) and proof of birth date (birth certificate, baptismal certificate, or passport). We would appreciate having immunization records also.

Please let any friends or neighbors who have eligible five-year-olds know about our registration dates.

CONGRATULATIONS MRS. DENNIS!

Mrs. Mary Ann Dennis is Somerville School's honoree in our district's Teacher Recognition Program. This is an honor she richly deserves for her dedication to our children and the stimulating instructional program that she provides. I know that you all join in extending heartiest congratulations to Mrs. Dennis.

STUDENT COUNCIL FOOD DRIVE

The Student Council will be conducting a spring food drive for the Center for Food Services. Please send only canned and dry, boxed foods to your child's classroom. The drive ends on March 29. It is heartening to note that our youngsters are willing to extend their efforts and energies to help those in need.

PROJECT CHILD FIND

Project Child Find is a service of the State Department of Education to help identify unserved handicapped children, birth through age three. If you have any concerns about important developmental issues for children in this age range, you can call Project Child Find at 1-800-322-8174.

SCHOOL ELECTION/BUDGET REFERENDUM

The school election/budget referendum will be held on Tuesday, April 13, from 2:00 to 9:00 PM this year. Polling places will be the same as those for the General Election in November and the June Primary Elections.

PTA NOTES

March is here already and it brings with it a number of PTA events. One of them is our fingerprinting program. Flyers will be going out shortly to register your child. Your child will be fingerprinted by a trained member of this committee, and the one and only copy of these prints will be mailed home to you. Chairperson for this committee is Sharon Mulhausen. Please leave her a message in the PTA mailbox if you have any questions.

March is also "Adopt A Note" month for our Music Boosters Committee. This is their major fundraiser for the year, and it enables them to purchase many items to enhance our wonderful music department such as instruments, instrument cases, and tapes, to name a few. Watch for flyers asking for your support. The Art Booster Plant Sale is rapidly approaching as well. Delivery of preordered flowers is in early May. Volunteers are needed to help on the day of delivery. Please contact the chairperson for this committee, Kate Kramer, 555-0155, if you are interested in helping. Please remember your PTA when you are planning your garden!

Donna Fox
PTA President

(Continued)

Figure 12.6   (Continued)

NEW SOMERVILLE STAFF MEMBER

Mrs. Kimberly Janoff has joined our staff as a sign-language interpreter. Having recently moved to our area from Illinois, Mrs. Janoff has served as an interpreter in several school and community settings.

Replacing Ms. Cheryl Bates, who recently resigned, Mrs. Janoff will be working with hearing-impaired students at our school.

- Emergency closing information
- Conferences and progress reporting practices
- Policies for visiting the school and classrooms
- School publications and newsletters
- The Parents Association: Functions, officers, committees
- Homework policy
- Testing program
- School records
- Health and safety procedures: School nurse, medications, insurance, bicycle rules, safety in the school and community, crossing guards
- School classrooms: Organization, schedules, and programs
- Assembly programs
- Behavioral expectations
- Special subjects and programs
- Field trips
- Special services: Remedial instruction, resource center, ESL, speech/language, counseling, gifted program, bedside instruction
- School governance and shared decision-making procedures
- Student council
- Peer mediation
- Classroom parties: Birthday, holidays
- School photographs
- Lost and found
- Bus procedures
- School contact information

To give the handbook a child-oriented look, a youngster's drawing of the school building can be placed on the cover. (You might even hold a contest for the drawing.) Producing this publication along with a parent or group of parents will engage others in understanding and appreciating school routines and procedures.

Just as teachers need to be aware of schedules within the school, parents also have to be kept abreast of what is happening in the school. Send home timely reminders about conference days, special programs, school celebrations, performances, and other items of general interest. For example, announcements about the Halloween Parade, the Student Council Election, or the first-grade play all need to come from the school office. Don't take for granted that students will convey schedule information to their parents.

Parents also like to be informed about special programs, staff news, or faculty changes. If teachers or other staff members are replaced during the year, letters should be written to the parent community, explaining (if appropriate) the details of the staff changes as well as something about the new individuals who will be employed. It is essential to anticipate what parents will be interested in and acknowledge their desire to be informed about important events in the life of the school.

FACE-TO-FACE COMMUNICATIONS

The majority of communications within the day of a principal will be face-to-face encounters. Whether it be conducting a meeting, speaking with a parent, addressing a professional association, or mediating a dispute among staff members, all such situations require verbal skills and an engaging, persuasive personality. Some individuals are more comfortable in this arena than others, but like it or not, such interactions are clearly part and parcel of the role of the principal.

In meetings with colleagues, parents, students, and community members, it is important to set the tone for the activity. State the purpose of the meeting and, depending upon your particular style (collaborative or authoritative) or the needs of the situation, set a timeline for what you hope to accomplish in a set amount of time. If the intent is to arrive at decisions about specific issues, be certain to elicit the ideas and thoughts of those in attendance. This will help to build commitment to whatever outcome is reached. Listening to others does not necessarily mean adopting their ideas, but important and prevalent viewpoints and ideas must be taken into account.

One of the most difficult interactions all principals face is the angry parent who parks him- or herself outside of the school office and will not leave until a meeting occurs with the person in charge. Such encounters are always emotionally charged, but the principal who has developed skills of diplomacy and tact can be assertive while at the same time demonstrating that the parent's ideas are being heard. Many times, an angry parent just wants to be heard, and once a rational discussion takes place, tempers will abate. Other times, however, which will call for every shred of your patience and understanding, you won't be so lucky. In those situations, it is important for you to keep summarizing what you think the parent is saying and ask if your perception of his or her view matches with what the parent is trying to convey. Taking the time to truly listen will at least convince the parent that you are being responsive to the concern. Then, state your own view of the matter and try to find any common ground. Offer several possible solutions and try to work with the parent to project how each alternative might help abate the problem. Pay attention to body language and don't let your own face, arms, and hands escalate the situation.

TIPS ON PREPARING PRESENTATIONS

Principals have countless occasions to offer congratulations (publicly) to staff members who have accomplished notable, outstanding service to the school or community, or have had a blessed event in their personal lives. Good news ought to be shared. Gather the staff together, even if only for a moment, and, with genuine enthusiasm, congratulate the individual. Sharing the good times and the accomplishments of others can help to promote staff morale and a sense of community.

There are also times when you have to announce a difficult piece of information—an ill staff member who has taken a turn for the worse, the death of a family member, a natural disaster, or budgetary cutbacks, just to name a few. How this information is conveyed, the tone of voice used, and the degree of sincerity and sensitivity expressed and implied can all go a long way toward easing the blow of learning about sad news.

Invariably, there will be times when all principals will be asked to address large audiences. Talks to committees, community groups, nursery schools, professional organizations, or the parent body from your own school are all quite common for elementary school principals. It is always appropriate for principals to honor teachers for awards and accomplishments, speak on behalf of retirees, or convey news of national or personal tragedy.

When called upon to prepare a presentation, a few simple tips can help the event to go smoothly:

- Outline your thoughts to make sure that your ideas are logical and flow in a coherent, sequential fashion.
- Prepare visuals, charts, slides, or other aids to clarify ideas or statistics.
- Rehearse and time your presentation. If you are given 30 minutes for your talk, make sure to convey your most important ideas within the given timeframe.
- If appropriate, engage the audience with an informal, conversational tone.
- Speak up, be enthusiastic, be positive, and, when possible, appropriately inject humor.

This may be hard for some principals, but with practice, a touch of humor, and genuine enthusiasm for the topic, your audience will follow you better. If you enjoy the experience, it will show.

ESTABLISHING A NETWORK OF "KEY COMMUNICATORS"

Most principals are well aware of the individuals within the school community who have influence and are well respected by their constituent groups. These people, who may be thought of as "key communicators," are essential contacts for the principal, and they should be contacted first when there is a need to disseminate important information—good or bad. Often, the best candidate for being a key communicator for the parent body is the parents association president, but we all know of situations in which this might not be the case. One way to start would be to ask eight or ten parents at random whom they would rely on for accurate, unbiased information about the school.

A key communicator should be identified for the parent community, the teaching staff, the nonteaching staff, the district administration, the nonparent neighborhood community, and the board of education. The reasons you might want to contact key communicators include the following:

- A rumor about something that happened in the school
- Breaking news about an important staff change
- An issue regarding a hazardous situation in the school (noxious fumes, a collapsed roof, storm damage, etc.)
- The effects of a budget proposal or referendum

You will not need to call all communicators for every situation as you will know which group needs to be informed regarding any particular issue.

People you rely upon as key communicators should also be asked to call you if they hear rumors or information that they feel you need to be aware of regarding the school, community, or individual families. The use of key communicators is an effective strategy for being informed about essential information regarding the school and will help avoid the unfortunate effect of rumors that can hurt the school, even if they are unfounded. Even in a rapid information age, verbal communications among individuals remain a critical vehicle for keeping attuned to important viewpoints, perceptions, and information that is "floating" about the community.

THE WRITTEN LETTER: A LOST ART

In our rapidly expanding information age, the written letter has become something of a lost art. There are any number of reasons and occasions that principals should write letters to members of the school community. Letters are very personal, and individuals appreciate them, especially when their purpose is to express thanks or to offer congratulations. Some principals find it easy to write brief, handwritten notes; others prefer to word process letters. In any case, the extra effort will be recognized by the recipient. Some of the very many reasons that principals might want to write a letter include

- expressing appreciation to a parent or teacher who has served on a specific committee,
- thanking a parent or teacher for volunteering time in support of the school,
- congratulating a student or teacher for receiving an award or some other recognition,
- thanking students for school service, and
- recognizing a special event in the life of a staff member such as a birth, graduation, or wedding.

Of course, the use of word processors can make writing personal letters much easier than before the advent of these essential administrative tools. Let's say, for example, that you wish to write a thank-you letter in June to everyone who has volunteered in the school during the year. You can use a standard opening paragraph, the same on all of the letters, and then individualize a middle paragraph by making mention of a particular area in which the individual has served the school. The final paragraph, again, can be standard for all of the letters. By saving the letter as a template, numerous letters can be produced in a reasonable amount of time. In the example in Figure 12.7, the middle paragraph is the one that is tailored to what the recipient has done for the school.

Figure 12.7   Sample Letter of Thanks to a Parent Volunteer

ELEMENTARY SCHOOL, OFFICE OF THE PRINCIPAL

June 18, _______

Mrs. Sandra Fielding

[Inside Address]

Dear Mrs. Fielding,

Now that another school year is about to end, I am reminded of the many individuals who have given so generously of their time in service to our school. At _________________ School, we have a long and happy tradition of parent and community involvement that helps to enhance opportunities for students and staff.

I am particularly grateful for your assistance this year in our school's media center. Such an ongoing and regular commitment truly makes a difference in school life at _____________________. I know that many youngsters have benefitted as a result of the generosity of your time and expertise.

Your help has been truly important and I very much appreciate your spirited dedication to our school. Please accept my best wishes to you and your family for a pleasant and fulfilling summer.

Sincerely,

Principal

Effective communication is an essential skill for principals—or almost any professional, for that matter. We cannot underestimate the effect that good communication can have. It can make a relationship or break a relationship. It can also be the difference between someone who is viewed simply as a concerned or competent administrator and one who is perceived as a great leader.

13

Promoting Positive Parent and Community Relations

Each principal is, in a way, an ambassador for the nation's education system. Good relationships with parents and the larger school community are essential for the success of any principal, and when such relationships are particularly productive, the entire profession will be viewed more positively. As school leaders, we can take deliberate steps toward building a positive image of our schools. We must not only maintain good relationships with parents of schoolchildren, we must also reach out to other taxpayers who support the school and its programs. A simple way to look at this is to view your school as your classroom. What is the culture and climate that permeates the building? What does the outside observer see when looking in? As open enrollment plans, school alternatives, magnet schools, and voucher programs become more popular, principals will have to "market" their schools.

Much as it runs against the grain of many school administrators' philosophies, competition among schools for students (and the tax dollars that follow them) is more and more a reality. This requires us not only to be aware of the image of the school, but also to take steps to promote it. Good community relations require planning, time, and patience; we cannot underestimate the importance or the amount of work we must devote to this essential aspect of modern school life.

Note: All forms, letters, and checklists included in this chapter can be found at corwin.com/elementary survivalkit.

BEGIN WITH YOUR OWN SCHOOL COMMUNITY

Maintaining a positive partnership and good relations with the leaders of the parent organization is an essential activity for principals. The elected leaders of the official organization need to be cultivated as key allies to promote the school. Take the time to bring these parents in, let them see the "inside view" of the school, and ask them to support the school. Sometimes, such individuals seek positions of power because they may have an ax to grind, hope to make specific changes, or want to initiate a pet project. As misguided as this motivation may seem at first, this situation does not necessarily mean that such parents cannot be helpful if they join the school team. Regardless of the intent, the fact of the matter is that a disgruntled parent is still a parent. By asking for opinions and advice on school directions and initiatives, you will help these parents to see that you are willing to work with them and to hear their points of view. In some cases, resolving communication problems is all that needs to be done to appease the parent. As was mentioned in Chapter 12, the art of communication is key to every school leader's success.

School leaders have an important role to play with the parent organization. Meet with the president or executive committee prior to each parents association meeting to set the agenda. This provides a good opportunity to head off any problems that may be brewing, or to explain the school's point of view about controversial issues. Make a brief presentation about items of general interest at each parents association meeting. It is important to prepare for these talks, but if they are too formal, they often lose their luster. Talk about homework policies, highlight a new instructional program, outline extra-curricular opportunities, explain specific teaching methodologies, or simply report on upcoming events. Informal presentations like these help to let the parents know that you are knowledgeable, involved, and willing to explain the operation of the school.

Work with the leaders of the parents association or specific committee chairs to plan school events, set the annual calendar, design newsletters or flyers, or organize volunteer programs. Demonstrate that you are willing to "roll up your sleeves," pitch in, and be a part of the operation of the parent organization. Offer your advice about what makes for successful school events, fundraisers, and volunteer programs. Parents will generally appreciate your being an advisor to them in their efforts.

Increasing the level of parental involvement should be a goal for any school leader. Studies have shown that student achievement is enhanced if parents are involved in the school. Active participation also allows parents to understand the inner workings of the school and to become more supportive because they feel a sense of belonging.

Parent involvement, in terms of volunteering in the school, goes a long way toward promoting positive public relations. However, with this added benefit comes an added responsibility. It will be your responsibility to ensure that three things happen in order to make this experience beneficial for both sides. You must exercise care when selecting parents to serve as volunteers, volunteers must be placed in classrooms where teachers want their support, and there must be an orientation to "show" the parents what will be expected of them. If any of these things are lacking, you undoubtedly run the risk of failure in this area. (A sample letter soliciting parent and community volunteers is shown in Figure 13.1.)

Figure 13.1 Sample Letter Soliciting Parent and Community Guests to Talk to Children

Name of School

Dear Resident,

At ________________ School, we are in the process of compiling a list of willing volunteers to develop a community Talent Bank. Many local citizens have expertise, talents, and interests that can be shared that will enrich our youngsters' educational experiences.

Volunteers can come to our school to talk about their careers or share collections, hobbies, travels, and other interests with our children. Parents, grandparents, retired citizens, businesspeople, or anyone who has a talent or skill to share is encouraged to visit our program.

Classroom talks can take place anytime during the school day. We will work to develop a mutually convenient time for your visit.

Please fill out the form below and return to:

______________ School Talent Bank

[Address]

* *

I am willing to share my talents and skills in one or more of the following areas (circle as many as you like).

Career	Travel
Performing Arts	Language
Hobby	Home Economics
Business	Craft
Fine Arts	Writing/Publishing
Collection	Technology
Science	Other
Photography	

What time(s) are most convenient for you? (Circle all that apply.)

Morning   Lunchtime   Afternoon

Name: ____

Address: ____

Town: _______________________ **State:** _______________ **Zip:** _______________

Telephone: Work: (____) ___________________ **Home:** (____) ___________________

DEVELOPING A UNITY OF PURPOSE

All members of the school community ought to know what the school stands for—its fundamental purpose or mission. The development of a mission statement (discussed in Chapter 3) can go a long way toward uniting individuals who are concerned with the welfare of the school. The process of defining a mission statement should be a collaborative one involving input from all segments of the school community. Once the mission statement is developed and published, it should be "tested" periodically to check whether or not it is still applicable. The school leadership committee is an ideal body for developing and assessing the mission statement. Each year, place an examination of the mission statement on the agenda and ask the following questions:

- Does this statement define the purposes for which we all strive at our school?
- Have we lost sight of our common ideals?
- Have any circumstances caused us to alter our mission?
- What can we do to redevote ourselves to our original mission if it is still appropriate?
- Should we "redefine" ourselves?
- If so, what is our new mission?

The mere act of checking that the school's mission statement is still appropriate helps remind people of the ideals and values of the school and can help to foster unity of purpose.

Many principals find that it is useful to have the school's mission statement placed on a large chart or poster, framed, and mounted prominently in the school. This announces that all the people in the school believe in the mission and are willing to make it public. It also serves as a continuing visual reminder of purpose. In a sense, the mission is the school's theme song.

THE IMPORTANCE OF
AVAILABILITY AND VISIBILITY

Another way that school leaders can foster positive public relations in the school community is by being visible and available. This does not mean that you should drop everything you are doing to answer every phone call or meet with every parent who walks through the office door. It does mean, though, that people should know that you are available for scheduled appointments and should also know how they can meet with you. Some principals like to maintain defined "calling hours," that is, a time of day when parents can drop in to meet with them to talk about any matter or issue.

If a parent comes to the school office and demands to meet with the principal, and you are available, it is not bad practice to see the parent right then and there. If, on the other hand, you are not available, then the school secretary should explain politely that you are at a meeting, in a conference, in a classroom (or whatever happens to be the truth), and suggest times when you can meet later. If the concern comes in as a phone call or e-mail, the protocol you follow should be the same, and communications should be returned in a timely fashion. Principals should be viewed as accessible and not aloof, and the office staff can readily convey this perception.

A positive public relations technique is to deliberately make telephone calls to parents to convey good news. When you notice a particular act of kindness on the part of a youngster, or an outstanding pupil report or performance, pick up the phone and simply tell the parent how delighted you were with what you saw. This will help parents to have the impression that you are an involved, active school leader who cares about student achievement and positive communication. A note home to parents and/or students when something special has been observed also serves to foster positive home-school relations.

Get to know your students—not just by name, but also their personalities, strengths, and vulnerabilities. When you see parents, say something personal about their children. This will let the parent know that you have taken the time to get to know their children as individuals. It is an instant way to gain credibility, because by knowing your students, you have shown the parents you are willing to take the time to make their child's experience personal.

Encourage teachers to call or meet with parents when they have concerns. Letting a situation fester can often result in its becoming bigger and more complicated than it actually is.

For example, let's say that a teacher has a practice of having students score each other's quizzes. One day, a child does not do well, and when the teacher asks the student whether or not he studied, the youngster replies, "My father says that you never look at the quizzes anyway, so what's the point of studying?" Such attitudes can grow if not confronted and discussed in a rational, reasoned manner. In a situation like this, you should ask the teacher to call the parent and explain that when children score their own quizzes (if indeed that is the practice), all of the answers are reviewed and the scoring is considered a learning experience that is not intended as a replacement to teacher assessment. Such an open, honest approach to communication can help to promote good relationships among teachers and parents.

Of course, on countless occasions situations will occur that go beyond the control of teachers, and parents will demand—legitimately—to meet with you. When you do meet with parents, listen to their concerns and their views. Offer solutions to problems. Being perceived as a listener and a problem solver is a very positive image for a principal to have. Gaining trust within the school community comes after many people have had fair experiences with the school administration. Trust is gained over time, but once it is earned, it will endure and help to facilitate respect and cooperation.

WORKING WITH A PRINCIPAL'S ADVISORY COUNCIL

A school leadership team (see Chapter 3) is an ideal forum for principals to understand the many viewpoints that are prevalent in the school community. There are, however, other constituencies that school leaders will want to use to stay in touch with concerns, issues, or community opinions.

Sometimes, principals want to meet with different groups to gain distinct viewpoints. For example, parents of children with learning differences, parents of children enrolled in a gifted/talented program, or parents of children who live in a particular neighborhood in the school community might all make for specific subgroups with which you might want to meet. The agenda for such a meeting can be structured or flexible, depending upon the particular needs.

School leaders who work with advisory groups convey to parents that they care about their points of view and feel that they have something of value to contribute to the principal's leadership in the school.

Some school leaders like to host "grade-level coffees." If this style appeals to you, you can hold these receptions anytime during the school day (or before or after school), with the goal of letting parents get to know the school leader better as an individual. Another benefit of a grade-level coffee is the opportunity to hear the concerns and aspirations that parents have for their children. In some schools, it may be a good practice to have an officer of the parent association cohost the event. The parent leaders can help the school leader keep the discussion on a professional level and remind parents not to allow the meeting to turn into a "gripe session."

Sometimes, you might want to invite a guest speaker or a special community leader to these informal get-togethers. In any case, inviting parents into the school for specific purposes helps promote interest, involvement, and positive public relations.

ESTABLISHING PROCEDURES FOR HANDLING PARENTAL COMPLAINTS

Few aspects of the role of principal are as frustrating as dealing with complaints, either legitimate or unfounded, about school employees. Devising a specific complaint policy, with consistent procedures for handling parental concerns about staff members, can help ease this potentially difficult situation. Begin with an attitude of genuine openness and the sincere belief that concerns expressed about staff members can result in improved professional performance and sensitivity. It is best to establish a clear, well-publicized policy for handling complaints about employees. Usually, principals insist that the person who has a complaint first meet with the person about whom they have a concern. In most cases, complaints can be resolved at such a conference. Sometimes, the issue is simply a matter of miscommunication. If the principal jumps in too early, before the complainant has had a chance to confer with the employee, the process can be undermined and options for compromise and recourse will be lost.

Only after the complainant has had a chance to speak with the employee should either party be entitled to call for a three-way conference. In this meeting, the immediate supervisor of the staff member (usually the principal) schedules the conference for the purpose of discussing the matter further and seeking resolution. Skills in active listening and compromise should be exercised. The supervisor should take a neutral tone. There will be times, however, when the complaint seems so unjustified that the supervisor may wish to actively support the employee. The supervisor should take notes on any agreements (or lack of agreement) that come out of this meeting. A letter summarizing the meeting should then be sent to both parties.

If the complainant is not satisfied with the resolution of the three-way meeting, he or she should have an opportunity to file a formal, written complaint. A sample complaint form appears in Figure 13.2. This form should be submitted to the employee's immediate supervisor, who will then review it and forward it to the superintendent or designee. At this point, the superintendent may act upon the complaint, probably by having a meeting with the complainant and the employee. In such cases, care must be taken not to violate any of the due process rights of the employee, and the employee should be invited to bring representation from his or her professional association. The superintendent should give each party a chance to state facts about the incident, problem, or concern. Each side should ask questions of the other to elicit relevant facts. The superintendent then may further investigate the matter by seeking legal counsel or by interviewing other associated

Figure 13.2 Sample Complaint Form

EMPLOYEE COMPLAINT FORM

This is the official form to be used for complaints against employees of the Sunnyside Public Schools.

Name of School Employee: ____

Person Filing Complaint: ____

   Address: ____

   Telephone: ____

Specific concern, problem, or dissatisfaction:

Details of relevant incidents or situations including date and time of incident, if applicable:

Witnessed by (Name[s]):

   Address(es):

Redress/resolution sought:

Signature of Person Making Complaint: ____

Date: _______________________

c: Superintendent of Schools, Complainant, Employee, Immediate Supervisor

parties. If a resolution is achieved at any stage of the complaint process, a form documenting the outcome should be prepared and filed. (See Figure 13.3 for a sample of such a form.) Within a reasonable period of time, a decision should be rendered and sent, in writing, to both parties. If the resolution is still not satisfactory, the complainant may have rights to further appeal the decision to the board of education or the state commissioner of education.

Handling complaints about school employees is rarely a pleasant task. However, if a procedure is in place that is clear to all members of the school community, public relations may actually be enhanced. Employees know that they have rights and protections from unfair and unfounded complaints, and parents or other community members know that they have a clearly defined procedure to voice their concerns.

Figure 13.3   Sample Resolution of Complaint Form

EMPLOYEE COMPLAINT RESOLUTION FORM

This form should be filed when a resolution is reached regarding a complaint against a school employee.

Name of School Employee: ____

Person Filing Complaint: ____

Persons Present at Meeting	Position	Reason for Presence
1.		
2.		
3.		
4.		

Resolution: ____

Presiding Administrator: ____

Title: _________________________

Date: _________________________

Submitted to the following parties/files: **Date:**

1. _________________________________   _______________

2. _________________________________   _______________

3. _________________________________   _______________

4. _________________________________   _______________

5. _________________________________   _______________

THE IMPORTANCE OF THE ROLE OF THE SCHOOL SECRETARY

Often, the very first impression that people have of a school comes from the school secretary or office staff. The secretary's role, and its importance in public relations, cannot be underestimated. A friendly, positive demeanor on the part of the school secretary is essential for a positive feeling about the school. A cheerful greeting and a willing interest in how the visitor can be assisted will go a long way toward promoting a good first impression. We all know that secretaries are always "in the middle of something," and when someone walks into the school office, it is difficult for them to drop what they are doing and turn their attention to the needs of others, but this is a critical aspect of the position. If a secretary keeps visitors waiting, or, worse yet, does not look up from what he or she is doing, this will reflect poorly on you and the image the school wishes to convey. One way to help your secretaries understand the importance of this aspect of school life is to ask how he or she would want to be treated when first entering their own children's schools.

The secretary is often the first person that a parent who is angry or upset is likely to encounter. Help to convince your secretary that the parent rarely has a difficulty with the secretary, so the initial contact should not be taken personally. The secretary is rarely involved in the conflict and can help to diffuse the situation by maintaining a friendly, helpful, and polite demeanor.

As school leaders, we must be aware that the general operation and appearance of the school office reflects upon the entire school. If the office seems cheerful, friendly, and inviting, this is the impression that the visitor will have of the school; if, on the other hand, the office is chaotic and disorganized, this will leave another kind of impression. We must recognize that school visitors—particularly community representatives and salespeople, among others—call upon several schools. These people are in a position to relate the way they were treated in different schools. No one wants to hear from a colleague that when a community recreation director went to your school, your secretary treated him or her rudely and abruptly.

Telephone manners can also have an important impact on general school relations. Secretaries—indeed, all school employees—should be instructed to answer the telephone in a polite, helpful manner. For example, a standard greeting should be determined and publicized—perhaps even posted on a card near each telephone. A possible telephone greeting might be: "Good morning, Springhurst School. This is Ms. Jenkins," or "Springhurst School. Good morning. May I help you?" Callers should not be left on hold for an unreasonable period of time. If a message cannot be taken right away, the secretary should offer to call back in a few moments. Just as when someone visits the school office, the impression given when someone calls the school will be lasting and can help to promote good public relations.

Principals know that the "buck stops" with them. They are the ones who have the responsibility setting the tone for the school and ensuring that office staff is polite and inviting. This cannot be taken for granted, so periodic meetings with the staff to outline and reinforce practices and procedures need to be scheduled.

DEALING WITH THE MEDIA

Many school leaders know how to use local media to promote positive public relations for their schools. Others have gotten "burned" because they were not aware of how to deal with the media. The most common activity for most school leaders is to inform local newspapers or radio and television stations about events in their schools. Some principals appoint a teacher as "public relations coordinator"; others simply collect information from teachers about upcoming events for which they would like publicity. Also newsworthy are special awards, presentations made, grants secured, or seminars attended. To streamline the effort, develop a form to collect timely, interesting information from staff members. If you design a form to gather this information, the preparation of a press release is expedited. In many districts, the central administration wants this information to come from one central source in the district. However, the form suggested can help you to collect information from within your building. (See sample of a Press Release Information Form in Figure 13.4.)

Once information about noteworthy upcoming events is gathered, contact the appropriate people at local papers or stations. It is wise to keep an updated list of the names,

---

Figure 13.4 Sample Press Release Information Form

Office of the Principal

PRESS RELEASE INFORMATION FORM

Today's date: _______________________________

Teacher, class: ____

What's happening?

Why is it newsworthy?

When (date and time)?

Where?

Do you need a photograph of the event? (If so, where, when?)

Background information:

Person preparing this form:

Please return to the principal's office at least two weeks prior to the scheduled event.

---

addresses, and phone and fax numbers of the contact individuals for these media. After a while, the contact people will come to know you and your school. Try to be aware of deadlines, especially in the case of weekly community papers. For example, if a local paper comes out on a Wednesday afternoon, there may be a 12:00 PM deadline on Tuesday for the inclusion of an item. This is especially important if you are submitting an item about a school event and you want people to know about it before it occurs.

When important stories develop in the local community, especially if linked to a natural disaster or emergency situation, expect to be contacted by reporters. Your school district should have a policy for who is authorized to provide information to the press. If you are unsure about your district's policy, ask your superintendent. It is common practice for the superintendent, the superintendent's designee, or a public information officer to be the only person in the school district who is authorized to speak with the press about emergency situations or breaking news stories.

If you are the person who is in contact with the press, be careful of what you say. School leaders often find that they are quoted out of context, especially if the reporter has a particular slant to the story that he or she is writing. Ask the reporter to repeat back what he or she heard you say. Clarify your points. Some principals often feel that they can say something to a reporter "off the record." This is a risky practice, as many have found that there is no such thing as "off the record" when an important story is breaking and the public is thirsting for information and particular points of view.

A good practice is to invite a local education reporter to school to meet you and have a tour of the school. This will help the reporter become acquainted with you on a personal basis. Developing personal, informal relations with local reporters will help you if you want publicity for a specific event or accomplishment. Many local newspapers run a "Back-to-School" issue in early September. Give reporters ideas by highlighting new school initiatives, significant enrollment shifts, new programs, or other matters that will be of general interest.

BECOMING SKILLFUL AT CREATING POSITIVE PUBLICITY FOR YOUR SCHOOL

You must be savvy about marketing your school. Promoting a school is an acquired skill. It is the rare school leader who is particularly adept in this area their first year at a school. Just getting through a day may seem like enough of a challenge, but when you think about it, time spent on promoting positive publicity for your school is time well invested. Schools are actively competing for tax dollars and state aid allocations. Also, "school bashing" has almost become fashionable, as parents and other community members sometimes like to blame all the ills of society on the schools, thus the need to promote schools and let people know about all of the positive things they are doing. You want to ensure that the public sees and appreciates the critical importance of quality education for the future of the entire nation.

Schools are active places in which teachers, parents, and students are busily engaged in meeting goals and working on behalf of children. You might feel that there is not much that's newsworthy about this. Some outstanding principals feel that they are simply "doing their jobs" and that there is nothing special to boast about. Well, all principals should take stock of the wonderful things that are happening in their schools each day and note special programs that are designed to help students grow and succeed.

Assess Needs

Have school budgets been routinely defeated? Does the community have a positive or a negative image of the school? Are citizens skeptical about the general effectiveness of their local schools? Do parents, by and large, seem to be satisfied with the instructional program, or do you feel like you are always fending off complaints? Does the community sense that the school is a safe, orderly place? These factors must be taken into consideration when assessing the need for a school public relations initiative. Ask others about their perceptions of the school, the concerns that they have, and what they perceive to be the school's strong points. This information can help in designing the right program to fit local needs.

Define the Audience

You must understand the various audiences that need to have accurate, positive information about your school. Parent groups, retired citizens, community service organizations, local businesses, and realtors are among the many different groups that you must consider. Once you've defined the various groups with which you should communicate, decide upon the appropriate vehicles. Some might include community newsletters, articles in a local newspaper, tours of the school, or school information nights or breakfasts.

The first audience to consider is the internal one—the school staff. Publicize the accomplishments of teachers. Highlight interesting events taking place in individual classrooms. Celebrate collegial projects. Making sure that all members of the school are aware of the positive things that are happening within it is the first aspect of any public relations effort.

Develop a "Press Packet"

Prospective parents, realtors, and businesspeople often call to find out more about the school. A convenient way to disperse information to various groups is to compose a press packet. Some of the components of such a packet might include

- an overview of school enrollment and staff,
- admission policies and procedures,
- a mission statement or school philosophy,
- a brief description of standard programs and special offerings,
- vital statistics about the school building and school district,
- highlights or unique programs of which the staff is especially proud,
- frequently asked questions, and
- school contact information.

The press packet can be easily assembled and placed into a pocket folder. In this way, whenever someone calls to inquire about the school, any staff member will have this vital information at his or her fingertips, or the entire packet can be mailed out to the interested party.

Make Connections to Service Organizations

Service clubs, such as Rotary, Lions, and Elks, all have vested interests in their local communities. School leaders would be well-advised to make contact with leaders of these organizations and perhaps make presentations about their schools. Such clubs are more than willing to get involved in projects that can help children in the community. For example, in one district, the Lions Club has supported eye examinations and eyeglasses for needy children. Another such organization provided an FM listening device for a hearing-impaired youngster. Nothing is lost in asking for assistance, and very often, such clubs are more than receptive to ideas for projects that will benefit the schools in their locality.

Forge Links With Local Businesses and Industries

Get to know the important businesses and industries in your local school community. Call the heads of these companies, or if they are large enough, the public information officers. Invite them to meet with you and visit the school. When possible, do business with the area merchants. Whether it is down at the local pizzeria or in the regional bank, oftentimes after you make a contact and get to know more about the company you can think about ways to form a partnership. Perhaps some of the corporation's employees can visit the school to talk with children about their work. Technical expertise can be shared. Employees can serve as mentors to students who are working on special projects, banks can work with the parent organization to set up savings accounts for students, and the pizzeria may offer reduced rates on pizzas to support a fundraising effort.

You must convince corporate executives of the benefits *to them* of such partnerships as well. (A sample letter to a company president inviting such a partnership appears in Figure 13.5.) These benefits include many possibilities, such as the following:

- Promoting positive publicity for the corporation
- Gaining a better understanding of the complexities of educating the nation's youth
- Contributing to the improvement of a national workforce
- Helping students understand career options and the need for good preparation to enter specific fields
- Possible tax write-offs for equipment that is no longer needed

Figure 13.5	Sample Letter to Corporate President Suggesting a School-Business Partnership

Office of the Principal

Mr. Jonathan Michaels, President
Acme Pharmaceutical Manufacturing Corporation
42 Downing Avenue
Sunnyside, NY

Dear Mr. Michaels,

As you well know, business, industry, and education all share a stake in the development of a skilled workforce to keep our nation's economy strong. Since your firm is located just blocks away from our school, I am writing to suggest that we set up a meeting to find ways to join together to develop a partnership between the Sunnyside Elementary School and Acme Pharmaceutical. As you may know, Mr. Roger Carroll, a parent of a child in our school, is a member of your research and development team.

You might ask why you would even want to entertain such a relationship. In answer to this question, corporations all over the country have found relationships with their local public schools rewarding in many ways. Some of the benefits include the following:

- It creates positive publicity for your company.
- It helps your employees gain a better understanding of the complexities of modern-day schooling.
- You will have the satisfaction of knowing that in some small way you are contributing to the development of a skilled workforce.
- You will be able to help youngsters understand a sampling of career options that might be open to them.
- Newspaper articles that emerge from such a partnership can serve to enhance the public image of your company.

The staff of Sunnyside Elementary School and I have been thinking of positive avenues for mutual involvement. We would like to begin by inviting you to visit our school to discuss possible ways to establish a mutually beneficial connection between Acme Pharmaceuticals and our school.

I will be calling you next week to set up an appointment for us to discuss this matter further.

Sincerely,

Principal

Once a relationship with a business or organization has been formed, the school leader can begin to think in terms of creating a formal proposal for some kind of involvement, grant, or donation from the corporation to the school. The needs of the corporation as well as the school must always be kept in mind in preparing the proposal.

If there is an institution of higher learning in the school vicinity, the opportunities for involvement and interchange are quite obvious. Not only can the school serve as a site for student teachers and interns, but the principal can work with college personnel to create professional development programs for teachers. In recent times, one of the criteria for securing corporate or government grants requires that schools form relationships or consortia with local colleges or universities.

Maintain a Web Presence

Most schools have Internet Web pages for public access. Such Web pages can contain countless items including

- up-to-date information about school events and programs;
- classroom news and special programs;
- explanations for homework assignments;
- opportunities to e-mail the principal, teachers, and other school personnel;
- photographs of the school;
- information about school closings or schedule changes;
- profiles of staff members; and
- vital statistics about the school such as school enrollment, class size, student-teacher ratio, budget information, test scores, and special awards received.

A Web presence makes the school accessible not only to existing parents, but also to others who might be interested in moving into the area or finding out more about the school. Opportunities also exist to provide access to global exchanges by having students and staff communicate with their peers and engage in cooperative ventures and projects.

Increasingly in schools, the primary mission goes well beyond educating children. Principals, and for that matter all school employees, must be aware of and sensitive to the way that the school is perceived in the community at large. As competition for resources in education increases, the need to establish a planned, coordinated program for promoting the school becomes essential. The more citizens and business groups learn about the school and feel part of its mission, the more likely they will be to support initiatives, capital improvements, and become involved productively in the school.

14

Technology and the Elementary School Program

Technology has firmly taken hold and has transformed the instructional landscape. By the time this book is printed, changes in and new uses for technology will have come about. Technology advances so quickly, and this presents a continual challenge as well as a great opportunity for school administrators. No book of this nature can offer a truly timely treatment of technology use in schools, so in this chapter, useful generalizations prevail. The focus is on how to help you keep your school on the move and aware of the rapid changes that will inevitably present themselves.

In its purest sense, technology is the application of scientific principles in everyday contexts. The thermostat that controls our heating system is a technological device. The wheel is a technological device. MRI (magnetic resonance imaging) diagnostic equipment is a common form of technology in medicine. The list is truly endless. In this chapter, though, the term *technology* is used specifically as it relates to computers, computer-related equipment, and how these devices can enhance and support the instructional program.

Computers first appeared in classrooms in the late 1970s and early 1980s. In many cases, this equipment was funded by parent organizations, as parents were eager to ensure that their children would be able to keep up, and parents wanted to offer them every advantage in a rapidly changing technological world. These initial trials were somewhat variable in their success, and it was not until teachers were convinced of how technology could help them in their classrooms that the movement toward greater use of computers really took off.

Computers are used to enhance and support instruction in a variety of ways. The use of technology can lead to increased enthusiasm, more intense engagement, and greater

---

Note: All forms, letters, and checklists included in this chapter can be found at corwin.com/elementary survivalkit.

263

investment on the part of students in their own learning. Included among the many technological tools commonly used in schools are

- computers,
- PDAs (personal digital assistants),
- DVD players and recorders,
- IPods or other MP3 players,
- LCD panels or projectors,
- interactive whiteboards or SMART Boards,
- telephones in classrooms,
- digital video recorders, and
- robotic devices.

Students use many other devices that can be considered part of a technology program, and it is handy to have all of this equipment available. However, unless the *purposes* of the use of technology are well thought out, even the best-equipped school can flounder in its applications.

CLARIFYING THE PURPOSES OF TECHNOLOGY IN THE SCHOOL

The purposes and the goals for the use of technology in the elementary school should be clear, or else the potential of this technology may not be fully realized. Without collaboratively developed goals, technological tools can come to determine the curriculum rather than having the technologies support the established curriculum.

A large, overarching purpose for the use of technology in schools might be for students to acquire the skills and knowledge needed by all citizens to thrive and contribute in a rapidly changing society. In order to achieve this comprehensive purpose, some definite goals need to be established. A list of appropriate goals for elementary school students includes

- helping students feel successful and competent in their use of technology;
- providing resources and support so that students can be engaged in rich, authentic learning experiences and participate successfully in a technological society;
- using technology to gather information through databases, archives, online services, and all components of the World Wide Web;
- gaining access to the inaccessible through simulations and virtual-reality programs;
- using technology as a tool for enriching and enhancing the curriculum and providing opportunities for students to extend learning, solve relevant problems, enhance thinking, and pursue independent interests;
- using technology for composition, including word processing, desktop publishing, drawing, musical composition, graphics creation, and the development of multimedia presentations;
- applying technological skills and knowledge to design, construct, use, and evaluate ideas, concepts, and data;
- benefiting from establishing global connections with students, scientists, experts, and other members of the world community;
- helping students understand ethical considerations in the use of technology, that is, the need to respect copyright laws and the development of appropriate etiquette in using the Internet;

- providing a basis for student evaluation of the advantages and some of the possible dangers of the proliferation of technology; and
- supporting educators in their assessment of student learning, administrative functions, and record keeping.

PLANNING FOR EFFECTIVE USE OF TECHNOLOGY IN SCHOOLS

Once the purposes of the use of technology have been determined, you must plan the best ways to deploy equipment in your school. Where to locate the various pieces of equipment is an essential question. What students will do with the technology is another area that must be defined.

Determining the Location of Technological Devices

When computers were first introduced in elementary schools, they were either located in a library/media center or shared between classrooms by placing them on carts. As computers became more available and affordable, administrators had to decide whether to place the computers in media centers, classrooms, or computer labs. When computers were placed in common areas, like libraries or labs, they could be clustered for common instructional activities. Usually, a schedule had to be developed so that classes or groups of children could be rotated in and out of the common area.

In recent years, there has been a trend toward having computers available in a variety of locations throughout the school. The benefits of having computers in classrooms are clear:

1. Software and online services can be incorporated into regular classroom instruction.

2. Connections to a network and the Internet can provide access for students in all classrooms to all the information available in the global community.

3. Children can use computers for more natural purposes and when the need arises as opposed to when they are scheduled to use them.

4. Teachers can monitor what students are doing with computers and look over their shoulders to ensure that Internet activities are not being misused.

When computers are in short supply, restricting their use to classrooms can reduce the amount of time that all students have for access to computers. The ideal situation is to have computers available in a variety of places—classrooms, special instructional areas, and media centers. The proliferation of wireless computer carts has also helped to provide computers when and where needed. When a relatively large number of computers are clustered, large-group instruction can be provided to introduce a new program, procedure, or device. Educators have considered the best numbers of computers for each classroom. It is not unlikely to imagine the day when, in addition to a desk or worktable, each student will have his or her own computer station or laptop. However, for the present, many teachers feel that the four- or six-computer classroom is ideal. If classrooms are set up into learning stations, then the computer station can provide ready access to a wide variety of functions. For example, children can draft some of their written work at tables, and then, when they cycle through the computer station, they will have their turn to word process their work. Teachers often develop rotation schedules for computer stations. In other situations, a computer station is used like a classroom library for when students need to access information for a particular purpose. The use of interactive whiteboards or SMART Boards can be used for group research, lessons, explanations, and exploration.

So far, this discussion has dealt only with computers—the most common form of technology found in schools. However, many other devices are in use in schools today, and the placement of this equipment must also be well thought out. LCD projectors, iPods, video cameras, DVD players, and other such devices may not be so broadly available that each classroom will have its own complete set of equipment. In some schools, teachers in the same grade level share the equipment. In other situations, such equipment is locked in a media cabinet and signed out as needed. Because such devices can break down from time to time, it is important that one person be responsible for maintaining an inventory of such equipment, checking it in and out, and determining if repairs are necessary. Sometimes, an administrator has this responsibility; in other cases, the librarian or media specialist will assume this duty; in still other cases, an "extra-compensated" or stipended position is created in which a teacher will oversee this operation. This person can also be responsible for providing brief training sessions for how to operate the equipment and simple troubleshooting techniques. Whatever the arrangement, a secure location for such technological devices must be maintained; otherwise, the equipment is likely to become lost, broken, or misused.

Defining the Purposes for Which Technology Will Be Used

After the main goals for the use of technology have been addressed, teachers and administrators should define the specific purposes that will be served through technology. One school's list includes

- Information Gathering

  electronic dictionaries, encyclopedias, and thesauruses

  online databases

  the World Wide Web and search engines

  school, districtwide, or commercial subscription networks

- Instructional Software

  problem-solving programs

  drill and practice programs

  informational programs

  software to accompany commercial instructional programs

  autotutorial programs

- Analytical and Information Processing Tools

  graphing programs

  spreadsheets

  database management programs

  statistical packages

  scientific instrumentation, for example, temperature or humidity probes

- Composition Tools
  word-processing programs
  desktop publishing programs
  graphics and art production programs
  musical composition programs
  personal digital assistants (PDAs)
  outlining aids
  multimedia tools and presentations

- Games and Simulations
  instructional games

  simulations, for example, stock trading programs, wilderness adventures, animal dissections, and virtual-reality programs

- Communications
  e-mail
  distribution lists
  RSS feeds
  blogs
  forums
  online databases
  podcasts
  school-to-home communications
  school publications, class or school Web sites, announcements

Developing Guidelines for the Use of Technology

Early efforts to integrate technology into classrooms failed because teachers were not provided with sufficient in-service experiences and assistance on how best to coordinate regular classroom practices and activities with technological devices. Teachers also require specific instructions on how to teach students the basic operations of computers and other equipment. Often, students who were expert users at home were much more adept than their teachers at using technology. Teachers and students are often collaborators in their exploration and understanding of how best to use technology. Yet teachers need to stay in the driver's seat, because if students alone lead the way, the purposes of technology could easily become compromised.

A committee of teachers, a director of technology (if your district has one), administrators, and perhaps parents should join together and develop procedural guidelines, or a curriculum, for technology use in the classroom. A sample of a second-grade computer curriculum appears in Figure 14.1.

Once a curriculum outline is established, implementation forms or checklists should be devised to assist teachers in monitoring student competencies and how they use computers. If teachers check these forms from time to time, they will know which aspects of the program require additional reinforcement or instructional emphasis. A sample of a second-grade computer competency checklist appears in Figure 14.2.

Figure 14.1 Sample Second-Grade Computer Curriculum Outline

COMPUTER TECHNOLOGY CURRICULUM: GRADE TWO

Learning Processes	Activities	Results	Assessment Type
Computer Literacy	1. Learn how to turn computer on and off	Successfully accomplishes activities specified	Teacher observation
	2. Name and define use of keyboard, monitor, disk drive, CD-ROM, and mouse	Successfully accomplishes activities specified	Checklist
	3. Carefully and safely insert and eject CDs		
	4. Demonstrate appropriate handling of CDs	Students will hold diskettes and CDs by edge and away from strong magnetic fields	
	5. Handle equipment with care		
	6. Save new or revised work in a file		
	7. Open and edit work saved on a file	Students will open and edit documents in progress	
Keyboarding	1. Know and be able to use return, space bar, cursor keys, shift, and caps lock keys	Successfully accomplishes activities specified	Teacher observation checklist
	2. Use mouse (pointing and clicking) to enter and exit programs, open and close windows, files, and graphics	Demonstrate use of mouse techniques	
	3. Know how to "drag and drop" items with a mouse		
	4. Enter text and select and change font name, font size, and text style	Produce a simple written text and change font name, size, and style	Examination of student document produced
Composition	1. Create a simple written piece using a word-processing program	Produce a simple written piece	Examination of student document produced
	2. Add a graphic element to the piece	Place a graphic element appropriately	
Information Retrieval	1. Locate information on an electronic encyclopedia	Find information for a stated purpose	Teacher observation
	2. Conduct a simple one- or two-word search using an appropriate browser	Select one or two relevant Web sites	
	3. Access a map using appropriate software or Web site	Find a map of a specific country	
Data Organization and Analysis	1. Use a graphing program	Enter data provided on a simple graphing program	Rating of student document with teacher-developed rubric

Figure 14.2 Sample Second-Grade Computer Skills Checklist

STUDENT NAME																	
Student successfully turns computer on and off.																	
Student names and defines use of keyboard, monitor, flash drive, CD drive, and mouse.																	
Student carefully and safely inserts and ejects CDs.																	
Student holds CD along outer edge.																	
Student demonstrates proper care of equipment.																	
Student demonstrates use of mouse to enter and exit programs, open and close windows, and in application of appropriate second-grade software.																	
Student can save and retrieve work.																	
Student can open and edit work.																	
Student can revise work and save to file.																	
Student successfully demonstrates entering text for written work and can select and modify font name, size, and style.																	
Student can select and insert a graphic or graphic element into a document.																	
Student composes and prints a short piece of writing.																	
Student can draw geometric forms or a simple figure by using a drawing or painting program.																	
Student can retrieve a map and information about a country using an electronic encyclopedia.																	
Student can conduct a simple one- or two-word search using an appropriate Internet browser.																	
Student can create a simple graph to represent data given or collected.																	

One of the ways to ensure that technologies are integrated into the regular classroom curriculum is to require that whenever a curriculum area is reviewed or new curriculum written, appropriate software, Web sites, and equipment are defined that will enhance the accomplishment of the desired skills and objectives. Although software offerings and Web sites will change from time to time, it is important to think through how technology can assist student learning in all areas.

INTEGRATING TECHNOLOGY INTO THE GENERAL CURRICULUM

Technology is not an end in itself. Rather, it is a means to an end. When equipment has been simply assigned to classrooms without adequate staff development and thought as to its purposes, this equipment will often be unused or misused. Careful thought must be devoted as to how best to integrate technology into the established program. Where does it best fit? What can it do to enhance opportunities for students and teachers? If technology is seen as an "add-on," its potential will hardly be realized.

Colleagues need to meet to define and plan for the best possible uses for technology in their current teaching situations. Teachers can imagine and create applications that will help in teaching, learning, and managing information and solving problems in all subject areas. Software must be evaluated in terms of how it can enhance opportunities to promote the existing curriculum. This is a perfect area of investigation for the school learning community. (See Chapters 3 and 11 for more discussion of professional learning communities.) As teachers review their instructional sequences in each curriculum area, they can discuss the possibilities offered by services, software, and Web sites within each discipline.

Some of the specific uses that may occur in classrooms include the following:

- *Word Processing and Publishing.* Word processors are used to assist student writing. The programs selected should be developmentally appropriate and serve the needs of the curriculum.
- *Drawing or Painting Programs.* If the class is studying shapes, then geometry programs or drawing programs can enhance the ways in which students can explore this topic.
- *Simulations.* If a social studies unit on basic economic principles is planned, then teachers can look for software that will allow students to conduct a simulation in which they will apply the concepts studied.
- *Blogs.* Students can share their ideas, thoughts, research, thinking, and reactions through the use of blogs. Any student can become a columnist. Teachers need to exercise caution in monitoring the content of student blogs and screen them before they are published for wider distribution.
- *Podcasts.* Students can create audio or video digital files that can then be shared with others over the Internet or downloaded to portable media players or computers. Podcasts can be used to summarize student research or to record the main aspects of a lesson, book discussion, or observation.
- *Internet Forums.* These bulletin-board systems allow students to react to one another's postings and continue an ongoing dialogue. Students from diverse areas

of the world can communicate and engage in discussions through such forums. Again, teachers should monitor such interactions.

- *RSS Feeds.* The initials RSS stand for "Really Simple Syndication." RSS feeds allow users to get timely updates and articles from favorite Web sites on specific topics. These can be quite helpful in conducting research or maintaining an awareness of new developments in a specific field.

These tools can enhance learning, open up the classroom, and engage students in their learning. They also have the potential to reach and stimulate learners who exhibit a broad variety of skills and interests. However, teachers need to find the natural connections between what they intend to teach and how technology can support that effort. Not every tool will fit every classroom endeavor.

Students must be guided to use technology to support their learning goals and the topics currently under study. It is easy to see how this scenario is different from simply having "free time" in which students are able to explore whatever they want that happens to be on the computer.

Student use of computers should also result in products that will enable teachers to assess their work and involvement. Written compositions, graphs, drawings, and spreadsheets can all be submitted, and the quality of the products can be evaluated and discussed with students with the goal of determining how the use of technology helped support the learning, and how the tools and programs were used and perhaps could have been used to better avail.

TECHNOLOGY AND EDUCATIONAL REFORM

The broad use of computers and other technologies has had an enormous influence on education in schools. Technology will continue to play a central role as we prepare our students for the skills necessary for life in the 21st century. Learning environments in which a bank of classroom computers used only for word processing or other simple tasks no longer fit the bill. Teachers today need a true vision for the use of technology as a means of supporting and enhancing teaching and learning. As more and more teachers have found natural ways to integrate computers into their instructional programs, the ability to retrieve information on a global scale has led to educational reforms. Inquiry-centered, process-oriented instructional methods have become more and more common, and these approaches have been aided and assisted by the use of technology. This has led to greater ownership and investment on the part of students in their own learning. They are making more decisions about what they will learn and how they will learn. As students search databases, work through simulations, manage data collected, and use word-processing tools, they are actively engaged in constructing their own knowledge, rather than simply acting as vessels of knowledge poured into them by teacher lectures or textbooks. This transformation of the elementary school classroom is unprecedented.

Skills for the 21st Century

Educators all over the nation are embracing an effort often referred to as 21st-century skills. These skills form a basis for being competitive in an ever-changing and increasingly technological workplace. These skills have also redefined the commencement outcomes of most school districts. In order to keep up with these changes, districts have found themselves increasing the rigor of what their students will need to do to reach high levels of competency throughout the core skills. Technology will continue to play a central role as we prepare our students for life well into the 21st century. With this generation of students growing up in the "digital age," it will no longer be acceptable for students to simply find information. Rather, they must be able to interpret, analyze, and synthesize information. Students must possess a deeper understanding of all content as it applies to the matter at hand as well as what it means in the greater society. Knowledge and understanding of core subjects will need to be woven across interdisciplinary themes. Being an agent of change, you will need to champion the cause for more than exposure and superficial learning within the classroom. The principal who is prepared to lead this change should look to see that the following skill sets are developed:

- *Technological Literacy:* Students will need to be proficient with digital media and information technology.
- *Innovative Thinking:* Nontraditional learning methods, creative thinking, and problem solving should be encouraged in both the classroom and outside the school walls. Risk taking and real-world problem solving only serve to enhance the student's intellectual capacity.
- *Interactive Communication:* Students will need to understand the importance of being an effective and articulate communicator in multiple settings and configurations, whether that is a one-on-one dialogue, communicating as part of a team, or weighing in on an issue of global importance as a matter of debate in a social setting.

These essential skills will undoubtedly prepare our students for the challenges they will face beyond the classroom. In order to fully develop those skills, though, it is imperative for you to create a learning environment that is prepared to foster the rigor of these new expected standards.

Maintain Focus on Curriculum

Of course, the teacher still orchestrates the kinds of inquiries students engage in, but the technological classroom has resulted in greater student choice and involvement in the learning process. This situation is not without its challenges. Sometimes, student interests and inquiries may steer them far from what the teachers have established as the curriculum to be learned. In such cases, the teacher must develop the skills to redirect student activities and bring them closer to the goals and objectives that have been established.

An additional challenge for teachers and administrators is to regularly sift through the vast amounts of information that has become available and accessible to students. This requires the teaching of a whole new set of skills to students. How do they evaluate the importance and relevance of materials they find as they travel along the information superhighway? Access is the first step, but once access is available, students need to be able to assess the value of the information with which they are confronted, and how well it relates to the topic they are researching. Teachers also have to spend additional time to assess and evaluate the software that they bring into their classrooms.

As exciting as these new methodologies are, no effective instruction can happen without adequate access to technological equipment and online services. If principals wish to see the kinds of reforms mentioned above, then their goal must be to secure the resources that will enable this to happen.

The Principal as a Model of the Use of Technology

If technology is to flourish in a school, then the principal must be viewed as a leader in the use of technology. Routine announcements can be sent to the staff by e-mail. Interactive whiteboards can be used for staff presentations and at faculty meetings. PDAs can be used during walk-throughs or teacher observations. Assessment data can be presented to staff using computer-generated graphs, tables, and charts. The active use of technology on the part of the principal sends a positive signal to the entire school community that technology is valued and used to good avail.

PLANNING FOR APPROPRIATE STAFF DEVELOPMENT FOR USING TECHNOLOGY

Study after study has shown that all of the best equipment placed in classrooms can have little or no educational impact if adequate staff development for the uses of technology is not provided. A wise superintendent once said, "We need to spend four dollars on staff development for every dollar we spend on equipment." Although that figure may be a bit of an exaggeration, the point is a good one. Without proper training and support, any investment in equipment will not be realized.

In every school, you will find teachers who are reluctant to learn about technology and its use in the classroom. Some feel that they are not technologically inclined; they are fearful and believe that they lack the orientation and proclivity to be adept in using computers and other technologies. Other teachers are resistant to change and find it difficult to incorporate new methodologies and approaches. In either case, these teachers cannot be shunned or ignored; they must be helped to develop positive attitudes and the skills required to make effective use of technology in their classrooms.

Designing a staff development program to help teachers use technology should take into consideration the fact that there is a broad range of familiarity and comfort among the staff in any school. Some teachers are experts; others are novices. A reasonable plan for a staff development program in a school or school district should include the following components:

Familiarity with the school's technology plan and expectations. The first step in any staff development program is to make sure that the participants are aware of the school's or district's technology plan. The goals for computer use should be made clear and be related to each employee's specific role in the school. Expectations for computer use should be specified and translated into how it can be achieved in the classroom.

Formal presentations. A staff development plan should include some formal presentations such as defining the most appropriate purposes and uses for technology, sharing successes and frustrations, and what specific equipment and programs can offer students and teachers. Using an interactive whiteboard to demonstrate the applications being discussed can model the effective use of technology.

Guided practice. In this aspect of the staff development plan, teachers practice new skills and are guided in their work by more experienced users, teacher coaches, workshop leaders, or others. If a district is fortunate enough to have a training center with several computer stations, the coach can go from learner to learner providing advice, assistance, and suggestions. If a training center is not available, then a few computers clustered together in a classroom or media center may serve the same purpose.

Collaboration with colleagues, staff developers, and technology turnkeys. Where staff developers or teacher coaches are employed, these individuals can provide training sessions and individual classroom visits to help teacher learners in their own environments. Many individuals have remarked that this is the most valuable kind of training, because the staff development focuses on how teachers are using technology in their own situations and questions are directed toward helping each teacher achieve success.

Where staff developers are not available, each school can name a group, or at least one individual, to serve as a computer "turnkey," or resident expert. These individuals may receive a small stipend for assuming this role, or they may simply help others because they are willing to share their expertise. Some of the duties that building turnkeys can assume include

- setting up equipment when it arrives in classrooms,
- loading software or showing teachers how to load their own software,
- simple troubleshooting for common problems,
- diagnosing more complicated problems and indicating what needs to be repaired,
- conducting brief workshops for colleagues,
- helping teachers select software and Web sites based upon predetermined criteria, and
- interpreting the district's technology plan and how it affects each classroom.

Independent Practice

Once teachers have been provided with some basic training experiences, they need to practice independently to become more adept at using technology. This can take place in their classrooms along with their students, at quiet moments before or after school, or at home. More and more schools are making laptop computers available for teachers to use at home so that they may prepare lessons or presentations and practice at their own pace. Even if all teachers do not have access to a school-supplied laptop, one or two, with appropriate software preloaded, can be "signed out" overnight, during a weekend, or for a few weeks at a time. When school equipment is loaned out, however, accurate inventory and records must be maintained. A sample Equipment Loan Request Agreement form appears in Figure 14.3. Securing laptops for teachers' independent practice might indeed be a fruitful grant idea for funding by a local foundation or corporation.

Figure 14.3 Sample Computer Loan Request Agreement

EQUIPMENT LOAN REQUEST AGREEMENT

Request is made to loan the following equipment for the time specified.

Name: _______________________________ **School:** _____________________

Description of Equipment	Make/Model	Serial #
1.		
2.		
3.		
4.		
5.		

From (date): ___/___/____   **To** (date): ___/___/____

Comments (condition): _________________________________

   I acknowledge receiving the above-described equipment and assume full responsibility for it during the time specified above. I further agree to indemnify the _______________ PUBLIC SCHOOLS for any loss or damage to the above-described equipment that might occur while I am responsible for it.

Signed: _________________________________ **Date:** ___/___/____

Issued by: _________________________________ **Date:** ___/___/____

____

Date Returned: ___/___/____ **Received By:** _____________________

Condition Received:

Any staff development initiative for technology must help teachers see that technology is used in sensible ways that are well articulated within the established program. Teachers must also have many opportunities for practice. There is just no substitute for spending time becoming acquainted with technology and its applications at an individual pace.

USING ONLINE SERVICES

The Internet has opened the world to each individual classroom. Students and teachers can access diverse information at their fingertips with lightning speed. Students can converse with their counterparts in schools in other parts of the world and take part in fascinating, enriching, and meaningful online projects. Discussions with scientists, data collection and sharing, and access to databases all serve to provide exciting, rewarding opportunities for students and teachers.

The uninitiated, however, must know how to start. There are some basics all users will need to know. How to log on? How to access e-mail? How to get onto the Web? Such questions must be specified, and the principal should be among the first to know the answers to these important questions.

Once online, teachers must know how to search for the information they need, connect with others, or join some of the very beneficial projects in which they or their students can engage. Below, a few basic terms are reviewed in terms of their application to classroom instruction.

Logging On

Regardless of the type of connection the school system provides, the first thing a user needs to do is log on to the system. Usually this involves entering a username and a password. Teachers should be careful to keep their passwords secret and secure. They should also teach students the "netiquette" of always looking aside when someone else enters a password. Once access is granted, mail can be checked and other applications can be accessed.

Search Engines

These are tools for accessing information on the World Wide Web. Different search engines operate in unique ways. Some search the Web by key words; others use whole phrases. Teachers and students need to learn how to search for specific information. Sometimes, the words entered must be linked to very narrow concepts if you want information on a very specific item. If you want to choose among a variety of possible articles or sources, then a broader range of terms should be used for the search. For example, let's say you want to find specific resources in your area to find out about dog breeds. You may be interested in the Dalmatian. You could enter the term *Dalmatian*, which will probably bring up lots of information about the breed. If, however, you enter *dogs* and *New York*, you might be more likely to find information about dog clubs in the area.

Blogs, Forums, and RSS Feeds

The Web allows you to maintain contact with hundreds—even thousands—of individuals who have similar interests by reading blogs or joining a forum, a newsgroup, or an RSS feed. Such memberships provide access to online discussions, articles of interest, or items entered by individuals who are responding to one another or an issue or topic.

Maintaining Safety

Safety on the Internet is a critical consideration. Teachers and administrators must employ certain precautions and safeguards to ensure that the content to which children are exposed is safe and appropriate. This is by no means an easy task as new sites appear on the Web each and every day.

Teachers, administrators, and media specialists must evaluate search engines and Web sites for the appropriateness of their content. Lists should be made of sites that are particularly helpful and meaningful, as well as those that should be avoided. Most school districts have invested in Internet protection filters, site blockers, or "nannies," which block out certain sites that contain inappropriate content. Schools can also subscribe to a variety of online management systems. These services screen content, filter inappropriate sites, and lock students out of them.

Developing Internet Usage Policies

Once access to the Internet became widespread in schools, parents, administrators, and school board members were confronted with the issue of establishing policies and procedures for appropriate use of this resource. Staff development about this issue is necessary and should grow out of local policy. If your district has not already done so, a committee of teachers, parents, administrators, and school board members should be formed to establish local policies. Some of the issues that should be addressed include the following:

- What are the purposes of student use of the Internet?
- Under what conditions will students be permitted access to the Internet?
- What online services will be permitted and made available in the schools?
- How will sites be filtered or screened? What security measures are in place?
- What are appropriate standards for online behavior and how can they be reinforced?
- What are the responsibilities if e-mail accounts are issued?
- How are students taught to understand the limitations of the use of copyrighted material?
- How often and under what circumstances will local policies be reviewed?

A sample Acceptable Use Policy for a school district appears in Figure 14.4.

Gaining Parental Permission for Students to Use the Internet

Once local policies for Internet use have been established, parental permission for student access should be secured. Parents must be made aware of the potential hazards that their children encounter while online. Aside from inappropriate language, content, and graphics, children are also exposed to advertising. The online marketplace has advertising that is aimed specifically at the lucrative 18-and-under market. Sometimes, children are asked to fill out forms online, and their names then become a part of a marketing database. *All students should be instructed never to give out personal information while online.*

Figure 14.4   Sample Internet Usage Policy

Board of Education

INTERNET ACCEPTABLE USE POLICY

Our students have access to many valuable instructional technology tools as well as Internet access in various areas of the school. Computer networks allow students to interact with others within the school and the larger global community. Our goal is teach students to use these resources responsibly to enhance the instructional program. This Acceptable Use Policy is necessary to outline the conditions for responsible, legal, and ethical use of our network resources.

Acceptable use includes

- using computer or network equipment for classroom activities or projects, including connecting to other systems and computers through the Internet;
- sending and receiving e-mail related to school activities;
- respecting and showing proper care and handling of all equipment; and
- observing copyright laws.

Unacceptable use includes

- using the network for commercial advertising;
- using the network to access pornography of any type;
- using the network to send/receive messages that are racist, sexist, and/or discriminatory in any manner;
- using the network to send/receive messages that contain obscenities;
- using the network to provide information that others may use inappropriately;
- using the network to send/receive inflammatory messages;
- loading or modifying software and/or settings without the consent of a staff member or administrator;
- using the network in any way that may damage its operation and stability, e.g., accepting a message containing a virus or loading a virus onto any workstation;
- using the network to send/receive a message with someone else's name on it;
- using the network to send/receive a message that is inconsistent with the school's code of conduct; or
- accessing the network from an unauthorized station.

Inappropriate usage of the network will result in disciplinary action as deemed necessary by the administration. It may also result in criminal and/or legal action taken against the violator.

The Board of Education and its employees are *not* responsible for any damage that may occur from the use of the Internet. The Board of Education is also not responsible for any inappropriate usage by the student. The Internet is to be used at the student's own risk and the student shall be held responsible for his/her own misconduct.

The type of permission that should be secured from parents for students to use the Internet will vary from district to district and will undoubtedly be somewhat different for high school students as compared to elementary school students. For students at the elementary school level, a rather simple "permission form" may be used to serve as a user's agreement. A sample of such a form, appropriate for elementary school students, appears in Figure 14.5.

Figure 14.5 Sample Internet User Contract for Elementary School Children

INTERNET USER CONTRACT, GRADES K–5

I, _______________________________, will obey the rules for using the Internet. I also understand that any behavior that is not acceptable may result in not allowing me to work online. I am responsible for all of my actions when using technology and online services.
   In using the school's network, I promise to

- use all equipment carefully and according to instructions;
- be respectful of the rights, the ideas, the information, and the privacy of others;
- never use a computer to hurt, frighten, or bully anyone;
- neither send nor receive information that is not related to my schoolwork or that can be hurtful or harmful to others; and
- report to teachers any sites or persons that demonstrate inappropriate use of online services.

Student Signature: _______________________ **Date:** _______________________

   As a parent/guardian of the above-named student, I have read and reviewed with my child the school district's Internet Acceptable Use Policy. I understand that access to the Internet is for educational purposes. I also understand that even though the school is providing supervision and guidance during my child's use of the Internet, complete blockage of all unauthorized material is not guaranteed, and I will not hold the school responsible for my child's access of unauthorized material. I have explained to my child that if he/she does not follow the rules outlined in the Acceptable Use Policy, access to the school's network will be denied. By signing here, I give my son/daughter permission to access the Internet through his/her school.

Signature of Parent/Guardian: _______________________________

Date: _______________________

Ethical use of the Internet and respect for copyright laws must be instilled in students from the beginning of their use of technology. Many students know how to copy programs and share them; they also must understand that they may not lift whole sections of content from a Webpage for a report. The illegality of these practices must be reviewed with students.

Guidelines for using the Internet, including respecting passwords, using proper language, and avoiding deliberate access of objectionable Web sites, must be firmly promoted and encoded into school policies.

EVALUATING CONTENT AND SOFTWARE PROGRAMS

Principals should lead staff members in continually evaluating Internet sites and software programs for instructional use. The constant proliferation of new Web sites makes this a difficult task, but teachers can form study groups to exchange the benefits of sites they have explored and how they have used them in their classrooms. One site often links to others—some are good; others are not. It is best for teachers to maintain a log of sites that they have visited and a brief comment about the quality of the content and ease with which students can navigate through the site. A sample of such a log appears in Figure 14.6.

Figure 14.6 Sample Internet Web Site Evaluation Log

INTERNET WEB SITE EVALUATION LOG

Name of Web Site	URL	Content	Quality	Ease of Navigation	Student Reaction

The assessment of computer software and appropriate Web sites also deserves careful attention when formulating new curriculum. This responsibility can become part of the charge to a curriculum development committee. The members of the committee can suggest software titles that teachers and students can use to support instructional units. The members of the committee should establish criteria for the review of software and Web sites. Many forms are available for this purpose, but those that suit local needs are best. A sample software evaluation form that can be easily adapted appears in Figure 14.7.

ENSURING THE PROPER USE, MAINTENANCE, AND INVENTORY OF EQUIPMENT

Technological equipment in schools represents a considerable investment of public funds. You must exercise responsibility to ensure that this equipment is properly secured and maintained. Teachers and students need some instruction in how to operate and care for this equipment. Many classrooms have lists posted that specify rules for using computers. Some of the possible items that might appear on such a list include the following:

- Turn computers and peripherals on and off in the correct sequence.
- Keep liquids away from computers.
- Always handle CDs by the edges.
- After using CDs, place them back in the appropriate containers.

Students can be organized into a technology squad and taught to provide routine cleaning and maintenance of school equipment and to note any problems that require additional attention. Youngsters generally love such responsibilities, and if properly trained, they can do quite a good job in helping to maintain school equipment.

In small schools, principals should consider purchasing service contracts for school equipment. In many school systems, this is a district function, but if not, the terms of the service agreement should be carefully reviewed and considered with the district business manager. If much of the equipment is still covered by manufacturer warrantees, then a service contract may not be a wise investment.

An accurate inventory of all school equipment should be maintained and updated whenever any new devices arrive. The inventory list should include the name and model of the piece of equipment, the serial number, the date of purchase, and the initial purchase price. This information will be necessary in the event of loss or theft and the school is insured for such losses. Maintaining an inventory is aided by keeping it on a word-processed document or in a database program. In this way, whenever a new acquisition arrives, you simply have to add the piece of equipment to the saved inventory and your list is immediately up-to-date.

As you get caught up in acquiring new technological equipment, you also need to think about developing a system for replacing equipment that is out-of-date. Many districts have devised five-year computer renewal plans in which older equipment is phased out and replaced by newer models according to a specified schedule. This can help to ensure that a certain number of devices will always be "state-of-the-art" and in peak condition. It may not be easy to convince those holding the "purse strings" to institute such a replacement program, but if you can, you'll be ahead of the game.

Figure 14.7 Sample Software Evaluation Form

SOFTWARE EVALUATION FORM

Name of Program: ____

Publisher: ____

Vendor Name/Address: ____

Subject/Topics: _____________________ **Copyright Date:** _______________

Grade Level(s): _____________________ **Price:** _______________

Type of Program (Check all that apply):

☐ Demonstration   ☐ Simulation   ☐ Skill and Practice

☐ Desktop Publishing   ☐ Database   ☐ Spreadsheet

☐ Information   ☐ Graphing   ☐ Data Analysis

☐ Other (Specify): ____

Brief description of program: _______________________________________

What are the best uses and curriculum connections of the program? _______________

What is the best feature(s) of the program? _______________________________

Other Assessments of the Software (rate each characteristic on a scale of **1–5**, with **5** being the highest rating):

1. Encourages critical thinking and problem solving.	
2. Allows for creative responses.	
3. Supports our district's learning goals.	
4. Encourages a high level of student interaction.	
5. Presentation is organized, easy to follow, and effective.	
6. Is engaging and stimulating.	
7. Provides for feedback and assessment.	

Student reaction: ____]

Recommendation: ☐ Yes ☐ Yes, for limited use ☐ No

Other comments: ____

Reviewer: _______________ **School:** _______________ **Date:** _________

The proliferation and use of technology in schools has resulted in unimagined opportunities and reforms in educational practice. Technology has promoted innovative practices and has in many ways transformed the administration of schools. Sometimes, development has been at such a quick pace that it has been hard for principals to keep up with the rapid changes, and to separate those aspects that truly result in educational improvement from those that are little more than games. A flexible attitude and a capacity to change and grow are clearly required. The challenge of technology is great, but the rewards are well worth the "growing pains."

EVALUATING THE SCHOOL TECHNOLOGY PROGRAM

Equipment acquisition and curriculum development in the area of technology represent important investments. As with any such program, its effectiveness should be assessed. A good place to start would be to look at the goals in the school or district technology plan. In that plan, were the means for assessing the achievement of the stated goals and objectives specified? Were benchmarks stated? How were they to be evaluated? There are a variety of techniques and devices that can be used to assess how well the school technology program is working. Among them are the following:

Surveys and Questionnaires. Staff and students can be surveyed to uncover the results and attitudes that are related to the implementation of the technology plan. How have student learning and achievement been affected? What evidence do we have for the impact of technology on the instructional program?

Assessment of Goals of a Technology Curriculum. Where schools have a technology curriculum, the goals and individual objectives in that curriculum should include achievement and performance measures.

Portfolios. Student work samples and projects can be assembled into portfolios to be examined to ascertain the degree to which technology has been integrated and used in student learning.

Rubrics: Student presentations using technological tools can be assessed according to teacher-designed rubrics.

Technology and Its Effect on Student Learning and Attitudes. Surveys and other instruments can tap into how technology has affected student achievement in a variety of areas, including

- oral and written communication skills,
- problem-solving skills,
- group work, and
- attitudes toward technology.

Teacher Logs and Written Reports. Teachers can maintain logs or prepare reports that document how computers have been used in their classrooms and other areas of the school.

Walk-Throughs. Principals can focus on the use of technology during their walk-throughs within the building.

Performance Samples. Students often use computers to create products. They can design presentations, drawings, reports, and other projects. Assessing these performance samples will provide information about the effects of the technology program on student learning.

As in any important school program, initiative, or effort, the impact on students and the school needs to be assessed. The results of such an evaluation can point the way toward programmatic improvement or, if needed, help to steer the project in new directions. Such an assessment may reveal achievements that were never anticipated.

15

Effective Budget Preparation and Control

Developing and controlling the school budget can help you get what you need to run an effective educational program. This is a very important process, and errors made early on in the process can make your position very difficult for a year or years in the future. Once the budget is set and approved, you have to live with it. Some school leaders simply do not pay enough attention to this area of school administration; others truly enjoy the process. In any case, budget preparation and control constitute an essential aspect of running an elementary school.

In recent years, the budget development process has been increasingly decentralized. Principals who had previously been "handed" their allocations by the business manager or superintendent were all of a sudden faced with the responsibility, and the *opportunity*, to prepare the budget for their own buildings. Many were not ready—did not know how to use this situation to involve staff and the community in the preparation of a budget proposal. There are many benefits associated with this process. It helps all stakeholders in the school to understand the complexities and the trade-offs in building a school budget. When one program has to be sacrificed in order to expand another, you'll have much greater support for this difficult decision if several key players have been involved in the budget preparation process. Even though the degree of individual school autonomy in proposing a budget is variable from district to district, decentralization is clear.

Once a budget is set, you must live within the specific allocations for each account— supplies, textbooks, equipment, and so on—for the school year. By their very nature, budgets do not allow for much spontaneity. Therefore, educating yourself on the budget and the process early and often will be critical. Meet with the assistant superintendent or business manager to learn the specific processes your district follows. Ask which accounts receive categorical aid and therefore should be exhausted annually to continue the aid formula working to meet the district's fiscal needs. Learn about previous budget history. How successful has

---

Note: All forms, letters, and checklists included in this chapter can be found at corwin.com/elementary survivalkit.

285

the annual budget vote been? Has it failed recently? If so, why? Taking the time to get clarity on these items will most certainly gain you an ally in the budget process; it will also invariably provide you with a perspective that will not come from looking at numbers on a spreadsheet. The budget process should also be viewed as a forum to educate others. At a staff meeting, you can discuss the importance of being fiscally responsible with the moneys you are allotted. Point out the correlation between that practice and providing quality and sustainable educational programs. Remind staff that the budget is funded with taxpayer money. Whenever possible, let your constituents know how fortunate you are for their commitment to meeting educational needs and district goals, and assure those same constituents that you are exactly the "watchdog" they want overseeing their moneys and how they are spent.

Working through the budget process requires a lot of foresight and vision; you must also allow time for reflection and revision. Both will serve you well when dealing with hundreds of thousands of dollars. Both should also help you overcome a challenge every principal will face—balancing the need for careful planning and the ability to be flexible about educational programming.

Planning is an essential aspect of the budget process, and there are deliberate steps that you must take in order to develop a responsible budget for the school.

ADVANCE PLANNING: THE FIRST STEP

Nothing can replace the value of careful planning in the budget process. The budget preparation process can be viewed as a cycle with a step-by-step sequence that repeats each year. The cycle suggested is outlined in Figure 15.1 and is summarized below.

Figure 15.1   Sample Annual School Budget Cycle

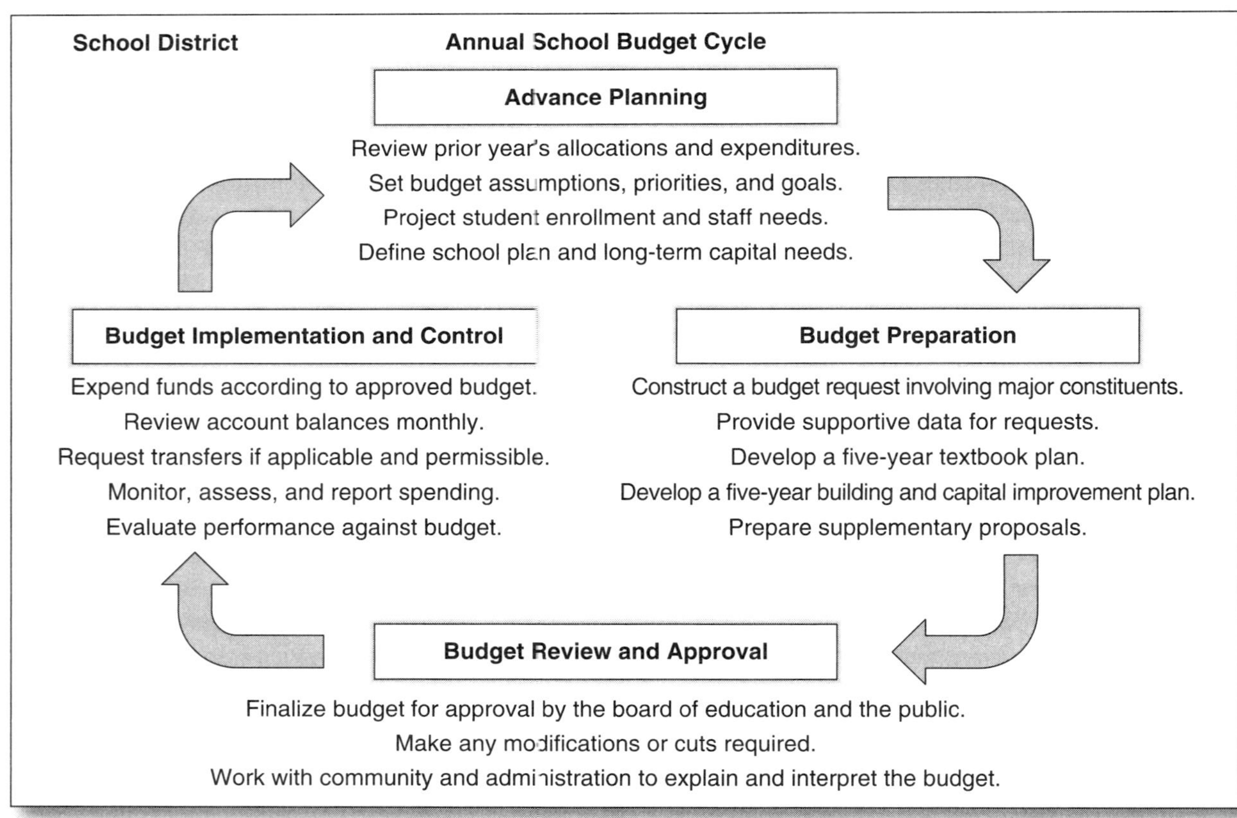

Set Budget Goals and Assumptions

As a first step in the budget process, administrators must be familiar with any local or state requirements that drive the budget process and procedures. Then, in accordance with these practices, develop a list of broad goals and assumptions that drive the priorities. What is the basic philosophy behind the budget? Is it a priority to refurbish older school buildings? Are technology upgrades essential? Have new instructional programs been recommended that will require significant new funding? Is reducing class size a major thrust in the community?

Providing input into budget priorities, assumptions, and goals is an appropriate area for staff and community involvement. These priorities should be discussed at faculty meetings, school leadership team meetings, and parents association meetings. At this stage of budget development, it may also prove useful to meet with nonparent members of the school community. What issues would they like to see addressed? Do they appreciate the fact that good schools will help maintain their property values?

Assemble all of the data and opinions gathered at this stage of the budget process and summarize them for consideration at the district level. District administrators can then consider the perceived priorities and, along with their own input, prepare a brief outline of budget goals and assumptions. (See Figure 15.2 for a sample of such a document.)

Figure 15.2 Sample Statement of Budget Assumptions and Goals

County School District

BUDGET GOALS AND ASSUMPTIONS

Assumptions

- State and federal aid levels will remain the same next year.
- Building improvements preserve community value.
- Enrollments will remain stable in the next three years.
- The community will support the budget at the polls.

Goals

- Maintain small class sizes at the primary-grade levels.
- Provide support for the district's long-term instructional goals.
- Improve services to meet the emotional and social needs of children and families.
- Meet the technological requirements of the school system.
- Maintain safe, clean, and attractive school facilities and grounds.

Review Prior Year's Accounts and Expenditures

The budget process usually begins by reviewing past expenditures. Were your estimates of needs accurate? Go through each account, line by line, to check whether or not your projections were adequate. For example, did you overestimate your need for textbooks and underestimate your need for computer software? If errors were made in the prior year's planning and expenses, were adjustments or corrections made in the current year's budget? A careful review of your prior year's budget and expenditures can help to answer these questions.

Anticipate Student Enrollment

Student enrollment projections need to be made. There are several methods for achieving accurate projections. Perhaps the easiest method is the straight-line projection. In this model, you simply promote the children from one grade to the next; that is, 72 third graders become 72 fourth graders. For your beginning grade, simply average the enrollment for that grade over the past three to five years and use this figure. The straight-line method, though easy to do, does not take into account past history of considerable influxes into a particular grade, new housing developments, and abrupt population spurts. A more sophisticated, comprehensive enrollment projection model is called the "cohort survival method." Although detailing this method is beyond the scope of this chapter, the basic premise in this model is to project grade enrollment by taking into account prior years' growth or decline within a given group of students (a cohort) moving from one grade to the next. Sometimes, this history might reveal a 10% increase in students from kindergarten to Grade 1. Or it might reveal a fall-off in enrollment from Grade 5 to 6. Such declines may have something to do with the availability of spaces at particular grade levels in competing parochial or private schools in the area.

This is where having very accurate census information becomes necessary. A conversation with the census keeper and attendance officer at this juncture might be wise if you were to follow this model. Their input may help alleviate underplanning or overestimating, both of which can be equally damaging to a building's budget.

Some principals are tempted to "pad" their enrollments by adding in an extra pupil or two at each grade level. If this is based on prior history, that's one thing, but if this is just a general "cushion," such a practice may come back to haunt you. For example, let's say that you have a current enrollment in first grade of 75 students in three sections of 25 students each. Assume for a moment that the district guideline calls for splitting classes when a primary-grade class size reaches 26. It might be tempting to project 79 students for second grade, thereby calling for four sections and the hiring of another teacher. You get approval and go ahead and hire the fourth teacher for the grade level, only to find that, in September, you have only 74 students. The superintendent asks you to reorganize back into three sections. Now you are faced with important staffing implications, new class configurations, and upset parents and teachers.

Another step in anticipating enrollment is to talk with neighborhood residents. Are new housing developments near completion? Are any major demographic changes apparent? If apartments and homes are turning over, is a new immigrant group moving in? For example, let's say that a particular area of your school community has become popular among Korean individuals who are moving into the area. If the individuals are new immigrants, this may well have an impact on the program for ELL students, and additional staff may be required. As you can see, obtaining accurate enrollment projections is an essential step in anticipating budget needs.

Projecting Staff Needs

Once the enrollment projection is completed, you must consider what staff you will need to service the student population. Are there class-size guidelines in the school district? If so, might you need another classroom teacher, or be able to have one fewer section of a particular grade level? Are any special needs anticipated, for example, if a new immigrant group seems to be growing in the student population? Sometimes, large class sizes may trigger the need to hire additional classroom aides.

Declining enrollments may offer some unique opportunities to fund new programs. For example, if you need one section fewer of third grade, the school board may expect you to return the funds for this position to the general budget. On the other hand, you may be able to retain the funds for this position and redeploy the staff member to serve as a technology specialist, provide extra assistance to at-risk pupils, or help out in the media center. All such considerations must be a part of the planning phase.

Define Plant and Building Needs

Another important aspect of the budget preparation process is to define plant and building needs. The next chapter addresses the school environment, but if you don't prioritize the building's physical needs as part of the budget, it is easy to deplete a substantial amount of capital before ever addressing academic needs. It is helpful to separate plant and building needs into three categories: immediate, short-term, and long-term needs. Immediate needs should be items that cost little money and are considered cosmetic issues, such as the painting of a few classrooms and replacing bulleting boards. Short-term needs can be categorized as items that require a moderate amount of money but may need to be planned for over one- to two-year budget calendars. These items can be things like replacing playground equipment, addressing the building's landscape needs, or sealing the school's parking lot. Long-range plans can cost a substantial amount of money and usually include large building projects or needs. These projects and needs should be developed in a five-year plan—specifying what ought to be accomplished each year. Major items should be specified in this plan, such as roof replacements, interior or exterior painting, furnace or heating system renewal, door or window replacements, school grounds improvements, a new lighting program, handicapped access improvements, floor and ceiling upgrades, and the like. Equipment and school furniture needs should also be anticipated and specified in a five-year equipment plan. Replacement of desks and chairs, photocopiers, office equipment, computers, and other such large equipment purchases should be specified. You, as the person who oversees the entire operation of the school, must have basic understandings of repair and improvement cycles and how to plan for them.

Before any large equipment items are detailed in a five-year plan, however, an accurate inventory and assessment of the condition of existing equipment must be made. This is a good time to work with the school custodian. Seek his or her input as to what needs repair or replacement. One of the added benefits of securing this information is that the custodial staff will realize that you value its input and advice, thus enhancing the feeling of these employees that they have value within the school culture.

Teachers and parents like to become involved in discussions about prioritizing such needs. Are playground improvements considered more critical than external door replacements? Is updating the furniture in the media center more of a priority than classroom carpeting? These items can be the center of a lively discussion, but in the end, you come out with a list of priorities that reflects input from staff and community members.

PREPARING BUDGET DOCUMENTS

A school budget may be likened to a tube of toothpaste; the amount of the contents remains fixed, but it can be squashed and reshaped to fit another form. One of the important aspects of working from a defined set of budget goals is that they are derived from established priorities. For example, if maintaining small class sizes is a budget goal, then some other programs may have to be sacrificed to free up sufficient funds to reduce class size. Perhaps certain clubs, athletic programs, musical instrument purchases, or extracurricular activities might have to be reduced or eliminated. This is, of course, a judgment call that a budget-setting group might have to make, but if priorities and goals were set, they can steer the budget process.

Provide Supportive Data for Budget Requests

Each school system will have its own forms for the development of budget requests.

A budget development worksheet for each line item for general supplies, audio-visual equipment, computer software, and so on should be completed. A sample of such a worksheet appears in Figure 15.3. If materials need to be reviewed, they should

Figure 15.3   Sample Budget Development Worksheet

BUDGET DEVELOPMENT WORKSHEET

Date: _____________________   Budget year: _____________________

School: _____________________   Location code: _____________________

Budget account number: _____________________

Description: _____________________

Items	Itemized Cost	Total
1.		
2.		
3.		
4.		
5.		
6.		
7.		
8.		
9.		
10.		
11.		
12.		
13.		
14.		
15.		

Rationale:

be distributed to staff allowing sufficient time to obtain feedback that can be helpful in making purchases. For example, certain grades of construction paper may be superior to others; the staff should assess writing paper; math manipulatives should be aligned with the math program and based upon teacher need. Of course, inventories of existing supplies and stockpiles should be checked and distributed prior to any new orders.

Backup data should be provided if requested budget lines are significantly different from the prior year's allocation. Is a new program being installed? Was the prior year's estimate of need insufficient to fund a particular category of items? Space should be provided on budget worksheets for a rationale.

Worksheets should also be devised to account for resignations, retirements, and leaves of absence. Requests for an increase in staffing should also be outlined on a budget form with proper justification for the increase. Multiyear purchases should also be separately specified. A sample of a multiyear purchase request form appears in Figure 15.4.

Figure 15.4 Sample Multiyear Purchase Budget Worksheet

BUDGET DEVELOPMENT WORKSHEET, MULTIYEAR PURCHASE REQUEST

Program name: _____________________ School/cost center: _____________________

Account number: ____

Item to Purchase or Lease	2009–2010 Amount	2010–2011 Amount	2011–2012 Amount	2012–2013 Amount	2013–2014 Amount
High-Capacity Photocopier with: Reduce/Enlarge, Automatic Feed, Automatic Stapler, Automatic Duplex, and Stapler Functions.	$1500	$1500	$1500	$1500	$1500
Includes service plan with all toner, developer, fuser, and other pertinent supplies included.					

Rationale: Our current photocopier cannot accommodate the increased demand. It is frequently being repaired. As we purchase more and more programs that come with "blackline masters" instead of individual books for students, we have used the current photocopier well beyond its stated capacity. Teachers have become more creative and innovative in terms of devising their own materials for classroom use that must also be photocopied. Automatic duplexing will save considerable amounts of paper.

Develop a Five-Year Textbook Plan

Some school districts require the specification of a five-year textbook plan. This allows for the anticipation of major textbook or programmatic adoptions in an orderly way. Usually more relevant at the high school level than at the elementary school level, planning long-term purchases can help to define future needs for replacements that might not have been taken into account.

Textbook plans should specify anticipated purchases, adoptions, or replacements of books and kits in all subject areas with costs projected over a period of five years.

Develop a Five-Year Capital Improvement Plan

All schools require ongoing maintenance. There are certain big items that require replacement at long-term intervals, such as heating/cooling systems, roofs, doors, and windows, among others. Items such as lighting upgrades, paint, and ceiling and floor renewals may need to be refurbished every 10 years or so. School leaders need to look at the whole school and anticipate needs for recurring maintenance and renewal. Usually, school districts hire a director of buildings and grounds. This individual may be very helpful in defining plant needs. Nevertheless, the principal, as the person who oversees the entire operation of the school, must have basic understandings of repair and improvement cycles and how to plan for them.

Prepare Supplementary Proposals

Supplementary proposals may be considered a program, equipment, or staff position that goes beyond the basic budget allocation for the school. Examples might include new office equipment, increased funds for technology updates, the addition of a guidance counselor, expansion of media services (equipment, materials, and personnel), or even the formulation of a preschool program. Such requests need to be well substantiated and supported with backup information and data. For example, if a request is made to expand an existing program, the following questions should be addressed:

Educational Rationale

1. How will the change improve conditions for teaching and learning?

2. How will the result of the change affect student performance?

3. How will the impact of this change be evaluated?

Financial Considerations

1. What are the financial implications associated with the proposed change?

2. Which cost centers (buildings or departments) are affected by the change?

Political Ramifications

1. What will be the impact on the school community?
   a. Students
   b. Parents
   c. Board of Education
   d. Community at Large
   e. Staff

Organizational Implications

1. What is the impact of the change on the structure of the organization?

2. What effect will the change have on other staff or programs in the school system?

3. Is the change associated with compliance to any national or state mandates or codes?

It should be apparent from the foregoing that several forms and worksheets must be assembled prior to submission of the school budget. Of course, each district will have its own set of forms and requirements, but the following is a list of the major components of a principal's budget request:

- ☐ Budget Development Worksheets for all supply and equipment accounts
- ☐ Resignations/Retirements and Leaves Worksheet
- ☐ Staffing Worksheets
- ☐ Five-Year Textbook Plan
- ☐ Five-Year Capital Needs/Improvements Plan
- ☐ Multiyear Purchase Forms
- ☐ Supplementary Proposals

BUDGET REVIEW AND APPROVAL

In some larger school districts, school leaders may be required to appear before a central-office review team, or even a board of education subcommittee, to defend their budget request. It is important to be prepared for such meetings. Occasionally, school leaders are caught off guard in these sessions if they have not prepared sufficient background information and rationale to support their requests.

District administrators and the board of education must finalize the budget document for approval. Sometimes, you will be asked to make cuts in budget requests. This requires going back to established priorities and the consensus reached in creating the budget. Areas that were not considered essential will have to be examined. In some cases, an across-the-board 10% cut in all supply categories may be enough for the reduction. In other cases, staff may have to be eliminated. This is always a difficult issue. Let's say, for example, a budget goal was to maintain small primary-grade class sizes. Now you have been told that a cut must be made. An area that was not considered a priority is instrumental music, so you go ahead and eliminate this program. Once this news is out, those who helped to establish budget priorities might rightfully object, saying that when they determined the priority for small class sizes, they did not know what they were trading off to achieve this goal. This is the time to call the major stakeholders together for continued discussion and decision-making.

In many communities, once the proposed budget is approved by the board of education, the voters in a special election or budget referendum must approve it. Your role is a sensitive one in promoting the budget. It is hard to imagine a principal who would not support passage of the budget at the polls, but where budget approval is a very sensitive issue—for example, when a large constituency is actively opposed to the school budget—school leaders might be well advised to tread carefully. In some districts, principals are encouraged to support the budget actively among the citizens. At the very least, you will be called upon to explain and interpret the key features of the budget. This might take place at a community forum, a question-and-answer session hosted by the parents association, or at a civic or service organization. You can explain the budget and encourage people to vote in the budget election without coming out and taking a definitive stand.

In some communities, principals are expected to write letters to the members of their own school communities to explain how passage of the budget will impact their local schools. A sample of such a letter appears in Figure 15.5.

Figure 15.5   Sample Principal's Letter Explaining School Budget Issues

School District Name
Elementary School Name
Office of the Principal

Dear Members of the School Community,

I am taking this opportunity to write to you about a very important matter—our proposed budget for the next school year. The School Board Election and Budget Referendum will be held in our middle-school gymnasium and is set for **APRIL 4.** Residents often ask me to outline some of the important features of the proposed budget that are designed to strengthen our instructional program. A few such items include the following:

- An increase of one staff member in our Resource Center program. Projected enrollment increases in this program will bring us beyond the legal class-size limit for this important program. In order to service our children who exhibit special academic needs, we need to hire this additional teacher.
- A teacher coach program to strengthen staff development in the areas of science, technology, and mathematics.
- Much-needed equipment including probeware for our science program, classroom furniture, musical instruments, athletic equipment, and a new photocopier for the school office.
- Capital projects would include repair of the slate roof at Trowbridge, new computer rooms at the middle and high schools, and continued efforts to ensure handicapped access to our school so that we may comply with provisions of the Americans with Disabilities Act.

Following are a few interesting facts you may wish to know about our budget:

- Projected enrollments are up, and yet the proposed budget does not raise revenues beyond the legal limit (CAP) imposed by our state legislature.
- The capital projects portion of our school budget has been extremely low in the recent past. The proposed budget will reflect the recommendations made by a citizen's group that studied physical and plant needs in our school district.
- The increase in the premiums we must pay for our employees' medical insurance will be about 12% next year.
- The increase in the proposed operating budget is the smallest rise than has been the case in the past four years even though inflation is at a four-year high.

We all cherish the right to vote on matters of public interest. Please remember to vote in the School Board Election and Budget Referendum at the middle school on **April 4** from 1:00 to 9:00 PM.

Sincerely,

Principal

IMPLEMENTING AND CONTROLLING THE BUDGET

Once a school budget has been approved, the time comes to spend the money. This can be an area for considerable creativity as you try to make funds go as far as possible. Most of the school budget is understandably devoted to salaries and benefits, but for the areas that you *do* control on a day-to-day basis, considerable discretion can be exercised. The majority of the nonsalary funds will probably be spent on books and supply items such as paper, manipulatives, pupil response books, art supplies, and so on. You must be careful not to spend down these accounts early in the school year to allow some funds for more spontaneous purchases. Let's say a group of teachers attends a conference. They return particularly enthusiastic about a program that will perfectly enhance one of the school's initiatives. If there is no money left in the various accounts, there is no opportunity for the trial of new approaches and ideas during the school year.

Expend Funds According to Budgeted Categories

All schools must establish a system for how teachers initiate purchase orders. In most schools, teachers must first complete a form specifying all of the required information, which, once approved by the principal, is given to the secretary for preparation of a purchase order. In more and more school systems, purchase orders are completed electronically and sent directly to a central purchasing office. The form that teachers (or other requesters) use is called a requisition form. (See Figure 15.6 for a sample requisition form.) The reason for this extra step is for the principal to review the order and code the budget account number (in the reference-number column) that best matches the use of funds. If you have such a system, you must also determine if sufficient funds are available in the appropriate account to support the order. Sometimes, there are purchases that could legitimately fall into more than one account. Let's say, for example, that a teacher is requesting a resource book on spelling. This could be a reading supply (because of spelling's association with the reading process), a general supply item, or even a professional book expense. Through such thinking, you can create more "space" in the budget for unanticipated expenditures.

The school secretary should have a system for recording the purchase orders and maintaining a running balance on each of the accounts. A simple ledger sheet—one for each of the various accounts—is an ideal way to keep track of orders. Another good practice is to add 10% or 15% to the total of each order for shipping and handling costs. If this is not taken into account, a purchase order can be rejected by central office for insufficient funds. This is an area that has caught many a principal off guard. They did not add shipping costs into their own records, only to find that their accounts were expended sooner than they had thought.

Review Account Status Monthly

In most systems, school leaders receive a monthly printout of the status of their budget account. Increasingly, school leaders can also check their accounts online. When you examine your printouts, study the history and patterns of your spending. Where is more needed? Which accounts are nearly expended? Where did you overestimate your needs? Where do you still have considerable balances?

It is also a good idea to sit down each month with your secretary (or whoever maintains the accounts for the school) and review outstanding purchase orders. If an order has

Figure 15.6 Requisition Form

REQUISITION FORM

Please fill out a separate form for each company/vendor you are ordering from. Also, please add 10% for postage and handling where appropriate.

Requested by: ____

Vendor code: ____________________ **Vendor name:** _______________________

Address: ____

Ref. no.	Quantity	Description	Unit cost	Total cost
Postage and Handling				
Total				

Approved by: _______________________________ **Date:** ________________

not been received after several months, it is possible that these orders became "lost" or never went out. At other times, there are problems with the vendor. Perhaps the item is out of stock, or the vendor lost the purchase order. Once a purchase order is initiated, your account is encumbered and you cannot use the money that is being held aside to fund an unfulfilled purchase order. It only makes sense to periodically review the status of these orders and cancel those that are long outstanding so that you can secure the needed items from another vendor or use the funds for something else.

Monitor, Assess, and Report Spending

Periodically, school leaders should assess their spending patterns and compare them to the allocations in their budget. Make notes on areas that were underestimated and overestimated for the development of next year's budget. Which areas can be reduced? Which need to be increased? Were any expenses a onetime occurrence that will not require continued funding in the future? Taking the time to monitor and assess your use of the budget is a very important exercise. In some school systems, school leaders must report on their progress in controlling their budgets, and the answers to these kinds of questions can become the basis of the report.

Request Transfers if Permitted

The ability to transfer funds from one account to another is a very powerful tool in making the most of the school budget. Not all school districts allow this flexibility. In such cases, the prevailing thought is that you estimated your needs when you prepared the budget, and any changes in these estimates are not allowed. The money returns to the "general coffers."

If transfers are permitted, there are usually forms to request reallocation. The account with the largest sum of money in most schools is the general-supplies account. Many principals try to keep balances in this account so that funds can be transferred to other areas where moneys may have been quickly expended but needs arise during the course of the school year. Of course, if you are relying too much on transfers during a budget year, it may be a sign that the budget was not prepared with enough care, planning, and forethought.

How to Deal With Cuts or Budget
Freezes in the Middle of the School Year

There are times when, due to unforeseen circumstances, the business manager and superintendent will enact a budget freeze, or, worse yet, call for cuts in the middle of a school year. This is never an easy situation. The first thing that school leaders can do in such situations is to freeze spending, that is, stop the issuance of all purchase orders, except for critical items, each of which must be reviewed carefully. Next, the usual course of action is to cancel all attendance at conferences and the use of consultants in the school.

If actual cuts must be made midyear, perhaps after-school programs, clubs, and other recreational initiatives can be suspended. All overtime expenses should be reviewed and cut back, if possible. The substitute accounts are another area that should be assessed. Perhaps in emergency situations, if teachers are absent, the youngsters in the class can be divided among other teachers in the school. If possible, the school leader or your assistant may also serve as a substitute. This demonstrates his or her understanding and willingness to pitch in to aid the general situation.

Evaluate Performance Against the Budget

Related to the area mentioned above about monitoring and assessing spending, you should evaluate your own performance at the end of the budget cycle. How well did you live within the budget? Which areas will need greater levels of funding next year? Which areas can be reasonably cut back? How good a budget manager have you been? Did you find areas to use the budget creatively? Were you able to allow for some flexibility, or were all funds expended at the beginning of the budget year? Sitting down and discussing such matters with colleagues and the district's business manager may help you gain new approaches and understandings about how to control the school budget.

The budget process holds many important responsibilities for school leaders. Those who are oblivious to fiscal realities often make blunders that can have a negative impact on their schools. School leaders who are adept, careful, and creative can find ways to make their budget dollars go further.

SECURING ALTERNATIVE MEANS OF FUNDING IN YOUR SCHOOL

A school where principals and staff have everything they could possibly want can hardly be imagined. In order to secure more equipment, supplies, and special opportunities for their students, many school leaders have become particularly adept at obtaining funds from outside sources. There are numerous grant opportunities available to principals, but be aware that writing grant applications can be time-consuming and will not always result in your being awarded the funds, equipment, or services you had hoped for. The best way to learn how to write successful grants is to attend a seminar or workshop that is geared toward this activity. There are also several books and online discussion groups that can assist in this effort. Another way to become more skillful at writing grant applications is to contact the funding agency, for instance, the state education department or a large corporation, and ask if you can examine the applications of those individuals or schools that were successful in obtaining grants. Take careful notes on what you see. Undoubtedly, you will see that the applications were focused, innovative practices and approaches were outlined, and an evaluation or assessment design was carefully spelled out. In grant applications, specific questions are usually posed. In successful grant applications, these questions are answered thoroughly and directly.

Gaining funds from outside sources does not always have to be so competitive. In some school districts, parents have established local foundations that support innovative projects. Sometimes, these organizations are just waiting for imaginative proposals and have funds available for their local schools.

Large corporate foundations are another source of funds, usually for specified projects, for schools. Call large corporations, especially in the vicinity of your school, and ask about any grant programs they might have. If they do not have such a program, propose that they establish one.

Another way of securing important donations for the school is by asking local businesses when they intend to replace their office furniture or equipment. Many school leaders have been successful in getting donations of perfectly good office furniture and technological devices that, though obsolete for the company, may well find good uses in elementary schools.

Finally, principals can appeal directly to their own parent body for items such as VCRs, televisions, carpets, and other such items. Parents sometimes replace these appliances while they are still in good condition and would be only too happy to donate them to their children's school. Publishing a "wish list" on a fairly regular basis in the school newsletter can have very fruitful results.

16

Maintaining a Clean, Safe, and Secure School Environment

The moment you walk into a school building its appearance conveys an important message about the care and pride invested in it by those who work and learn there. You must strive to maintain an aesthetically pleasing school building, regardless of its age. The level of care defines the general morale and the relationship of physical spaces to the instructional program. A school with polished floors, clean grounds, attractive spaces, and functioning equipment conveys pride, respect, and a sense of care about the environment in which children learn and grow. Beyond cleanliness and safety, it is essential for school leaders to be involved in the development of school security plans for extraordinary events that require immediate response and mobilization of staff. Unfortunately, this has become more and more a reality in today's schools.

In terms of school cleanliness, sometimes, an individual custodian will exercise an unusual level of stewardship for the school building, but this cannot be taken for granted. Such commitment must be fostered deliberately through words and deeds on the part of the school leader and the entire school community. Custodians must be included and helped to feel that their roles are essential to the success of the school and the educational program. Everyone in a school has a stake in its appearance and maintenance, and if you value an attractive, well-maintained building, you must work toward achieving this goal.

Note: All forms, letters, and checklists included in this chapter can be found at corwin.com/elementary survivalkit.

CARING FOR THE SCHOOL BUILDING

If you are seen picking up a scrap of litter from the hallway floor, you convey through your actions that you care about the appearance of the school and are willing to work toward that end. You should have a role in defining the cleaning and maintenance schedule for the building and be aware of needs, problems, and long-range plans.

Just how the school leader works with custodial and maintenance personnel requires expertise and sensitivity. Sometimes, these individuals feel that they are not as important as the certified teachers in a school. You must help them to realize that their jobs are essential and that all human beings who work in a building have a stake in its success. Sitting down and having regular conferences with maintenance personnel helps them to know that their work and advice are valued.

Walk through the building frequently, oversee the custodial schedules, talk with staff about the care and condition of the school, and help define ways in which students can contribute to and take pride in the appearance of their school. Each class in the school can be organized to create an outdoor cleanup schedule. The children can be issued trash bags and asked to help to clean up the school grounds. Students can also be involved (with supervision, of course) in planting and general beautification efforts on the school grounds.

In the lunchroom, students can be asked to wipe the tabletops and sweep debris from under the tables. With sponges, small plastic pails, brushes, and dust pans supplied by custodians, students help care for and clean their lunchroom. Of course, they cannot substitute for professional cleaning, but their efforts can instill a sense of responsibility.

MAXIMIZING THE USE OF BUILDING SPACE

Flexibility in the use of building space is a goal toward which all principals should strive. Educational practice has swung back and forth, from open-space configurations to more traditional classrooms, and many arrangements in between. Many of these trends have been promoted by school architects, the best of which always consult with educators as to the priorities and needs of the instructional program. In any building, though, the challenge is to use space to maximum advantage so that it supports the primary purposes of the school.

Movable furniture, bookcases, room dividers, and other such furniture can help to define space for distinct purposes. The key to wise use of space is to maximize flexibility. Teachers should have the ability to open up areas or define space as needs dictate. Space arrangements can facilitate groupings of students for independent or cooperative work, for teacher-student conferences, and for large-group discussions, learning centers, displays, computer areas, and classroom libraries.

In some schools, principals have to deal with underutilized rooms; in other schools, a shortage of space is the problem. Where an excess of space is available, think of how the extra space can serve the educational program or the general school community. When additional rooms are available, the following alternatives are among those that can be considered:

- A computer room
- An annex to the school media center
- A science room
- A school museum
- A parent meeting room
- A space devoted to adult education or parent education programs

- Meeting rooms for guidance, support services, psychologists, and so on
- A teacher workroom with materials and technological equipment
- Space for university-sponsored courses

The greater challenge facing most school leaders, however, is a shortage of space. Sometimes, two programs (for example, ESL and remedial reading) may have to share one instructional area. Be ready to help solve some of the conflicts that often accompany the sharing of space. Room dividers, creative arrangements, and a good measure of mutual respect will help when teachers find that they are conducting their programs alongside another professional in the same room.

Sometimes, good scheduling practices can alleviate some of the problems with sharing space. For example, let's say that a guidance counselor is assigned to your school on Mondays and Wednesdays. This individual will clearly need a space in which to have private sessions with students, teachers, and parents. If a speech-language pathologist is also assigned to your school two days per week, it makes good sense for these two individuals to share the same space on different days. Thoughtful planning of the schedule as well as some friendly agreements on storage spaces and the use of desks, tables, and the like will help to facilitate the process of sharing space.

Under ideal circumstances, elementary schools will have separate gymnasiums, auditoriums, and lunchrooms. This ideal, though, is rarely the case. Most schools do not have the luxury of large areas for each of these purposes. More likely is the situation where a school has a multipurpose room. Chairs on carts can be set up for assembly programs, lunchroom tables can be wheeled out at lunchtime, and the floor can be cleared for physical education classes. Such shared facilities do have important scheduling implications since the physical education program can hardly take place while the space is being used for lunch or for a school assembly. Such factors must be taken into consideration when planning the school schedule. Also, the custodial staff will need some time to roll out and set up lunch tables.

Students can help in setting up and taking down chairs before and after school assemblies. This is an appropriate form of school service and the members of a "chair crew" can be recognized at an annual awards assembly.

WORKING WITH THE CUSTODIAL STAFF

It is essential that school custodians and maintenance workers feel that they are a part of the team—that their work is critical for the school to achieve it basic mission. It is not a bad idea to occasionally have breakfast with your custodians to get to know them better as people. This will convey to them that you value them as human beings as well for the important work that they do. Find out about the satisfactions and frustrations associated with their jobs and do what you can to be an advocate for their position. One principal found out through such conversations that a faulty vacuum cleaner and inadequate supplies were making the school custodian feel resentful. Once these issues were attended to, job performance improved. Had the principal not taken the time and shown the interest to find out about such matters, the situation might have festered and the bad feelings might have grown to unnecessary proportions.

We all like to feel appreciated for the work that we do, and custodians are no exception. Consider declaring a "Custodian Appreciation Day." Students can be asked to make signs, letters, or posters in which they express their gratitude for the work that the custodians perform. Perhaps a brief assembly can be organized in which students read sentiments of appreciation.

You can recognize the day's events by honoring the custodial staff, explaining their importance in the total school program, and writing a letter to express your own appreciation. (See Figure 16.1 for a sample of such a letter.) You have a key role in modeling respect for the custodial staff and stressing the importance of the work that they perform.

Figure 16.1 Sample Letter of Appreciation to a School Custodian

_________________ **Elementary School**

Office of the Principal

Date

Mr./Ms. ____

Custodian

______________________________Elementary School

Dear _______________________________________,

Today, on Custodian Appreciation Day, I want you to know how very much I appreciate the services that you provide to our teachers and students each and every day. You exercise care and concern for our school building and it shows. Whenever guests visit our building, they remark upon the fine condition in which it is kept—especially for a 70-year-old school! You take pride in your job and you fulfill all of your duties with skill, enthusiasm, and expertise.

Teaching children is a difficult job, but you make all of our jobs so much more rewarding by providing safe, clean, and attractive spaces in which our children can learn and grow. The children are all so fond of you and know that they will have an opportunity to express their gratitude during this special day. The entire staff appreciates your assistance, good sense of humor, and sense of responsibility.

For my part, I want you to know how very much I appreciate all that you do day in and day out—not only today on Custodian Appreciation Day, but throughout the year.

Sincerely,

___________________________________ (Principal)

Sit down with the custodial staff at the beginning of the year and set goals for the appearance of the building. Perhaps the floors can be maintained with a new finish. Maybe paying additional attention to surface areas in classrooms will be a new emphasis. Such goals should be arrived at mutually and after an honest assessment of building needs and priorities. You may also help to organize the custodian's work day, understanding that the custodian will probably know best what needs to be done and how best to do it, but also bringing to bear your own organizational skills. School leaders and custodians should conduct periodic building walk-throughs together to assess the maintenance needs of the school. The criteria for such inspections should be arrived at jointly and then plans for improvement made if any needs are noted.

In cases where custodial staffs do not have adequate training in the use of equipment, cleaning chemicals, and other supplies, the principal should try to arrange for appropriate in-service education. Custodians, like all school personnel, require on-the-job coaching to help them perform their duties more effectively.

Custodial duties ought to be well-defined with respect to the kinds of building repairs that can be performed. Sometimes, custodians are willing to take on jobs that more appropriately lie within the domain of district maintenance personnel; each principal should understand the types of repairs that custodians can reasonably be expected to perform and those that need to be referred to the maintenance department. Occasionally, a willing and cooperative custodian may worsen a situation by attempting to make a repair that he or she is ill equipped to do.

All school personnel ought to know how to ask for routine assistance. Whether it is moving classroom furniture, repairing a window shade, or replacing light bulbs, a system should be established for such requests. Many schools use a system of work orders that are forwarded to the principal or custodian, who then decides whether or not the job can be performed by school personnel or district maintenance workers. (A sample of such a work order appears in Figure 16.2.)

Figure 16.2 Sample Work Order Form

CUSTODIAL/MAINTENANCE WORK ORDER

_______________ **Public Schools**

WHITE: Custodian's Copy; YELLOW: Maintenance Copy; PINK: Principal's Copy

Building: _______________________________________ **Date:** _______________________

Please indicate the details: location, source of trouble, etc.

It is requested that the following repairs be made:

Location: _______________________________________

Description of work to be done:_______________________________________

Comments: _______________________________________

Desired completion date: _______________________________________

____
(Initiator)

____
(Principal)

(do not write below this line) _______________________________________

Date Received: _______________________________________

Approved: _______________________________________

Assigned to: _______________________________________ **Date:** _______________

Completed: _______________________________________

NO. _______________________________________   **PRIORITY**   1   2   3   4

SECURING, STORING, AND MAINTAINING AN INVENTORY OF CUSTODIAL SUPPLIES

When the school budget is prepared, school custodians should be involved. They will alert you to chronic problems in the building or capital items that need consideration. Also, allowances must be made for custodial supplies and equipment. Discuss the kinds of supplies, vendors, and quality of materials with the custodians. Their input will be invaluable as you prepare this aspect of the school budget.

Once custodial supplies arrive, they must be stored. Many of the fluids and substances used are toxic or corrosive and must be kept in special locked storage cabinets where children cannot access them. Some states have laws that require proper labeling for any reactive substances. Paints and other flammable materials should be stored in a heavy metal cabinet designed for that purpose. Some custodians may need assistance in developing a system, or a format, for maintaining an accurate, up-to-date inventory of custodial supplies, and here, too, you can be helpful.

MAINTAINING A SAFE AND CLEAN SCHOOL SITE

The school grounds must also be kept safe and clean for students. Plan this activity with the custodial staff. Periodically tour all outdoor areas with the head custodian or personnel from the district's maintenance department. Make note of any needed repairs or hazards. Inspect for graffiti that must be removed. A routine for the removal of trash and debris should be developed, and students can be asked to help in this effort as a school service.

All playground equipment must be inspected with particular vigilance. Make sure that all moving parts in jungle gyms are operating correctly and that no nails or bolts protrude that can cause harm to children. Maintaining good ground cover under jungle gyms is also necessary. In recent years, many recommendations have been made (sometimes conflicting) as to the safest ground material. At one point, sand was the recommended material. However, sand can pack hard and children may become hurt if they fall onto it. Pea gravel is another alternative. Shredded rubber or wood chips are also recommended, although some say that wood chips become moldy. It is best to read safety bulletins from your state education department for the current recommendations. Once your ground cover is in place, it will require periodic cleaning and replenishment. Compliance with the Americans with Disabilities Act (ADA) is another essential consideration.

A planting program to beautify school grounds should be a perennial matter. Parents and students can be enlisted to support this effort. Perhaps the student council can sponsor an annual planting-day program in which trees, shrubs, or ground cover is planted. Local 4-H clubs, garden clubs, or soil conservation agencies may be helpful in this effort. The enterprising school leader need only to look at community or county resources to secure assistance for school beautification.

IMPROVING THE APPEARANCE OF INDOOR SPACES

There are many things that you can do to make school buildings—even the oldest ones or most starkly modern ones—seem more attractive and appealing. Indoor spaces can be livened with attractive bulletin boards that are both nice to look at and educational. Each teacher should be assigned a bulletin board and asked to change it and maintain it throughout the year. Some teachers create interactive displays; others post items of general interest to members of the community; still others display pupil work based upon a classroom study or investigation. Ask teachers to create displays around a particular theme. When all of the bulletin boards are ready, each class can take a "trip" through the school to "read the walls." Many teachers who are skeptical at first about such an idea later find that the project is both stimulating and instructionally valuable.

To make indoor spaces livelier, some teachers have children paint hallway ceiling tiles and decorate window shades. Whether or not teachers and students are allowed to make such permanent decorations, however, should be a matter of local discussion and policy.

Showcases and displays are another means to make a building more attractive and inviting. Teachers can be assigned the responsibility of creating displays in showcases on a rotating basis. Sometimes, the art teacher will want to assume this responsibility. Parents who bring in costumes, artwork, or artifacts from a particular culture can also be invited to maintain a showcase.

Sometimes, a particular area of the school requires a bit of "tender loving care." Perhaps it is an auditorium lobby, a back hallway, or a stairwell. Teachers can "adopt" this space and put up samples of student artwork, mobiles, or stories in the shape of stars, fish, baseballs, or other appealing shapes. Public acknowledgment of the teachers' efforts will help to motivate others. You can promote attractive hallway spaces by writing letters of appreciation to teachers thanking them for their work in creating displays that truly add to the general appeal of the school building.

Office displays also need to be well thought out. Bulletin boards near the school office should contain items of community interest, notes about recreational activities, and information from civic organizations. The parents association should also have a space to hang important flyers and notices. You should also have an area where monthly newsletters and school district publications and news can be posted. Some principals like to create their own corners, a bulletin board that reaches out to the children in which brain-teasers, optical illusions, "match the teachers with their baby pictures," and other such activities can be posted. A "guess the number of beans in the jar" or other such contest can also generate enthusiasm and connection between you and your students.

As efforts are initiated to make school spaces more attractive, students should be actively involved. This will help to instill in them a sense of pride in their school and respect for the displays created by others. All staff members should model care for the school building, an appreciation for cleanliness, and a desire for orderly, appealing classrooms and hallways.

LONG-TERM PLANNING AND CAPITAL PROJECTS

A key administrative responsibility that all school leaders must fulfill is to plan ahead for long-term projects and capital needs within their buildings. Schools are community investments, and just as residents take pride in maintaining their homes and neighborhoods, so, too, should they take pride in maintaining their schools. School leaders have an important role in convincing the public of its obligation to care for this collective property.

As school finances become scarcer, and are subjected to continual scrutiny, you must be aware of the capital needs of the buildings and help to determine what proportion of funds must be devoted to building needs versus salaries and instructional materials. If a program of top-notch ongoing maintenance has been in place, chances are that more funds can be devoted to the instructional program. If, on the other hand, building needs have been continually deferred, leaking roofs, broken furnaces, and other such major expenses will put pressure on the instructional budget.

In many school systems, a five-year capital plan is formulated in which building needs are anticipated and defined. Along with the assistance of maintenance personnel, business managers, and perhaps architects, principals must be involved in helping to determine and plan for these needs.

Involve members of the community in planning for building maintenance and capital improvements. Many talents may be available—architects, engineers, and electricians, among others—who can offer invaluable expertise and assistance in this effort. Undoubtedly, building improvements will have to be funded by the members of the community, and the more involved they are in the process, the more that they are likely to support the projects.

The scope of the work to be done should be outlined after conducting an assessment of the needs and conditions that exist in the school. Five-year capital plans can take many different forms, and each school system will have its own methods for specifying the needs. Resource people will need to be consulted in arriving at estimates—which must, of course, be adjusted for inflation.

In areas where population growth or decline may significantly impact what is needed in school buildings, accurate enrollment projections must be an integral part of long-term planning. If a population surge is expected, then school additions may need to be planned well in advance of the expected influx of students. On the other hand, if classrooms are expected to be vacant, plans can be made to lease or find alternative purposes for these spaces. (See Chapter 15 for a discussion of enrollment projections and space utilization.)

Once a long-term plan is established, its funding must be secured. In some school districts, such needs are addressed each year as part of the regular budget development process. Other districts must put forth a special bond issue or referendum to supply the needed funds for school improvements and upgrades. In any case, you must be involved in helping to convince the public of the need for these funds. Formal presentations before parent and community groups, "cottage parties" in which informal discussions are held, letters to parents, and even architectural models of anticipated improvements all need to be considered in the effort to promote public spending on capital projects.

Occasionally, school leaders are fortunate enough to witness a renovation of the school building. Again, careful planning should occur. Instructional needs should first be defined and projected for a number of years. Flexibility in the use of space to respond to a wide variety of needs and imagined approaches should be taken into account. When planning a school renovation, you should work closely with architects and emphasize that "form must follow function." As the renovation proceeds, students may have to be relocated to other buildings, placed on split shifts within the same building, or placed into alternative spaces during certain phases of construction. Involvement in a school renovation is an exhilarating opportunity, but it must also be accompanied by judicious planning, anticipation of needs, and continual attention to preserving the instructional program.

SAFEGUARDING SCHOOL EQUIPMENT AND MATERIALS

Any modern school contains many thousands of dollars of educational equipment. This equipment, as well as the safety of students, of course, is a concern of the elementary school principal. Many schools today have alarm systems. If your school does, you need to know exactly how this system works, who has the alarm codes, and how to contact the alarm maintenance services. It is an important responsibility to make sure that if you are the last person to leave the building in the evening or the first to arrive in the morning that you activate (or deactivate) the alarm system. Code numbers must be kept under lock and key. Despite the temptation to allow teachers and other staff members to enter the school building on weekends by giving out alarm codes, many principals find these numbers are quickly passed around, and it is not long before the entire security system is compromised.

Simpler, more commonsense approaches to maintaining school security also need to be in place. Many schools have a "locked door" policy. All outside doors are locked (from the outside only, of course) after students arrive in the morning, then any visitors must be buzzed in through an intercom located in the school office. Sometimes, mirrors are installed that allow school office personnel to see who is entering the building. Signs may be posted instructing all visitors to go to the main office before proceeding to other locations in the school. Once visitors arrive at the office, many schools maintain sign-in books in which visitors must enter their names and the time and purpose of visit.

Below is a checklist for principals to use to monitor school security:

- ☐ Check that all doors are in good repair and close tight when released.

- ☐ Have the operation and integrity of the alarm system checked periodically.

- ☐ Ensure that intercom systems are working properly.

- ☐ Provide "walkie-talkies" or other communication devices for those staff members who supervise students outside of the school building in situations such as school recess periods, outdoor physical education periods, and so on.

- ☐ Make sure that all staff members are alert to strangers in the building and aware of basic safety procedures.

- ☐ Have the custodian make a morning and afternoon building security check.

- ☐ Make sure that all teachers close any outside doors that remain open.

- ☐ Have visitors proceed to the main office to sign in upon entry into the building.

- ☐ Have bathrooms and other unsupervised areas checked periodically throughout the day.

- ☐ Review safety procedures with substitutes or have a handout prepared for them.

It is also wise to solicit suggestions from teachers, custodians, and other school employees on how to improve school security. Sometimes, a wonderful idea has not been thought of before and may be relatively easy to implement.

SCHOOL SAFETY AND EMERGENCY PLANNING

Ensuring the safety of students is a primary responsibility, and as principal, you must develop (or play a key role in the development of) procedures to fulfill this responsibility. The purposes and procedures for fire drills, bus dismissal, traffic flow around the school, school closings, emergency evacuations, bomb threats, lockdowns, shelter-in-place, and other such matters should be on the agenda of this committee.

The following is a list of some of the guiding principles that can be followed when planning for school safety and violence prevention:

- School safety plans should be developed with broad participation with teachers, administrators, custodial staff, parents, public safety agencies, local law-enforcement departments, and other community members.
- Planning should be thorough and comprehensive and include activities that involve early prevention through crisis response.
- Roles and responsibilities should be clearly delineated. There should be backup for people with key roles who might not be available in an emergency situation.
- School data should be incorporated into safety planning including such items as building floor plans, a list of entrances, fire doors, assembly areas, accommodations for students with physical handicaps, and so on.
- The plan developed should be easily understood by all parties and widely disseminated so that all members of the school community accept the plan and work toward its implementation. Copies of the plan should be on file in school district offices, local law-enforcement agencies, and first responders.
- A staff development component should be provided so that all members of the school community can become familiar with and review the roles and responsibilities within the plan. This should be included in a school's or district's annual staff development plan. "Tabletop" exercises, in which a variety of hypothetical school safety situations are presented and participants practice how they would respond, should be a part of the staff development.
- Once procedures are set and disseminated, the committee should review its implementation of the plan periodically.

Some of the situations for which emergency planning is necessary include

- fire;
- bomb threat;
- presence of an intruder;
- loss of heat, water, or electricity;
- external threat, for example, an active armed person in the vicinity, or a nearby crime scene;
- severe weather, for example, tornadoes, hurricanes, earthquakes, electrical storms;
- chemical or biological incident;
- major act of violence; or
- act of terrorism.

Depending upon the specific situation, possible responses include

- school evacuation,
- early dismissal,

- reverse evacuation,
- lockdown,
- shelter-in-place, and
- contacting school and local authorities.

Any emergency plan will include forms that outline procedures for all of these situations. In many schools, a booklet that details these procedures is developed and located near the door of every room within easy reach of teachers, aides, and substitutes.

A checklist that you might use to ensure that these strategies and procedures are in place appears in Figure 16.3.

Figure 16.3 Checklist for Review of School Emergency Plan

CHECKLIST FOR DEVELOPMENT OF SCHOOL EMERGENCY PLAN

1. Does the plan include specific and detailed descriptions of the roles and responsibilities of each individual?

2. Does the plan make provisions for overlap in the event that a key individual is not present or available?

3. Does the plan take into account a review of the local emergency agency and first-responder procedures that exist in the community?

4. Have safety surveys of the facilities been conducted?

5. Has the plan been developed with assistance from
   - local emergency management agency,
   - local law-enforcement agencies,
   - the local fire department,
   - local emergency medical services, and
   - the local public health agency?

6. Has the plan been developed with assistance from
   - school security officers,
   - school facilities personnel,
   - transportation coordinators,
   - school nurses,
   - risk management personnel,
   - special-needs personnel,
   - finance officials, and
   - school district public information personnel?

(Continued)

Figure 16.3 (Continued)

7. Does the plan include provisions for the following types of incidents?
   - Severe weather
   - Chemical or biological incidents
   - Bomb threat
   - Fire
   - Earthquake
   - Disruption of electricity, heat, and/or water
   - Major act of violence in the school or vicinity
   - School intrusion
   - Act of terrorism

8. Have procedures been specified for
   - lockdowns,
   - shelter-in-place,
   - evacuation, and
   - reverse evacuation?

9. Has a copy of the plan been issued to all employees of the school district and appropriate local agencies?

10. Have staff development exercises been conducted to ensure that all personnel are familiar with and have practice with the plan including tabletop exercises, functional exercises, and full-scale exercises?

11. Have provisions been made to review and update the plan as needed?

Also following are two sample procedures for an elementary school: Figure 16.4 deals with fire drill procedures and Figure 16.5, bomb threat procedures. A procedure for a crisis response team that can be called into action in the event of a natural disaster or family crisis was outlined in Chapter 12.

Parents and community members often voice their concerns about what procedures are in place for the safety of their children while they are at school. You should first and foremost help parents to understand that their child's safety is of utmost importance and that all situations have been planned for. While the school's plans should be shared, it is also important, for security reasons, that specific details (for example, assembly areas within a building, evacuation routes) remain confidential, known only to members of the emergency response team. A sample letter to parents outlining the plans that are in place and communication procedures appears in Figure 16.6.

Figure 16.4 Sample Fire Drill Procedures

_____________ **Elementary School**

FIRE DRILL PROCEDURES

We are required to hold one fire drill each month that school is in session. When the fire alarm sounds:

1. Take your attendance cards.
2. Close the classroom windows.
3. Lead your class to the assigned exit door.
4. Close the classroom door.
5. Walk to the designated area outside of the school building.
6. Take attendance to make sure that all children are accounted for.
7. ESL and special-services teachers will check the bathrooms to make sure that all children have left the school building.
8. Talking is NOT PERMITTED at any time during a fire drill.
9. Children must walk in an orderly fashion and listen carefully for additional instructions.

Exit Procedures

Kindergarten: Use own doors

Rooms 201, 203: South front door

Rooms 209, 211: South front door

Rooms 212, 213, 214: North front door

Rooms 103, 107, 109, 111: Rear southwest door

Rooms 120, 122, 124: Rear northwest door

Art Room, Music Room: Rear northwest door

Library, Computer Room, Room 113: North driveway door

Auditorium, Orchestra and Physical Education: Classes exit from auditorium driveway

Other Procedures

1. Children will be expected to exit along with the teacher of a special class they may be attending.
2. In the event that a child is unattended (in the lavatory, nurse's office, main office, and so on) when the fire alarm sounds, he or she should leave the building through the nearest exit and quietly find his or her way to the class's normal lineup area.

(Continued)

Figure 16.4   (Continued)

3. At times, an exit or hallway will be obstructed. Teachers are expected to react calmly and make a decision as to an alternate route. Questions to discuss with children at the beginning of the year include:

   a. What would you do if our regular exit is blocked?

   b. What would you do if you were in the library? Computer room? Resource center? Lavatory? Delivering a message?

4. In the event that a fire drill takes place when the children are at an assembly, each class will exit the auditorium doorway nearest where it is seated and then proceed quickly through the auditorium driveway doors down to the northern perimeter of the school building.

Figure 16.5   Sample Bomb Threat Procedures

_____________________________ **Elementary School**

BOMB THREAT PROCEDURES

The school's safety committee has prepared the following procedures in the event that a bomb threat is received. These procedures take into account the fact that the school is responsible for a large number of students, teachers, and other staff, and that administrators must do all that is prudent and possible in the event of imminent danger. Please read these procedures carefully.

I. When a call is received.

   A. The person receiving the call should make every effort to connect the caller with the principal, assistant principal, or teacher in charge.

   B. If the person receiving the call is unable to accomplish the above, he or she should gather as much pertinent information as possible, including the following:

      1. Site of the bomb

      2. When is it set to "go off"

      3. What kind of device it is

      4. Name, sex, and location of caller

      5. Approximate age of caller

      6. Voice tone, accent, background noises

      7. Exact nature of threat

   C. Immediately after the call is received, the person should give information to the principal, assistant principal, or teacher in charge.

II. Principal notifies the superintendent, who will initiate procedures based upon his or her judgment.

III. Search and evacuation procedures

   A. The fire alarm will sound.

   B. Teachers not responsible for exiting a class will scan the floor in which they are located before exiting and notify the principal's designee outside of the school building immediately if anything looked suspicious.

   C. Custodial personnel will search boiler rooms, janitorial supply rooms, sink closets, waste containers, and other areas as directed.

   D. In the event that no bomb is found, a search of all lockers may be ordered.

   E. **No one is to handle any suspicious-looking package or device.**

IV. Reentry after evacuation

   A. The highest-ranking police department official shall inform the principal that a reasonable search has been conducted.

   B. Based upon such information, and in consultation with police and fire department officials, the principal shall decide when it is appropriate to reenter the building. If the decision is made not to reenter the building, instructions to proceed to the designated evacuation site will be given.

Figure 16.6 Letter to Parents Outlining Emergency Planning

September ____________________

Dear Parents,

I would like to take this opportunity to share with you a brief description of the school district's "Emergency Plan" for our school. Although, for reasons of security, I believe it best not to share specific details of the plan, I would like to provide you with a few essential features. Please be aware that this plan was developed in collaboration with local law agencies.

The plan includes safety procedures for staff and students to follow depending upon the nature of the emergency at hand. A copy of the plan has been distributed to and reviewed with each staff member. Should an emergency occur, our Emergency Response Team will be responsible for oversight and implementation of the plan.

Please be assured that we have done our utmost to ensure your child(ren)'s safety. All instructional rooms are equipped with an emergency kit, and all staff members have copies of their own plan.

Should an emergency occur, information as to a specific area for parents to gather would be designated at that time. The exact location to gather will depend upon the circumstances of the particular emergency. Please check the district Web site or call our emergency hotline for the designated location to meet with school administrators and first responders. Should the emergency require the school to go into a lockdown procedure to protect the children, please access the district's Web site or call the emergency hotline to obtain updated information.

Respectfully,

____________________, Principal

If you make the safety of children a priority, staff, parents, and community members will appreciate your dedication and understanding of this basic concern.

17

Developing and Implementing Effective Class Placement Policies

As with all important policies established in schools, class placement practices and procedures must be well thought out. In some cases, districts have specific policies for class placement, and those policies will drive your own process. In other cases, the placement process is decided upon at the building level. Regardless of the situation, decisions that are made for the grouping of students should aim for increasing instructional effectiveness and maximizing the use of resources available. There are several questions that must be considered when formulating class placement policies: How will students be grouped in classes? Who will form the classes? How large will classes be before they are divided? What are the criteria that govern the assignment of students to various teachers?

At the conclusion of placement proceedings, you should be able to answer whether or not your groupings addressed the following: Did the groupings allow you to enhance a student's ability to learn? Will these groupings offer intellectual challenges to students of all ability levels? How will these groupings facilitate planning and instruction for the teacher?

FAIR AND APPROPRIATE ORGANIZATION OF CLASSES

One of the very first decisions that principals must come to grips with in organizing classes is to determine the premises that will guide this activity. If your school district has not

---

Note: All forms, letters, and checklists included in this chapter can be found at corwin.com/elementary survivalkit.

established guidelines for class sizes, this is a worthwhile endeavor. When such guidelines are in place, they permit rational decisions that are fair and equitable and can help to avoid the controversies that often occur when a group of parents feels that their children are in classes that are too large. (A sample set of class-size guidelines appears in Figure 17.1.) Again, local policies will determine such guidelines.

Figure 17.1 Sample Class-Size Guidelines

Name of District

ELEMENTARY SCHOOL CLASS-SIZE GUIDELINES

The following numbers will apply to elementary school class size with the understanding that these numbers will be used as guidelines by the administration. The factors of educational suitability, physical plant, and fiscal constraints will also be taken into consideration.

Grade	An aide will be added when the class reaches	A new class will be formed when enrollment reaches
Kindergarten	24	28
One	24	28
Two	24	28
Three	25	29
Four	26	30
Five	26	30
Six	27	30

Special Considerations

A. If a new student enrolls in the middle of the school year, and that student would cause a new class to be formed, that student will be offered free transportation to attend another elementary school in the district.

B. If a class that was provided an aide drops at least three students below the "trigger" number for an aide, then the aide will be discontinued by the December recess.

C. A two-grade combination of three classes should be considered in the primary grades for a number fewer than 61 students.

D. The class-size guidelines will be reviewed every three years, taking into consideration current trends and relevant educational research.

With class-size guidelines in mind (either formal or informal), you and staff members should establish the criteria upon which classes will be formed when children are promoted from one grade to the next. The once-common practice of grouping children according to ability is rare in schools today. Within a class, there may be occasions to work with a specific group of youngsters either to reinforce or reteach a particular skill or to provide enrichment, but most classes are heterogeneous in their makeup. There is a distinction between "random heterogeneity" and "deliberate heterogeneity." When students are grouped randomly, but without attention to perceived ability or specific interests, the resulting groups might not be comparable. On the other hand, if composing heterogeneous classes is indeed the goal, then specific steps must be taken to ensure this outcome. What many teachers do is to rank the children in the sending grade according to performance and perceived ability. Then, when forming new classes, a balance is created by selecting equal numbers of students from the top, middle, and bottom of this ranking. If student interests, self-confidence, and related social skills are also taken into account, classes will more likely be well balanced than if random assignments are made. Gender and ethnicity should also be balanced, as well as the English-language ability of the students. In some schools, where differences in neighborhood or economic factors result in distinct populations, these groups should be balanced as well. A heterogeneous group represents a true cross section of the student population at the particular grade level(s). Of course, if students are grouped into multigrade classes, these same factors should be balanced as well as the age span for the grades that are combined.

Parents should be involved in discussing the various factors that go into creating classes. If they are a part of frank discussions of the policies and procedures for class placements, they will better understand the delicate balances that are created, and will perhaps go on to defend the school's decisions to those who might register complaints or try to tamper with the process. It is also important to make public the criteria used in arriving at class placements. A sample letter to parents explaining these policies appears in Figure 17.2.

Figure 17.2   Sample Letter to Parents Explaining Class Placement Policies

---

Name of Elementary School

OFFICE OF THE PRINCIPAL

June ___________

Dear Parents,

  Each spring there is considerable discussion about placing children in classes for the next school year. This is a matter that we do not take lightly at ______________, and the staff and I spend countless hours in forming well-balanced classes in which all children will have an opportunity to learn and to grow in their academic and social skills.

  It is hoped that a frank review of our procedures for class placement of students will obviate the need for parents to individualize their concerns or make requests for specific teachers.

  When classes are structured, we follow a clear set of guidelines. Classes are formed into deliberate heterogeneous groups with the following in mind:

- An even boy/girl balance
- A full range of aptitudes within each class
- An even proportion of abilities and learning styles across the classes at each grade
- An equal number of pupils in each class on a grade level
- An even proportion of children with English-language proficiency

  Once these factors have been considered, teachers begin to "build a class" of children who show promise of working well together. At this point, attempts are made to match pupil and teacher personality and style. Quite naturally, these decisions are based upon observations made by the teachers during the course of the year. While we welcome your input about your child's individual learning needs, we trust that you understand that your comments are but one of the many factors that we consider in forming classes. The final decision on class placements will reside with the school.

Sincerely,

Principal

INVITING PARENT INPUT INTO CLASS PLACEMENT: BENEFITS AND DRAWBACKS

One of the issues that most elementary school principals face is the degree of parental input that should be allowed when teachers form classes. This can be a very controversial matter. On the one hand, if you invite parental opinion or input, it may raise the expectation that their comments will result in their child's having the teacher or group that they requested. On the other hand, if parental input is denied, the staff may be losing some important information about children—as well as losing the opportunity to avert potential problems of which teachers might not be aware. For example, let's say that a parent and a teacher were involved in a dispute—or even a lawsuit—some years previously. Placing that parent's child with that same teacher may only be looking for trouble.

If it is clearly understood that the ultimate class placement decision resides with school personnel, there are some distinct advantages to seeking parental input into the process. A parent input form may be sent home with a request that parents return the completed form in an envelope via the student or mail it to the school's main office. Parents can describe a child's learning style, home situation, and classmates with whom he or she has worked particularly well—or those with whom their child has had chronic difficulty. Parents should be cautioned not to request specific teachers, but rather to write about general learning characteristics. Providing such information should be optional on the part of the parent. After building a cooperative relationship during the year, teachers are often put into awkward situations that relate to placement, and a parent input form may prevent these situations from occurring. Should a parent discuss placement with a teacher, the teacher should be careful not to imply that any promises are made or input automatically translated into guarantees for class placement. Parents will sense, however, that teachers are taking their comments seriously if the teacher takes notes about relevant comments in the conversation. The information gained through this process can be quite helpful when teachers form classes. A sample of such a parent input appears in Figure 17.3. During this

<table><tr><td>**Figure 17.3**</td><td>Letter Inviting Parental Input Into Class Placements</td></tr></table>

Name of Elementary School and District

There are many factors that staff examine to determine the best placement for every child, one being parental knowledge of their children. Please fill out the form below and return it in an envelope to the *Main Office* no later than *date.* We welcome your input, but please do not request a specific teacher. Thank you.

In what kind of setting has your child worked successfully?

In what kind of setting has your child encountered difficulties?

Is there anything else you think that we should know about your child that will help our decisions in class placement?

Do you plan to move to another community before the beginning of the next school year?

time, it is helpful to ask parents if they are planning to move to another community before the start of the next school year. Knowing the full scope of the student body will help you balance classes even more accurately.

DEVELOPING CLASS LISTS

When teachers finally do form class lists, they should have gathered information about each youngster. In many schools, teachers begin by making an index card for each child. On these cards, they can indicate the child's birth date, gender, and reading and math levels. Then, the names of youngsters with whom they have worked particularly well in the past can be listed, as well as those children with whom same-class placement should be avoided. Relevant ethnic, special-education, geographic, and family information should also be included. Finally, there should be some indication if the child's family may have had unusual problems in the past with a particular teacher that might need to be taken into consideration. With all of the cards filled out, teachers and principal should meet and place the children in classes, weighing and balancing the various factors. Make sure that ability/achievement levels are equally distributed and that those students who tend to require a great deal more attention than others are not all in the same class. Some attempt should also be made to match teacher and pupil learning style; however, discretion must be exercised in discussing such matters within the group of teachers. This can be a delicate issue, since public evaluations of other teachers' strengths and personalities can quickly be broadcast back into the faculty lounge.

Another approach is to have a team of teachers use the index-card information to form classes. The team often consists of a teacher representative from each grade level, the school psychologist, reading and math specialists, special educators, and a school administrator. Once class lists are formed, individual teachers can review the list for apparent errors.

Once class lists are formed, they should be double-checked for the factors that went into their creation. Is the boy/girl balance equal? Are English-language learners evenly distributed? Does one class seem to have an advantage over others? Did all of the "behavior problems" wind up in the same class? These are the kinds of questions you will want to ask when reviewing the draft lists. Special notations can be made regarding students whose placement should not, under any circumstances, be changed. Youngsters who must be separated, families that have had significant difficulties with a particular teacher, and other such matters should be noted in some sort of code—an asterisk next to be child's name or some other indication that the principal will clearly understand.

Staff should be cautioned not to discuss class lists with parents. Once placements leak out, you are likely to be barraged with requests for changes or an explanation of how certain decisions were made. Under no circumstances should students be permitted to see these lists. Class placements should be done in one central location so the confidential information remains confidential.

FORMING INCOMING KINDERGARTEN CLASSES

When forming kindergarten classes, principals usually do not have as much information about children as when they have already spent a year or more within the school. Some schools have prekindergartens, and these teachers may provide important input into class placement, but in most schools, the incoming kindergartners are new. There are, however, several factors that you and your teachers can keep in mind when developing kindergarten class lists.

Many of the considerations that go into forming upper-grade classes also apply to kindergarten classes, that is, boy/girl balance, ethnic balance, English-language ability, geographic balance, and other such matters. Each child's birth date should be placed next to his or her name so that you can form classes of children with the full range of birth dates within the group. Especially with the youngest students in a school, having mostly older children in one class and the younger ones in the other can lead to imbalanced groups. Another consideration that principals look at is where (and whether) the children attended nursery school. If there are three or four popular preschool programs in the area, it would be wise to note which school each child attended. Then, it is best to keep a few children together who may have known one another in the past. This may help to alleviate early adjustment problems. Care should be taken, however, not to put four or five children from one nursery school in one class and only one in another. The child who does not see any familiar faces may feel isolated. If you do consider the nursery schools that youngsters attended, try to ensure that each class formed has a few children from each of the predominant preschools.

Another way to find out information about incoming kindergartners is to use a screening process. This may involve inviting registered children to school in the spring prior to their kindergarten year on a day in which they will meet teachers and perhaps social workers, learning specialists, and speech/language pathologists. Many schools develop a screening program in which children's verbal, motor, and perceptual skills are assessed through standardized or local inventories. Health screening may also occur during this time period. The information gained during such sessions may not be entirely reliable or predictive, but it will give the professionals a chance to meet the incoming students and perhaps note some outstanding observations that may assist in the placement process.

It is helpful to hold a parent meeting while the students are being screened. The parents are bursting with questions that can be addressed during that time. Key staff members can be introduced, questions can be answered, and a brief tour of the school can be conducted. This meeting goes a long way toward making parents feel comfortable in the school at a very early stage of their children's education. Parents who have already had children in the school often answer the new parents' questions. This meeting can make new parents feel that they are part of a supportive school community and thus starts a positive relationship between you and the incoming parents.

Many schools also use parent questionnaires to provide background information that may assist in the formation of classes. Such inventories can be designed to provide important details about a child's development, health information, and other factors that teachers, nurses, and principals should know before the opening of school. A sample of such a developmental questionnaire appears in Figure 17.4.

Figure 17.4 Sample Developmental Information Form

Name of District

KINDERGARTEN DEVELOPMENTAL INFORMATION

Name of child: ________________________________ **Birth date:** __________ **Age:** ________

Address: ______________________________ **Sex:** __________ **Phone:** ________________

Has your child attended nursery school? Yes: ____________ No: ____________

Name and address of school: ____

Number of years attended: ______________________

Days per week: ______________________________

Family History

Father: ____________________ Occupation: ____________________ Birthplace: __________

Mother: ____________________ Occupation: ____________________ Birthplace: __________

Marital Status of Parents: Married ☐ Separated ☐ Widowed ☐ Divorced ☐

Guardian (if other than parents): ____

Who is responsible for child if parent(s) work outside of home? ____________________

Other adults living at home: ____________________ Relationship: ____________________

Language(s) spoken at home: ____

Brothers and/or sisters of child: ____

Full Name	Age	Any Speech, Hearing, Reading, or Other Educational Difficulties

Are any children in your home adopted or foster children? Yes: __________ No: __________

If yes, please provide names: ____

Is there a family history of any of the following? (Please explain.)

(1) Seizures ____________________

(2) Asthma ____________________

(3) Diabetes ____________________

(4) Tuberculosis ____________________

(5) Congenital Defects ____________

(6) Scoliosis ____________________

(7) Visual Problems ____________

(8) Hearing Loss ______________

(9) High Blood Pressure __________

(10) Other ____________________

Prenatal and Birth Information

Were pregnancy and delivery normal? ________ If not, give details:

Child's Medical History

Has your child had any unusual illness or injuries? Yes: _______ No: _______

Has your child had any convulsions or seizures? Yes: _______ No: _______

Is your child on long-term medication for any condition? Yes: _______ No: _______

Has your child ever been hospitalized? Yes: _______ No: _______

Has your child had any psychological or neurological evaluations? Yes: _______ No: _______

Has your child had any evidence of a hearing problem? Yes: _______ No: _______

Does your child have any physical defects? Yes: _______ No: _______

Has your child had any evidence of vision problems? Yes: _______ No: _______

Does your child have any speech difficulties? Yes: _______ No: _______

Does your child have any allergies? Yes: _______ No: _______

Does your child take any medications? Yes: _______ No: _______

Please provide details for any area(s) checked "yes."

Developmental Information

Sleep Habits (Check those that apply):

Sleeps Well ☐   Naps ☐   Sleepwalks ☐   Sleeps Restlessly ☐

Comments:

Developmental Concerns (Check those that apply):

Overactive ☐   Short Attention Span ☐   Bed Wetting ☐

Separation Difficulties ☐   Temper Tantrums ☐   Tics ☐   Nail Biting ☐   Thumb Sucking ☐

Comments:

Developmental Milestones:

At what age did child

Teethe ____________ Sit Up __________________ Walk ___________________

Toilet Train ____________ Speak Words ____________ Speak in Sentences ____________

Social and Emotional Information

Does your child have any specific fears?

Please comment on any social and emotional factors you feel would be helpful to us in providing an appropriate and supportive climate for your child. Please attach any additional pages and relevant preschool records or reports.

Signature of person completing report: ____

DEALING WITH THE RETENTION OF STUDENTS IN A GRADE

One of the issues related to class placement is the matter of students who are retained at a particular grade level. This is never an easy decision. Although current research indicates that any benefits from retaining, or holding back, a pupil are short-lived, the practice is still somewhat common in elementary schools. There is considerable anecdotal evidence that placing a child who has experienced academic or social difficulties in a new group that is less socially and intellectually mature can be advantageous. The student can have an opportunity to shine and to exercise leadership.

Because retention can be emotionally painful to students, the decision should never be taken lightly. Many factors must be kept in mind when considering retention. Among them are

- the child's chronological age in comparison to the others in his/her group,
- the child's level of social maturity,
- the child's physical size,
- the child's level of academic achievement,
- the availability of support services to help the youngster in any grade or class,
- the parents' attitude about retention,
- the child's own attitude about retention,
- the school's or school district's philosophy on the practice of retention,
- the child's classification as a regular-education or a special-education student, and
- the ages and grades of the child's siblings.

Whenever retention is considered, early discussion about the matter is essential. In some school districts, retention must first be mentioned or considered in March of the school year prior to the year of retention. Several meetings with parents, and ongoing assessments of progress throughout the spring, should occur to ensure that the decision is a sound one. Retention must be viewed as a decision for the next school year, but its ramifications should be projected long into the future. Will the child be likely to reap long-term advantages in 5 or 10 years? Will the "gift of a year" be helpful to the child as he or she enters the adolescent years and beyond? How have other children in the school reacted to children who have been retained?

Perhaps one of the most important factors is the parents' attitude toward retention. If parents resist the idea and do not see the benefits of retention, the idea is likely to be sabotaged, and in the end will not benefit the child. On the other hand, where parents see the advantages of retention and support the plan, it has the best chance of benefiting the child. To help you in the process, there are professionally developed questionnaires that you can use along with teachers and parents to guide this decision.

ANNOUNCING CLASS PLACEMENTS TO PARENTS

The timing for informing parents of class placements for the new school year is usually a matter of local policy or practice. In many schools, children's next year's placement is noted on the final report card at the end of the school year. Other schools mail home the notifications during the summer, sometimes along with a letter from the child's new teacher. In some schools, class assignments are posted on a notice board, and then the principal goes away for a few weeks. There are even a few schools, although they are not in the majority, where students receive their class assignments on the first day of school as they enter the school building. Whatever the notification process, lists should be checked and double-checked before students are informed of their classes. Errors in this all-important process should be avoided. A sample assignment letter from the principal appears in Figure 17.5.

Figure 17.5 Sample Letter to Students Announcing Class Placement

Office of the Principal

Date

Dear Girls and Boys,

I hope you have been enjoying a great summer. My family and I went to the shore, and my five-year-old son learned to swim on his own. It was a great event for our family!

School will open in a few short weeks and I am looking forward to hearing all about what you did during the summer—especially the books that you read!

You will find the name of your new teacher and room number at the bottom of this letter. Please go directly to your classroom on *date*, the first day of school. There will be many people there to help you find the right room. Your new teacher will be waiting to greet you at the classroom door and then let you know about all of the learning adventures that lie ahead in the new school year.

I extend a particularly warm welcome to all of our new students and know that you will quickly feel right at home.

Your Principal,

____

Student's Name has been assigned to Grade _______________. Your teacher's name is _______________________________.

Your classroom number is _________________.

One benefit of sending out placement announcements at the end of the summer is to allow you the flexibility to make changes due to unforeseen occurrences during the summer. If several students move during the summer and a number of them are from the same class, you can keep class size balanced by considering moving other students. Another possibility is that several students move into the district. Rather than place new students randomly, you can place them in classrooms that best serve their needs.

HANDLING PARENT COMPLAINTS ABOUT CLASS PLACEMENTS

One of the most frustrating aspects of the role of the principal is the onslaught of telephone calls and complaints that accompanies the announcement of class placements. Some parents may be upset that their children did not get a favored teacher; some children may be angry because they are separated from their closest friends; still others may be disappointed that they have been placed with other youngsters with whom they did not want to spend another year. In any case, such concerns and complaints are usually directed at you. The first principle in handling complaints about class placement is to listen. Parents need to feel that their concerns have been heard. It is best to provide reasons for placement of a student, reiterating the school's class placement policy. Often, when parents understand the many complex factors that go into creating well-balanced classes, they become more reasonable. It may be wise to say that, as principal, you do not want any child to be miserable but that, in your experience, waiting a few weeks usually results in more positive attitudes. You can further assure parents that, most often, children were placed where they were for very good reasons, and it's best to give the situation a chance.

Whether or not to make changes in class placements is a matter for each principal to decide for him- or herself. Some principals stubbornly refuse to make any class changes regardless of the validity of the request; others may be too willing to make accommodations and changes in order to "keep everybody happy." Most experienced administrators, however, have found that if word gets out that all parents need to do is to exert sufficient pressure on the principal, and class placements will be changed, the results can be quite problematic. Honored requests may herald a stream of others to follow, and the all-too-agreeable principal may find that his or her "flexibility" has created an impossible situation.

PLACING STUDENTS WHO ENTER DURING THE SCHOOL YEAR

Another challenge in class placement is how to assign students who enter the school in the middle of the school year. In schools with a high rate of pupil turnover, this can be a persistent dilemma. Whenever a new student enrolls in a school, any school records that have been provided should be examined with the aim of getting to know more about the child's performance. If the child enrolls without prior records, you can conduct a brief screening. After welcoming the youngster and putting him or her at ease, you might sit down with the child and discuss his or her interests and favorite aspects of school. You can ask the child to read a brief passage from an engaging book and perhaps prepare a short math worksheet—one appropriate for the child's grade level and time of year. Once you have a sense of the new student's abilities and personality, examine your current class lists in the applicable grade. Go back to the factors that are considered in initially forming classes. Will this child fit into one class better than another? If the child has limited English-language ability or diagnosed learning difficulties, will his or her presence affect the balance already created? How have the existing classes fared during the school year? In some classes, where boy/girl balance is uneven, or social interactions have become "locked," a new face on the scene can have a very positive effect upon the class's general demeanor. Always introduce the new child to his or her new classmates and tell them something about the new child's background. You can do a great deal to model a welcoming spirit and warm acceptance of new students.

REVIEWING AND EVALUATING CLASS PLACEMENT PRACTICES

As with all important school practices, class placement policies should be reviewed periodically to ensure that they are appropriate and being fairly implemented. Are the policies clear to all of the constituents? Does the system seem to be serving the students well? Do classes seem to be well balanced? Are grouping practices well understood and consistent? An ideal place to raise these important issues is with the school leadership team.

It is healthy, in any organization, to examine existing practices and check whether or not they are consistent with the overall mission and philosophy. Student grouping can affect the self-esteem of the youngsters and the perceptions of parents. When changes in grouping practices seem to be called for, they should be carefully planned and made public.

18

Effective and Creative School Scheduling Practices

What children do in the course of a school day and when they do it are issues of prime concern to school leaders. The schedule of the school day can have a critical impact on how the educational program is delivered. Alternative scheduling practices may not add hours to the school day, but they can improve the ways in which teachers and students spend their time together. School scheduling practices should be consistent with and support the school's basic philosophy. If a school's mission is to provide a quality educational program in the core curriculum area, for example, to refine children's use of language (and all of its ramifications), then special classes should be scheduled around protected time for core curriculum instruction. Be sure, when you are developing guidelines for school scheduling, to consider the school's philosophy, mission statement, or identified values.

SETTING GOALS FOR THE SCHOOL SCHEDULE

As in all aspects of educational planning, specific goals can be accomplished through the school schedule. These goals, emanating from the school's philosophy or mission, should drive the development of the schedule. Some such goals might include

---

Note: All forms, letters, and checklists included in this chapter can be found at corwin.com/elementary survivalkit.

- providing as much unfragmented classroom time as possible,
- allowing for common planning time among teachers at the same or adjacent grade levels,
- reducing pupil-teacher ratios in certain subject areas by scheduling reading and/or math at designated times so that specialists may "push-in" and conduct small-group instruction in the regular classroom,
- increasing student time on task,
- decreasing the number of student "pullouts," and
- honoring specific provisions of the teachers' contract.

Once these important considerations, or goals, have been defined, they should be kept in mind as the school schedule is planned. For example, what will have to happen to reduce student pullouts? How will the schedule have to be configured to allow for maximum common planning time for teachers at the same grade level?

THE EFFECT OF THE SCHEDULE ON THE CLIMATE OF THE SCHOOL

Many school leaders underestimate the importance of a school schedule and its effect upon the general climate of the school. Teachers often complain about the schedule; they may not like the time when they have their preparation periods, and it may be inconvenient for them or for the children. Some teachers like to engage students in long, uninterrupted periods of inquiry, and they resent having the classroom seem like a revolving door, through which students leave and reenter throughout the entire day. How often have we heard teachers say, "If only I had my entire class with me for a whole uninterrupted hour!" These comments are quite common, and although careful, intelligent scheduling will not be a panacea for all individuals in a school, a broad understanding of some of the limits and trade-offs that come with developing school schedules will help staff members to appraise the constraints and perhaps develop creative, innovative approaches. Be careful, though, not to make any guarantees when soliciting input. One of the most discouraging aspects of inviting suggestions for school scheduling is the expectation that might arise from the invitation. Teachers may feel that their input will automatically be put into action. Make it clear that everyone's preferences cannot be honored, but at least they can all be considered.

DEFINING PREMISES, ASSUMPTIONS, AND CONTRACTUAL CONSIDERATIONS

After a careful look at the school's philosophy and mission, some premises should be defined to guide the development of the school schedule. Following is a checklist of the matters that should be considered when developing a school schedule:

- ☐ Should common planning time for teachers at a grade level be accommodated?
- ☐ Are the early mornings left uninterrupted in primary-grade classes so that reading instruction can be conducted in predictable time blocks each day?
- ☐ What are the contractual considerations that must be honored?
- ☐ How long is the time block for each special class?

- ☐ What are the requirements for planning time for special teachers?
- ☐ Are there any requirements for Resource Center (special education) classes that will determine when special classes can occur?
- ☐ Are special teachers assigned to the school on specified days of the week that must be taken into account when developing a school schedule?
- ☐ Are there special programs, such as gifted/talented, instrumental music, assembly times, that must be taken into consideration before developing a school schedule?
- ☐ Are there any time and space constraints that must be considered? For example, if the gymnasium and the lunchroom are in the same space, then what are the hours that the lunchroom cannot be used for physical education?
- ☐ Are there state regulations that mandate how much time a student must engage in a particular subject area?

Involving Staff in the Development of the School Schedule

It is usually fruitful to involve the staff in defining the premises that drive the school schedule—and indeed, in developing the schedule itself. The staff should have a key role in coordinating the human resources assigned to the school in a way that best serves the educational program. When all stakeholders understand the complexities of developing a school schedule, they are more likely to devise some creative solutions and be less likely to consider the schedule something that is "engineered" by the principal to make their school days frustrating.

A committee of staff members should be formed to study the following:

- Grouping patterns in the school
- The amount of time classroom teachers have their entire classes with them
- Time-on-task research
- The roles and deployment of special teachers
- The impact on youngsters of pullout programs
- Parental opinions regarding various scheduling patterns
- Space utilization and constraints
- Ideal time blocks for instruction
- State, local, or national mandates

The school scheduling committee should also study various models for school schedules and consider the benefits and drawbacks of each. The members of the group should call or visit other schools that have used unique models. If such a group is empowered to conduct "action research" and bring data back to the entire staff, the whole question of scheduling will benefit from diverse, examined alternatives and new, creative models tailored to each school's unique situation.

To obtain appropriate data for its study, the group may interview parents to gain their understanding of how the school schedule impacts students. It should also interview students (particularly in the upper grades) to collect data about their own thoughts and opinions. Three questions that might be asked of students include the following:

- How do you feel about being pulled out for special classes or lessons?
- Do you have any problems coming back into class after being out of the room?
- Do you have any suggestions?

We should not be too surprised that students often have viable suggestions for reducing the impact of pullouts. After all, they are the ones who are most affected.

If a group of teachers will be developing the school schedule, they should be given a written copy of the premises and assumptions that must be considered prior to scheduling. For a sample of such a memo, see Figure 18.1.

Figure 18.1   Sample Memo to Scheduling Committee

Dear Members of the Scheduling Committee,

You are about to embark upon an important activity—developing the school's master schedule. There are some important matters that you must consider before you work on the schedule. Please keep these many factors in mind as you proceed:

1. Note the days on which our special teachers are assigned to our school.

Staff Member A	Physical Education	Monday through Friday
Staff Member B	Librarian	Monday, Tuesday, Wednesday (AM)
Staff Member C	Art	Wednesday (AM), Thursday, Friday
Staff Member D	Vocal Music	Monday, Wednesday (AM), Thursday
Staff Member E	Instrumental Music	Tuesday, Wednesday (PM), Thursday
Staff Member F	Remedial Instruction	Monday through Thursday
Staff Member G	Resource Center	Monday through Friday (AM only)
Staff Member H	Speech/Language	Tuesday, Thursday

2. Set aside assembly time on Thursdays from 9:00 until 10:15 AM. Do not schedule any special classes during this time.

3. Avoid all AM specials for the following classes: 3-S, 3-D, 4-K, 4-H, and 5-F since these classes have children who attend the Resource Center and this is a replacement program. Since the teacher is here only in the mornings, these youngsters *must* have reading, language arts, and math in the mornings.

4. Make sure that all teachers are provided with sufficient special classes to comply with the contractual requirement of 200 minutes of planning time each week. Planning time for classroom teachers must be in blocks of at least 30 minutes. The instructional day begins at 8:30 AM, so special teachers may have planning time from 8:30 to 9:00 AM, thus beginning the special schedule at 9:00.

5. The gifted/talented program will operate on Tuesday mornings for fourth and fifth graders. Try to avoid special classes for students in this program before 11:00 AM. (See the gifted/talented teacher for a list of the students in this program and the classes to which they are assigned.)

6. Prepare the master schedule on a grid sheet and check for conflicts (for example, the same class being scheduled for more than one thing at a time, the lunchroom being scheduled for classes when it is not available) and for compliance with the teachers' contract in terms of planning time.

(Continued)

Figure 18.1 (Continued)

7. One option for fulfilling teacher planning time may be as follows:

Special Subject	*Grades K–2*	*Grades 3–5*
Physical Education	2 × 35 min = 70 min	3 × 30 min = 90 min
Art	1 × 40 min = 40 min	1 × 50 min = 50 min
Vocal Music	2 × 30 min = 60 min	1 × 30 min = 30 min
Library/Media	1 × 30 min = 30 min	1 × 30 min = 30 min
TOTALS:	**200 min**	**200 min**

8. In the schedule grid, list the class designations by grade and teacher initial, for example, K-S, K-W, 1-B, 1-M, 2-G.

9. Although we prefer not to do so, special classes may be scheduled until dismissal time, 3:00 PM. If this is the case, children pack up their belongings just prior to going to the special class and are ready for dismissal at 3:00 PM.

Understanding the Roles of Special Teachers

In forming or overseeing the work of a school scheduling committee, be cautious about the unique interests and conflicts that may occur between classroom and special teachers. The importance of all school personnel must be respected, and the roles of each group of individuals should be discussed and viewed in terms of how each individual contributes to the entire school program. When considering scheduling models, a distinction is usually made between special teachers who work with an entire class—such as physical education teachers, librarians, art teachers, music teachers, global language teachers, or technology specialists—and other kinds of special teachers who usually work with small groups of children or individual students. Among this set of teachers are special-education teachers, remedial reading or math specialists, speech/language therapists, guidance counselors, ESL teachers, and instrumental music teachers. The ways in which special teachers work, and the group sizes that they see, have important implications for studying school scheduling patterns and alternatives.

If all participants in a school scheduling committee or study group are charged to put aside individual agendas and work toward the improvement of the instructional program by considering scheduling models and alternatives, the results are likely to be positive and productive. One of the associated outcomes may well be a renewed respect for the contributions made to the school by all members of the staff.

MODELS AND APPROACHES FOR SCHOOL SCHEDULING

There is no single approach to school scheduling. In most schools, a variety of models are adapted to fit local needs. Individual situations will often require modifications to what might seem like a very specific system or model. With the involvement of staff, the best practices can be brought to even the most problematic and fragmented schedule. Again, it is important to keep the mission of the school in mind and make scheduling decisions based upon the premises imbedded in that mission.

Parallel Block Scheduling

One of the promising practices to reduce instructional fragmentation is parallel block scheduling. Simply put, this approach preserves a block of time for instruction in a particular area. For example, let's say that 9:00 to 10:00 AM is set aside for teaching reading in Grade 1. No special classes would be scheduled during this time and all teachers—classroom teachers, special-education teachers, remedial reading teachers, and ESL teachers—would work with the first graders during this time. This has the added benefit of reducing group sizes so that attention may be focused on instruction in the particular area by all of the teachers mentioned. In three classes of 25 students each, the classroom teachers might work with 15 students during this time period; the ESL teacher might work with 11 students taken from the three classes; and the special-education and remedial reading teacher might work with the remaining 20 students. Of course, students who would be best served by the particular specialists should be assigned to them. In some schools, an enrichment teacher or librarian also works with the class during the time block, therefore further increasing individual attention and opportunity. This person can provide advanced work, reteaching or guided practice, and other forms of individual or small-group assistance. In this plan, the class could have a special period at the same time each day, thus allowing predictability of the schedule and common planning time for teachers at the same grade level. A sample of a time block for a typical elementary school of three first-grade classes is outlined below. Such a schedule can be created for each grade level in the school.

Time Block	*Class*		
MONDAY	*1-B*	*1-M*	*1-S*
9:00–10:00 AM	Reading Classroom Teacher (15) Staff Member B (ESL) (3) Staff Member C (Resource) (2) Staff Member D (Rem. Reading) (5)	Reading Classroom Teacher (15) Staff Member B (ESL) (4) Staff Member C (Resource) (3) Staff Member D (Rem. Reading) (4)	Reading Classroom Teacher (16) Staff Member B (ESL) (4) Staff Member C (Reading) (2) Staff Member D (Rem. Reading) (4)
	Mrs. Reed (Librarian) conducts enrichment and research as needed.		
10:00–10:30 AM	Physical Education	Vocal Music	Computer
10:30–11:15 AM	Math	Math	Math

The sample is for a hypothetical Monday. On other days of the week, the special classes from 10:00 to 10:30 would be rotated. The only disadvantage that might be seen is that the special teachers will not have one section of a grade level following another. Art teachers, for example, might argue that if they have a first-grade class followed by a fifth-grade class, they will be spending needless time changing the setup for each class. Many principals find that this type of scheduling results in improved student behavior because the pupil-to-teacher ratio is reduced, and children are not left to work independently while the teacher works with subsets of the class or individuals. As more teachers take on the responsibility for primary instruction in reading, for example, it becomes even more important for teachers to have common preparation time when they can discuss student goals, grade-level outcomes, and the use of materials. Parallel block scheduling requires considerable planning and flexibility. If it is a priority, however, the benefits can be quite rewarding.

Four- or Six-Day Cycles

The most common school schedule usually encompasses a five-day, Monday-to-Friday plan. In some school systems, however, Monday may be the day of the week when most school holidays occur. If, for example, an art teacher sees students only once each week on a Monday, it would not be too long before the program for those students begins to look somewhat different from the program for students who have art on a Wednesday. One approach to deal with this problem is to develop a four- or six-day schedule. In this approach, a complete cycle of all classes occurs every four or six days. The schedule for the first Monday, let's say "day one," will not always fall on a Monday, and so the special program will be more equitably distributed. Building a five-day schedule often results in being able to provide a special class to students "two and a half times" each week. This usually requires unnecessary and confusing "A Week/B Week" cycles. Physical education, for example, is offered three times one week and two times the next. School teams that have developed four- or six-day schedules have found that fitting in all the classes is an easier task than when dealing with a five-day schedule. Principals sometimes worry that children and teachers will have difficulty adapting to the rotation, but most schools that have tried such approaches find that everyone quickly becomes used to the new scheduling arrangement.

The "Four-Block" Day

Another scheduling concept that is gaining in popularity is a "four-block" day. In this approach, the school day is divided into four 90-minute time blocks. One block is routinely devoted to language instruction; a second block can be an alternating science and social studies time (or integrated units); a third block (slightly longer in time) can be devoted to mathematics and lunch (45 minutes for lunch and 60 minutes for math); and the fourth block can be devoted to special subjects or other options such as clubs or interest groups. Teachers at the particular grade level can lead the interest groups, and these can be rotated throughout the year. This type of arrangement is particularly suitable to intermediate or upper-elementary school students. A sample four-block day is outlined here:

Time	Monday	Tuesday	Wednesday	Thursday	Friday
8:30–10:00 AM	Language Arts	Language Arts	Language Arts	Language Arts	Language Arts
10:00–11:30 AM	Science	Social Studies	Science	Social Studies	Science or Social Studies
11:30 AM–1:15 PM	Lunch Math	Lunch Math	Lunch Math	Lunch Math	Lunch Math
1:15–2:45 PM	Physical Educ. Music	Art Interest Club	Physical Educ. Music	Library Interest Club	Computer Lab
2:45–3:00 PM	Preparation for Dismissal	Preparation for Dismissal	Preparation for Dismissal	Preparation for Dismissal	Preparation for Dismissal

One glance at the above schedule reveals that it is predictable and unfragmented, and that it allows for reasonable time blocks for students to explore and integrate their learnings.

Providing Planning Time for Special Teachers

Exactly when in the course of the day to schedule planning time for special teachers is another matter that needs to be addressed. In some schools, providing this planning time first thing in the morning can be most productive. Not only does this allow classroom teachers to start the day with their classes outlining the day's plans, it also has the advantage that special teachers will have common planning time. This might be an ideal time for the principal, guidance counselor, learning specialist, or other individuals to meet with all of the special teachers to discuss individual pupil needs and programming strategies.

You should consider two matters, however, before using this obviously efficient approach. The first is that classroom teachers and special teachers will not be available at the same time to discuss concerns with pupils or plans for integrated studies. The other consideration is that in some teacher contracts, special teachers cannot see more than four classes in a row without a break. Early-morning planning time may require some special teachers to work with five groups before a lunch break.

Keeping All Special Subjects of Equal Time Length

In schools that have studied scheduling patterns, it has been found that the task of scheduling, as well as the flow of the day, is facilitated if special periods are all the same length of time. Half-hour sessions seem ideal, but many art teachers would argue that by the time they distribute materials and have the youngsters clean up, this is not sufficient time for a meaningful experience. One way to mitigate the effects of having 30-minute,

40-minute, 45-minute, and 50-minute periods for special subjects is to plan them in increments of 30 minutes. Thus, all special periods will either be 30 minutes or 60 minutes. This will allow for a smoother flow of the schedule, less fragmentation, and greater flexibility in scheduling pullout programs around the master schedule.

"Pullout" Teachers Planning Their Schedules Together

One of the difficulties that often arises in school scheduling occurs after the master schedule is developed. The master schedule usually specifies when each class, as a whole, goes to a special subject area such as physical education, art, library, music, computer lab, and so on. Pullout teachers such as special-education teachers, ESL teachers, guidance counselors, instrumental music teachers, and speech/language therapists then need to know, "When can I get your kids?" This is when the day is likely to become chopped up for classroom teachers.

Principals have found it useful to have these pullout teachers plan their schedules together. In this way, they can see what is happening to any particular child. For example, suppose that Jane Smith is pulled out of her classroom for speech therapy from 10:00 to 10:30; then the instrumental music teacher wants to see Jane in her woodwinds group from 10:50 to 11:20. What happens to Jane from 10:30 to 10:50? She reenters the classroom, tries to catch up to where her classmates are, and then once she reorients herself, she must leave again for instrumental music lessons. If pullout teachers complete their schedules together, they can look at what happens to individual children, confer with classroom teachers about the best times of the day for pullouts, and perhaps alternate the days in which they see students from a particular grade level so as to reduce the impact of fragmented instruction.

"Pullout-Free" Time Blocks

One possible approach to reducing the fragmentation of the day is to define, ahead of time, certain time blocks when students may not be pulled out of their regular classrooms. If you use "pullout-free" time blocks, this information can be provided to all teachers before schedules are defined. In this way, classroom teachers can plan on uninterrupted instructional time with the entire class present. A sample memo to teachers in which "pullout-free" blocks are announced appears in Figure 18.2. As a courtesy to all, though, this information must be provided before any "pullout" teachers attempt to arrange their schedules.

A "Pullout" Block of Time:
Both Support and Enrichment for All

Another scheduling concept is to insert a block of time for each grade level when all pullouts occur. All students who attend special-education classes, reading and math support groups, instrumental lessons, and others can be pulled out during this time. Students who are not pulled out for anything on a given day can attend "enrichment-for-all" classes developed by staff members and based on state standards. These classes can run for six-, seven-, or eight-week time periods and then another group of students can attend. On one of the days, music lessons for a particular group of students can be given, and the student can attend an enrichment class on the other days of the week. Enrichment

Figure 18.2   Sample Memo Specifying "Pullout-Free" Time Blocks

Name of School and District

MEMORANDUM

Date:

To: All Teachers

From: Principal

RE: "PULLOUT-FREE" TIME BLOCKS

In an attempt to provide teachers at each grade level with uninterrupted instructional time with all of their children present, a plan for "pullout-free" time blocks has been devised and approved by our school's leadership council. Initially, it was hoped to provide the same time block to each grade each day, but upon further discussion with the staff and the council, it was decided to vary the times each day so that all grades might benefit from some pullout-free time blocks in the morning. The schedule outlined below has been built around the school's master schedule.

Special teachers are asked to look at the times indicated below and to avoid scheduling any children for individual or small-group music lessons, speech/language therapy, ESL, counseling, or remedial instruction during the specified time blocks. If you find that your schedule (or time allocation in our building) simply does not allow for you to comply with this arrangement, please speak with the classroom teacher and me so that we can mutually arrive at the best times for pullouts. With your cooperation, we can all work toward an improved quality of instructional time for all pupils.

Grade	Monday	Tuesday	Wednesday	Thursday	Friday
One	9:00–10:00	10:30–11:30	10:30–11:30	10:30–11:30	9:00–10:10
Two	10:15–11:15	9:00–10:00	9:00–10:00	2:00–3:00	11:00–12:10
Three	1:00–2:15	8:55–9:55	10:30–11:30	1:45–3:00	10:15–11:30
Four	9:30–10:30	9:00–10:00	12:30–1:45	10:30–11:30	10:30–11:30
Five	9:00–10:30	10:00–11:30	9:00–10:30	12:30–1:45	9:00–10:30

classes should not form the basis of any regular classroom teaching because several of the students who get support services will not have experienced the activity.

Instrumental Music Rotation

One novel approach that has been used in several schools is the idea of developing a rotating schedule for instrumental music instruction. For example, instead of determining that all woodwinds will have their group lesson on Tuesdays at 2:00 PM, the time slot rotates throughout the week. In this way, children do not miss the same part of their regular classroom experience each week. Many teachers have argued that if an instrumental music lesson is scheduled each week at the same time, some students will miss a significant portion of their science, social studies, or math instruction. The rotating schedule works in time blocks that alternate on eight- or nine-week cycles. In this way, children who are pulled out of their classrooms for individual lessons will miss something different each week. In some schools, this rotation can also cut across other special classes; for instance, once each eight or nine weeks, the child who goes for instrumental music lessons may also miss a physical education period or an art period. Some people consider this a fair and equitable approach.

To implement this arrangement, teachers and students must be provided with the schedule in advance. It can become confusing, but if the schedules are published and posted, everyone will get used to them. Teachers should post the lesson schedules in their classes so that substitutes and students can check it each day.

Using Before- and After-School Times

Another practice that can be a great help in scheduling the school day is to conduct certain classes before or after the official opening or closing of the school day. For example, rehearsals for all instrumentalists to practice as a school band or orchestra can be held 45 minutes before the official start of the school day once or twice each week. In this way, there is less classroom disruption. In some school districts, remedial teachers and speech/language specialists have the flexibility to begin their days earlier and end them earlier than classroom teachers. Sometimes called flexible (or "flex") time, this arrangement allows these specialists to work with youngsters before the opening of the school day, thereby eliminating the need to pull them out of their regular classrooms. Admittedly, this plan can be problematic where the majority of students are bused to school, but, nonetheless, it is another innovative practice that can help to increase the amount of time that youngsters spend in their classrooms.

GETTING DOWN TO BUSINESS: DEVELOPING THE MASTER SCHEDULE

Clearly, there are countless factors to consider before developing a master schedule for an elementary school, but once all of these factors have been taken into account, the time arrives to come to grips with the actual task of creating the schedule. The mechanics of completing a school schedule require concentration and attention to detail, even if you use a software program to develop the schedule.

One way to begin to develop a schedule manually is to list the number of classes that must be scheduled and the time allocations for each of the special teachers. Then, a grid should be produced that should exist as an electronic file so that changes can be made, and so that it can be projected on a screen or interactive whiteboard for group work. The grid can be filled in by hand or by using a computer. See Figure 18.3 for a sample of a scheduling grid that includes physical education, vocal music, art, and library. In the sample that follows, the time grid is produced in five-minute intervals. Within each column, a block is drawn with the class designated that attends the special subject during the times specified. See Figure 18.4 for a schedule form that is already completed. For example, on Tuesday afternoons, class 5-G has physical education from 2:00 until 2:45 PM.

Figure 18.3   Elementary School Scheduling Grid

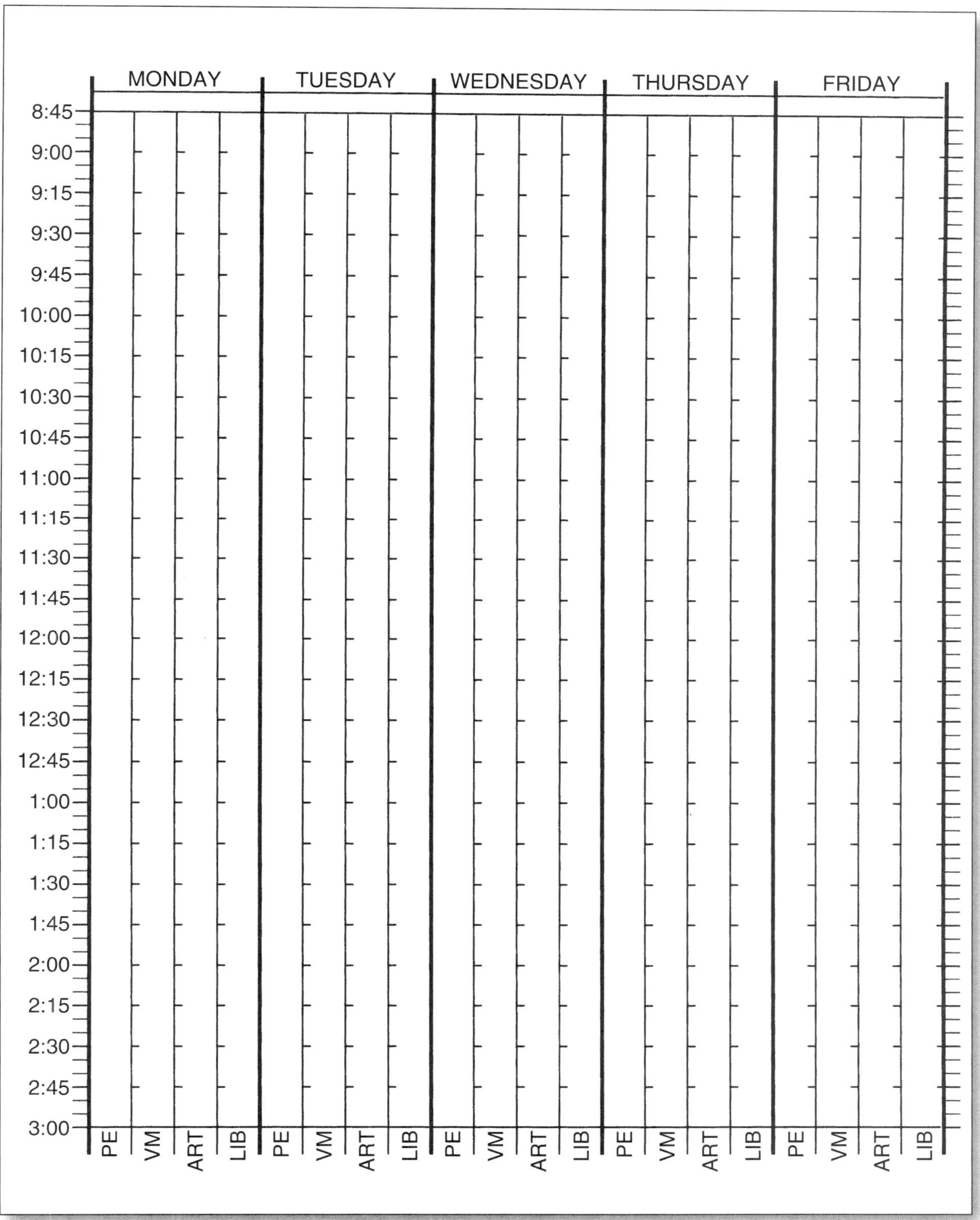

Figure 18.4   Sample Completed Master Schedule

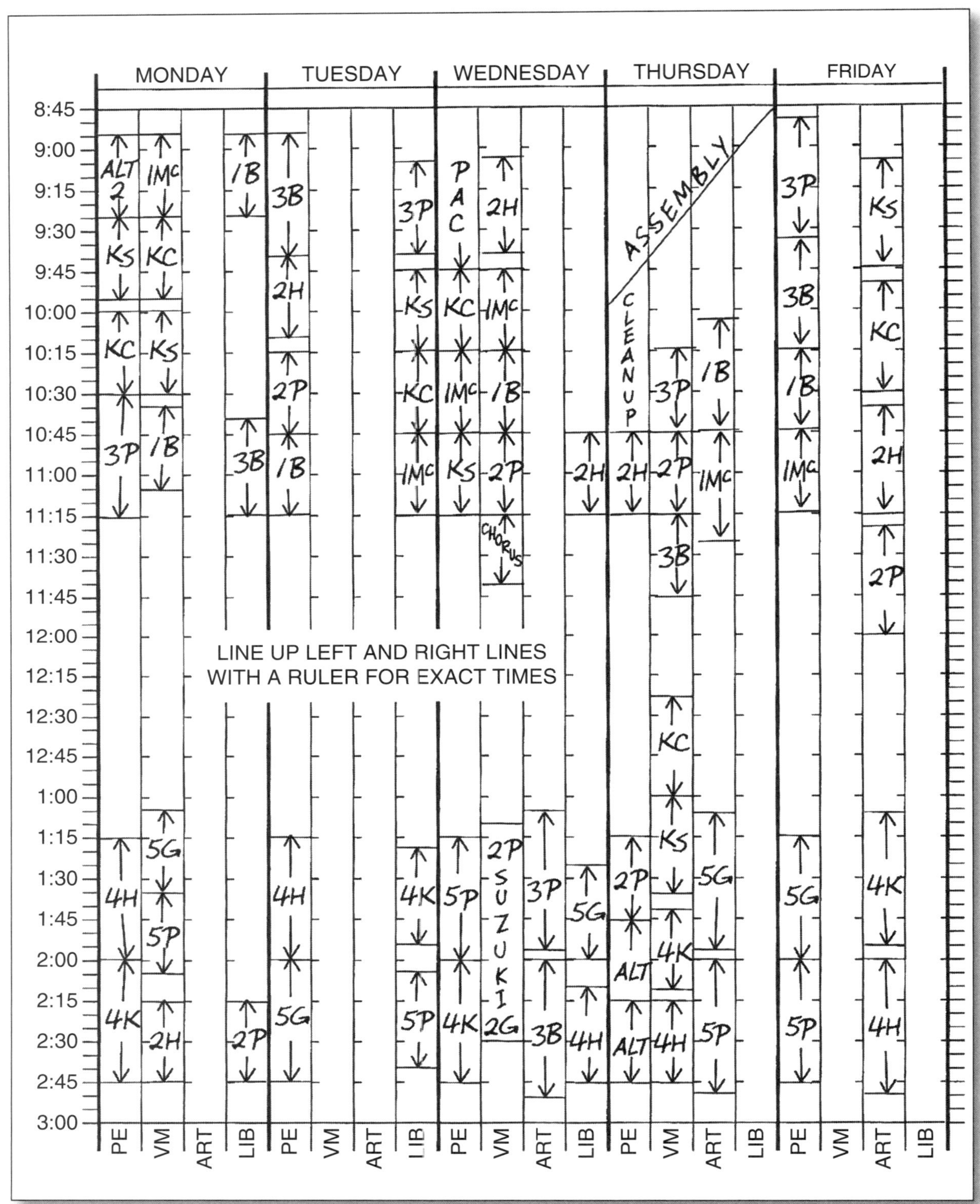

The best way to begin to schedule is to first fill in the classes for special teachers who are not assigned to the school for the whole week. For example, if special staff are shared between schools, and an art teacher is assigned to the school for only two and a half days, then you should begin to schedule art first since this is the subject that will "lock" early on in the development. There is more flexibility in scheduling for teachers who are assigned to the school for a full, five-day week. After this, it is essential to make a list of how often each class is supposed to attend each special area and for how long. (See Figure 18.1.)

When preparing a schedule, there are several details that need to be checked. Some of these include the following:

- Check horizontally across the grid for conflicts; that is, is the same class scheduled more than once during the same time period?
- Make sure that all contractual requirements in terms of teacher planning time are honored.
- Make sure that all special teachers have the required amount of planning time.
- Make sure that classes do not have more than one special period each day, unless they are scheduled for more than five each week.
- If classes are ever doubled in a particular subject, check the enrollment to make sure that only the smallest classes are ever doubled.
- Double-check the time bands defined in the scheduling grid to make sure that they conform to the prescribed period length for each special at each grade level.
- If your school has more than one specialist for a subject, physical education, for example, and a class is scheduled to have physical education twice each week, it is better if the class sees the same teacher each time.

Preparing a Schedule for Shortened School Days

Many elementary schools have several days during the course of the year in which students are dismissed before the end of the normal school day. These shortened days are usually scheduled so that teachers can engage in staff development activities, conduct parent conferences, or even get an early start to a holiday, such as the day before Thanksgiving. This situation has important implications for the school schedule. Let's say that the school day ends at 1:00 PM on such a day instead of the normal 3:00 PM dismissal. Some schools will simply cut off the day at 1:00 PM; that is, all special classes that would have occurred prior to dismissal time take place. Those that were scheduled after the early dismissal time are simply canceled. Certainly, the simplicity of this arrangement makes it appealing. However, more careful thought about the structure of the school day will reveal that some children are continually placed at a disadvantage under this plan. If there are six or eight shortened days during the school year, and they repeatedly occur on the same day of the week, children who are scheduled for once-a-week specials (such as art) may find that their overall program becomes substantially different from their peers whose special classes take place earlier in the school day.

A convenient solution to this problem is to create a compressed schedule for early dismissal days. Simply shave off 5 or 10 minutes from each special class— 5 minutes for special classes that are normally less than 40 minutes long and 10 minutes for classes that are greater than 40 minutes long. In this way, all special classes will take place during an early dismissal day, but they will just be a bit shorter in duration. A compressed schedule must be developed for every day of the week on which an early dismissal occurs.

Scheduling Around the Master Schedule

Once the master schedule is developed, it becomes the foundation upon which all other schedules are based. Pullout programs need to be scheduled around the master schedule. Normally, youngsters who go to speech/language classes, ESL, remedial reading, individual counseling, and others are pulled out of their normal classroom time—not out of a special class, such as art, physical education, or music. In current practice, however, there is a growing trend to reduce pullouts by having special teachers "push-in" and collaborate with classroom teachers to deliver these special services. Despite this trend, there are still situations in which freedom from distraction makes it preferable for students to be removed from their classrooms for these special sessions.

There are countless other reasons that principals need to schedule around the master schedule. Days on which individual and class photographs are taken, book fairs, bake sales, student workshops, visits of "artists in residence," and guest speakers all require that special schedules be developed. School leaders need to refer to the master schedule when developing the time slots for these visits and be mindful of when students would normally be engaged in special classes. Scheduling for such events and visitors needs to be done in advance. Teachers do not like surprises, and the administrator who does not develop schedules for special events in a timely fashion can be seen as disorganized and inconsiderate. Usually, classroom teachers or special teachers can accompany students to a special event depending on the time that the event is scheduled for the class.

Developing a projected master schedule based on a district's demographic data early in the school year can help you project staffing needs for the following school year.

THE TREND TOWARD YEAR-ROUND SCHOOLING

Although the arrangement of days in the school year is not directly related to the everyday school schedule, the trend toward year-round schooling affects how we organize the instructional program. The traditional 9- or 10-month school year followed an agricultural calendar. Many youngsters were needed at home during the summer to help run the farm. Ask any teacher who has moved up from grade to grade with her own class about "summer learning loss," and that teacher is likely to attest to the degree of reteaching that is necessary at the beginning of the school year. "What happened? I know that they knew this material at the end of the school year!" is a comment often heard.

In response to this educational need, as well as a more contemporary view of society, many states and school districts now offer year-round programs. This does not necessarily mean that the number of days in the school is increased, but that the distribution of school days is more even. In some plans, students attend school in eight-week stretches, punctuated by two-week intersessions or vacation periods. There are many variations of this arrangement currently in practice. There are also many advantages to a year-round schedule, including the following:

- "Summer learning loss" is reduced or eliminated; there is less need to reteach concepts and skills at the beginning of the school year.

- Student interest in learning is sustained throughout the year.
- Individual assistance or remediation can occur throughout the year.
- Enrichment classes or clubs can be planned for intersession periods.
- Staff development programs for teachers can be scheduled during intersession periods.
- The plan may be more convenient for working parents.

Clearly, curricular adjustments and modifications would be necessary in year-round schools. Unit planning will take place in different chunks of time. Intersession schedules are often developed. In some cases, special subjects are rotated throughout the year and this, of course, will have scheduling implications. For example, if a school is run on eight-week cycles, it is possible to schedule students for an intensive eight-week exploration in art followed by an eight-week exploration in music, and so on. This arrangement may also help to improve efficiency of staff deployment.

The school schedule determines the times in which students, teachers, and curriculum interact. Not only does the schedule dictate when teachers and students join together for the important work of the school, it also provides the time that teachers need to plan, collaborate, and meet with parents. Any school schedule should be consistent with the philosophy and needs of the educational community. The schedule is a driving force in how schools deliver and interpret the instructional program.

19

Staffing and Hiring

Critical Decisions for Principals

Perhaps one of the most important decisions that school leaders make is the hiring of new staff. Each time a new staff member is secured, there is an opportunity to enhance the educational community, to advance the goals of the school, and to select an individual who can contribute to the overall tone and climate of the school. Great care should be exercised in hiring, and the needs within an individual school may change from year to year. For example, if the school does not have many teachers who are adept with modern technologies, you might want to seek a teacher who has had considerable experience in incorporating such approaches into classroom instruction. On the other hand, if a school goal is for teachers to learn more about cooperative learning, then you might want to find a candidate who has used this practice successfully in past experiences. Sometimes, a neophyte straight out of college is what is needed for a particular situation. You must build balance and harmony into a school staff, so it is always important to begin with an analysis of staff needs.

PROJECTING STAFFING NEEDS

Sometime around the middle of the school year, school leaders begin to anticipate which teachers might retire, which might not be rehired, and which ones might resign or request a leave for a variety of family reasons. It is never too early to think about such needs. Many principals send a letter to the staff asking about requests for grade changes or transfers to other buildings in a school district. Such voluntary transfers can often be very refreshing for staff members who have had the same assignment for several years. However, be sure to consult your colleagues in other buildings about this practice.

Each year offers a new opportunity for principals to take a fresh look at school organization. Perhaps you want to consider a multiage class. Nongraded primary classes have

Note: All forms, letters, and checklists included in this chapter can be found at corwin.com/elementary survivalkit.

proven very successful in some communities, and with such a structure comes the chance to redeploy teachers and reorganize assignments and offerings.

Once staffing needs are determined, develop a list of the vacancies for the coming year. (Experienced principals also know that "surprises" are also likely, despite their best planning.) If a teacher hiring procedure is not in place in your school or school district, it's a good idea to define one. Such a document outlines the steps involved in selecting new staff. It should be clear and sequentially organized. A sample Teacher Hiring Procedure appears in Figure 19.1.

Figure 19.1 Teacher Hiring Procedure

Name of School and District

TEACHER HIRING PROCEDURE

Activity	*Staff Involved*
1. Position is posted internally and advertised. (Postcard acknowledgments are mailed to applicants.)	Personnel department
2. Paper screening of résumés received.	Administrator, supervisor, or selection committee
3. Interview committee is formed. (Consider size, participation, questions to be asked.)	Administrator and committee
4. Establish criteria for selection. (Consider background, recent courses, experiences, specific competencies, professional organizations.)	Administrator and committee
5. Schedule initial interviews.	Administrator
6. Conduct initial interviews. (Standard interview form used.)	Administrator alone or with committee
7. Decide which candidates to call back for second interviews.	Administrator alone or with committee
8. Conduct second interview and teaching demonstration.	Administrator and committee
9. Select one or two finalists.	Administrator and committee
10. Check references by telephone.	Administrator
11. Call back finalists to complete formal application and writing sample.	Administrator
12. Complete candidate profile and hiring recommendation.	Administrator
13. Superintendent (or director of personnel) interviews the candidate and sets salary.	Superintendent or personnel director
14. Candidate is presented to board of education for hiring.	Superintendent
15. Administrator completes personnel flowchart listing gender and race of all applicants interviewed and submits it to personnel office.	Administrator or designee
16. Follow-up letters are sent to all candidates interviewed.	Administrator

FORMING A SELECTION COMMITTEE

Local practice will determine whc will serve on a teacher selection committee, but it is usually good practice to include teachers and perhaps a parent, at least for some parts of the hiring process. If you're looking to hire a new third-grade teacher, it might be wise to include another third-grade teacher, or a teacher at an adjacent grade level, on the selection committee. Sometimes, contractually, you must ask the teachers' union to assign teachers to serve on the selection committee. If this is not the case, you may wish to ask the school faculty to make recommendations for teachers to serve on the committee. Classroom teachers understand the demands of the position and can frame some very important questions. This process can often become political, in the sense that teachers may perceive that their colleagues who serve on a selection committee might give preference to candidates who espouse a particular approach or have specific kinds of training and experiences. It should be made clear that the process of hiring new staff is to be an objective one, based upon desired traits as established in a candidate profile that will be developed by the selection committee.

The size and membership of the selection committee depend on the position you are seeking to fill. If you're looking to hire a classroom aide or assistant, you and the teacher who will be working with the aide might be enough. If, on the other hand, the position is for an assistant principal, a teacher coach, or a team leader, the committee will undoubtedly include several representatives. If the school has a tradition of shared leadership that includes parental representation, then parents may well be a part of the selection committee for any such position.

Once the membership of the selection committee is established, bring everyone together to review the search procedure and stress the confidential nature of the process. Prepare a timeline for each phase of the hiring process. A sample timeline is outlined below:

Date	Activity
March 3	Send out letter to seek volunteers for selection committee.
March 12	Choose members of selection committee.
March 19	Meet with selection committee to outline candidate search process and to develop a candidate profile. Outline time frame for search. Develop interview questions.
March 20	Prepare posting notices and advertisements. Contact college placement services. Set deadline for receipt of résumés.
April 15	Screen paper résumés with subcommittee of the selection committee. Choose candidates for initial interviews.
April 22–26	Call candidates for initial interviews.
May 6–10	Conduct initial interviews.
May 13	Meet with committee to review interview performance and to decide upon candidates for second interviews. Prepare schedule for interviews and demonstration lessons.

Date	Activity
May 14	Contact candidates to arrange for second interviews and demonstration lessons.
May 20–22	Conduct second interviews and demonstration lessons.
May 23	Meet with committee to decide on selection of one or two finalists. Make written recommendations to superintendent.
May 24	Contact finalists and arrange for them to meet with superintendent, prepare writing sample (if appropriate), and complete application.
May 28–30	Superintendent or designee meets with finalists.
May 31	Superintendent or designee consults with committee, if necessary, and makes hiring recommendation to board of education.
June 4	Send letter of regret to unsuccessful candidates. Send letters of appreciation to members of the selection committee.

DEVELOPING A CANDIDATE PROFILE

What qualities and experiences are you seeking in an ideal candidate? This question should be considered by the members of the search committee. Do you want to hire someone with a great deal of prior experience, or do you want to hire a recent graduate? Are you seeking an individual who has familiarity and experience with a specific instructional program or approach? Is a college degree with a particular major important? Do any specific colleges provide the kinds of training and experiences that are aligned closely to the position you are seeking to fill? One way to make sure that the selection committee stays on course through the hiring process is to develop a candidate profile that outlines the desired traits that you are seeking in an ideal applicant. (A sample Candidate Profile appears in Figure 19.2.)

Discussion should occur among the members of the selection committee about the desired traits, and some consensus should be reached about the ideal candidate. Of course, there may be times when the personality and interview responses of an applicant may sway members of the search committee, and some deviation from the outline of desired traits may occur. This is fine, so long as all candidates are compared similarly with regard to this useful tool. Sometimes, an outstanding strength in one area may outweigh a deficiency in another area. For example, a primary-grade teacher applicant may be a true expert in early intervention strategies in reading, but may not be as adept as you would like in the area of technology. You must consider such trade-offs in any hiring process.

In addition to a candidate profile, most school districts establish formal job descriptions for each position. These are often created by individuals in the personnel office, but principals should have input into the process. (A generic job description for a teacher appears in Figure 19.3.) A candidate profile differs from a job description in that the profile is likely to be more closely related to a specific vacancy—not a general job title.

Figure 19.2   Candidate Profile

Name of School and District

CANDIDATE PROFILE

Vacant Position/Location: ____

Check all that apply:

1. Educational Background   __BA   __MA in Progress __MA __MA +

2. Experience   __0–1 yr.   __ 2–5 yrs.   __ 6+ yrs.

3. Technology Skills   __Not Essential __Somewhat Essential __Essential

4. Specific Skills Sought:

	No Knowledge	Beginning Use	Mastery
a. Differentiated Instruction			
b. Portfolio Assessment			
c. Hands-On Science			
d. Authentic Assessment			
e. Curriculum Standards			
f. Specific Programmatic Approaches: ________________			

5. Professional Responsibilities

	No Knowledge	Beginning Use	Mastery
a. Instructional Skills			
b. Human Relations			
c. Child Development			

6. Professional Affiliations: ___Not Necessary ___Holds Membership ___Active

7. Other Traits Desired in Candidate:

Administrator: _________________________________   **Date:** _______________

Figure 19.3 Teacher Job Description

Name of School and District

TEACHER JOB DESCRIPTION

Title: Teacher

Qualifications:

State teaching certificate

Demonstrated knowledge of effective teaching methods and developmentally appropriate classroom activities

Ability to maintain a positive learning environment

Strong interpersonal and communication skills

Required criminal history background check

Reports to: Principal or designee

Supervises: Pupils, and, when assigned, student teachers and classroom aides

Job Goal: To implement an approved educational program and establish a class environment that fosters integrated learning, thinking, cooperation, and personal and social growth; to help pupils to develop skills—technology, attitudes, and knowledge—needed as a foundation for continued education; and to maintain good relationships with parents, other staff members, and the community.

Teacher Responsibilities:

Curriculum:

Reviews/revises/writes curriculum.

Achieves district educational goals and objectives by promoting active learning and thinking in the classroom using board-adopted curriculum and other appropriate learning tools.

Develops lesson objectives and/or unit plans, uses instructional materials, provides individualized and small-group instruction, and adapts the curriculum when necessary to meet the needs of each pupil.

Systematically measures student performance by means of a variety of assessment tools such as teacher-made tests, standardized tests, and/or alternative assessments to measure learning.

Students:

Implements current best practices to promote student learning.

Budgets class time effectively.

(Continued)

Figure 19.3 (Continued)

Plans lesson presentations, class activities, and assessments for the class that meet group and individual needs, interests and abilities.

Uses technology to enhance instruction.

Monitors pupil academic progress and personal growth toward stated objectives.

Identifies pupil needs and cooperates with other professional staff members in assessing and resolving learning issues.

Establishes and maintains standards of pupil behavior to achieve a classroom climate conducive to learning.

Maintains records of pupils' educational progress in class record books, portfolios, and/or board-approved forms, and summarizes such progress for reporting purposes.

Devises written and oral assignments and tests that require analytical and critical thinking as well as factual knowledge.

Works collaboratively with resource personnel.

Communicates with parents through conferences and other means to inform them about the school program and to discuss pupil progress.

Professional Growth Standards:

Maintains professional competence and continuous improvement through active participation in professional development activities.

Participates in faculty meetings, councils, and district and school committees.

Makes effective use of community resources to enhance the instructional program.

Upholds and enforces school rules, administrative regulations, and board policy.

Performs other duties within the scope of his/her employment and certification as assigned.

Actively promotes professional growth, revision and improvement of curriculum, and shared decision-making.

Terms of Employment: Work year and salary to be determined by the board of education.

Evaluation: Annually in accordance with state law and the provisions of the board of education's policy on evaluation of certificated staff.

RECRUITING SUITABLE CANDIDATES

School districts vary in their approaches to recruitment. In large districts, recruitment may be a centralized function, but you should be assertive in expressing your desire to have a role in this important function. Often, personnel offices maintain a file of résumés and applications. Some may have been unsolicited. This does not necessarily mean that they should be ignored, but they should be checked to see that they are current.

The process of recruitment can take many different forms. Placing advertisements in newspapers is the most common way to secure likely candidates for positions, but it is by no means the only way. "Word of mouth" among principals is often an effective means of developing a list of applicants. One of the best teachers I ever hired was recommended by a principal in a neighboring community. The teacher had been a maternity-leave replacement and the individual for whom she was filling in was returning from leave. The principal wanted to make sure that this fine young teacher would not be lost from the profession, so he called a few colleagues to see if there were any staff vacancies.

Formal advertisements are usually used to gather résumés of likely candidates. Work along with the personnel office on the exact wording of the advertisement. You might want to specify a grade level or an early-childhood or intermediate-grade teacher. If a specific skill or competency is required, this can be mentioned in the ad. More and more, ads mention the necessity of an online application.

Where to advertise is another consideration. If your school is near a large metropolitan area, you will probably want to place ads in a major newspaper there. This can be costly, and the benefits of wide coverage must be weighed against the general quality of the applicants attracted by advertising in such newspapers. Personnel directors generally have good experience in knowing the yield from ads in specific local or regional newspapers.

Another source of good candidates is the placement offices of colleges, universities, and teacher training institutions. Again, experience will probably allow you to draw some conclusions about the general quality of candidates drawn from specific colleges. It is a good idea to find out about the teacher training programs that exist in your area. Developing relationships with the heads of the placement offices of local colleges can make for good matches as you describe the position you are seeking to fill. Cultivate these relationships. They will undoubtedly serve you well.

Early in February, you should watch for local job fairs where your district can set up a space to welcome teachers who are looking for jobs. They are usually well attended, and initial screenings at the fair can be helpful to both you and the potential candidate. In some regions, there are also online application systems to which districts can subscribe. Principals can print out only those résumés that seem to indicate a good fit for the job being filled.

Contacting professional associations can lead to another source for likely candidates. For example, the National Science Teachers Association maintains a registry of members seeking positions as science teachers or specialists. Other professional organizations have similar services for their members.

PAPER SCREENING

Once a stack of résumés has been received, the next step in the process is to conduct paper screening for potential candidates. You need to establish a few important guidelines for this activity. First, decide who will be involved in the process of paper screening. Sometimes, a subcommittee of the selection committee is involved; in other situations, all members of the group review all of the applications. If hundreds of résumés are received and you are interested in hiring a teacher with only a few years' experience, you may wish to ask someone in the personnel office to make the first cut by removing the résumés of applicants who do not have prior teaching experience. This can save time.

It helps to go back to the candidate profile previously developed as you screen the résumés. Remind yourself of the desired traits that you deemed important for the position. Let this profile guide you as you go through the résumés. It is easy to be influenced by an attractive, "glitzy" résumé, but the essence of the candidate's training and experience may not be consistent with the traits that you previously defined.

One way to proceed is to place the résumés into one of three piles: "Yes" for candidates whose résumés clearly exhibit all of the desired traits; "Maybe" if some of the desired traits are evident; and "No" if there does not appear to be a match between the candidates' background and the qualifications you previously defined. If several individuals are involved in paper screening, each person can sort the résumés and place his or her initials next to a "Yes," "No," or "Maybe" notation. Then the group can compare the level of agreement. If broad disparity exists among the placement of résumés, it may be worthwhile to review the candidate profile.

It is not a bad idea to go through the piles once more for a second check. Aim for agreement among the paper screeners to select the résumés of candidates you definitely want to interview. Achieving consensus at this stage is important, since it may be an initial test of how well the selection committee will function.

Candidates with outstanding credentials may be applying for more than one position simultaneously, and they may no longer be available when you call to schedule an interview. For this reason, it is wise to keep a few more résumés in your "Yes" pile than you think you can reasonably interview.

DEVELOPING INTERVIEW QUESTIONS

Another important function of the selection committee is to develop a set of interview questions. These will guide the interview and ensure a level of consistency that will permit an objective comparison of candidates after the interviews have taken place. The questions should be broad enough to allow each candidate's personality to come through, yet specific enough to provide information about the applicant's general level of competence and skill.

The first question or two should help you gain information about the candidate's educational background and professional experiences. Then, as you get to more specific aspects of the position, the questions are more detailed and are tailored to the position you are seeking to fill. Questions should also test the applicant's classroom management skills, values and standards, and tact and diplomacy.

If time permits, generating the interview questions should be a collaborative effort of all of the members on the selection committee. (A sample of interview questions for a classroom teacher is reproduced in Figure 19.4.) Each member of the committee may choose to specify the question(s) that he or she would like to ask. Some people have favorite questions.

Each person involved in the interview process should be given a sheet of the interview questions. It is helpful to take notes on these sheets so that specific answers and impressions can be recorded. If you are seeing a large number of candidates, reviewing these papers after all the interviews are conducted will prove to be invaluable in terms of remembering who said what. The brief rating scale at the bottom will also allow a comparison of your overall impression of each candidate.

Figure 19.4 Teacher Interview Form

Name of School and District

CLASSROOM TEACHER INTERVIEW QUESTIONS

Applicant: _______________________________________ **Date:** ___________________

1. Educational background:

2. Professional experience:

3. Describe a typical day in your classroom:

4. Describe your ideal reading/writing program:

5. What are you most proud of in your recent teaching experiences?

6. What has been your most significant problem, and how did you respond?

7. What accommodations do you make for a wide range of abilities within a class?

8. How would you deal with a child who continually forgets his/her homework?

9. What would you say to a parent who challenged the way you teach spelling?

10. What would you like us to know about you that we have not already discussed?

11. What questions do you have for us?

Information we provide:

Time frame of search	Salary to be set with superintendent
Number of candidates	Benefits
District priorities and goals	Information about school and staff

Overall Rating: 0——1——2——3——4——5   **Interviewer:** _____________________

DEVELOPING AN INTERVIEW SCHEDULE

The next thing you do is develop the schedule for interviews. This is not as easy as it might sound. Time slots and availability should be first decided upon by members of the selection committee. Then, each of the candidates must be contacted and an interview time offered. (Occasionally, candidates can be eliminated on the basis of the telephone contact. A brief conversation might reveal that the applicant is not well suited to the position, is longer available, or—once he or she hears more about the position—may not feel that it is a good match.)

Initial interviews can be scheduled for half an hour, with 10 or 15 minutes between them in case the interview runs over or someone arrives late. Members of the selection committee often like to share comments and impressions between interviews, but it is best to withhold judgment until all of the candidates have been seen. Don't expect the interviews to proceed like clockwork; often they do not. One way to avoid late arrivals is to have the school secretary prepare written or Internet directions to the school from major highways or streets. This set of travel directions can be sent to all candidates before the interview. It is also helpful to include other details such as where to park, which door to use to enter the school, the room where the interview will be held, and the school's telephone number.

Have a place where applicants can sit if they arrive early and provide some information about the school for them to read. We have often found that applicants appreciate a packet with the school handbook, some demographic information about the school district, and perhaps a recent school newsletter.

If second interviews and teaching demonstrations are scheduled, this can be more complex. More people are usually involved, since the schedules of teachers whose classes will be used for the demonstration lessons will have to be consulted and perhaps adjusted. The individuals on the selection committee and the school secretary will undoubtedly benefit if the interview schedule is developed in advance and distributed to all parties affected. (See the Sample Schedule for Candidate Demonstration Lesson and Second Interview in Figure 19.5.) Begin each session with a general briefing in which you provide background information about the candidates who will be seen and the classrooms in which they will be observed.

Figure 19.5   Sample Schedule for Candidate Demonstration Lesson and Second Interview

Name of School and District

SAMPLE SCHEDULE FOR CANDIDATE DEMONSTRATION LESSON AND SECOND INTERVIEW

Time	Candidate	Activity	Staff Involved
Date (Monday Morning)			
8:45–9:00		General Briefing—Location	Name
9:00–9:30	Candidate A *(name)*	Teach Lesson in Grade 4—Room 214	Name

Time	Candidate	Activity	Staff Involved
9:35–9:55	Candidate A *(name)*	Interview With Committee—Location	Name
10:00–10:30	Candidate B	Teach Lesson in Grade 4—Room 218	Name
10:35–10:55	Candidate B	Interview With Committee—Location	Name
11:00–11:30	Candidate C	Teach Lesson in Grade 4—Room 214	Name
11:35–11:55	Candidate C	Interview With Committee—Location	Name
Date (Tuesday Afternoon)			
1:00–1:10		General Briefing—Location	Name
1:15–1:45	Candidate D	Teach Lesson in Grade 2—Room 103	Name
1:50–2:10	Candidate D	Interview With Committee—Location	Name
2:15–2:45	Candidate E	Teach Lesson in Grade 2—Room 107	Name
2:50–3:10	Candidate E	Interview With Committee—Location	Name
3:10–4:00		Summation and Recommendations	Name

CONDUCTING INTERVIEWS

The interview can fulfill several functions. First, it provides an opportunity for the members of the selection committee to meet with the candidates and gain a sense of their relative strengths and weaknesses. Apart from the applicants' answers to the interview questions, the meeting allows a glimpse into their interpersonal skills and personalities. Matching a new teacher's personality and style to the culture of the school is a very important aspect of building a staff. Remember, however, that sometimes you and the selection team will want to hire someone who may expose existing staff members to new ideas and approaches.

Interviews should be professionally conducted. New applicants are usually nervous, so it might be a good idea to try to put the person at ease by inquiring about how easily he or she found the school. A bit of tasteful humor always helps to set a more relaxed tone. Provide information on how long the interview is expected to take and how it will proceed. The candidate should first be asked to tell the interviewing committee something about him- or herself. Then, each person on the committee can ask one of the predetermined questions.

The interview is also a time for the candidates to gain information about the position. They might come to realize on their own that they are not well suited to the position; or on the other hand, once they hear more about the requirements of the job, they might be able to articulate the kinds of skills and special qualifications they can bring to the position. Always allow time for applicants to ask questions of the interview committee. Conclude the interview by outlining the search process—how many candidates are being seen, what the timeline is for making a hiring recommendation, whether second or third interviews will be required, and the like. Depending upon the district, you may also be able to provide information about the salary and benefits provided. Often, this is reserved for someone else at the district level. The candidate should also know who will make the final recommendation to the board of education. Will it be you and the selection committee, a central-office administrator in charge of personnel, or the superintendent?

At the end of each block of interviews, take a few moments to share and summarize your impressions of the candidates. If you are interviewing for more than one day, ask the members of the committee to resist the temptation to come to premature conclusions about recommendations until all of the candidates have been seen.

After the first round of interviews is complete, the selection committee should deliberate, compare each of the candidates in terms of their relative strengths, and decide which applicants will be asked to return for a second interview or a teaching demonstration. If no clear priority ranking of candidates is apparent, the principal may wish to make a chart of the rating given to each candidate (on a 1 to 5 scale) by each member of the selection team. Then, when the points are tallied, a priority order of candidates will emerge.

When candidates are asked back for a teaching demonstration, they should be told the grade level they will be teaching, the amount of time they will be allotted, the number of students in the class, and perhaps a guideline as to the kind of lesson. Sometimes, a writing activity, math lesson, or reading experience is desired. The more specific you are about the type of lesson you would like to see, the more easily you will be able to make objective decisions about the candidates. If a teaching demonstration is not practical due to geographic distance or time, ask the candidate to submit a video of a lesson conducted with his or her own class or another group.

After the demonstration lesson, the committee members can meet again with the applicant for an abbreviated interview. This provides the committee the opportunity to comment upon the lesson observed and ask questions about it. The second interview is also a time to clarify any lingering questions that may have come out of the initial interview.

When all interviews and demonstration lessons have been completed, it is time for the committee to deliberate and decide which applicants should be considered further. The committee can make a hiring recommendation pending the reference checks. This is a good time to return to the candidate profile and check each applicant's qualifications and skills against the criteria that you set at the outset of the selection process. Try to gain consensus on a hiring recommendation. Unanimity among the members of the selection team makes the recommendation stronger. Before a hiring recommendation is made, be sure to check the applicant's references.

CHECKING REFERENCES

School leaders occasionally find that when they call the individuals who prepared written recommendations for applicants, they get a different view as a result of the telephone conversation. Most people are uncomfortable giving a person a written reference in which weaknesses or professional needs are outlined; however, they are more willing to discuss them in a telephone conference. Always contact the individuals who have written references that are given to you by candidates. It is essential to make sure that at least one, and preferably two, of the references checked is for someone who knows the applicant in a professional capacity.

Before calling to check references, review your interview notes. Prepare specific questions that will enable you to probe issues that left you with questions or concerns on the basis of the interview. Ask the person you are calling to be frank, and emphasize the importance of references. If the applicant is leaving his or her current position, you may wish to probe for the reason. Does it match with information that the candidate provided? Assure the person that comments made to you will be held in the strictest of confidence, and not revealed to the applicant. This practice will give you the best chance of getting honest, helpful comments.

Usually, the instincts of the selection team will be reaffirmed by the reference checks, but occasionally surprises may emerge. If you derived information about an applicant that may cause you to reconsider his or her candidacy, reconvene the selection committee and review the information you received. This may result in a new recommendation.

MAKING A HIRING RECOMMENDATION

Once references have been checked and the results confirm the impressions and initial thinking of the selection committee, a hiring recommendation is prepared. You should write a hiring recommendation listing the members of the selection committee, the number of applicants considered (paper screening as well as interviews conducted), the number of teaching demonstrations observed, and the reasons that the recommended applicant is best suited to the position. In some districts, the superintendent or designee may wish to see the top two candidates. This practice varies from district to district. A sample of a hiring recommendation appears in Figure 19.6.

In some school districts, candidates must complete a writing sample as a part of the formal application process. This extra step helps to ensure that the applicant can express him- or herself well in writing and use proper grammar and spelling. The applicant is called back and asked to write a page or two, in his or her own hand, about a predetermined issue. Topics you can use include the following:

- What do you think is the most critical issue in American education today, and why?
- If you could change one thing about American education today, what would it be, and why?

No principal wants to be embarrassed by a teacher who sends home notes or letters to parents that are filled with spelling and grammar errors. It is far better to know this before you hire the individual. A potential teacher who makes such errors might not

Figure 19.6   Sample Hiring Recommendation Memorandum

Name of School and District

MEMORANDUM

Date:

To: *Name*, Superintendent

From: *Name*, Principal

RE: HIRING RECOMMENDATION, *Name of Candidate*

I recommend that *Name of candidate* be hired to fill the second-grade vacancy at *Name of school* for the ____________ school year. The selection committee consisted of the following individuals:

List of names on selection committee

Over 700 résumés were reviewed by the committee in May and 12 candidates were selected for interviews. These initial interviews took place on June 1 and 2. Five candidates were then called back for second interviews and teaching demonstrations on June 8 and 9. Based upon this extensive process, the selection committee unanimously recommends that we hire *Name of candidate*. *Name of candidate* has taught third grade in California for six years and she and her family are relocating to our area. She possesses all of the qualities we defined in our Candidate Profile: extensive use of the cooperative learning method, relevant experiences in portfolio and other authentic assessments, and knowledge of several hands-on science programs. She performed well in the interviews and answered our questions directly and with confidence. Each of her responses reflected a thoughtful practitioner who is always seeking to refine her craft. She was recently selected as Teacher of the Year in her current school in California.

Reference checks revealed that *Name of candidate* is a dedicated professional who always strives to improve her instructional skills. She takes part in countless professional development opportunities and is considered one of the very best teachers in her current school. Her principal is sorry that she is moving. She relates well to students, colleagues, and parents and is very well respected in the community. *Name of candidate's* writing sample—attached—is outstanding, as are her application and résumé. Should you have any questions, please call me.

automatically be disqualified, but if the application is in other ways outstanding, it can be made a condition of employment that corrective action is taken. The writing sample can be collected at any stage of the interview process to cut back on the number of visits a candidate must make to the district.

NOTIFYING APPLICANTS OF THEIR STATUS

Applicants have a right to know their status as soon as possible. Aside from its being a courtesy, some candidates may have applied for several positions. Because of this, early notification can be helpful not only to the applicant but also to others within the profession. One of the issues regarding notification concerns the time when you can inform applicants with assurance. Some principals do not release any candidates until the board of education has officially hired the individual for the position. Other principals inform candidates who are not likely to be called back that they have not been selected for the position prior to board action. The best compromise is probably to give early notification to those candidates whom you do not feel you would call back under any circumstances. You can telephone those applicants who may not have been recommended to the board but whom you would consider in the "next string" should anything go wrong with the hiring recommendation. Occasionally, the candidate you recommend may reject the offer; make sure that you have a backup candidate or two.

Applicants may be informed of their status by telephone, but in our experience, people who have given their time to come in for an interview, and perhaps to teach a demonstration lesson, appreciate a personal letter. The use of word-processing programs allows you to compose just one letter, and then have it sent to each of the applicants who are no longer being considered. Occasionally, you may wish to personalize one of the paragraphs in such a letter. A sample "rejection" letter appears in Figure 19.7.

Figure 19.7   Sample Teacher Candidate Rejection Letter

Name of School and District

Date

Name of candidate

Candidate's address

Dear *Candidate's Name,*

Thank you for taking the time to come to our school to meet with members of the selection committee in connection with our search for a second-grade teacher. We appreciated the opportunity to meet you and learn about your educational views, perspectives, and professional experiences.

We received over 700 résumés as a result of our advertisements, and it is because of your fine credentials and experiences that we wanted to pursue the possibility of your employment at *name of school*. Please know that we were impressed with what you had to say during our discussion as well as with your positive outlook on education.

The hiring decision was a very difficult one because of the very large pool of qualified candidates. I wish to advise you, though, that after much deliberation, you are not among the list of individuals recommended for further consideration to fill this vacancy. Your résumé will be kept on file for future reference.

I wish you well in all of your future endeavors and appreciated the opportunity to have met you.

Sincerely,

Principal

Figure 19.8   Sample Letter Informing Candidate of Hiring

Name of School and District

Date

Name of candidate

Candidate's address

Dear *Candidate's Name,*

At last night's meeting of the board of education, you were officially hired to fill the second-grade vacancy at *Name of school.* Congratulations! As you may recall, we received over 700 responses to our advertisements, and you emerged as the outstanding candidate from a pool of highly qualified applicants. You will be joining a distinguished faculty, and we look forward to the contributions that you will undoubtedly make as we move our school forward.

Our personnel office has several forms that you must fill out within the next few weeks to complete the processing of your employment in our school district. Please call *name of staff member* at *phone number* to arrange for a mutually convenient appointment. Also, there will be an orientation program for all new teachers on *date.* The program will take place at 8:30 AM in the administrative conference room at the board of education building. Please plan to attend this important session.

Our parents association would like to host an informal reception in honor of our three new staff members. This will be held at the *location* on *day of week, date, time.* Whereas we would be delighted if you could attend, this is by no means a requirement. Please call *name,* our school secretary, to let us know if you can join us.

We are proud to have a mentor program for new teachers to our district. After a mentor has been selected, you will receive the necessary contact information.

In the meantime, I wish you a very pleasant and relaxing summer and look forward to our work together in the future. Please know that I stand ready to assist you at any time and I am committed to helping you succeed as a teacher at *name of school.* If you have any questions, please do not hesitate to call me. And again, many congratulations.

Sincerely,

Principal

It is also a good idea to write a letter to the successful candidate, once the hiring is official. This sets the tone for a positive working relationship and also provides the opportunity to give some important information about upcoming events or tasks to be completed. All new teachers will have to complete some paperwork concerning their new positions. It may be necessary to inform the new teacher about this requirement in the congratulatory letter. In some instances, new teachers may have to attend an induction program. This information can also be provided in the letter. A sample letter congratulating the successful applicant appears in Figure 19.8.

ANNOUNCING HIRING DECISIONS TO THE SCHOOL COMMUNITY

Parents and teachers in the school will be interested in the final outcome of the search for new staff members. Rather than let the information trickle out into the community, it is wise to inform everyone at the same time. In some situations, the parents association organizes an informal tea or reception to introduce the new staff member to the community.

Write a letter in which you let the school community know about the new staff member and mention something about the process that was followed. You can also provide some information about the background of the new teacher. Before you include any details of the teacher's personal life, you should check with the individual to make sure that he or she has no objections. (Some individuals might not want you to divulge information about their marital status or their own children.) A sample letter introducing a new teacher to the school community appears in Figure 19.9.

Figure 19.9   Sample Letter Announcing Staff Hiring

Name of School and District

Date

Dear Members of the *Name of School* Community,

    I am pleased to inform you that after a rather extensive search, *name of new teacher* has been hired to fill the second-grade vacancy created as a result of the retirement of *name of staff member*. A selection committee composed of teachers, parents, and administrators followed a very rigorous process. We examined over 700 résumés, conducted 12 initial interviews, and 5 subsequent interviews and teaching demonstrations. *Name of new teacher* emerged from a pool of highly qualified candidates as our choice to work with our children and staff at *name of school.*

    A graduate of the University of California at Davis, *name of new teacher* taught third grade in Irvine, California, where she was a highly valued educator. She comes to us as a result of her family's relocation to our area—and how fortunate we are! A mother of two sons, *name of new teacher* was very active in her local scouting program. She is an active runner and has completed three marathon races.

    Our parents association will be hosting an informal reception in our library in honor of *name of new teacher* and our other new teachers for next year. This event will be held on *date and time*. All parents are invited to attend. This will provide an opportunity for you to meet *name of new teacher* and welcome her to our school community.

Sincerely,

Principal

ORIENTING NEW STAFF MEMBERS

Hiring the best candidates is only the beginning of building a top-quality staff. The next step, and an important one, is the orientation of new staff members. The goal of any orientation program should be to eliminate obstacles and assure success. During the interview process, the candidate is likely to sense what is important in the school. Certainly, if several people were involved in the interviews, then it would be apparent that collaboration is valued. Undoubtedly, some information about the school and its programs would have been shared during the interviews.

Once the teacher is hired, there is much information that needs to be conveyed. Here, you set the tone; be helpful and maintain a warm, friendly, yet professional relationship. Go out of your way to make the new teacher feel at ease adjusting to a new community. Ask if there are any issues of a personal nature with which you can provide assistance: housing and neighborhoods, local banks and other services, carpools, service organizations, and so on. Many principals offer to drive new staff members through the school community, pointing out the various neighborhoods, shops, library and other municipal services, student "hang-outs," and other such features. In some districts, this becomes part of the summer orientation program for all new hires.

There is also a great deal of useful written information that new teachers will need—a staff handbook, the board policy manuals, a copy of the appropriate curriculum guides, and teacher editions of textbooks or program materials. If the staff member can visit the school during the summer, this is an ideal time to go over these documents. On the other hand, if a summer visit is not practical, these materials can be boxed and shipped out to the teacher so he or she can review them at leisure during the summer.

The school district may operate its own orientation program, and advance notice of the dates and details about such a program should be provided. At the opening school faculty meeting for the year, introductions are made. You or one of the new teacher's colleagues can make the introduction, providing some details about his or her background, family, and prior experiences. If your school has a social committee, they might give a small welcome gift to the new staff member—a coffee mug filled with candy, or a desk organizer, for example. Whatever the gift, the spirit in which it is given—along with best wishes for success—is always appreciated. Such small tokens and gestures go a long way toward making the new staff member feel welcome. Using the hiring process described in this chapter gives the staff a feeling of having a stake in the new teacher's success.

Arranging for a mentor teacher is essential. All new teachers need a close colleague with whom they can share joys and frustrations and feel free to ask the hundreds of questions that come to mind during the opening weeks of school. It is usually preferable for the mentor teacher to be on the same grade level, but if that cannot be arranged, teachers of adjacent grades often work well in this capacity. In some school systems, where a formal mentoring relationship exists, the mentor teacher may conduct observations and coach the new teacher. Such arrangements are particularly helpful. It is wise for a school or district to train cadres of mentors in the process of new teacher induction and how to have helpful, nonjudgmental interactions.

Be sure to let new staff know about in-service courses, university or college opportunities, workshops, or any other meetings that can help in the orientation process. New teachers also become "socialized" to their new settings through school newsletters, bulletins, memos, staff lounge discussions, and faculty meetings. Through these means, the culture of the school and the professional expectations become known. If a new teacher does not seem to be picking up the mores of the school from these devices, then direct discussions between you and that teacher about expectations are necessary. You may have to be explicit in going over shared values, the school's philosophy, and faculty behavior.

You also have a more formal role in providing ongoing orientation and staff development. Classroom observations and pre- and post-conferences are most helpful to new teachers and are required in most school systems. In addition to scheduled observations, principals ought to drop in on classes frequently and offer encouragement and constructive feedback. Regular meetings, scheduled at strategic intervals, also help to orient new teachers. Plan one meeting before back-to-school night to make sure that the staff member knows about the expectations for the evening. Another good time to meet is just before the first round of report cards is issued or parent conferences are held. Again, a review of procedures and practices will ease the way.

As you observe that new teachers are adjusting well to their new assignments, it is common to pay less attention to orientation activities. However, new teachers need ongoing guidance and support. Continue to meet throughout the year to ensure that concerns are raised and questions are answered. It is best to err on the side of providing too much rather than too little support for new staff members.

EVALUATING HIRING AND ORIENTATION PRACTICES

The process outlined for the recruitment, hiring, and induction of new staff may seem elaborate, but if it results in the selection and maintenance of high-quality staff members, it is well worth the effort. The sense of broad involvement and collaboration alone makes a statement. It says that you value shared leadership and group decision-making. It also sets a tone of professionalism and conveys to applicants that the hiring process is organized and well thought out. Teachers who are involved in the hiring and orientation processes feel as though they have a stake, even a responsibility, for the new teacher's success.

Ask your new teachers to provide feedback about the hiring process and the orientation program—both formal and informal aspects. This information should be discussed and goals set to improve practices. If possible, it is most helpful to reconvene the selection committee to evaluate its operation and decisions. This cycle of feedback, continued discussion, and frank self-assessment can only serve to improve the hiring process.

20

Fostering a School Culture

Traditions and Ceremonies

The culture of any school has an important effect on the way it is viewed and perceived. Traditions and ceremonies contribute to the development of a distinct school culture and give a sense of what is valued within the school community. School traditions don't just happen by themselves, however; they must be deliberately built and fostered over a number of years. From the very inception of a new school, the school leader should work toward the development of a distinct and shared culture.

MAKING SCHOOLS GREAT AND MEMORABLE WITH TRADITIONS AND CEREMONIES

Walk into any school building and you quickly get a sense of what it's all about. You can feel what is valued, what is deemed important. Principals often wonder how this comes to be. Beyond the definition of a school mission, vision, and philosophy, the maintenance of traditions and ceremonies can go a long way toward promoting the school and making the time spent there time by students, staff, and parents rewarding and valuable.

A school tradition is an event, a ceremony, or an activity that is repeated over and over, year after year. The members of the school community come to anticipate the tradition, whether it is an opening assembly, a back-to-school picnic, an awards day, or the performance by a kindergarten rhythm band. Traditions convey an important message; they perpetuate those events that are broadly valued.

Note: All forms, letters, and checklists included in this chapter can be found at corwin.com/elementary survivalkit.

Not all school events become honored traditions. If you listen carefully, you will come to know which activities capture what the school represents. If an event is antithetical to a school's basic mission or vision, the mismatch will be palpable. For example, if a school values cooperation and collaboration among students, then an event in which students are honored for selling the greatest volume of gift wrap or reading the largest number of books might not be in keeping with the school's basic philosophy.

DEVELOPING A SCHOOL CULTURE

Each school has a culture that can be identified. You want the culture of your school to be a positive one, but, unfortunately, this is not universally the case. There are definite things that a school leader can do to modify or improve the culture of a school. The first, most obvious thing is to lead by example. If you want the school to be a "caring place," then that caring must be demonstrated. You can go out of your way to remember birthdays and important events in the lives of staff members and build a culture for recognizing the efforts and accomplishments of others. Significant life events can be celebrated publicly at faculty meetings and staff gatherings and in written communications. If you remind staff members to send greetings or flowers to colleagues who are ill, eventually, the expectation will catch on. This can help to build positive morale. If a social committee is formed, its mission and tasks can be defined collaboratively. Back-to-school get-togethers, holiday parties, and end-of-year parties all help to develop a culture of collegiality. Some principals may feel that they do not have a role in promoting or organizing such events, but if you connect the value of these gatherings to the morale of the staff, you will quickly realize that their efforts will be met with handsome rewards.

You can also instill a sense of service in your students. By bringing worthy causes to the attention of a student council or other student organization, you can convey the message that charity and service are important. Whether it is earthquake relief, collections for flood victims, or assistance for individuals who need food or clothing, such projects create an attitude that something important is being accomplished. By setting such collections into motion, you demonstrate that caring about others is valued and essential for the moral development of students. Annual food or clothing drives can become traditions that others will continue once students and staff associate such activities with positive feelings and a sense of purpose.

Honoring school employees—teachers, aides, secretaries, food-service workers, and custodians—can lead to traditions that will be kept from year to year. Whether it is a giant card that all students sign for Custodian Appreciation Day, a list of services that students can perform to help the secretarial staff, or holiday gifts made for school aides, such acts, if promoted by you, send a message that recognizing the efforts of others is expected and appreciated. If such events and values do not exist in a school, they can be initiated and fostered; someone must pay attention to such matters if they are to become part of your school culture.

Bulletin boards can be organized in appreciation of school staff members. For example, an "Employee of the Month" or a "Volunteer of the Month" display can be set up including some background on an employee, that employee's history in the school, perhaps some photographs of the employee's family, and words of appreciation written by students. If you recognize those who give of themselves to the school, an example of appreciation is established and promoted.

Setting a tone of professional conduct can also be promoted by the school leader. Professional appearance, respectful conversational tone, and setting a norm for initiating discussion about educational matters can yield successful results. These seemingly simple gestures can go a long way toward building a positive school culture. They can help to build a collective perception that will provide motivation and energize others to carry on the traditions and norms that are valued by you and the organization as a whole.

PLANNING FOR CEREMONIES AND MAINTAINING TRADITIONS

You can do many things to make school ceremonies and traditions special. All it takes is a little ingenuity and creativity. For example, if the school has a front lawn, it can be used for an awards ceremony. In one school, each June, a special awards assembly is called "The Gathering on the Lawn," because chairs are set up for the entire student body by the members of the school orchestra, who arrive at school one hour early just to make this a very special event.

An ensemble of a school orchestra can be prepared to perform for special events such as a school "planting day" or a dedication of a "library corner" or hallway. Bringing such attention to school events and ceremonies makes them important for the members of the school community.

Special printed programs can be developed to accompany school performances and assemblies. For example, let's say that the school has a tradition of presenting a Martin Luther King Jr. assembly each year. A program can be developed that is distributed to staff members and guests. A sample of such a program appears in Figure 20.1.

Figure 20.1 Sample Program for a Martin Luther King Jr. Assembly

Name of School and District

MARTIN LUTHER KING JR. ASSEMBLY

Orchestra: March of a Festival

Introduction: Staff Member's Name, Librarian

Kindergartens: Song: "I Am Freedom's Child"

First Grades: Poem: "Dreams" by Langston Hughes

Second Grades: Choral Reading: "All the Colors of the Earth"

Third Grades: Drama: Montgomery Bus Boycott

Fourth Grades: Choral Reading: "I Am a Man: Ode to Martin Luther King, Jr."

Biography: The Life of Rosa Parks

Fifth Grades: Poem: "The Way I See Any Hope for Later"

Martin Luther King's Jr.'s "I Have A Dream" Speech

All Grades: Display of quilt depicting scenes from the life of Martin Luther King Jr.

Onstage: The Twenty-Foot Book with artistic representations by the students of Dr. King's Dreams

Communal Songs: "If I Had a Hammer," "We Shall Overcome," "This Land Is Your Land"

Closing: Principal

The wise school leader begins to build cherished traditions by selecting staff or parents to lead special events and ceremonies. These individuals will then be committed to the event and will assume continuing responsibility for its success. Participation should be as broad as possible to gain enthusiasm for the tradition. In some cases, it might be appropriate to invite special guests or dignitaries to the event to lend an air of importance. For example, in some schools, the chief of police is asked to attend a ceremony to "induct" the members of the school safety squad.

EXAMPLES OF SCHOOL TRADITIONS AND CEREMONIES

Special events and ceremonies should be tailored to emphasize the values that are shared among the members of the school community; thus, not all ceremonies will be appropriate in all schools. The following list provides a sampling of the kinds of events that might be supported in an elementary school. The events appear in alphabetical order.

Annual Birthday Party

An interesting tradition some schools have is an annual birthday party. This may be intended to supplant the celebration of individual birthdays in each classroom. A committee of parents and teachers can plan the annual event, which can include a special lunch, some form of entertainment for the children, a large "birthday cake," decorations, favors, and the like. The theme for the birthday can be kept a great secret, and children will look forward to the annual birthday party with great anticipation. These events can become truly spectacular, and good feelings will be had by those who plan the day, as well as by the children. Students' individual birthdays can be announced during the morning announcements, and they can go to the office to receive a birthday pencil or button.

Awards Assembly

To honor students who have served the school in a variety of capacities, an Awards Assembly can be held toward the end of the school year. Certificates of recognition can be ordered from a printer or made with a desktop publishing program, and these awards can be presented to each child who has done something to serve the school community.

Begin the ceremony by talking about the awards tradition in the school, and then those staff members who have led student activities can be called upon to make their presentation and call the students up to receive their certificates. An Awards Assembly is an ideal vehicle for recognizing the efforts of those students who have served the school, and for promoting enthusiasm for service activities among the younger students. A sample program for an Awards Assembly appears in Figure 20.2.

Figure 20.2   Sample Awards Day Program

Name of District and School

AWARDS DAY

"Gathering on the Lawn"

Flag Ceremony

"America"

Our Awards Tradition	Principal
Student Council Awards	Student Council Leader
School Chorus Awards	Chorus Teacher
School Orchestra Awards	Orchestra Teacher
Student Mediator Awards	Staff Member
Safety Committee Awards	Staff Member
Library Squad Awards	Staff Member
Tech Squad Awards	Staff Member
Field Day Captain Awards	Staff Member
Recycling Squad Awards	Staff Member
Other Special Awards:	Principal

- Office Messengers
- Attendance Monitors
- Newspaper Deliverers
- Fire Drill Timers

Honorable Mention:	Principal

- Chair Squad
- Cleanup Crew
- Kindergarten Buddies

"America the Beautiful"

Back-to-School Night

A common tradition in most elementary schools, Back-to-School Night ought to be an evening in which parents meet the school staff and hear about the activities and programs offered in the school. Usually, Back-to-School Night combines a general meeting in which parents are introduced to the school staff and hear about programs sponsored by the parents association. The principal might make a brief talk and discuss school goals and initiatives.

Classroom visits are the norm for most Back-to-School Nights. Teachers are usually cautioned not to conduct individual conferences, but rather to discuss the plans for the year, homework expectations, and the curriculum in general. You can do many things to make Back-to-School Night special and innovative. Consider the following items:

- Show a video of school life during the opening days of school.
- Greet all parents in the hallway and be visible during the evening.
- Conduct a science or math activity that demonstrates a part of the school curriculum.
- Have a table in a lobby where parents can join the parents organization.
- Set up a display that highlights something special about the school.
- Put out a sign-up sheet for "conferences with the principal."
- Prepare and serve a special dessert or refreshments.
- Invite school "alumni" to speak and share their experiences at the school.
- Set up a large mural on which parents can write a brief note to their youngsters.
- Demonstrate a new piece of equipment or a new technology.

Put a sign-up sheet in each room so that parents can sign up for the first round of parent conferences.

Class Plays

Although having class plays may not seem like anything unusual, when they are anticipated and expected, they quickly become school traditions. The children in each class or grade can be involved in making a presentation for the school. It does not necessarily have to be a play or musical; it can be a program about a famous hero, a reenactment of a story, a "teaching program" about ecology, or a program about the history of the town, among countless other themes. The parents of the children in the class can plan a little reception for the performers after their play or program.

The way you introduce such presentations is also a part of the tradition. Comments about the efforts of the children and the teachers are always appreciated. Parents love seeing their children perform or make a contribution to school life. If such presentations are encouraged and supported, they will become valued traditions.

Closing Exercises or "Moving Up" Day

At the end of the school year, most elementary schools conduct some sort of ceremony to send off the students in its top grade as they move on to middle school or junior high school. Each school develops its own tradition for this ceremony, but, usually, it involves a farewell address by the principal. Sometimes, the school superintendent or member of the board of education will talk to the students. In some cases, an alumna of the school is invited back to address the graduates. The children themselves often share their memories of their years at the school.

In one example of a closing assembly, the students sing a song as they proceed into the auditorium. An introduction is provided by the president of the student council. Then, all of the students share their memories of the school in a choral speaking piece. A few songs are presented that are appropriate to the occasion. The principal offers a "farewell," and then each student pulls a long-stemmed flower from a vase atop the piano and gives it to a staff member or school volunteer in the audience. Another part of this particular tradition is to have a PowerPoint slide show (or computer graphic presentation) of photos of the graduates as babies or very young children. (This portion of the program tends to be a tearjerker.) Then, the students leave the auditorium as they sing a song. The teachers follow the students out as they shake hands, congratulating one another on having led another set of students through their final year. A written program for this kind of closing assembly appears in Figure 20.3.

Figure 20.3   Sample Closing Assembly Program

Congratulations

CLOSING ASSEMBLY

DATE

Processional: "_________" (Name of a song)

Introduction: _________ (Name of student council president)

"Years of Memories:" All fifth graders share their memories of their years at _________ (Name of School).

Songs: Name of a song

        Name of a song

Farewell: Principal

"Flowers to the Flowers": Ceremony in which students present flowers to the school staff.

Slide Show: "The Way We Were"

Recessional: "We're on Our Way" (or another song)

Custodian Appreciation Day

Organizing an annual Custodian Appreciation Day can model for students that all personnel are appreciated and recognized. Here again, a school tradition can be readily established. One possible way to make this ceremony special would be to hold a brief assembly and assign a special task to the students at each grade level. For example, the kindergartens can create a mural in which they depict custodial tasks; first graders can recite a poem of appreciation; second graders can make greeting cards, and so on. You can be the "master of ceremonies" for the assembly. Perhaps the staff will purchase a gift basket for the custodians. Such traditions can help to instill an appreciation for the dignity and importance of hard work, improve the morale of the custodians, and demonstrate that in your school, people who help are valued.

Earth Day

Elementary school children love to become involved in projects designed to improve the environment. Teachers can lead students in an Earth Day celebration that includes several valuable activities. Students can conduct a "teach-in" and help younger children understand the concepts they have learned; displays can be set up; games can be organized; environmental skits can be presented; a songfest can be conducted. In some communities, high school students plan activities to teach environmental concepts to elementary school children. Such interchanges are rewarding for both older and younger students. With the infusion of lessons about sustainability, Earth Day is an important day to recognize.

Family Picnic

In many schools, parents plan a social event early in the year to bring the members of the school community together. Such events can foster school spirit and a sense of belonging. Family picnics can be organized around any sort of theme, and the dinner can be a potluck; each family signs up to bring a special dish, appetizer, or dessert. Of course, some activities should be planned for the children as well as events that involve students and their parents. This is a particularly valuable event for parents and students new to the community. If a friendly, welcoming tone pervades such events, families will look forward to them, year after year, as a time to come together as neighbors and friends and support the school.

Field Day

Field days are common in elementary schools. The extent to which they are competitive usually reflects the school's philosophy in this area. Different formats for field day become traditions unto themselves. Students look forward to field day, the fun and games, and the school spirit that it engenders.

One model for a "working together" field day that has become a respected tradition in several schools follows:

The students in the school are divided into 20 teams or squads. Each team is composed of equal numbers of students from each of the grade levels in the school. The students at the oldest grade level are trained to serve as "captains." The "captains" help to set up for the event and explain the various stations and are charged with the responsibility of encouraging the younger students and modeling good sportsmanship.

The outdoor area is divided into 20 activity stations. Most of these involve some sort of relay activity such as a potato sack race, a marble-on-the-spoon relay, throwing small balls into wastebaskets, obstacle courses, and so on. Two "rest stops" can be set up, and these count as stations. Each team rotates through the stations, conducting as many successful completions as the time will allow. A sample instruction sheet for such a field day is as follows:

1. The outdoor field will be set up into 20 stations. Two of the stations are "rest stops," where parents have been enlisted to provide water and/or juice.

2. The children from all grade levels will be divided, as evenly as possible, into 20 teams with approximately the same number of students on each team.

3. The teams will move from one station to the next in a clockwise fashion.

4. Each station has a station manager (teacher or assistant). The manager marks the number of successful completions on the score card for each team. The manager must enforce the rules of fair play.

5. Each team has a team captain who will explain and demonstrate the activity at each station when the team arrives, carry the score cards, and ensure that each student gets to take a turn.

6. Timing for each event is as follows: 1 minute—explanation; 3 minutes—continuous activity; students, in line place, rotate through as many successful completions as they can during the 3-minute period; 2 minutes—score activity and move on to the next station.

7. Teams follow their leader from one station to the next. They sit in file order to await instructions.

8. All scoring is done by counting the number of children on a team who complete the event within the 3-minute period.

9. The overall score is the sum total of points awarded for all of the events.

Having the school band conduct opening exercises in which they play a sporting theme, a patriotic song, and a school-spirit song can enhance events like field day. At the end of the program, the principal can announce the teams that gained the greatest number of points all the while praising the level of cooperation and enthusiasm noted.

During a field day, it is wise to have school nurses close at hand with complete first-aid kits and cell phones for emergency purposes.

Fifth-Grade Debate

In schools where the students at the top grade level are interested and capable, a junior debating society can be organized by a staff advisor. The person who runs the debating society should be well grounded in the rules of debate and also enjoy bringing such programs to young children. The students can decide upon an issue and have a debate at a school assembly. Publicity for the event can be planned in advance, and an awareness of the issues can be fostered among all teachers. If this kind of activity gains appeal in your school, it can become a tradition highly valued by students, staff, and parents alike.

Flag Ceremony for Assemblies

In many elementary schools, each assembly begins with a flag ceremony. There are many ways that this can be accomplished. The flag can be kept in a stand at the side of the auditorium, and the youngsters can be asked to stand and recite the Pledge of Allegiance led either by you, a music teacher, or an assembly leader.

To make the occasion more "ceremonious," however, three students (usually upper-grade-level youngsters) can be chosen on a rotating basis and asked to leave the auditorium with the flag prior to the assembly. Then, when all of the children are seated, you or your designee asks everyone to rise, and the three selected youngsters enter the auditorium through the center aisle—led by the child bearing the flag. The three children turn to face the audience, and one of the youngsters gives a command. It could be "Attention, salute" or "Ready to salute the flag." The Pledge is recited (which, by the way, is required in many states), and then the children are asked to remain standing to sing a patriotic song. When the song is completed, another member of the trio might say, "Retire the colors," and then the flag is replaced to its stand. When the flag is returned, you or the assembly leader signals the children to be seated.

At the end of the assembly, the flag bearers once again get the flag and then remain at the center of the auditorium until it is silent. Then, upon a cue from the assembly leader, they leave the auditorium. This signals the end of the assembly, and the other children march out. As contrived as this flag ceremony might seem, many principals find that such a practice not only instills patriotism and respect, but it also helps to calm and settle the children at the beginning of an assembly program and readies them for what is to follow. Younger students may look forward to the day when it is their turn to be leaders in the flag ceremony. Such practices help to build school traditions.

Kids' Days

A student organization can run various "kids' days" throughout the year. Such days can be "earned" by the students and involve their input and planning. Some possible themes for a kids' day are

- an ice-cream sundae party;
- a "turn-around" day, in which students and teachers reverse roles and the students assume the responsibility for teaching all day;
- bringing a stuffed animal to school and writing about the creature or performing dramatizations using the toys;
- wearing clothing inside out or backwards for a day; and
- bringing certain games to school and allowing time for the students to play with them.

Kids' days can take any number of formats, but they should be well organized, viewed as earned privileges, and approved and supported by the school staff.

Kindergarten Buddies Day

"Kindergarten Buddies" is a wonderful program in which students from the highest grade in the school are paired with the youngest students. After a few sessions in which students get to know each other, the partnership can be forged. Teachers can plan joint activities; the older children can serve as scribes to the kindergartners as they attempt to write stories; kindergartners can draw pictures for their buddies. In some schools, the buddies have lunch together. Such partnerships have tremendous benefits for all participants. The kindergartners feel a true kinship toward their buddies, and kindness, compassion, and a sense of caring are fostered among the older students.

Special events can be planned for the buddies. For example, at a spring concert, the pairs of students can sing a song together. The kindergartners can also prepare a send-off gift or sing a farewell song at the older students' graduation ceremony. Parents, students, and teachers alike find such interchanges heartwarming and look forward to continuing the tradition.

Kindergarten Roundup

Once kindergarten registration has taken place, many principals invite the incoming children and their parents to school for an orientation visit. One successful model is for each child in the current kindergarten to be paired with an incoming student. The older child can show the newcomer the classroom and a sample of the kinds of activities that occur. (These, of course, should be adapted for the age of the younger students.) The teacher, who has prepared name tags for the new students, can then gather them together and read a book, do a puppet activity, and in other ways make the youngsters feel at home.

While the children are visiting the kindergarten class, the principal and representatives from the parents association can conduct a simple reception in which the kindergarten program is explained and opportunities to become involved at school are offered. After the brief session, the parents can meet their children back in the kindergarten room. Parents should be informed that a child's visit to a kindergarten teacher's classroom for the Roundup does not imply that the student will be assigned to this teacher's classroom when school begins in the fall.

Martin Luther King Jr. Assembly

Each January, around the birthday of Dr. Martin Luther King Jr., the students and staff can prepare a special assembly program to honor this great civil rights leader. The event can help foster sensitivity among the students and be the culmination of varied studies. Often, the best assemblies honoring Dr. King are the "homegrown" ones, in which each class or grade makes a unique contribution to the program. See Figure 20.1 for a sample program for a Martin Luther King Jr. Assembly.

Morning Announcements and Opening Ceremony

If opening ceremonies are held in classes each morning, a feeling of community is built if everyone joins in at the same time by having students recite the Pledge over the public address system and lead the singing of a patriotic song. A flag should be displayed in every classroom. The classroom teacher supervises the announced commands to "rise" and "be seated." Pertinent, short informational announcements related to the day can be included in the daily opening ceremony. "Have a great day!" is a good way to end the announcement. There should be no further public address interruptions during the day unless there is an emergency.

Open House

Most schools conduct an "open house," a time for parents to visit classrooms in action. There are several ways to organize this event. Teachers can send home a notice, in which the schedule of classroom activities is outlined. In some cases, members of the student council serve as "receptionists," escorting visitors to classrooms and other areas. Passes can be distributed and limited to 5 or 10 per classroom so that the rooms do not become overcrowded. If parents have to wait to be admitted, furnish a comfortable waiting area with coffee, tea, and cookies. Special teachers may wish to distribute their own schedule of events and encourage parents to visit their rooms. A sample invitation to an Open House appears in Figure 20.4.

Figure 20.4 Sample Invitation to Open House

Name of School and District

SCHOOL OPEN HOUSE

Date: (Tuesday, November ___)   **Time:** (8:45–1:00)

Please come to our school's OPEN HOUSE! All parents are welcome to visit our classrooms for 30 minutes anytime between 8:45 AM and 1:00 PM on ELECTION DAY, Tuesday, November ___.

Our **MUSIC BOOSTERS** will also be holding their annual Bake Sale in the Auditorium Lobby, so please stop by on your way to the polls and give your support to this dedicated group of parent volunteers.

To make classroom visits as meaningful as possible, we ask our guests to:

1. Take a seat in your child's classroom.

2. Please refrain from entering into conversation with other guests, your child, or the teacher.

3. Observe your child as objectively as possible. Remember, your presence in the classroom may alter typical classroom behavior.

4. Observe your child as he or she relates to assigned work and peers.

5. Try to picture the setting in which school experiences take place as they are related to you at home.

6. Visit special-subject classes if they are scheduled.

Opening Assembly

It is never too early to begin building a sense of community among students and staff. An ideal event is an opening assembly on the first or second day of the school year. Depending on the size of the school, all staff members can be introduced, and students new to the school can be introduced by their teachers. The opening assembly is a natural time to establish and explain assembly expectations—where students sit, how they file in and exit, a flag ceremony, and general school behaviors.

At an opening assembly, the principal can explain, in "kids' language," the school goals for the year. It's also a time to introduce those staff members who sponsor student activities such as the student council, the orchestra and chorus, the safety committee, the recycling squad, the technology squad, and so on. Generating enthusiasm for the school year and establishing essential routines should be among the goals of the opening assembly. A sample program for an opening assembly appears in Figure 20.5. If your school is large, you may consider dividing the school into two groups for assemblies.

Figure 20.5   Sample Program for an Opening Assembly

Name of School and District

OPENING ASSEMBLY PROGRAM

Flag Ceremony	The Color Guard
Welcome	Principal
Introducing Staff and New Students	Principal
Student Activity Leaders	Principal
School Chorus	Staff Member
Orchestra	Staff Member
Safety Committee	Staff Member
Library Squad	Staff Member
Technology Squad	Staff Member
Recycling Squad	Staff Member
Student Council	Staff Member
Student Mediation	Staff Member
Computer Club	Staff Member
"What's New at School This Year"	Principal
School Goals	
Lunchroom Procedures	
New Programs	
Building Improvements	
Return of the Flag	The Color Guard

Presidents Day Assembly

Just before Presidents Day weekend, the students can plan an assembly program to honor famous U.S. presidents. Such events help students understand the significance of these great figures and why they have the day off from school. In most states, Presidents Day is in honor of George Washington and Abraham Lincoln, both of whose birthdays are in February, but schools can establish a tradition to learn about and honor any number of presidents. Each class can take a small part in the program, or the program can be assigned to the students at a particular grade.

Principal's Coffee

Some principals like to host "coffees" at which they meet parents, listen to concerns, and talk about the mission of the school. In some cases, a separate coffee is held for the parents at each grade level in the school. The PTA can be asked to help out with the refreshments, and perhaps the PTA officers can talk about their functions and becoming involved in the school.

Staff Get-Togethers

Many principals underestimate the value of planning social events for the staff. Such occasions can help to boost morale and let the staff know that its members are appreciated. If you and your staff live within reasonable proximity, you can host a simple Friday night or Sunday afternoon get-together. You can serve light refreshments, or give a dinner party, if that is your style. If the party is scheduled for just after the opening of school, it gives people a chance to reunite after the summer vacation. If the get-together is scheduled at holiday time, or at the end of the year, other purposes are served. It is true that such events require extra effort on your part, but they do demonstrate in a very real way how much you value the members of the staff as individuals. Such graciousness is remembered by the staff. Of course, make sure that all staff members realize that attendance is optional.

Student Council Elections

Student council elections can be held with little or no fanfare, but they can also be conducted in such a way as to generate considerable enthusiasm and excitement in the school and teach important lessons about representative democracy. Candidates can be selected in a variety of ways, but once they are announced, the campaign begins. Candidates need guidelines for how to conduct their campaigns. Perhaps one or two posters can be allowed, or a flyer in which the candidate's platform is defined. The candidates can make scheduled visits to classrooms to answer questions about their experiences and why they feel qualified for the office. On the day of the election, the student council advisor can conduct an assembly program at which each candidate delivers a brief campaign speech. In schools that have closed-circuit television capabilities, the campaign speeches can be televised.

Student council elections can be the topic of considerable controversy in elementary schools. Some parents will undoubtedly feel that they are too competitive; others will strongly support the importance of direct lessons in participatory democracy. Whatever the staff and community decide is the best way to conduct such activities, the ceremonies and traditions should be followed and supported. Changing the rules year after year not only weakens the positions of school leaders, but also does not help to build meaningful traditions. However, traditions can be revisited periodically to evaluate how they can be improved in light of a changing society.

Winter or Spring Concerts

Most elementary schools have orchestras or bands and a chorus. These groups usually perform a concert at holiday time or in the spring. These events also become honored traditions, and younger students look forward to the day that they, too, will be able to perform for an audience. Some schools have a tradition of conducting a "sing-a-long" during such concerts. This can help to generate enthusiasm, joy in music making, and community spirit.

The concert can be introduced by you, with appreciation expressed to the music teachers and others who may have assisted in the effort. Some school leaders like to acknowledge grandparents or other guests who have traveled some distance to attend the concert. The parents association can be asked to provide refreshments for the concert goers.

The examples above are just a sampling of the types of school traditions and ceremonies that might occur in an elementary school. Each school will develop its own traditions that reflect the values of the staff and the community.

PASSING DOWN SCHOOL TRADITIONS FROM ONE GENERATION TO THE NEXT

School traditions should be so well ingrained that they exist regardless of the principal or faculty. They just continue on their own. When a principal is new to a school, it is important to find out about the existing traditions that are valued. Care must be taken not to forget about or eliminate honored traditions. Think, for example, of the first-grade students who may have been so impressed by the closing exercises that they look forward with anticipation to the day when they will be students who are leaving the school and being publicly honored.

When conducting school ceremonies, the school leader should point out during the event that this tradition is a part of the school's culture and that it has been valued by members of the school community. If older students are being honored or recognized, let the younger students who witness the ceremony know that they, too, will be a part of such a tradition in years to come. As a principal new to a school, you must watch the traditions unfold for a year. Then, any changes that you think should be made can be discussed with the school council and the staff.

Photographs and videos of school ceremonies should be maintained and catalogued. A staff member may choose to become "the keeper of the traditions" and organize scrapbooks, notes, and photo albums in which these ceremonies and events are captured and captioned. Designating a "school historian" can help in the effort to celebrate a school's past and ensure cherished traditions for the future.

All principals should be concerned about the culture of their schools. The principal's attendance and leadership at such events send an important message to staff, students, and parents; they convey that these traditions are important and need to be maintained and nurtured. Enthusiasm for the school's tradition can be transmitted through word and deed. Underestimating the importance of traditions in a school, or being indifferent to them, can be a critical mistake for school leaders. The values held within a school and the traditions and ceremonies that define the ethos of the school can make the difference between a good school and a great school. Do all that you can to make your school a great school.

The Corwin logo—a raven striding across an open book—represents the union of courage and learning. Corwin is committed to improving education for all learners by publishing books and other professional development resources for those serving the field of PreK–12 education. By providing practical, hands-on materials, Corwin continues to carry out the promise of its motto: **"Helping Educators Do Their Work Better."**